Documents of the American Revolution

Volume II

Transcripts
1770

DOCUMENTS
OF THE
AMERICAN REVOLUTION

1770–1783

(Colonial Office Series)

Volume II
TRANSCRIPTS
1770

Edited by
K. G. DAVIES

IRISH UNIVERSITY PRESS
Shannon Ireland

© *1972*

Irish University Press Shannon Ireland

All forms of micropublishing
© *Irish University Microforms Shannon Ireland*

ISBN 0 7165 2085 0 Set
ISBN 0 7165 2087 7 Volume II

Irish University Press Shannon Ireland

T. M. MacGlinchey Publisher

Filmset and printed in the Republic of Ireland at Shannon
by Robert Hogg Printer to Irish University Press

CONTENTS

ACKNOWLEDGEMENTS

The typing of this volume was done by Miss Teresa Hall of the Irish University Press and by Mrs Elaine Porter; and the copy-editing by Miss Clare Craven also of the Irish University Press.

INTRODUCTION

The Transcripts

This volume consists of 143 documents chosen from those which have already been described, in calendar form, in Volume I of the series. All are of date 1770, though some are preserved in the Public Record Office in the form of enclosures to covering documents of 1771. Each document selected for inclusion in this volume has been printed *in extenso*, except that the formal and protracted valedictions with which some letters conclude have in most cases been excised. Where, as is occasionally found, these valedictions are grammatically joined to preceding matter of substance they have of course been allowed to remain in the transcript.

The following conventions of transcription have been employed:

(1) the spelling of common English words has been modernized;

(2) the use of initial capital letters, indulged in by eighteenth-century correspondents with a profusion likely to be rebarbative to present-day readers, has been brought into closer conformity with modern practices;

(3) where, as is often the case, the punctuation of an original document is more confusing than helpful, punctuation has been supplied by the editor with full awareness of the responsibility thereby assumed;

(4) the paragraphing of the original documents has been retained;

(5) proper names, both English and American, of persons and places have in most instances been printed as written. Among exceptions to this rule are the correction of obvious mistakes (such as General Gage's habit, whether conscious or not, of referring to Lieut.-Governor Elias Durnford of West Florida as 'Dunford'); the rendering of the capital city of South Carolina as 'Charleston', though in 1770 it was still commonly written 'Charlestown' or 'Charles Town'; and the preference of 'Choctaws' to 'Chactaws'.

The complementary relationship between the *Calendar* and the *Transcripts* needs to be emphasized, the former providing the necessary context for the latter. Data, such as endorsements, location of alternative versions of a document etc., already supplied in the *Calendar*, have not been repeated in the *Transcripts*. The omission from the *Transcripts* of a document described in the *Calendar* does not mean that it is necessarily devoid of historical interest. There are documents, and not a few, which are of great importance but which are couched in so formal a style as to render transcribing them a wasteful exercise.

1

Orders in Council, for example, the kernel of which is often contained in a few words, are generally more eligible for the *Calendar* than for the *Transcripts*. Richard Jackson's reports on colonial laws, some of which recite without comment the full titles of twenty or thirty acts submitted for approval before coming to the one or two on which substantive observations are to be made, are of the same nature. Thus, for a document to have failed to qualify for transcription does not denote degradation.

In choosing the documents for this volume, no account has been taken of previous publication. To have done so would have conflicted with the aim of presenting as full a picture of the British administration of North America as the Colonial Office records permit. It is hardly necessary to add that every document appearing in the *Transcripts* has been edited from the original in the Public Record Office or from a photo-copy thereof.

Although any selection of records must to some extent reflect the interests or prejudices of the selector, the editor of these documents has tried to keep in mind the broad purpose of this series: to recreate the situation as regards information in which the Secretary of State for the American Department found himself. This has meant giving attention to problems and documents which seemed important to participants in 1770, and not merely selecting those which have acquired unforeseen or special importance as the result of later events. While the strains and tensions which five years later produced a revolutionary situation in America are, it is hoped, fairly represented in this volume, at least as far as the limits of the series allow, some documents have been included in the *Transcripts* which have no bearing or only indirect bearing on the crisis but which contributed to the variegated picture of the lives and strivings of the King's subjects in America which was assembled at Whitehall. Such are Governor Lord William Campbell's plan to form an Indian village near Halifax, Nova Scotia, modelled on those of New England and Canada;[1] Governor Grant's concern for the welfare of the Greek settlement at New Smyrna, East Florida;[2] Governor Carleton's quarrel with the Commissioners of Customs at Boston;[3] and a number of documents bearing on Indian affairs which are no more than indirectly connected to the American Revolution.

This said, it remains true that the bulk of this, or any, selection from the Colonial Office records of this date must above all reflect the three dominant themes of North American history at the beginning of the 1770's: the opposition which had arisen in the seaboard colonies to British policy and British administration; the problem of what, if anything, was to be done with the Mississippi Valley; and the settling of the affairs of Quebec and the King's 'new subjects' there. It is not the purpose of this Introduction, by seeking to supply a comprehensive guide to the contents of the volume, to usurp the function of the Index; much less to attempt to summarize the main events in North America

1   Below, No. CXLI.
2   No. LXXXVIII.
3   No. LXI.

in 1770. Nevertheless, for any user of the volume who is not familiar with the Colonial Office records, a brief statement of these themes, as they are developed in the documents, may be of some service.

The Seaboard Colonies

1770 was a year of decision in the campaign for non-importation of British goods, launched in protest against the Townshend Duties. References to this subject are plentiful in the correspondence of Massachusetts, Maryland, Pennsylvania, South Carolina, New York, New Hampshire and Georgia, though the governors of the last two were at pains to emphasize the tepid support for the boycott. Governor James Wright insisted that non-importation resolutions, though framed in Georgia, remained unsigned, attributing this to his own cleverness.[4] In New Hampshire, Governor John Wentworth's dispatches suggest that he hoped to make some advantage by dwelling upon the loyalty of his province. Though the news of the Boston Massacre gave the colony for a time the appearance of a 'troubled ocean', by October Wentworth was able to report that he had removed the prejudices and bad impressions 'artfully infused into the minds of the people'.[5] Both these colonies, from Whitehall, looked fairly safe.

Massachusetts, South Carolina, New York and Pennsylvania looked anything but safe. Despite Lieut.-Governor Thomas Hutchinson's sanguine hope that 'non-importation cannot hold another year', and despite the presence in Boston of perhaps as many as fifty merchants who wanted to import,[6] Massachusetts in 1770 did not have the appearance of a community in retreat. Hillsborough in Whitehall was aware of it. 'It is but too apparent . . .' he wrote of the House of Representatives in another connection 'that they . . . really mean to promote distress to the mother country', and placed his hopes for the future in constitutional reform, that is to say, in alterations to Massachusetts' charter.[7] Far from going backwards, there was a scheme in Boston to punish New Hampshire for not adopting non-importation by breaking off all commercial intercourse between Massachusetts and that province, and persuading other colonies to do the same.[8] In South Carolina, too, we learn from Governor Wright's letter of 20 July, though not from Bull's dispatches from Charleston, that an extension of non-importation was under consideration, in this instance to the West Indies.[9]

In the summer of 1770 it seemed as if the non-importation question might be settled one way or the other by the decision of the two mercantile colonies, New York and Pennsylvania, which were poised either for advance or retreat. By July the news of the British government's intention to remove duties on glass, paper and painters' colours, but not on tea, had been fully assimilated, and it was also clear that for the time being this was all that could be expected by way of concession.

---

4   No. XLIV.
5   Nos. XVII, XXXII, CXIII.
6   Nos. X, L.
7   No. C.
8   No. CXIII.
9   No. LXXIV.

Decision could be no longer postponed. The outcome, however, was probably the one least expected, more a draw than a knockout. New York decided to import, Pennsylvania to maintain and extend non-importation.

The resolution taken in New York on 9 July to import all British goods except tea was briefly reported by Lieut.-Governor Cadwallader Colden and by Lieut.-General Gage,[10] but there is a fuller account of the house-to-house poll in New York City, resulting in a 'great majority' for importing, by Alexander Colden, deputy Postmaster-General.[11] We owe this letter to the administrative requirement of explaining to the Postmaster-General in London the circumstances in which packets were detained from sailing: in this case the *Duke of Cumberland* was held back in order to carry merchants' requisitions for goods.

New York's decision, welcome as it was in Whitehall, did not have the expected effect in swaying opinion elsewhere; in the short run it was counter-productive. The merchants of Philadelphia, on first hearing that the duty on tea was to be retained, had chosen to wait and see what other colonies would do, the implication being that they would follow a lead.[12] They finally made up their minds on 19 July, and to judge by their resolutions were more influenced by abhorrence of what New York had done than by any other consideration. New York's vote was denounced as 'a sordid and wanton defection from the common cause' which had 'weakened the union of the colonies, wounded the public character of America, strengthened the hands of our enemies and encouraged them to prosecute their designs against our common liberty'. Not only was Philadelphia to continue non-importation: a restricted form of it was to be extended to New York 'until they return to their agreement or until the Act of the 7th of George the third is totally repealed'.[13] Thus in the second half of 1770 two American colonies, Massachusetts and Pennsylvania, were contemplating commercial boycotts against two others, New Hampshire and New York.

South Carolina was another colony where 'the late infamous revolt in New York' was resented,[14] but here reactions were slower and more confused. At a meeting of 'planters, merchants and mechanics' held in Charleston on 13 December, the non-importers were conclusively enough beaten for Bull to believe that 'the Association will now be wholly at an end.'[15] This news was perhaps by way of a bonus to Whitehall and brought the year to a reasonably satisfactory end. Little had been hoped for, nothing gained, from Massachusetts, while Pennsylvania's decision had been a defeat for British policy, though Hillsborough hoped not a final one.[16] On the other hand, New York had taken a long step back to normal and South Carolina had made a move in the same direction.

10   Nos. LXVII-LXVIII.
11   No. LXIX.
12   No. XLIX.
13   No. LXXII.
14   No. CIX.
15   No. CXXXVIII.
16   Vol. I, No. 724.

Non-importation came nearest to furnishing a common issue in dissensions between royal governors and popular assemblies in 1770. The difficulties of the governors (and the difficulty they sometimes had in convincing Hillsborough of the need for tactical concessions to the popular voice) are a staple item in the Secretary of State's correspondence. Massachusetts, New York, South Carolina and Georgia supply most material under this head, but neither in New Jersey, North Carolina nor West Florida, can it be said that harmony prevailed between executive and legislature, while in Virginia the House of Burgesses weighed in majestically with a petition to the King for repeal of the duty on tea.[17] Lord Botetourt, Governor of Virginia, blamed this on the malignant influence of the 'patriots' in England,[18] an opinion with which Hillsborough concurred.[19] The same explanation was offered on behalf of Massachusetts and accepted by the Secretary of State,[20] and something like it was suggested by Colden to account for Philadelphia's *volte-face*.[21]

In several colonies there existed or arose local matters of contention which at times eclipsed more general issues, including non-importation. In Massachusetts there was prolonged and wearisome wrangling over the summoning of the General Court to Cambridge instead of to Boston, a point on which Hutchinson would probably have liked, but did not dare, to give way.[22] In Georgia there was the campaign for no taxation without the representation in the Lower House of Assembly of the four southern provinces, St David, St Patrick, St Thomas and St Mary.[23] And in South Carolina it was the claim of the Commons House to order payment of money out of the public Treasury without the concurrence of Governor and Council that opened a breach between legislature and executive never to be healed.

This last issue deserves a comment not only for the number of documents it generated but also for the demonstration it provides of the swift and brusque response which Whitehall was capable of making when stung in a sensitive place. The *fons et origo* of the dispute was the resolution of the Commons House of South Carolina of 8 December 1769, reported in Lieut.-Governor Bull's letter to Hillsborough of 12 December. Because there are so many references to this resolution in 1770 and later, and because it falls just outside the chronological plan of this series, the text is worth recalling here:

> Ordered, that the public Treasurer do advance the sum of £10500 currency out of any money in the Treasury to be paid into the hands of Mr Speaker, Mr Gadsden, Mr Rutledge, Mr Parsons, Mr Ferguson, Mr Dart and Mr Lynch, who are to remit the same to Great Britain for the support of the just and constitutional rights and liberties of the people of Great Britain and America.[24]

17 Below, No. LIX.
18 Vol. I, No. 444.
19 Below, No. XCIX.
20 Nos. XLVIII, LXXVIII.
21 No. LXV.
22 Vol. I, No. 1269.
23 No. XLV.
24 Public Record Office, C.O.5/379, fo. 76.

Bull's dispatch, or rather its duplicate, was received in Whitehall on 3 February 1770, and the following recorded acts ensued: 13 February, Order of Committee of Council for Plantation Affairs referring Bull's letter to Board of Trade;[25] 13 February, Attorney-General's opinion given on the matter;[26] 17 February, letter from Hillsborough to Bull conveying the royal displeasure;[27] 23 February, Board of Trade's report to Committee of Council;[28] 3 April, Order of Committee of Council to Board of Trade to draft additional instruction to Governor of South Carolina;[29] 4 April, Board's draft of the instruction;[30] 5 April, Order in Council approving instruction and directing that the Treasurer of South Carolina should be prosecuted;[31] 14 April, letter from Hillsborough to Bull, sending the instruction.[32] This string of administrative acts, reeled off in two months, may be compared with the Board of Trade's protracted consideration of the Ohio land question, not to mention the dispute regarding the lands west of Connecticut River.

The Treasurer of South Carolina died before he could be prosecuted, but predictably the Commons House found the instruction unpalatable and the ensuing wrangle continued to fill Bull's dispatches for the rest of the year;[33] by the end of 1770 the matter had been widened and rendered virtually insoluble by the Commons' demand not only for the recall of the instruction but also for an order to be issued by the King to the Governor of South Carolina to communicate to the House any representation he might make to Whitehall concerning its proceedings.[34] It is of interest that Bull noticed in the assemblymen as individuals a wish that the resolution of 8 December 1769 had never been passed but at the same time a collective determination not to rescind it,[35] a posture he thought characteristic of popular assemblies.[36] This was also Lord Charles Montagu's opinion[37] when he returned to his governorship in September 1771, though it is not clear whether he thought it up for himself or took it over from Bull as a useful formula, when reporting to the Secretary of State, for slightly softening the contumaciousness of an Assembly. A breakdown in relations with the legislature was bound to reflect in some degree on the executive, and more than one royal governor can be found urging mitigation, much as the headmaster of an unruly school, without condoning disorder, might plead to the police for his charges. All the interested parties, Secretaries of State, Governors and Assemblymen, had faces to save.

The opposition so far touched upon was developed more or less within the traditional constitutional and legal framework, though here

25   Vol. I, No. 98.
26   Vol. I, No. 99.
27   Below, No. XVI.
28   Vol. I, No. 145.
29   Vol. I, No. 234.
30   Vol. I, No. 236.
31   Vol. I, No. 239.
32   Vol. I, No. 268; below, No. XXXV.
33   Below, Nos. XXXVII, LXXXVI, XCI.
34   No. CXXVI.
35   No. LXXXVI.
36   No. XXXVII.
37   Vol. I, No. 1528.

and there the rules of the game were transgressed by one side or the other. In 1770, however, demonstrations of a different kind, by street-mobs, were also reported to Whitehall, especially from Boston. In New York, according to Colden's letter of 21 February, a major affray between townspeople and British troops was narrowly averted by the prompt action of the magistrates,[38] and in Philadelphia on 13 November there was a riot involving Customs officers in which, it was alleged, the magistrates failed to do their duty.[39] Dereliction was frequently charged against the magistrates of Boston also, and was held by some to be responsible for the 'unfortunate affair' of 5 March, when the skirmishing between soldiers of the 14th and 29th regiments and some of the townspeople culminated in the most dramatic event in North America in 1770, the Boston Massacre. The document entitled 'State of the Disorders, Confusion and Misgovernment etc.'[40] provides an introduction to political events in Massachusetts, as seen from White-hall, but apart from the three last paragraphs has nothing to say about the street brawling that took place on and before 5 March. For this, reference must be made, first, to the affidavits of the officers and soldiers concerned,[41] next, to Lieut.-Governor Hutchinson's letter to General Gage written on the day following the Massacre[42] and his dispatch to Hillsborough of 12 March,[43] and lastly, to the narrative of Lieut.-Colonel William Dalrymple and the 'Case' of Thomas Preston, the officer commanding the party that fired on the crowd in front of the Customs-house.[44] All these were eye-witnesses, in whole or in part, of what they described. Secretary Andrew Oliver's Record of the Pro-ceedings of the Council of Massachusetts[45] tells the story, though in a way members of that board did not much like, of the pressures on Hutchinson to have the troops withdrawn from the town to Castle William on the day after the shooting.

Hillsborough's immediate response to the news that two British regiments had been routed by an urban mob was fairly strongly-worded,[46] but the administrative reaction was something of an anti-climax. The Committee for Plantation Affairs duly considered the 'State of the Disorders' and recommended that Castle William (a provincial fort) should be garrisoned by regular troops and that Boston Harbour should be made the rendezvous of H.M. ships in North America. These proposals were turned into an Order in Council on 6 July.[47] Although it thus became necessary to evict the provincial garrison, one officer of which had been there for nearly fifty years, which gave Hutchinson an attack of conscience and engendered some resent-ment in the Boston populace, the fact was that the British regiments

---

38 Below, No. XX.
39 No. CXL.
40 No. LVIII.
41 Vol. I, Nos. 181–201, 709i-lxxiv.
42 Below, No. XXII.
43 No. XXVI.
44 No. XXVII.
45 No. XXIII.
46 No. XL.
47 No. LXII.

had been at the Castle since 6 March: ordering them to take it over was not a particularly masterful move. As for the proposed concentration of naval might in Boston harbour, some effect might be looked for in a check to smuggling; but if the townspeople had failed to be overawed by two regiments in their streets, they were not likely to be scared by ships lying offshore. These rather feeble reactions to a major blow to British prestige proved, however, to be the right ones: despite Paul Revere's widely circulated print of the affair (made by Henry Pelham, so he claimed, and copied from him by Revere)[48], much of the steam of the Boston Massacre evaporated in the summer and autumn of 1770. Preston's acquittal in October after a trial during which, Hutchinson admitted, the behaviour of the public was 'remarkably decent',[49] and the acquittal a few weeks later of all but two of the soldiers (convicted of manslaughter only) implied a realization that the affair had been more a clumsy accident than a declaration of war.

Far from the cities, on the frontiers of the seaboard colonies, there were law-enforcement problems of a quite different kind, the result of settlement having outstripped government. Here Americans clashed with Americans in a way that held no promise of concerted action in the future against an external enemy. Three such frontier regions were prominent in 1770: Orange County in North Carolina, the lands west of Connecticut River, and the 'Eastern Country' of Massachusetts, though in the last of these anarchy reigned more at the expense of the Crown than of American property-rights.

In North Carolina the Regulators took a step nearer the civil war which was to have its climax at the battle of Alamance on 16 May 1771. The petition of the inhabitants of Orange County of September 1770 is a fair statement of their grievances:[50] with its insistence that 'laws themselves when against reason and justice are null and void' and its complaints of the tricks and extortions of sheriffs and law-officers, this document could have been the manifesto of almost any group of peasant-rioters in England or France from the 15th to the 18th centuries. It was presented on the occasion of a riot of Regulators at Hillsborough, N.C., on 22 September, when the sitting of the Superior Court was interrupted, windows broken, and an assault made on the person and property of Edmund Fanning, all of which was described graphically, if with some exaggeration, by Associate Judge Richard Henderson.[51]

What the Regulators did at Hillsborough, other rioters did in Cumberland County, N.Y., where on 5 June armed men forced the

48   Henry Pelham to Paul Revere, 29 March 1770, Public Record Office, C.O.5/39, fo. 1d. 'When I heard you was cutting a plate of the late murder, I thought it impossible as I knew you was not capable of doing it unless you copied it from mine . . . I . . . find myself in the most ungenerous manner deprived not only of the proposed advantage but even of the expense I have been at as truly as if you had plundered me on the highway. If you are insensible of the dishonour you have brought on yourself by this action, the world will not be so.' But the world was.
49   Below, No. CXIV.
50   No. XCIV.
51   No. XCVII.

adjournment of Chester Inferior Court. The long-standing dispute between the provinces of New York and New Hampshire about lands west of Connecticut River, which gave rise to or anyway was the pretext for this incident, is represented in this volume by affidavits dated 9 August[52] describing the riot at Chester and a kidnapping in the same town in May: both documents belong to a file of papers on this dispute sent to the Secretary of State by Governor Earl of Dunmore in 1771.[53] Dunmore's first reactions to the state of anarchy in Cumberland and Gloucester Counties, on arriving in New York to take up his governorship, are contained in his dispatch of 12 November 1770.[54] An earlier instruction from the King to the Governor of New York prevented him for the time being making grants of land in these counties and kept alive the hope of those who held under New Hampshire grants that the territory might one day be awarded to that colony. Settlers under New York grants were too few for it to be possible to appoint magistrates: hence the riots. The rescinding of this instruction continued to preoccupy Dunmore throughout his short administration of New York.

In Eastern Massachusetts there were no riots comparable to Orange or Cumberland Counties reported, but the want of order and government disturbed both Hutchinson and Hillsborough. Here, it was not merely that an extensive and remote region served as asylum for debtors and criminals; more alarming was the fact that 'intruders' i.e. persons with grants from the General Court of Massachusetts but without confirmation from the Crown, encouraged 'the waste and destruction of that timber, the preservation and supply of which is become a matter of the most serious consideration in respect to the naval strength of this kingdom.'[55] It was to protect this timber that John Wentworth, Surveyor of Woods, visited the territory in the summer of 1769, an experience which he described at length in a dispatch of 22 October 1770.[56] Wentworth, as he told it, quelled the rustics by the force of his character and the majesty of his cause, but this does not mean that there was no problem of law and order in the 'eastern country'. Jonathan Longfellow, Justice of the Peace for Lincoln County, was beaten up by a number of the inhabitants of Machias; and Hutchinson feared that unless checked the settlers there would become as dangerous as Regulators.[57] One suggested solution was to partition the area, Massachusetts quitting all claim to land east of Penobscot in return for an 'absolute property' in the lands between Penobscot and Kennebec. This plan found surprising favour with Hillsborough[58] but, despite the 'fondness for land-jobbing' which Hutchinson hoped would incline the General Court of Massachusetts to compliance, no progress was made in that direction.

52 Nos. LXXX-LXXXI.
53 Vol. I, No. 1047.
54 Below, No. CXIX.
55 No. LXIII.
56 No. CX.
57 Vol. I, Nos. 759, 759i-ii.
58 Below, No. LXIII.

Because it was not the usual practice of governors of colonies to report in detail on the peaceful prosperity which undoubtedly existed in many colonies, there is a tendency for the American correspondence of the Secretary of State to concentrate on the dramatic and the alarming; and this tendency has perhaps been heightened by the selection of documents for inclusion in the *Transcripts*. It may be well, therefore, before leaving the seaboard colonies, to direct attention to two dispatches from the acting Governor of South Carolina, William Bull.[59] A third-generation American, educated in Europe, Bull alone among Hillsborough's correspondents tossed Latin tags into his dispatches and extracted compliments from Whitehall for what he wrote. The first of these letters, written after a tour of 350 miles through the province, by chariot to prove that the roads were better than reputed, reported a scene of 'great, growing prosperity'; while the second, the long dispatch of 30 November, gives as good a picture as could be wished of South Carolina in her centennial year. Bull must surely have exaggerated in claiming that the developments he lovingly described had all taken place 'since the birth of many a man now alive'; but there were grounds for his complacency. How else could the United States have afforded rebellion?

The West

An important exchange of views took place in 1770 between Hillsborough and Lieut.-General Gage on the subject of a British military presence in the Upper Mississippi Valley and the related questions of the fur trade and possible colonization of that region.[60] Fort Chartres in Illinois was no more to Hillsborough than 'a mere mark of possession' and a graveyard for British troops. On the other hand, to plant more troops in better-sited forts at the mouths of the Illinois and Ohio Rivers would cost too much. The only way to keep costs down and at the same time guarantee British authority would be by controlled colonization, against which Hillsborough was as firmly set as he had ever been. Aside from other objections, the trade of such a colony might benefit Spain (via Louisiana) more than Britain, unless it could be diverted from New Orleans to West Florida by a canal joining the Iberville and the Mississippi. Gage was invited to look into this possibility, but one may perhaps read between the lines and infer that Gage was being told to assemble all the arguments he could find against it.

Gage's reply to the Secretary's dispatch ranged over all the arguments in favour of western military posts, disposing of most of them though arguing that the forts had some use in keeping the French in subjection and the Indians in 'some sort of awe, though by it we destroy that confidential friendship we wish to establish'. He too was against 'colonization' in the Illinois Country, not only on political grounds—remoteness leading to independence—but also because he wanted to let 'the savages enjoy their deserts in quiet' for the sake of a fur trade

59   Nos. LI, CXXVIII.
60   Nos. LXXVI (Hillsborough), CXVII (Gage).

that would surely shrink if they were driven from the forests by settlers. 'I conceive' he wrote 'that to procure all the commerce it will afford, and at as little expense to ourselves as we can, is the only object we should have in view in the interior country for a century to come, and I imagine it might be effected by proper management without either forts or settlements.'

Hillsborough, if one may judge by his official archives, was less interested in the Lower than in the Upper Mississippi. In 1770–71 sixty-nine letters were written to him by the governor and lieut.-governor of West Florida while he replied with only seven, a disproportion appearing nowhere else in his correspondence. Yet West Florida was at an extraordinarily interesting and critical stage of development, not to be obscured by the rather absurd quarrel between Montfort Browne and Elias Durnford, the retiring and incoming lieut.-governors, with which the year 1770 opened.[61] To begin with, Indian problems were many and pressing; and here Hillsborough, in his letters to John Stuart, exerted himself so far as to keep alive the war between Creeks and Choctaws, and to add a little weight to Governor Peter Chester's plans for Indian congresses. These gestures, however, amounted to the merest containment. On the vital question of settlement Hillsborough had little to say. Coastal West Florida as an agricultural colony had not hitherto been a success, owing in Chester's opinion to the barrenness of the seaside and the unhealthiness of the lands about Mobile:[62] Pensacola in 1770 was no more than a garrison-town. On the other hand, there was good land on the bank of the Mississippi and elsewhere west of Mobile, some of it patented but hardly any in effective occupation. Towards this region settlers were moving: witness the arrival at Natchez in July 1770 of 79 whites and 18 slaves who had travelled overland, and a report that 100 families in Virginia and Pennsylvania were thinking of following this lead.[63]

The proximity of Louisiana may have deterred some settlers. The crisis in Anglo-Spanish relations, bringing the two countries to the edge of war over the Falkland Islands, came too late in the year to have much influence on the events with which this volume is concerned, but even in peacetime Spain could be represented as a threat, for example, through her intrigues with Creeks and Choctaws, who were invited to New Orleans and even Havana, given presents and arms, and generally courted. This danger, whether real or imaginary, was used to support West Florida's claims for more British troops and particularly for the re-establishment of Fort Bute, near Baton Rouge, proposed by Durnford,[64] by the Council of West Florida,[65] and by Chester.[66] Soldiers were wanted in West Florida to protect the colony from Indians and keep new settlers in order, and because they were good for trade, as well as to balance the Spanish troops in Louisiana; and they were

61 Vol. I, No. 113.
62 Below, No. XCV.
63 Vol. I, Nos. 618, 618i-ii.
64 Below, No. XI.
65 No. LXVI.
66 No. XCV.

wanted just as much there (or in East Florida or in the Island of St John) as they were unwanted in Boston or New York.[67]

The other remedy for West Florida's troubles canvassed in 1770 was the Mississippi-Iberville canal,[68] to which reference has already been made. Little hard information was available on this subject until Durnford's survey of the following year, and extravagant claims could be made for its practicability. Hillsborough, we have seen, was interested in the project, but more for its implications in considering the problem of the Illinois Country than for any effect it might have on West Florida. This colony was in a state of peculiar dependence on Whitehall, but it is difficult to find anything deserving to be called a Lower Mississippi policy. 'East Florida' wrote Governor Chester 'has had much more countenance and encouragement than this province (perhaps we have not hitherto deserved it) . . . we remain here, instead of improving, in much the same situation we were in some years ago.'[69] In part at least this stagnation resulted from the lack of such a policy.

Hillsborough shows to no better advantage in his handling of the Ohio question in 1770. The application of Thomas Walpole, Benjamin Franklin and others, for a grant of the lands on the Ohio ceded by the Six Nations at the Treaty of Fort Stanwix in 1768 figures hardly at all in the Secretary of State's correspondence. His dislike of the scheme was well-known but must have been expressed in ways other than through his official letters: for example, by delaying the matter as much as he could, which is the burden of Walpole's complaint of 16 July,[70] and by briefing persons going to the colonies to gather evidence of un-favourable reactions there to the proposed grant. An instance of the latter is furnished by Dunmore's dispatch from New York less than a month after his arrival.[71] 'I have made it my business' he began 'to enquire and to find out the opinion of people here on the scheme in agitation for establishing a colony on the Ohio', and went on to say that it alarmed 'all the settled parts of America' for fear that the lower classes would be drained away to the Ohio and land values fall: an interesting hint of the possibility of common ground between Whitehall and Eastern landowners and businessmen against Western expansion. Frederick Smyth's letter[72] of 5 October 1772 on the same subject shows that Dunmore was not the only person Hillsborough invited to report on this subject.

Part of Hillsborough's difficulty in deterring the Ohio project arose from the approval given by the Treasury on 4 January 1770 to the suggested purchase-price of the lands in question. Though the Treasury reserved the matter of quitrents and deferred to other department on the issue of principle, the applicants were undoubtedly encouraged by this favour. The whole of 1770, however, was taken up by referring the matter to Virginia, the colony with the greatest interest in the

67   Vol. I, Nos. 634, 686, for references to East Florida and Island of St John.
68   Below, No. XCV.
69   *Ibid.*
70   No. LXXI.
71   No. CXIX.
72   Vol. V, No. CIII.

disposal of the lands;[73] and it is this reference that brought the name of George Washington, for the only time in the course of this year, into the Secretary of State's correspondence.[74]

Each of these aspects of the Western problem in 1770—the role of the British Army in the Illinois Country, the policy (if any) to be taken in the Lower Mississippi, and the disposal of the Ohio lands—had implications in the confused field of Indian relations. The documents in this volume reveal more of Indian affairs in the Southern District than in the Northern. This is not the result of biased selection but a reflection of the fact that Superintendant John Stuart wrote more letters than Superintendant Sir William Johnson, and enclosed many more supporting papers with his dispatches. Johnson's reports can to some extent be amplified by Gage's frequent references to Indian problems; and while Gage's news and views were largely second hand, being founded chiefly on what the Superintendents told him, his orderly presentation gives them a certain value.

Much the most arresting theme in Indian affairs in 1770 was the attempt by the Western Indians, Delaware and Shawnese especially, to form some kind of confederacy against the Six Nations and the whites. The impetus of the plan was resistance to white encroachments on Indian lands and disgust with the Six Nations for their too close relations with the whites and particularly for their cession at Fort Stanwix of lands over which other nations claimed rights. From this diplomacy—'a notable piece of policy' Gage called it[75]—sprang many of the problems of the superintendants in 1770. Johnson's task was to counter the Western initiative and at the same time dissuade the Six Nations from launching a pre-emptive strike, while Stuart had to discredit Western emissaries in the South and to extract from the Cherokees a cession of land to Virginia without this appearing too blatantly to be just the kind of demand the Western confederacy was forming to resist.[76] Stuart's congress with the Cherokees at Congarees in April proved abortive in this respect[77] and, though he met them again at Lochaber in October and got most of what he hoped for, he did not get all.[78] This, he complained, was 'the first instance of any nation having shown a reluctancy to treat with me, it is the only one of my having failed in carrying a point with Cherokees'.[79] In writing to Governor Lord Botetourt, Stuart blamed his partial failure on Virginian land-grabbers,[80] but his report to Hillsborough suggests that Shawnese diplomacy had made the task harder.[81] Later, in April 1771, after the Cherokees had shown a disposition to renegue on the concessions made at Lochaber, Stuart used the propaganda of the Western

73 Below, Nos. XXVIII, LXXIII, LXXVII.
74 Nos. CII, CIV.
75 No. CIII.
76 *Ibid.*
77 No. XLII.
78 No. CV.
79 No. CXII.
80 *Ibid.*
81 No. CXXV.

Indians as the principal explanation of the reluctance of Indians to part with lands.[82]

From Whitehall's point of view, schemes to confederate the Indians raised issues of principle and policy. 'We appear to be thrown' Gage wrote in January 'into the disagreeable alternative either to permit the Indians, or perhaps encourage them, to go to war with each other, or by uniting them to endanger our own tranquillity and turn their arms against ourselves.'[83] Johnson used more forceful words to say the same thing.[84] Whitehall's reaction was predictably realistic. Justice and humanity might require that the Indians should be stopped from fighting each other and even that they should be allowed to confederate; but self-preservation came first.[85]

As it turned out, the Western initiative and the proposed confederacy did not get very far in 1770, but an interesting application of Whitehall's doctrine of divide-and-rule arose in connection with the Creek-Choctaw war. Governor Wright of Georgia, in a letter of 20 July, was one of the first to raise the alarm that this war might soon end, freeing the restless Creeks to attack his province.[86] With Durnford calling for more attention to Indian affairs in West Florida, Hillsborough wrote reproachfully to Stuart on 30 October: 'The peace between the Choctaws and Creeks which . . . I was led to consider as an event of advantage to us, appears though not yet brought to a final conclusion to have produced effects dangerous to the safety of West Florida.'[87] Charles Stuart's letters from Pensacola of 12 June and 17 June make it perfectly clear that it had indeed been the policy of the Southern District to put an end to this war.[88] Now John Stuart had to try to extricate himself by assuring Hillsborough, first, that mediation between Creeks and Choctaws had been undertaken only to remove the suspicion that the British were 'the incendiaries who kindled the war'; and, secondly, that the intervention had been no more than a token gesture towards adversaries who were anyway going to make peace.[89] Charles Stuart's position, on the receiving end of what must have looked from Pensacola to be a *volte-face*, is shown by a comparison between his letters of June and December. In the first he was congratulating himself on having brought the two sides together;[90] in the second he was expressing relief that he had managed to keep them apart.[91]

Hillsborough was not convinced by John Stuart's pleadings. His further thoughts on the subject did not come until 4 May 1771, and took the form of a fairly definite pronouncement to both Stuart and Johnson in favour of non-intervention in Indian affairs: 'if we persist in making ourselves parties in their politics, either directly or through

82 Vol. III, No. XXXVIII.
83 Below, No. III.
84 No. XIII.
85 No. XXXIII.
86 No. LXXIV.
87 Vol. I, No. 481; C.O.5/71, Pt. 2, fo. 59.
88 Below, Nos. LIV, LVII
89 No. CXXIX.
90 Nos. LIV, LVII.
91 No. CXLIII.

the intervention of any particular tribe in which they know us to have a particular confidence, it is impossible to say to what consequences it may lead.'[92]

Unfortunately non-intervention was scarcely a practical policy when traders were continually being involved in deplorable incidents with the Indians, hunters roaming over Indian lands, and settlers, as Attahkullahkullah put it, 'coming into our houses and encroaching on us greatly'.[93] Johnson addressed a long, somewhat rambling, letter to Hillsborough on the abuses committed by white traders,[94] which the Secretary made the subject of a circular to all colonies involved in the Indian trade.[95] The former decision, to leave the regulation of that trade to the colonies, had produced no results apart from a single Act, good in intention but ineffectual, passed by West Florida. Complaints against the traders came both from colonial officials and from the Indians themselves: the need for control was obvious. Yet the only move made in 1770 in the direction of regulation was one with which Hillsborough had no sympathy at all and which he did his best to discourage. New York and Virginia passed Acts to appoint commissioners to meet representatives of other interested colonies in order to consider ways of controlling the trade. A meeting was called, and actually took place in New York on 12 July, with Patrick Henry as one of the Virginian delegates. But, though Pennsylvania and Quebec had shown interest, neither sent delegates and the congress adjourned with nothing done.[96]

Cadwallader Colden, reporting the passing of the New York Act to regulate the Indian trade, clearly thought he was bringing good news.[97] Hillsborough's reply was chilling: 'I have at least great doubts of the propriety of giving encouragement to such a congress . . . it is past a doubt that you ought not to have given your assent to any law for such a purpose without His Majesty's directions.'[98] Colden, like John Stuart in the affair of the Creek-Choctaw war, had guessed wrong. Colden's reply, not unlike Stuart's, was to say that the congress would probably never take place, or if it did that no common plan would be found.[99]

Quebec

The affairs of Quebec are under-represented in this volume, mainly because Governor Guy Carleton departed for England in August 1770, leaving Hector Theophilus Cramahé, President of Council, later lieut.-governor, to conduct a holding operation while the politicians in London supposedly got on with the job. One step towards a settlement

---

92   Vol. III, Nos. XLV–XLVI.
93   Below, No. CV.
94   No. LXXXII.
95   No. CXX.
96   Vol. I, Nos. 963, 963i, 1015, 1015i–vii.
97   Below, No. XX.
98   No. XXXIV.
99   No. LXV.

of Quebec's problems was, however, taken before Carleton's departure: the issue of the Ordinance for reforming the administration of justice and regulating the courts of law.[100] Carleton's comments on this measure, and his strictures on carpet-bagging Protestant Justices of Peace, are contained in a dispatch of 28 March,[101] to which the Governor's report of objections made against the Ordinance forms an appendix.[102] This attempt to put right some of 'the distresses of the Canadians and the cause of much reproach to our national justice and the King's government' was provisional and no substitute for concluding in London the protracted consideration of Quebec's future; but it was something, and it is worth noticing that it received Hillsborough's approval by return of post.[103]

100   Vol. I, No. 221ii.
101   Below, No. XXX.
102   No. XXXVIII.
103   Vol. I, No. 401. Carleton's letter with the Ordinance arrived in Whitehall 4 June, Hillsborough's reply was dated 12 June.

LIST OF DOCUMENTS

TRANSCRIPTS 1770

I

Governor William Tryon to Earl of Hillsborough (No. 45, duplicate)[1]

1 January, Brunswick

My Lord, I am to acknowledge the honour of your lordship's duplicate, No. 27, received 28 November last. The original and duplicate of 26 and original of 27 are not yet come to hand.

I entirely subscribe to your lordship's reasonings with respect to the necessity of the colonies providing for their own security by keeping their fortifications in repair and making the necessary provision for the defence of them.

At the last Assembly I persisted in urging to the Lower House the necessity of making provision for ammunition for His Majesty's service and the defence of the province but was mortified to find by their address that the argument on which they founded their refusal was the reason why they ought to have granted an aid for that service.

I understand a great objection to a Tonnage Bill proceeds from an unwillingness to tax the vessels owned in the country. By His Majesty's instruction No. 32 (a most equitable rule) I am directed not to give my assent to any law wherein the inhabitants of North Carolina are put on a more advantageous footing than those of Great Britain etc. This prevents my passing a bill making a distinction and probably the acquisition of a partial Tonnage Bill.

The country continues in extreme want of a larger medium of trade. When His Majesty shall think fit to grant the Assembly's petition for a new emission of currency, it may be thought expedient that a stipulation be made in the grant that the paper currency now in circulation, big with mischiefs from its counterfeits, should cease to be a legal tender within a limited time after the emission of the new, and be bought up by the Treasurers with the new currency in order to be destroyed. *Signed.* [C.O.5/313, fo. 29]

1 Signed original in C.O.5/301, fo. 120, is dated 6 January 1770. Entry, in C.O.5/328, p. 175, is dated 1 January.

II

George Croghan to Lieut.-General Thomas Gage[1]

1 January, Philadelphia

Sir, since I came to this place I have had several letters from Fort Pitt, Detroit and from several traders in the Indian country, all agreeing that the Indians behaved very quietly late in the fall before they went out a 'hunting, but every person who has wrote to me observes that they have been very constant in private councils and very reserved to their most intimate friends amongst the traders and have been purchasing up powder and lead all fall for their peltry, and likewise offering their horses for ammunition, which is very uncommon, and I think discovers a design of an open rupture in the spring. They purchased no goods from

1 Enclosure to Gage's letter to Hillsborough, 21 February 1770: Vol. I, No. 139.

any of the traders but ammunition, of which they are laying up great quantities.

A party of the Ohio, Senecas, Shawanese and Delawares, have been this fall at Detroit and had a private council in the Huron village with the Hurons, Chipawas, Ottawas and Putiwatimies, in which council they complained to these nations, saying the English had made a large purchase of lands from the Six Nations, and that the Six Nations had shamefully taken all the money and goods to themselves and not shared any part thereof with them though the most part of the country which was sold was their hunting-ground down the Ohio, and that by that sale a great number of their people which have lived on the East and West Branches of Susquehannah have been so encroached upon by new settlements that they have no hunting-grounds left, and requested of the Hurons to give their people some lands near Guiqaliaga to plant and hunt on, and that they would go and remove them from the Susquehannah. This request the Hurons granted and gave them a large belt of wampum, and Mr McKee who is just come down from Wioming and Fort Augusta saw the Indians that came from the Ohio to take all the Shawanese and Delawares away from the branches of the Susquahannah who told him their business, and he saw about fifty families set off with them and the rest is to go early in the spring.

At this meeting in the Huron village, the Hurons, Chipawas, Ottawas and Putiwatimies agreed to confirm a peace with the Cherokees as soon as they return from amongst the Six Nations, which I think must be detrimental to the public interest.

Mr McKee says that the Indians he met upon Susquehannah from the Ohio spoke of the Six Nations with great disrespect and resentment, and calls them the slaves of the white people, that in the beginning of the late war they were as humble as dogs to the French, and that now they were the same to the English for what they could get, and yet when they came amongst the western nations, they spoke the worst they could of them and was always breeding quarrels between their nations and the English.

Mr McKee will set off this week for Fort Pitt and I have prepared some council-belts to send with him and a letter to Captain Edmonstone with speeches to the several tribes. Mr McKee, who was formerly commissary there, understands the several languages and knows their customs and manners and has an influence with them, will I hope be able to find out what they are determined on in the spring. I have wrote to Sir William Johnson and given him an account of everything that came to my knowledge. *Copy.* [C.O.5/88, fo. 44]

III

Major-General Thomas Gage to Earl of Hillsborough (No. 39)

6 January, New York

My Lord, I have had the honour of your lordship's letter No. 23, which containing no particular commands, I am to wait some future opportunity to know His Majesty's pleasure on the contents of the several dispatches of which your lordship is pleased to acknowledge the receipt.

I may reasonably hope your lordship will receive advice of the landing of the 9th Regiment in Ireland before this letter gets to your hands. Your lordship has been informed of the unavoidable accidents which retarded the embarkation of that corps, and our last attempt to effect it by means of small vessels from South Carolina has been attended with some misfortune. Three out of four vessels employed got safe into the harbour of St Augustine, the fourth with sixty persons on board belonging to the 21st Regiment was drove on the coast of Florida about sixty miles distant from the fort. Clothing, arms, baggage etc. were lost, but happily no lives; and the people made their way through the woods to St Augustine. The shallowness of the water at the entrance of that harbour admitting only vessels of small burden and the danger of anchoring large ships on the outside of the bar where the swell is prodigious, an immense sea rolling in unbroke almost from the coast of Africa, has been often reported and our experience has evinced the truth of it; and although we have made a trial in a season remarkably tempestuous and the risk might not be so great in the summer months, yet upon the whole I am humbly of opinion that all embarkations and disembarkations at St Augustine would be more sure and safe by making use of small craft from South Carolina and Georgia where the larger transports should land and receive the troops.

The autumn has been so remarkably dry as to disappoint my endeavours to send clothing and other necessaries to Fort Chartres, and the detachment appointed to escort them is obliged to remain at Fort Pitt, not being able to proceed ten miles down the Ohio. It is the more unlucky as the troops at the Ilinois have been again afflicted with a dreadful sickness which would probably continue till the beginning of winter. I have yet only heard of the death of one officer, and hope the sickness will not prove so fatal as the last year. During this calamity a number of savages crossed over the Mississippi to attack the Indians of the country, who fortified themselves near the fort with great expedition; and the enemy retired without making any attempt upon them through fear, it is said, of disobliging the English. The few British inhabitants took refuge in the fort, but Lieutenant-Colonel Wilkins complains greatly of the behaviour of the French who could not be persuaded to speak to the invaders, though the domestic Indians declared any Frenchman might go in safety. He says, in those disagreeable circumstances, he summoned the militia, encouraged and threatened, but met with little better than an absolute refusal and he was shortly after informed and for a certainty that one of them declared the inhabitants would rebel. It is reported that the Spaniards intend to send 300 men to St Louis above Fort Chartres, which it's apprehended may prove detrimental to the trade from their taking a position which will enable them to intercept the Indians who bring peltry from the upper parts of the river, and is one reason why the Colonel recommends the building a post at or above the Ilinois River. He sets forth that the trade has been increased by traders stationed some leagues above the fort at Kaho, or Kahokia, a place he says become respectable from the numbers that have emigrated from Canada in spite of every effort that can be used to prevent it.

The works undertaken to preserve Fort Chartres from the floods of the Mississippi have not been attended with all the success we could wish. The stones and rubbish laid to defend the bank, having no firm foundation, mostly gave way in the last flood in July and sunk two fathoms under water, and the bank which is composed of mud, sand, and other loose stuff, is continually washing away. When His Majesty's troops first took possession of Fort Chartres they found a space of 250 feet between the south bastion and the river, of which there is now only 30 remaining.

In my letter to your lordship No. 32, I mentioned the claim of the inhabitants of the Detroit to Hog Island, which His Majesty has granted to Lieut. Macdougal. And having since acquired further information in that matter, I am to acquaint your lordship that after having the registers examined in Canada, no grant of said island to the inhabitants can be discovered but grants thereof to particular people have been found and marked *cancelled,* as the inhabitants allege they have been upon the representation of the settlers. Major Bruce now commanding at the Detroit likewise writes that the inhabitants have no paper to produce in favour of their claim, and Monsieur de la Motte's grant was according to what he can discover only a verbal one, and that the people acknowledge their only pretension is the possession of the island for sixty years, which they think gives them a sufficient right. The matter therefore seems to rest upon the title of sixty years possession, the validity of which I can't pretend to judge of. The Indians who were supposed to have had some claim to the island in consideration of some presents have conveyed all their right to it to Lieutenant Macdougal.

The last letters from the distant posts relate no extraordinary occurrences, everything was quiet, and the annual supplies were lain in.

Your lordship will have observed in some of my letters that our Indian affairs in the Northern District were in a precarious situation. The congress at Onandaga between the Six Nations and the Cherokees is over and your lordship will be informed of the result of it in the copy of a letter to me from Sir William Johnson which is sent herewith. We appear to be thrown into the disagreeable alternative either to permit the Indians, or perhaps encourage them, to go to war with each other, or by uniting them to endanger our own tranquillity and turn their arms against ourselves. Some of the nations threatened by this confederacy seem to have been acquainted with their danger and to have been preparing against it, for we were informed some months ago that the Western Indians had confederated, and two chiefs of the Shawnese were at the Detroit the end of September where in a public speech to the Indians of the Lakes they begged for peace with the nations of the Ouabache and introduced the cession of lands made to the English by the Six Nations. As far as I can understand these affairs the cession abovementioned is the cause of all the commotions that have lately happened among the Indians. Great part of the lands ceded were claimed by the Six Nations by right of ancient conquest, and though the tribes who resided near them admitted the right they felt no inconvenience from it further than being forced to acknowledge a superiority in the Six Nations. But now that the Six Nations have sold the lands as lords of the soil, kept all the presents and money arising from the sale to their own use, and that the white people are expected in consequence of it to settle on their hunting grounds, these dependent Indians are exasperated to a great degree. The Cherokees have engaged from the strong desire of cultivating the friendship of the Northern Indians and to secure allies against their enemies on the Ouabache and other nations with whom they have been long at war.

Mr Stuart writes that he has the satisfaction to acquaint me the Indians in his department are well disposed, and nothing but encroachments and want of attention to the disorders of the traders will induce them to break with us. There was a meeting at Augusta in November with the Upper Creeks and Cherokees at which they enumerated some grievances, chiefly respecting irregularities in the trade, which Mr Stuart has laid before the respective governors in his district in hopes that the Assemblies will pass proper laws to restrain the traders from the commission of irregularities so disagreeable to all the Indians and care will be taken to put the laws in force. *Signed.* [C.O.5/88, fo. 26]

IV

Lieut.-Governor Cadwallader Colden to Earl of Hillsborough (No. 8)

6 January, New York

My Lord, I have the honour of your lordship's letter of the 4th of November, No. 34. At this time when difficulties in the administration are unavoidable the assurances your lordship is so kind to give of your support and protection gives me strength in performing my duty.

When the bill for supplying the troops quartered in this place was brought into the Assembly the party in opposition made a violent effort to disconcert all the present measures by exciting the people to appear against the bill. For this purpose the enclosed printed paper [Vol. I, No. 12i] directed "*To the betrayed Inhabitants of the City and Colony of New York*" was in the night before the last packet sailed dispersed through the town. I transmit your lordship likewise two proclamations [Vol. I, No. 12ii-iii] issued on this occasion.

Though some of our newspapers make the meetings of the Sons of Liberty, as they call themselves, on this occasion to be numerous and of consequence the party was really disappointed. The numbers who appeared were too small and inconsiderable to have any weight or be of any service to their purpose. They have been farther disappointed in three attempts since made. People in general, especially they of property, are now aware of the dangerous consequences of such riotous and mobish proceedings.

The supply of the troops is unpopular both in town and country. You know, my lord, it is very generally an unpopular subject in the English Government, and much pains is taken to work upon the prejudice of the people here. However, the party in the Assembly did not think proper to oppose the supply directly but proposed that it should be paid out of bills of credit to be emitted by a bill then in the House, in which case that Act must take effect immediately or there could be no supply. This made it necessary for the friends of government to compromise the matter by granting one thousand pounds out of the Treasury and one other thousand pounds out of these bills of credit, and even with this compromise the bill for supplying the troops was carried by a very small majority; and it could not have been carried had I not given the friends of administration expectations that I would assent to the bill for emitting bills of credit if it were in the same terms with the bill passed in the preceding session and transmitted to your lordship by Sir Henry Moore, and six months allowed to know His Majesty's pleasure before the bills of credit can be emitted.

Yesterday, my lord, I passed the bill granting £2,000 for supplying the troops quartered in this place with necessaries; and the bill for emitting £120,000 in bills of credit being ready for my assent, I called together the Council who all attended except Sir William Johnson who is at 200 miles distance. His Majesty's instruction of July 15th 1766 for creating and emitting paper bills of credit was laid before them. After having considered the same and reasoned thereon, the gentlemen of the Council unanimously advised me to give my assent to the bill for emitting £120,000 in bills of credit as being absolutely necessary in the present circumstances of this colony; and I accordingly gave my assent to it in the usual form.

It is the same with the bill transmitted to your lordship by Sir Henry Moore (except in two or three immaterial clauses on the appointment of loan-officers in the cities of New York and Albany, and unavoidable alterations in time) which the Lords Commissioners for Trade and Plantations must have had under consideration before this time. The bills of credit to be emitted by this Act are to bear date the 10th of June next, the interest is to arise from and the emission to be on the last Tuesday of that month, which is near six months from this time. This is equivalent to a suspending clause till His Majesty's pleasure shall be known; for His Majesty's pleasure certainly may be transmitted before that time. I now, my lord, transmit an exemplified copy of the Act under the seal of the province in a box directed to the Board of Trade and Plantations. No public business could have been carried on in the Assembly without my assent to this bill. The call for it both in town and country was so general that the friends of government in the Assembly would not have been supported without it, and the administration must have been made very uneasy to me. Your lordship may be assured I discover nothing in it prejudicial to His Majesty's service, and as the interest-money arising from these bills of credit cannot be disposed of without the governor's consent it may be a fund hereafter for supplying the troops. The King's approbation will give general satisfaction, and when people are in good humour His Majesty's service may be carried on more effectually than when they are in a contrary disposition.

I enclose another printed paper [Vol. I, No. 12iv] that your lordship may see the temper of the party who oppose the measures of government. At the same time it may not be improper to tell you that no governor-in-chief has been at any time attended by greater numbers on

New Year's Day than I was on the last with their compliments on the season. When what appeared in this place in past times is considered, my mentioning this will not be thought to proceed merely from vanity.

The Assembly are still sitting, they have passed none but the usual bills except those which I have already mentioned to your lordship. What remains to be done for His Majesty's service in this session I expect will be done without difficulty. I shall think myself extremely happy if my endeavours in the performance of my duty obtain His Majesty's approbation. Without doubt your lordship perceives the difficulties which attend the administration of government at this time in all the colonies, and therefore I flatter myself with your most favourable construction of the measures I have thought necessary for His Majesty's service. *Signed.* [C.O.5/1101, fo. 21]

V

John Stuart to Governor Lord Botetourt[1]

13 January, Charleston

My Lord, I am honoured with your excellency's letter of 18th December with the address and memorial of the House of Burgesses of the colony of Virginia, praying for a greater extent of boundary than that pointed out in the report of the Right Honourable the Board of Trade and directed by His Majesty to be ratified and marked as signified by the Earl of Hillsborough in his letter of 13th May 1769.

I must beg your lordship will be persuaded that in negotiating a boundary line between the Indian nations and the different provinces I have solely been actuated by principles of duty in conforming as nearly as possible to His Majesty's ideas and orders, so fully and clearly expressed in his additional instructions to all his governors in 1761, by his royal proclamation of 7th October 1763, and by his orders relative to the report of his Board of Trade contained in the Earl of Hillsborough's letter of 15th of April 1768, which evince his most gracious purpose of protecting and rendering strict justice to the Indians, thereby to remove their jealousies and apprehensions which our encroachments on their hunting grounds too well justified, and from which that dissatisfaction and hostile disposition which proved so expensive and destructive to His Majesty's subjects principally arose. I am therefore extremely mortified when from these considerations my reasoning on the subject of a more extended boundary must differ from that of so respectable a body as the House of Burgesses of the dominion of Virginia, whose view and wishes I can have no motive to obstruct or oppose except what arises from an earnest desire faithfully to discharge the trust reposed in me.

I beg your lordship's permission to represent that from the knowledge of the disposition of the Indian tribes within the Southern District which my office of Superintendent has enabled me to acquire,

1 Enclosed in Botetourt's letter to Hillsborough, 22 February 1770: Vol. I, No. 144.

I am persuaded the Cherokees will never consent to give up the territory pointed at in your Assembly's memorial, because:

First, a continuation of the line dividing your colony and North Carolina from the point where it intersects Holsten's River in a due western course can never touch the Ohio but will run within less than sixty miles of the Cherokee Towns and fall upon the Cherokee River a little below Chuola or the Chickasaw Landing.

Second, said line would cut off from the Cherokees and Chickasaws their only valuable hunting grounds, it being a fact well known that they always hunt at the distance of one or two hundred miles from their villages, for an obvious reason, the scarcity of deer near the dwellings of a nation of hunters.

Third, besides the distress which the Cherokees and Chickasaws would certainly be subjected to by the loss of their hunting grounds, the settlement of these lands by adventurers from your colony who are likewise hunters and in other respects disagreeable to the Indians would prove an insurmountable obstacle.

These difficulties, my lord, would operate immediately with the Cherokees and Chickasaws, but the jealousies and apprehensions of every tribe on the continent, especially of those within this district, would be again revived by such an extension of territory, although they are almost effaced by His Majesty's having most graciously directed to settle and mark distinct boundaries; and in whatever manner the cession pointed at in the memorial might be obtained from the Cherokees there is the greatest reason to apprehend that it would be productive of a general rupture with and coalition of all the tribes on the continent, for however Indians may quarrel amongst themselves yet an encroachment on the lands of any nation becomes a common cause and attracts the attention of the whole.

The Creek nation, consisting of four thousand gun-men, have lately complained to me of settlement being made by emigrants from Virginia on the unceded lands on the Mississippi. The Chickasaws and Choctaws are more immediately affected by such settlements and also express their uneasiness. At this very time there are in the Creek nation deputies from the Shawnese, Delawares, and other Northern tribes, accompanied by some Cherokees, endeavouring to form a general confederacy on the principle of defending their lands from our daily encroachments. The principal chiefs of the Cherokee nation sent me the enclosed message [Vol. I, No. 144iii] in July last, and immediately afterwards Ouconnastotah the principal leader set out with 30 canoes of armed men to reconnoitre the settlements on Holsten's River and see how far your inhabitants had extended beyond the line agreed upon by the treaty in November 1768. These circumstances appear to be worthy of your excellency's attention, and I hope will serve to evince the propriety of my declining to recommend the proposed extension, and here permit me, my lord, to express my great sorrow for being obliged to refuse my assistance of whatever weight it may be in obtaining for the colony of Virginia a boundary to the extent of their wishes. My sentiments on the proposal I shall candidly submit to His Majesty's ministers and be extremely happy in carrying whatever orders they may think proper to give me relative to it into execution.

I hope your lordship will think it for the good of His Majesty's service to restrain adventurers from your colony from settling beyond the line already agreed upon until His Majesty's ultimate orders can be received.

From the supposition in the memorial that the line therein proposed would fall upon the Ohio, I must conclude the plan referred to to be erroneous, for the division line between Virginia and North Carolina appears by the map to be in 36° 30': the Cherokee Towns are situated between 35° and 35° 40'.

I enclose your lordship my bill on his excellency General Gage for the amount of the bill of expenses contracted by direction of Mr Cameron. PS. I have chosen rather to send my bill upon my agent at New York for the amount of the bill of expenses abovementioned being £33 York currency, which will certainly be paid duly. The abstract of the additional instruction and proclamation I send merely to save your lordship the trouble of looking for the original. *Copy*. [C.O.5/1348, fo. 75]

VI

Governor James Grant to Earl of Hillsborough (No. 34)

16 January, St Augustine
My Lord, I have had the honour to receive your lordship's letter No. 24 by the November packet. Our planters flatter themselves that they are entitled to the premiums mentioned for indigo in the plan for laying out the sum allotted for the encouragement of useful articles of culture which I had the honour to transmit to your lordship with my letter No. 29.

The indigo crop consisting nearly of ten thousandweight is to be sent to London on board a vessel of Mr Oswald's, which arrived here lately from the coast of Africa with a cargo of very fine slaves: they have been sold and come cheaper than in the neighbouring provinces, exclusive of the advantage and satisfaction which the planters have in receiving their negroes without risk and upon the spot. This is the third vessel which Mr Oswald has sent to this place, 'tis to be hoped he will find his account in it as much as his brother planters do, who are much obliged to him for the assistance he has given them in the negro way. They or their agents are in the country hard at work preparing their grounds for the planting season which comes on early in March.

Plantations have been put into order, and everything appears to me at present to be in such forwardness that I am very sanguine in my expectations of the produce of indigo this year.

What is sent I flatter myself will in general be equal to any that is carried from America, and if gentlemen do not still improve this year in the culture of it I shall be much disappointed. I never intended to plant an acre in the province, but I thought we got on slowly, I became impatient and bought negroes, formed a plantation in November 1768, undertook in conversation to send produce to London within the year, and had my indigo crop ready to ship within the time, which I am assured is worth five shillings a pound. The example has been of use and gives a spur to other people which in fact was what I aimed at.

Mr Rolle, poor man, will not contribute to our exports; he has been here. I did not see him or hear from him directly but I have reason to believe that he is at last convinced of his error in some points. I agreed to everything his agent applied for in his name—he has a great passion for land and having already sunk £10,000 for which he has nothing to show, he is gone home to buy up some of His Majesty's orders for land in this province which have not been located by the gentlemen to whom they were granted.

Five companies of the 31st regiment are under orders to go to West Florida. This garrison will then consist of the 21st regiment and two companies of the 31st; but barracks are going on for another regiment which 'tis to be hoped will soon be sent from the northern provinces: they will be as much pleased to get rid of them as we are desirous to have them. *Signed.* [C.O.5/551, fo. 15]

VII

Earl of Hillsborough to Governor William Tryon (No. 30)

18 January, Whitehall

Sir, your dispatch of the 22nd of November, No. 39, containing an account of what passed on the meeting of the General Assembly of North Carolina on the 23rd of October and of your having dissolved them in consequence of the very extraordinary proceedings of the Lower House was received yesterday and immediately laid before the King.

It has given His Majesty great concern that his colony of North Carolina, whose conduct has hitherto been so decent and moderate and distinguished by its respect for the supreme legislature of the British Empire, should have been induced by the ill example of its neighbours to adopt and concur in measures and resolves so unbecoming and unwarrantable.

There are many circumstances which give but too just ground to apprehend that these violences do not arise merely out of the force of example but are the effects of false and, I am justified by a discovery made in one of the Departments in which I serve in saying, treacherous misrepresentations and letters of encouragement from this side of the water.

These wicked and factious designs will however I hope soon cease to have their effect and that it will not be long before the colonies see more clearly how severely their interests are prejudiced by suffering their conduct to be influenced by such artifices.

With this hope it is that His Majesty, at the same time that he thinks the dissolution of the Assembly was a measure which their own intemperate behaviour rendered unavoidable, does intend that it shall not operate to interrupt such necessary business of the colony as depends upon the full exercise of legislative power, and therefore I am commanded to signify to you his royal pleasure that you should as soon as it may be necessary and convenient issue writs for a new election of Representatives to meet at such time as you shall, with the advice of the Council, think most proper, at which time you will be cautious of saying more to them in your speech than will be necessary to express your resolution to concur in all such measures as may best promote His Majesty's service and the interests and happiness of his people under your government.

Enclosed I send you the King's gracious speech to his Parliament at the opening of the session on the 9th instant together with the addresses of both Houses and His Majesty's gracious answers thereto.

The King having thought fit to take the Great Seal out of the hands of Lord Camden, it was yesterday delivered to Mr Charles Yorke, and it is His Majesty's intention that he should be immediately called up to the House of Lords. *Draft.* [C.O.5/313, fo. 1]

VIII

Earl of Hillsborough to Lieut.-Governor Cadwallader Colden (No. 36)

18 January, Whitehall

Sir, I have received and laid before the King your dispatch No. 5, enclosing your speech to the General Assembly at the opening of the session on the 22nd of November and the addresses to you from both Houses.

The late governor in a letter to me dated the 19th of July last acquaints me that my circular letter No. 29, of which I now enclose to you a copy although I presume you are in possession of the original, had been communicated to the Council and had given great satisfaction, and I have also observed that the purport of that letter has been repeatedly printed in the newspapers on the continent of America. As the contents of it cannot therefore be unknown to you and are, I am certain, so clearly expressed as not to be misunderstood I must desire you will enable me to inform the King upon what authority you have taken upon you to declare in your speech to the General Assembly that there is the greatest probability that the late duties *(without distinction)* imposed by the authority of Parliament upon America would be taken off in the ensuing session; I very sincerely wish you may have it in your power so to explain and justify this proceeding as to remove the appearance of your having acted in a manner highly unbecoming your situation.

After what I have said on this subject it gives me much concern to find occasion to animadvert on any other part of your conduct, but it is not fit for me to pass unobserved your having omitted to take notice in your speech of the steps taken by the late governor and by yourself in respect to the Paper Currency Bill passed in the former session of Assembly; had this been done the Assembly could not have had the colour of a pretence for so irregular a proceeding as that of framing a new bill pending His Majesty's consideration of the former one, and if it shall appear that you have suffered the Assembly to proceed upon this business without using your endeavours to dissuade them from it, it will be such an aggravation of your imprudence and want of attention as cannot fail of exposing you to His Majesty's just displeasure. Upon what ground it is that you suppose this new bill will receive the Council's concurrence I am at a loss to guess; but I trust that they will not be influenced by any consideration to a conduct inconsistent with a due respect to the Crown.

His Majesty hopes that the account you give of the temper and disposition of the majority of the new Assembly will in the end be justified by their actions, but their having adopted and concurred in the resolves of the Virginia Assembly of the 16th of May is not a very favourable omen that their proceedings will have so desirable a conclusion.

Enclosed I send you the King's gracious speech to his Parliament at the opening of the session on the 9th inst., together with the addresses of both Houses and His Majesty's gracious answer thereto.

The King having thought fit to take the Great Seal out of the hands of Lord Camden, it was yesterday delivered to Mr Charles Yorke and it is His Majesty's intention that he should be immediately called up to the House of Lords. *Draft.* [C.O.5/1101, fo. 8]

IX

Earl of Hillsborough to Lieut.-Governor Thomas Hutchinson (No. 31)

18 January, Whitehall

Sir, enclosed I send you the King's speech to his Parliament at the opening of the session on the 9th inst., together with the addresses of both Houses and His Majesty's gracious answers thereto.

The notice which is taken in the King's speech of the Associations to obstruct and distress the commerce of Great Britain with her colonies, and what is expressed in the addresses of both House of their resolution to take such steps as shall discountenance and make effectual provision against these unwarrantable measures, render it unnecessary for me to trouble you with any observations of my own upon what you state in your letters, Nos. 9 and 10, respecting such Associations and the violent acts and proceedings of those who countenance them.

I trust that the measures of Parliament will be such as will be effectual to suppress these confederacies, to give support to lawful authority, and that relief and protection to the honest subject which he is justly entitled to from the government under which he lives.

The step His Majesty has thought fit to take in recommending the state of his colonies to the consideration of Parliament necessarily suspends all further determination upon it in any other way; it is therefore His Majesty's pleasure that the sitting of the Assembly should not be postponed beyond the time of its usual meeting or to which you may have prorogued it in consequence of my letter to you of the 4th of November; and His Majesty is not without hope, from the reliance he has on your prudence and discretion, that the public business of the colony may be carried on with temper and moderation and a due respect to the laws and constitution.

It has given the King great concern to find by dispatches from Major-General Gage that, notwithstanding the decent and exemplary behaviour of the troops at Boston, they have been exposed to very great insult and indignity from the populace, without any protection from the civil magistrate.

The reports of the commanding officer at Boston contain many facts and apprehensions relative to these insults that are very alarming, and therefore, though none of your letters to me contain any intelligence of this nature, yet His Majesty has thought fit in consequence of those reports to command me to recommend to Major-General Gage a careful attention to what passes at Boston and to reinforce Col. Dalrymple in case it shall appear to be necessary; and though the King is sensible of the weak state of his government in the Massachusetts Bay, His Majesty nevertheless expects that you should in both your capacities exert the utmost activity in supporting the constitution and in giving to all his subjects that protection which the authority of the chief magistrate may be liable to afford them.

The King having thought fit to take the Great Seal out of the hands of Lord Camden, it was yesterday delivered to Mr Charles Yorke, and it is His Majesty's intention that he should be immediately called up to the House of Lords. *Draft.* [C.O.5/759, fo. 21]

X

Lieut.-Governor Thomas Hutchinson to Earl of Hillsborough (No. 3)

24 January, Boston

My Lord, I have formerly observed to your lordship that after the agreement made by the merchants not to send for or import any goods from Great Britain until the first of January 1770, many persons who did not approve of the measure and had imported goods in the course of the last summer acceded so far as to promise not to sell them until the agreement of the merchants expired. The intent no doubt was that they who first agreed and they who afterwards acceded should all be upon the same footing. Six or eight of those who acceded really thought they were at liberty to begin the sale of their goods the first of January and did so, but a far greater number under the same circumstances were contented to wait until those who had first agreed could have time sufficient to send for and import goods after the first of January. The merchants' committee called a meeting last week in the town of Boston of merchants and others connected with trade which included the inhabitants in general. This meeting was as numerous as a town-meeting and consisted of much the same sort of people, hath no foundation in law, and their proceedings, though without any degree of tumult, in going in great bodies to two or three persons and among the rest to two of my sons who were of the number of merchants who had sold, and who live in my family, and demanding of them a compliance with their agreement, was altogether unwarrantable. My sons, at the first of the meetings, upon being applied to, thought it best to give up the point they had contended for, to prevent a tumult, and without my privity conceded to keep their goods as long as the rest who had been under the same circumstances with them; but as some had agreed their goods should be in the hands of the committee and others in their own hands a new misunderstanding arose. I found that whilst my family was interested in this dispute I should be under much greater difficulty both from the Council and every other quarter than I should be if they were out of the question, and upon inquiry into the agreement

I found it taken in different senses, and as it could make no material difference whether they complied in whole or in part I was not unwilling to be rid of any incumbrance on their account. The others who were in the contention saw the reason of it and I assured them of all the protection in my power, and they persevered to the end. After assembling three or four days, the meeting suffered itself to dissolve, a great part of the proceedings having been illiberal, puerile and very dishonorary: among other instances, much time was spent in debating whether Colonel Dalrymple, who with great discretion avoids all unnecessary irritations, did not deserve to be cashiered for quartering the troops in the town when barracks were provided at the Castle, and whether he had not exceeded his authority when some of the corps were allowed to be in the house of one of the obnoxious persons. They dropped this debate without a question.

I thought it of great importance that due testimony should be borne against those innovations. By the minutes of the Council [Vol. I, No. 56i], which I shall transmit, your lordship will see I could have no aid from them. They differed from me in sentiment. I have no doubt of their doing what appears to them to be right. Without the aid of the Council, I am so restrained by the charter and constitution I can do nothing except in what relates to military authority. I sent to the Justices of the county to attend me and showed them that the continuance of this assembly from day to day was the continuance of a breach of law, and desired them to consider by themselves the duty which the law required of them and act accordingly, but they were of opinion that it was not advisable to interpose unless there should be something more disorderly than yet had been.

I warned the moderator and some others, in private, of the danger to which they were exposed, that their professed design was to reform the law by effecting the repeal of the Revenue Acts, that any violences from any of the inferior people who were among them would in my opinion involve them all in the guilt of high treason, and I sent by the Sheriff to the moderator in the meeting a declaration [Vol. I, No. 56ii] which I required him to read, and which was done accordingly; and notwithstanding it did not convince them of the illegality of their measures, it made them more anxious to restrain all disorders at their breaking-up.

I daresay the affair of non-importation cannot hold another year: the merchants who are engaged in it nevertheless obstinately persist until the first agreement expires, and I am told that by this vessel near fifty tons of goods are reshipped to Bristol, having been imported contrary to the agreement. And so infatuated are the tradesmen that although they are destitute of work, yet when a Scotch merchant offered to build 4 or 5 ships in the town provided he might be at liberty to sell his goods, they chose he should contract for his ships somewhere else rather than the agreement entered into here should be infringed.

My situation, my lord, has been peculiarly difficult. If the Council had been in sentiment with me, I think this assembly might have been prevented or soon dispersed. Left alone, I had to consider the danger from such meeting from day to day, which I knew to be against law, and yet it consisted of several Justices of the Peace who ought to execute law, several professed lawyers, and a great number of inhabitants of property together with three of the Representatives of the town and a mixed multitude warmed with a persuasion that what they were doing was right and that they were struggling for the liberties of America. I considered also the uncertain consequence of anything tragical from the troops in suppressing acts of violence if the temper of the people should rise to it, occasioned by a dispute upon a point in which so many colonies warmly interest themselves, and I have acted upon the whole according to the best of my ability. *Signed.* [C.O.5/759, fo. 36]

XI

Lieut.-Governor Elias Durnford to Earl of Hillsborough (No. 3, duplicate)

3 February, Pensacola

My Lord, by the last opportunity which offered I had it not in my power to write your lordship many particulars of the province, and am now scarcely clear of the confusion which hath hitherto reigned here; nevertheless think it my duty to inform you of our present state although my time will not permit me to do it with that clearness I could otherwise wish.

There are two matters which I shall beg leave to lay before your lordship as they appear to me services which are absolutely necessary to be carried into immediate execution. The first is the re-establishing the post at Fort Bute and laying out a town at that place, as it will be the means not only of establishing our trade on the Mississippi, of encouraging a number of useful settlers, and of annually consuming a large quantity of British manufactures, but likewise of having the greatest part of the most opulent French inhabitants with their slaves and effects coming to settle on our side of the river if they see but the least prospect of their lives and property being protected.

I have wrote to General Gage on this subject and think that £700 will be sufficient for this post until it is properly established, and if a small post at the entrance of the lakes with an armed batteau was to be ordered it would be a sure means of keeping everything quiet in that quarter and I flatter myself will open the communication with the Mississippi by the Iberville.

The second matter that I take the liberty of communicating to your lordship is of the advantages that will accrue to this province by the establishing a town on the east side of the Bay of Mobile, below a place called the Red Clifts, as the unhealthy situation of the present one makes such a measure necessary. The place I now mention to your lordship hath ever been pointed out as the only proper one by all who have seen it; both the Brigadier-Generals Haldimand and Taylor had each given orders to have barracks for the troops which were appointed for the service of Mobile to be fixed here, but were countermanded by some unforeseen orders just as they were going to be put in execution.

By the next opportunity I shall send your lordship a sketch of the Bay of Mobile with the situation of the ground which is well known to be very healthy.

There would in another case be some objection to a town's being fixed there, which is the lands being granted near it, but the spot I speak of is at least a mile in front, with a depth of four or five miles back, and a mile more might be added from the adjacent lands as they are only French grants, one of them purchased by Mr Wegg to whom I have spoke of giving up part of his land if required, and the other by myself, part of which I formerly offered to Brigadier-General Haldimand on his proposing to fix a post near this spot. A town thus situated, where there is ten or twelve feet water within half a mile of the shore and a tolerable depth close in with it, would have great advantages over this place by its contiguous situation to the good lands of the province, likewise by reason of its inhabitants being constantly supplied with all kinds of provisions at a very easy rate, and the wellknown healthiness of the air would be the means of saving a number of lives. Add to this that the communication with this place would be trifling to what it now is with Mobile.

The old fort at Mobile is now falling to decay, and the materials might be used in making barracks for the troops or any other public buildings; indeed there is plenty of stone and the necessary materials for that business on the spot, and there is no part of the province that I know of where building can be carried on at so cheap a rate as at this place. It would be likewise necessary to have a post of 25 men and a town fixed up the River Mobile, which post might be relieved monthly or every fortnight either by land or water, which would be a means of keeping the troops in motion and of making them acquainted with the country, at the same time contributing to their health.

These thoughts I have long wished to communicate to your lordship and am truly sensible their being carried into execution must be of considerable advantage to this colony. Were the three companies last ordered for this province arrived and the smallest means in my hands to carry on this duty, I should not hesitate a moment at risking part of my own small property to carry this essential service into execution, flattering myself it would meet with His Majesty's approbation.

The trade of the River Mississippi hath of late years been very considerable, and as we are enlarging our fur-trade at the Illinois, which furs are usually sent to Orleans and fall into the hands of French factors, I should imagine if orders were given to the commanding officer at the Illinois to oblige all persons sending peltry down the Mississippi to give bond to leave them at Fort Bute or the town which might be fixed there, in order to be shipped for Great Britain or her colonies (which is not always the case at present to our no small loss of that trade), it might be a means of forwarding this settlement and a general advantage to the colony.

I must request your lordship's pardon for the trouble I give you, but being perfectly sensible of your great desire to promote the prosperity of His Majesty's American dominions and this infant colony in particular, I am therefore the more emboldened to write my sentiments more freely to your lordship and wish only that my conduct may meet your lordship's future countenance. *Signed.* [C.O.5/577, p. 217]

XII

Adam Stephen to Governor Lord Botetourt[1]

9 February, Winchester

My Lord, in obedience to your lordship's commands I have made all the enquiry into the circumstances of Indian Stephen's death that could be obtained without being on the spot.

One Gamble appears to have been principally concerned: in their way to commit the murder they asked a young man, Benjamin Harrison, to go along with them, telling him what their intentions were; he refused to join them and unless his evidence can be of weight against them no testimony can affect them.

The steps taken by your excellency and government has entirely satisfied the Indians.

The news of the murderers being apprehended, put in irons and sent down to Williamsburg to be punished gave them great pleasure.

They declared their great satisfaction in your lordship's pains taken to do them justice, asked what sort of men the Black Boys were that interrupted the trade and destroyed the ammunition intended for them.

Upon their being told that they were disorderly people who would be punished as soon as they were apprehended, they offered your lordship as many men as you should have occasion for to apprehend and reduce them to order.

I hope the outrages are entirely suppressed and there will be no more occasion to trouble your lordship with these fellows. In the meantime I beg leave to observe to your lordship that the sending Ingham to Williamsburg jail has had a very good effect upon the Indians and that it has probably prevented a great deal of trouble to your lordship and to me. Had he been recommitted to Winchester jail the passions of the people and their obstinacy was so great at that time that I should have been obliged to kill parcel of them to prevent another rescue.

When your lordship's proclamation was carried to Pittsburgh, an Indian of good education who was in London about two or three years ago happened to be at that place and was very active in explaining the proclamation to the Indians and quieting their minds. *Copy.* [C.O.5/ 1348, fo. 81]

1   Enclosed in Botetourt's letter to Hillsborough, 22 February 1770: Vol. I, No. 144.

XIII

Sir William Johnson to Earl of Hillsborough (No. 12)

10 February, Johnson Hall

My Lord, in my last of the 26th August (No. 11) I gave your lordship an account of my journey through the country of the Six Nations to Seneca with my proceeding at several conferences with the Indians, and acquainted you that deputies were arrived from the Cherokees etc. to request a meeting with the Six Nations and Canada confederacies at Onondaga, which has since taken place agreeable to their desire; the result of which I waited for, as judging it might be necessary for His Majesty's information. At this congress the Cherokees spoke on twenty belts to the Six Nations etc. to renew and strengthen the late treaty of peace entered into between them, and earnestly to request that in consequence thereof the Six Nations etc. should unite their arms with them in order to attack several of the Southern and Western nations who had acted as enemies to both. After some time spent in deliberation, the Six Nations returned for answer that before they could come to any resolution, agreeable to their former engagements they must first confer with me on the subject, to which end they would take care of their belts and calumets and send deputies to me to desire a general congress in my presence; and accordingly their deputies have since come here with some of the Cherokees, earnestly requesting on the part of the whole that I would as speedily as possible assemble the two confederacies and after hearing what they had to say give them my advice and opinion on the subject. To support their request they observed that we were as much interested as themselves in the matter, having suffered repeated insults from these people, as they instanced in Mr Croghan's being attacked, several of his party killed, and himself made prisoner by them on his way to the Illinois, and in their attacks upon our traders on Ohio. In short I observed that they were much inclined to unite and attack those people which gave me the more concern because I knew that when Indians were resolved on war, if they could be diverted from their favourite pursuit, they would be apt to turn their arms another way, perhaps against ourselves. Besides I was sensible of the great expense that must attend such a congress although of their own proposing, and that what could be spared out of the fund allowed for the Department could not defray the charge of so large and unexpected a congress. In this situation I consulted General Gage who is of opinion that as any sum can be spared out of the annual allowance will be inadequate to the expense that may attend it, I should first obtain His Majesty's orders for that purpose; but as the Indian deputies are very pressing and that it will not be in my power to have an answer within sufficient time to satisfy their importunity, whilst on the other hand I cannot refuse their request without occasioning a general discontent amongst them, I have resolved to treat with some of the chiefs only with all the economy possibly can consistent with the public safety, trusting that His Majesty will be graciously pleased to consider the peculiarity of the occasion and not suffer me to be a loser through the necessary discharge of my duty.

It is a disagreeable circumstance that we must either agree to permit these people to cut each other's throats or risk their discharging their fury on our traders and defenceless frontiers, for certain I am from the disposition they are in and from the conduct of the back-settlers, the latter may prove the case; but however disagreeable the alternative is, common policy and our own safety requires it, and under such circumstances I shall endeavour to govern myself in the manner that appears best calculated for the general security of all His Majesty's subjects here.

The situation of affairs since I had last the honour of addressing your lordship on these subjects has not varied materially. Although the severity of the season and the embassy from the Cherokees keep them at present quiet, yet the motives for their discontents still subsist, and the lawless conduct of the frontier inhabitants is the same when ever an opportunity offers, so that the event depends upon circumstances that are as hard to foresee as to prevent, and as there is no prospect of any immediate remedy to be applied for these disorders and the licentiousness of many of our own people, my endeavours must be directed to prevent their operation on the minds of the Indians till a more favourable period when the orders of Government will be treated with more respect and the people brought to a better sense of their duty. *Signed.* [C.O.5/71, Pt. 1, fo. 73]

XIV

Information from Mr Rawle[1]

10 February, Secretary's Office
Colonel Luttrell having yesterday mentioned to Mr Pownall at St James's that Lieutenant-Colonel Burgoyne had informed him of some circumstances relative to certain orders given by North American merchants to different tradesmen, and particularly to one Rawle living in the Strand, to get ready large quantities of arms and accoutrements for a number of troops to be raised in America, Lieutenant-Colonel Burgoyne attended Lord Hillsborough this morning and related what he knew of this matter, and of which he had taken memorandums in his pocket-book. For the greater certainty, however, he brought Mr Rawle to the Secretary's office, who gave the following account vizt.

That some days ago when Lieut.-Colonel Burgoyne was at his house, there came to him one Mr Blackburn, a merchant in Bush Lane, who told him that a thousand light horse were raised or raising in America to be under the command of Sir John Johnson, that he should want a thousand swords, a thousand helmets, and other accoutrements in proportion, and desired him to let him have patterns of said arms and accoutrements which were to be all of the best sort, superior to those furnished to the King's troops, that if these patterns were approved he should have further orders to give him as two other regiments were to be raised and accoutred in the same manner, that these regiments were to be raised at the expense of the people but not without the consent of government.

Mr Rawle further related that about three months ago he had an order from a gentleman whom he understood to be an agent for the people of Boston, but could not recollect his name, for patterns for accoutrements for 4,000 infantry, which patterns were accordingly delivered and that he every day expected an order in consequence thereof, that these troops were to have caps with this motto in the front *Vim Vi Repellere Licet*, that he had frequent conversations with this gentleman who constantly complained of the hardships put upon the Americans, and that his conversation seemed to imply an intention of resistance. [C.O.5/88, fo. 38]

1   Enclosed in Hillsborough's letter to Gage, 17 February 1770: Vol. I, No. 116.

XV

Earl of Hillsborough to Lieut.-Governor Cadwallader Colden (No. 37)

17 February, Whitehall

Sir, your dispatches [Vol. I, Nos. 5, 12; Vol. II, No. IV] numbered 6, 7, and 8, have been received and laid before the King.

At the same time that the King saw with satisfaction the commendable disposition of the Assembly to make provision for the troops, the giving part of the money for this purpose out of a fund that was to arise from the establishment of a paper-currency, the bill for which was depending at the Privy Council Board, was a circumstance that could not escape His Majesty's observation, and which your letter No. 6 did not enable me to explain; for it was impossible for me to suppose that, under the restriction laid upon you by His Majesty's instructions of July 1766 and informed as you was that the bill which passed the Council and Assembly in May 1769 was under His Majesty's consideration, you could have taken upon you without further directions to have given your assent to another bill for the same purpose without a clause suspending its execution until His Majesty's pleasure could be known; and I am yet at a loss to guess at the reasons which induced the members of the Council to advise you to a step so contrary to your duty and to your instructions.

Your conduct on this occasion has justly incurred His Majesty's displeasure which I am commanded to signify to you, and to observe to you that although the King considers the preserving the colony in tranquillity as a very desirable and commendable object yet His Majesty can never approve of any governor seeking the attainment of it at the expense of his instructions.

The merit, however, of your former services and what you say in respect to the time fixed by the Act for its operation, which you state as an excuse for your conduct, prevail with His Majesty to forbear any further marks of his displeasure, trusting that you will not for the future suffer yourself to be withdrawn from your duty by any motive whatever.

It is necessary I should acquaint you that the bill transmitted by Sir Henry Moore had received the fullest consideration at the Council Board before your letter to me, No. 8, and that to the Lords of Trade enclosing the Acts assented to by you were received, and that the Lords of the Council had as you will see by the enclosed Order [Vol. I, No. 84] advised His Majesty to reject it.

The ground for this advice was that those clauses by which the bills of credit are made payable at the Treasury and Loan Office were contrary to the Act of Parliament which restrains paper bills of credit from being issued as a legal tender in payment of any debts, dues or demands whatsoever; and therefore this objection does in its nature show in the strongest light not only the impropriety of your having assented to this Act but the risk to which you personally stand exposed by the terms of the Act of Parliament in consequence of having given such assent.

Under the circumstances of the disallowance of the former bill for the reason abovementioned, no time was to be lost in laying before His Majesty the Act transmitted by you to the Lords of Trade, and His Majesty having in consequence thereof been pleased to disallow the said Act, enclosed you will receive the Order in Council [Vol. I, No. 101] for that purpose which you will cause to be promulgated [MS: promulged] with all possible dispatch. But such is the paternal attention of His Majesty to the wishes of his subjects in New York and his royal disposition to concur in this object of them that, notwithstanding the steady opinion of all His Majesty's servants that it is against the true interest of the colony to have a paper-currency attended with any degree of legal tender, yet I have reason to believe the Parliament will be moved to pass an Act to enable the legislature of New York to carry into execution the bill they appear to be so desirous of.

The request of Lieutenant Crukshanks and others expressed in the petition [Vol. I, No. 5i] enclosed in your letter No. 7 appears to be founded in justice and equity, and I have His Majesty's commands to refer the said petition (together with a copy of your letter) to the Lords Commissioners for Trade and Plantations, and I shall not fail to recommend to their lordships to take the whole of what regards the settlement of the country to the west of Connecticut River into their consideration so soon as other matters of great importance now before them will admit of it.

In consequence of the death of Mr Yorke a few days after he received the Great Seal, His Majesty has thought fit to commit the custody of it for the present to Commissioners; and the Duke of Grafton having been permitted by His Majesty to retire from the Treasury Board, Lord North is become in consequence thereof First Commissioner at that Board. *Draft.* [C.O.5/1101, fo. 42]

XVI

Earl of Hillsborough to Lieut.-Governor William Bull (No. 33)

17 February, Whitehall
Sir, I have received and laid before the King your dispatches Nos. 19, 20, 21 and 22 [Vol. I, No. 18].

His Majesty saw with equal approbation and satisfaction the attention of the Assembly at their first meeting to those commendable objects of true commercial policy which you had so prudently and properly recommended to them with a view to divert them from the invidious idea of introducing American manufactures and to fix them in a pursuit of those more solid advantages which a series of improvement in the articles of rice, indigo etc. has opened to them, and in which the colony has made so rapid a progress.

After so pleasing a prospect of future advantage and prosperity to the colony which your good sense and discretion had pointed out, it could not but be very mortifying to you to find the session close with so extraordinary a resolution of the Commons House of Assembly as that they came to on the 8th of December.

You will readily suppose that a proceeding of this nature so unwarrantable upon every idea of the true spirit of the constitution, whether it regards the vote itself simply considered as a vote of the Lower House for issuing public money not concurred in by the Governor and Council, or whether it regards the purposes intended thereby and mentioned therein, which convey the most unjust suspicions of and the most disrespectful insinuations against His Majesty's government, could not but be matter of great concern and surprise to the King, and His Majesty after having taken the sense of that Committee of his servants to which affairs of the greatest importance are referred has thought fit to direct me to lay this matter before the Privy Council, where although it will doubtless meet with all possible dispatch in the consideration of it yet it cannot receive a final decision time enough for this packet, but I will not fail to press a speedy resolution upon it so as that the necessary instructions in consequence thereof may reach you before the middle of May.

I should however but ill obey my royal master's commands if I delayed to signify to you his entire approbation of your conduct, which has upon this occasion as well as in the manner of communicating the instruction contained in my letter No. 24 been distinguished by the greatest prudence and discretion; and you do no more than justice to the conduct and opinion of His Majesty's ministers in supposing that they do not expect you should, in order to make your representations of the state of the colony appear more agreeable, make them less consistent with truth and the real situation of public affairs in it.

In consequence of the death of Mr Yorke a few days after he received the Great Seal, His Majesty has thought fit to commit the custody of it for the present to Commissioners, and the Duke of Grafton having been permitted by His Majesty to retire from the Treasury Board, Lord North is become in consequence thereof First Commissioner at that Board. *Draft*. [C.O.5/393, fo. 18]

XVII

Governor John Wentworth to Earl of Hillsborough (No. 29)

18 February, New Hampshire

May it please your lordship, as the vessel intended for London when I had the honour to write your lordship, No. 28, altered her voyage, and this is the first direct opportunity since, and the quiet, peaceable and orderly state of the province leaving me nothing of importance to communicate, I have therefore deferred intruding on your lordship's time.

Permit me to acknowledge the honour done me in your lordship's very obliging letter No. 25. His Majesty's most gracious condescension to approve my humble zeal in his service confers the greatest reward and most inestimable happiness and causes in me the profoundest veneration and thankfulness for this repeated instance of his royal benignity, which powerfully animates and strengthens the unalterable diligence of the humblest and most devoted of his servants. Thus gratefully impressed with the highest sense of your lordship's goodness in this communication, and in the sentiments conveyed so favourably for me as is in the transcript enclosed to me of your lordship's letter to the Right Honourable the Lords of His Majesty's Treasury respecting my conduct in the Surveyor-General's office, I have not terms equal to my respectful gratitude; neither can time or circumstance diminish my obligations which will ever lead me to every acknowledgement and the most unfeigned hopes and desires for your lordship's prosperity.

The General Assembly of this province met the 9th January last, and after a few days employed in hearing petitions from parishes and private people upon various internal casualties, also telling over and burning what paper bills had been received into the province-treasury since the last session, they voted to present a petition to His Majesty for the payment of a sum of money about six thousand pounds sterling, being a proportion of the Parliamentary grant to the colonies for their aid in the last part of the late war, of which sum the province of New Hampshire only has not been in the least profited. It was also mentioned to pray His Majesty would be graciously pleased to annex that district west of Connecticut River to twenty miles of Hudson's River to this province; but this passed over upon my pressing a Supply Bill for next year, the House of Assembly requested it might be deferred and to be adjourned until March or April, by which time they were in hopes to receive a confirmation of the Act for dividing this province into counties passed the last session by His Majesty's permission. As the operation of this Act if His Majesty is pleased to grant it must necessarily augment the Supply Bill, and as the extreme and unusual rigour of the season prevented a full attention to public business, I thought it for His Majesty's service to adjourn them until the 20th March next; at which time they and indeed the whole province express the most sanguine expectations to be met with the royal allowance of the County Act which will spread an universal joy through every street in New Hampshire, and I believe tend greatly to His Majesty's service in facilitating the administration of justice in the remoter districts of the colony, who without some such assistance will certainly grow savage and ungovernable as Indians. As soon as the General Assembly have gone through the session I shall immediately collect, state and transmit all the public transactions to that day which have been done since the last general letter I had the honour to write your lordship on this subject. There have not been any new manufactures set up in New Hampshire since my residence here. One man in this town of Portsmouth has attempted to make nails and for a month or six weeks employed two men at it. But as the nail-rods are imported from Philadelphia the business soon declined and the man now chiefly pursues common blacksmith's work, his former business. There are not any non-importation committees or Associations formed in this province, though daily solicited; whence some Scotch merchants have been led to import their European goods hither, where they buy and sell without the least molestation, and have already remitted much of the specie that was in the province which the commerce does not replace but daily diminishes.

I have heard that the inhabitants on the lands west of Connecticut River have prepared a petition to His Majesty praying a confirmation of their titles and to be re-annexed to this province. They have for two years past had petitions before the General Court, many to the Governor and Council which we could not act upon and have constantly declined. But those people are become so importunate and exhibit such circumstances of distress and misery, suggesting that their titles were through this government, and thence so strongly urge a consideration that the Council have resolved to form a just state of the case that your lordship may the better judge of the merits of the petition and solicitations which may be preferred thereupon. When this is completed it shall be transmitted. In the meantime permit me to assure your lordship that however those poor people may succeed in their title, yet they are certainly objects of real compassion. Already many of them fill our streets, and should they finally be ousted, some many hundreds will inevitably perish by famine, and despair urge multitudes to fall victims to the laws. Mr Colden writes me they begin to resist the laws and apprehends dangerous consequences from executing them, in dividing the lands these men have cleared and cultivated to and among others who have obtained patents of them under New York. I have constantly recommended and urged the fullest obedience and acquiescence to the laws of the province wherein they are assigned, and to rely on a final determination of the courts. In this I have been so very positive that it is almost proverbial among them. I cannot adequately describe the confusion and wretchedness of this district, neither is it an exaggeration to assure your lordship that terror and uncertainty is largely striding to desolate that district which will soon perfectly resemble a military devastation more than a fertile peaceable country unless they should happily become the objects of your lordship's favourable representation to His Majesty for relief. I presume not to enter into the merits of their case but am persuaded if it could be justly described that your lordship's well known humanity and benevolent inclination for the welfare of all His Majesty's subjects would most assuredly conciliate your lordship's compassionate interposition in their behalf.

I have not any further communications to lay before your lordship and only to beg leave to entreat your lordship will be pleased to represent that this His Majesty's province of New Hampshire are most happy in their highest obedience and strictest veneration of His Majesty and the laws of his Empire, and that my unceasing zeal and fidelity in His Majesty's service cannot fail ever to influence and happily direct me in the faithful execution of the trusts committed to my administration. *Signed.* [C.O.5/937, fo. 3]

XVIII

Some Thoughts on the Indian Trade by Lieut.-Governor Elias Durnford[1]

[18 February]

On seriously considering the nature of the trade and situation of this province [West Florida] with the neighbouring Indian nations, many difficulties appear which without the interposition of the legislature of

---

1 Enclosed in Durnford's letter to Hillsborough, 17 February 1770: Vol. I, No. 134.

Britain will ever be obstacles to prevent that tranquillity taking place with them which it is so much the interest of the colony's to promote. The present order of putting the Indian concerns into the care of the different provinces will if properly managed by them be of great advantage, but the strong desire of gain which reigns in the human breast, I am apprehensive, will prevent those good consequences flowing from it which otherwise would, unless the following regulations take place vizt.

1st. That each province shall only be permitted to send traders into certain towns which ought to be specified and which actually are nearer to the town where they land their goods from Europe than those of the neighbouring colonies; that very severe penalties be laid upon any trader who shall send any goods to the Indians of a town not belonging to the province from whence he receives his licence, let it be either in the town where he resides or in the woods.

2dly. That the tariff with each tribe of Indians be the same and fixed in such a manner as to put it out of the trader's power to deviate from, I mean those of the different provinces who may trade with the same nation.

3rdly. That no more than a small quantity of rum be permitted to be carried into the nation by each trader for his private use; that one commissary or more if necessary be allowed to each province with an interpreter and armourer to reside therein, and for each town he visits once a year in that nation he should have an additional allowance exclusive of his pay which would be a strong inducement for him to pay due attention. These commissaries would prevent many parties of Indians from coming down to the seat of government which they do as often as they have complaints to make, the which is attended with considerable expense in provisions and presents. Commissaries would greatly prevent, if not put a stop to, many abuses and irregularities committed by the traders in the different Indian nations, as they may be armed with the power of magistrates and immediately send down to the capitals of the provinces any offenders, where their bondsmen should not only be prosecuted but corporal punishment be also inflicted upon the delinquent, which might be done in consequence of provincial Acts. Great care should also be taken that very little or no credit be given to Indians which might be done by not permitting too great quantities of goods to be carried amongst them, whereby they would find it necessary to pay more attention to their hunting to supply themselves, and the traders would always make proper returns to their merchants (which at present is not always the case).

With regard to the province of West Florida a congress is absolutely necessary with the Lower Creeks in order to obtain more of the interior part of the country for the use of settlers. A congress should also be held with those tribes who reside on and near the banks of the Mississippi in order to fix limits there. The lands granted by the Choctaws on the Mobile and Alabama Rivers are sufficient for the present. *Signed.*
[C.O.5/577, p. 343]

XIX

Deputy Governor Robert Eden to Earl of Hillsborough (No. 5)

21 February, Annapolis

My Lord, from my situation here as governor of this province it is incumbent upon me to give your lordship immediate information of a late transaction of a committee of the Associators here relative to the brig *Good Intent,* William Errington, chartered by John Buchanan, merchant in London, with goods to sundry merchants here.

Previous to the arrival of the above brig, Messrs. Dick and Stewart, merchants in this city and attornies in fact for Mr Buchanan, gave notice in our *Gazette* that such a vessel was expected and that no goods should be landed for twelve days after her arrival in order to allow a free inspection of her papers etc., for which advertisement I refer your lordship to the enclosed *Gazette* [Vol. I, No. 142i] of the 25th January.

In consequence of this advertisement, very soon after the vessel arrived four commissioners from each of the three counties principally interested in the importation met here, for whose resolves (in consequence whereof the brig returns to England) I also refer your lordship to the other enclosed *Gazette* [Vol. I, No. 142ii] of the 15th instant.

I think, my lord, I can venture to assure you that this step of the committee far from being the general sense of the province has not been attended with the approbation they expected. The merchants concerned, from their situation, were obliged to comply with the determination of a committee whose election perhaps was partial and hasty, whose resolution was not unanimous, and which I really believe the most violent of them are now sorry they entered into, although they are ashamed to recant.

I can give your lordship but little information of their proceedings except from the enclosed prints; they were so close as never to allow more than one of the merchants concerned to attend them at one time.

As soon as the issue of their deliberation was made public I endeavoured as my duty to my Sovereign and the colony required to persuade them to reconsider the matter, and I for that purpose laid before some of them extracts of your lordship's two last letters to me, but could not convince them of the impropriety of their conduct on this occasion when they have the greatest reason to expect that the Act they complain of as a grievance is already or shortly will be repealed.

The arguments had no effect, and the brig sails tomorrow for England, liable to be seized in the first English port she enters for carrying back India goods and other things contrary to the condition of the bonds given on shipping them, liable also to actions on every bill of lading given by the captain who could act no otherwise than he has done, any more than the merchants concerned.

I will just beg leave to observe that Mr Buchannan signed the City address, which gave great offence to many of his employers here. How far that may have contributed towards the virulence of this proceeding I will not take upon me to determine although the committee calls this *a premeditated design to subvert the Association.*

The Collector and Surveyor of this port, Messrs. Calvert and Eddis, have wrote fully on this head to the Commissioners of the Customs in London who probably will apply to your lordship for your directions how to act with respect to the vessel. I can only say, my lord, that the captain was obliged to act as he has done and that, as neither he nor his employer are to blame, the compulsion upon them will I hope entitle them to some indulgence.

I will send your lordship the pamphlet advertised at the bottom of the above account as soon as it comes out. *Signed.* [C.O.5/1283, fo. 23]

XX

Lieut.-Governor Cadwallader Colden to Earl of Hillsborough (No. 9)

21 February, New York
My Lord, I have the honour of your commands, No. 35, of the 9th of December, with His Majesty's additional instruction to me, which shall be punctually obeyed.

I know not how the objection made to the bill for emitting £120,000 in bills of credit can be removed, for unless the bills be received in the Loan Office and Treasury they cannot be paid in or sunk, nor can the interest be applied to the use for which it is designed. The making of them a tender is carefully avoided. Nor can they be a tender in any sense by this Act in any contract whatsoever, the Loan Office and Treasury only excepted; but though those offices are obliged to take them in, no person is obliged to receive them from either the one or the other. Nor can they be a tender of any duty, quitrent or fine. By the preceding packet I transmitted to your lordship the bill under the seal of the province with my reasons for giving my assent to it, which I hope will be satisfactory. It is a consideration of some importance to the government that as the interest-money cannot be applied without the consent of the governor the supply for the troops quartered in this place may for the future be secured, which has at all times met with opposition in the Assembly and has been difficultly obtained.

The session of Assembly ended the 27th of January to general satisfaction, notwithstanding the assiduous endeavours of a party in opposition to government to embarrass affairs. A great number of bills were passed at that time for continuing or reviving former bills, and on subjects which relate to particular counties, none of them of consequence to deserve your lordship's attention except two. One entitled "An Act declaring certain persons therein mentioned incapable of being Members of the General Assembly of this province", an attested copy [Vol. I, No. 140i] of which I enclose as the Acts passed last session could not be transcribed for the seal before the packet sails. By this Act the Judges of the Supreme Court and some other officers of government were made incapable of being elected members of Assembly. The Council amended the bill by striking out all the other officers of government, to which amendment the Assembly agreed.

The reasons given for this bill are:

1st. That none of the Judges in Great Britain or Ireland are allowed to sit in the House of Commons.

2nd. That in good policy, legislation and the execution of the laws ought not to be in the same person.

3rd. That in all elections the Judges must have an improper influence on the electors.

Lastly, it has been observed that in former Assemblies where the Judges have had seats they became attached to or leaders of parties or factions in the House. This gave a suspicion that they were often biased in their judgement on the bench in favour of a party interest. All cause of jealousy of this kind ought to be avoided.

The present Assembly have repeatedly refused to admit Mr Livingston, who is a Judge of the Supreme Court, to have a seat in their House upon a resolve made by them in their former session: this may be an unconstitutional power assumed by the Assembly and is therefore much more safely vested in an Act of the legislature. At all events I thought it for His Majesty's interest that I should give my assent to the bill as thereby the matter is subjected to His Majesty's pleasure which it was not while it stood on a resolve of the Assembly.

The other bill which may deserve your lordship's attention is entitled "An Act to enable all persons who are His Majesty's liege subjects either by birth or naturalization to inherit and hold real estates notwithstanding any defect of purchase made before naturalization within this colony". While this bill was before the Council I told them that though the bill in my opinion was framed with much equity and not liable to the same objections with the bill to which Sir Henry Moore refused his assent, yet as the King's interest may be affected by it, I would not give my assent without a suspending clause was added, which they did by an amendement and the Assembly agreed to it. On this occasion I think it my duty to inform your lordship that the reason of the Assembly being averse to suspending clauses is, they tell me, that such bills have often hung long in suspense without being taken into consideration.

All the bills passed the last sessions will be ready to be transmitted by the next packet.

I enclose your lordship the copy of an agreement [Vol. I, No. 140ii] made between General Gage and me in pursuance of the Act of Parliament for applying the money granted by the last Act of Assembly for the troops quartered in this place. I doubt not it will give your lordship pleasure to find this affair put upon a certain and regular footing for the present and which must probably produce the like for the future.

I have the satisfaction to inform your lordship that among the bills passed this session is one for appointing commissioners to meet commissioners from the neighbouring colonies to fix on a general plan for regulating the Indian trade. This was the best measure that could be taken upon His Majesty's gracious reference of this important affair to the legislatures of the several colonies; and if properly adopted by all concerned may produce the most beneficial plan. I have sent copies of our Act to the governors of the neighbouring colonies and have pressed them to procure the like to be passed in their governments.

My lord, it is my duty to inform your lordship that a violent party continue their assiduous endeavours to disturb the government by working on the passions of the populace and exciting riots though in every attempt they have hitherto been unsuccessful. The last might have been of fatal consequence, if not prevented by the prudent conduct of the magistrates and officers of the army. A new humour had been artfully worked up between the townspeople and soldiers which produced several affrays, and daily by means of wicked incendiaries grew more serious. At last some townspeople began to arm and the soldiers rushed from their barracks to support their fellow soldiers. Had it not been for the interposition of the magistrates and of the most respectable inhabitants and of the officers of the army, it had become a very dangerous affair. As it was only a few wounds and bruises were received on both sides. A very respectable number of the principal citizens publicly met together and sent 42 of their number to the mayor to assure the magistrates of their assistance in preserving the peace of the town, and the officers of the army were no less assiduous in quieting the minds of the soldiers and in guarding against every accident which might renew any dispute with the townspeople. Since which the place has remained quiet. It is not doubted here that these disturbances were promoted by the enemies of government in order to raise an indignation against the Assembly (then sitting) for granting money to the soldiers who were represented as ready to cut the throats of the citizens.

The persons who appear on these occasions are of inferior rank but it is not doubted they are directed by some persons of distinction in this place. It is likewise thought they are encouraged by some persons of note in England. They consist chiefly of Dissenters who are very numerous especially in the country and have a great influence over the country-members of Assembly. The most active among them are Independents from New England or educated there and of republican principles. The friends of the administration are of the Church of England, the Lutherans and the Old Dutch Congregation with several Presbyterians. From this the reason will appear of some bills having passed the House of Assembly in favour of the Dissenters and in prejudice to the few ministers of the Church of England who have stipends by a law of this province. There was less opposition to them in that House from the confidence they had that they would not be passed by the Council. They were accordingly rejected there. I must leave it to your lordship's judgement whether these things deserve His Majesty's attention and I transmit to the Plantation Board a printed copy of the Journal of the Assembly to enable you to form your judgement thereon.

In my letter of January 6th, No. 8, I enclosed a printed copy [Vol. I, No. 12i] of a libel directed *To the betrayed Inhabitants of the City and Colony of New York*, with a proclamation I issued with the advice of the Council and on an address of the Assembly offering a reward of £100 for the discovery of the author. One Alexander McDougal is now in jail, committed on the oath of the printer and his journeymen as the author and publisher of that libel. He is a person of some fortune and could easily have found the bail required of him but he chose to go to jail and lies there imitating Mr Wilkes in everything he can. When he comes to his trial it will appear what dependence we may have on a jury of this place. The most respectable persons in the place openly declare their opinion that he highly deserves punishment.

My lord, I now expect soon to remove from the administration on the arrival of the Earl of Dunmore. It gives me great satisfaction that in this short administration I have had an opportunity of doing something of importance for His Majesty's service, that a good agreement has been supported between the several branches of the legislature, the friends of government encouraged, the promoters of discord checked. His Majesty's gracious approbation of my conduct will make an old man happy, and will prevent the unfavourable impressions which a sudden removal from administration may occasion. *Signed.* [C.O.5/1101, fo. 45]

XXI

Lieut.-Governor Thomas Hutchinson to Earl of Hillsborough (No. 4, duplicate)

28 February, Boston

My Lord, by the December mail I have the honour of your lordship's letter No. 30 in which you are pleased to express your sentiments of the expediency of my meeting the General Court at Cambridge to obviate any objections on account of the troops and to show a proper resentment of the behaviour of the inhabitants of Boston, unless I shall think there are reasons to the contrary of such a nature as to outweigh these considerations. I apprehend, my lord, that when the main guard is removed from the courthouse I shall meet with little or no trouble on account of the troops, and I am sensible that removing the Court out of town will be disagreeable to most of the members. I doubt, notwithstanding, after mature deliberation whether I can be justified in not conforming to a measure which appears to your lordship to be highly expedient and therefore I have issued a proclamation proroguing the Court to the 15th instant to meet at Cambridge.

I shall also govern myself by your lordship's opinion with respect to such persons as may be elected Councillors who have been active parties in the late combinations. If I should refuse all who are concerned or who are favourers of them, I think I shall have no Council for in the present temper of the people I have no reason to think that any other will be offered to me for my consent.

I am very sorry that I must acquaint your lordship with the continuance of disorders in the town of Boston by exhibitions of pageantry before the doors of the few persons who venture to sell the goods they have imported contrary to the agreement of the merchants. Lads and children are employed on these occasions who collect in great numbers, and the civil magistrate will not oppose the popular prejudice and attempt to disperse them. A person offered to remove one of these shows and being obstructed by those who had the charge of it and at length pelted and drove into his house, and then having his house surrounded and, as he says, his windows broke and his person in danger, he fired upon the multitude and killed one lad and wounded another. He was soon fetched out of his house and committed to prison. The lad was buried a day or two after and his funeral the largest perhaps ever known in America.

All this tends to increase the discontent which before was very great in the town, and I thought it necessary to convene the Council and to propose to them to issue a proclamation against these disorders, but it did not appear to them to be necessary and, after two days consideration, they advised me to send for the Justices and Sheriff and exhort them to do their duty. This was done and had repeatedly been done before to no purpose. Some of the Justices openly justified the proceedings.

All this disorder is owing to a general disposition, not in the body of the people only, but in those to whom the administration of government by the constitution is entrusted, to favour the measures of the merchants as the only means to preserve the rights of the people and to bring about the repeal of the Revenue Acts and other Acts called unconstitutional. In other matters which have no relation to this dispute between the kingdom and the colonies, government retains its vigour and the administration of it is attended with no unusual difficulty. *Signed.* [C.O.5/759, fo. 57]

XXII

Lieut.-Governor Thomas Hutchinson to Maj.-General Thomas Gage[1]

6 March, Boston

Sir, I beg leave to refer you to Col. Dalrymple for the particulars of a most unfortunate affair which happened the last evening, so far as they relate to the troops under his command. So far as they respect the inhabitants and my own conduct, I must acquaint you that just before ten o'clock the bells of the town were rung as is usual in case of fire, but I soon found there was another cause and one upon another came running to my house to inform me that unless I went out immediately the whole town would be in arms and the most bloody scene would follow that had ever been known in America. I went immediately abroad and met vast crowds of people running for their arms and prevailed on them to turn back and follow me to King-street promising them justice should be done. I found two persons killed, a third mortally wounded and a fifth Mr Payne, a merchant of the town, shot in his arm and the bone splintered as he stood at his door. The people were enraged to a very great degree and could not be pacified until I assured them immediate enquiries should be made by the civil magistrate, which was done and the body of them retired; about 100 only remained until the examination was over, which lasted till 3 or 4 o'clock in the morning. I ordered a Council to be summoned to meet

1   Enclosed in Hutchinson's letter to Hillsborough, 12 March 1770: Vol. I, No. 177.

today at 11 o'clock: when I came to them I found the selectmen and the Justices waiting for me to represent that the inhabitants had insisted upon a town-meeting and that it would not be in their power to keep them under restraint if the troops were not removed to the barracks at the Castle. I told them this was not in my power. In a short time I received a message from the town-meeting, which I shall enclose. The committee consisted of the principal inhabitants, several of them in plain terms declared that they knew the people not only in the town but all the neighbouring towns were determined to unite and force the troops out of the town. I told them that an attack upon the King's troops would be high treason and every man concerned would forfeit his life and estate, but what I said had no effect. Upon consulting the Council, Col. Dalrymple and Col. Carr being present, they expressed unanimously their desire that the regiments might be sent to the Castle. As the principal if not all the quarrels of the inhabitants had been with the 29th, Col. Dalrymple so far yielded to their desire as to consent that the 29th should be quartered at the Castle and promised further that the 14th should be kept in the barracks at Wheelwright's Wharf and all occasions of difference with the inhabitants prevented. This the committee of the town were informed of and reported to the meeting, but it proved not satisfactory and in the afternoon a second committee came to me in Council, Colonels Dalrymple and Carr and also Capt. Caldwell of the *Rose* being then present, and laid before me another vote of the town declaring they were not satisfied etc., which vote I could not avoid asking the opinion of my Council upon. They not only unanimously declared their opinion that it was absolutely necessary that the troops should be in the barracks at the Castle, but most of them declared they had the greatest certainty that the inhabitants of the town and of the towns of Charlestown and Cambridge, Dedham, Roxbury, Dorchester etc. would infallibly unite and at all events drive the troops from the town and that it would admit of no delay; they were sure the night which was coming on would be the most terrible that had ever been seen in America. Two of the Council from Charlestown and Dedham confirmed what had been said of the disposition of the people of those towns and everyone in the most earnest manner pressed me to communicate their opinion and advice in a formal way to Col. Dalrymple and to pray him to cause both regiments to remove to the barracks at the Castle. I did not see how I could avoid complying with this unanimous advice of the Council under the circumstances of the town and province, especially as I had opportunity of consulting so many servants of the Crown, together with the Secretary who is not of the Council, and who all saw the matter in the same light that I did; and I am very certain that Col. Dalrymple was influenced to a compliance with the measure from the representations made in Council of the desperate state of the people and the desire they so strongly expressed which he thought necessary to justify him in his compliance.

I shall immediately represent the state of this affair to the Secretary of State. A vessel I am informed will sail for London in eight days. PS. March 7th. I am informed that four persons are dead and a 5th lies very dangerous, and that several more were slightly wounded. *Copy*. [C.O.5/759, fo. 61]

XXIII

Record of Proceedings of Council of Massachusetts by Andrew Oliver, Secretary[1]

5 March, Massachusetts Bay

The lieutenant-governor having summoned a Council to consider what was proper to be done in the state of disorder and confusion the people are at present in, occasioned by the troops firing upon the inhabitants the last evening, thereby killing 3 or 4 persons and wounding others: previous to the debate, moved that Lieutenant-Colonel Dalrymple and Lieutenant-Colonel Carr might have notice to attend in Council if they saw fit. They attended accordingly, when the matter was largely discussed in Council, and while this was doing a committee of the town desired to be admitted, who came in and delivered a message declaring it to be the unanimous opinion of the meeting that nothing can rationally be expected to restore the peace of the town and prevent blood and carnage but the immediate removal of the troops. The committee withdrew while the matter was debated in Council and Colonel Dalrymple having signified to the lieutenant-governor that he was willing the 29th Regiment who had rendered themselves in a special manner obnoxious to the people by the concern they had in this unhappy affair should be placed in the barracks at the Castle till he could receive orders from the general, the lieutenant-governor acquainted the committee accordingly and the Council was adjourned to the afternoon.

In the afternoon the lieutenant-governor received another message from the town acquainting him that it was the opinion of the meeting consisting of near three thousand people that nothing but a total and immediate removal of the troops would satisfy the town; and Mr Adams, one of the committee, told Colonel Dalrymple that if he could remove the 29th Regiment he could also remove the 14th, and that it was at his peril if he did not. The lieutenant-governor laid the answer of the town before the Board who after fully debating the matter unanimously advised him to pray Colonel Dalrymple to order the troops down to Castle William.

Previous to this advice Mr Tyler had said that it was not such people as had formerly pulled down the lieutenant-governor's house who conducted the present measures, but that they were people of the best characters among us, men of estates and men of religion; that they had formed their plan and that this was a part of it to remove the troops out of the town, and after that the Commissioners; that it was impossible the troops should remain in town, that the people would come in from the neighbouring towns, and that there would be ten thousand men to effect the removal of the troops, and that they would probably be destroyed by the people, should it be called rebellion,

---

1 Covered by Lieut.-Governor Hutchinson's certificate, 13 March 1770: Vol. I, No. 178.

should it incur the loss of our charter, or be the consequence what it would. Divers other gentlemen adopted what Mr Tyler had said by referring expressly to it and thereupon excusing themselves from enlarging. Mr Russell of Charlestown and Mr Dexter of Dedham confirmed what he said respecting the present temper and disposition of the neighbouring towns; every gentleman spoke on the occasion and unanimously expressed their sense of the necessity of the immediate removal of the troops from the town and advised his honour to pray that Colonel Dalrymple would order the troops down to Castle William. One gentleman [*Margin:* Mr Gray] to enforce it said that the lieutenant-governor had asked the advice of the Council and they had unanimously advised him to a measure, which advice in his opinion laid the lieutenant-governor under an obligation to act agreeably thereto. Another gentleman [*Margin:* Captain Erving] pressed his compliance with greater earnestness and told him that if after this any mischief should ensue by means of his declining to join with them the whole blame must fall upon him, but that if he joined with them and Colonel Dalrymple after that should refuse to remove the troops the blame would then lie at his door. The lieutenant-governor all along declared that he had no authority over the troops, yet as the Council knew by what had passed that upon this desire Colonel Dalrymple would consent to remove them, he on this emergency told the Council he would comply with their advice and would desire it of him accordingly; and the colonel declared that upon receiving a letter from the lieutenant-governor to that purpose he would do it. These declarations were made to the town's committee and were by them said to be reported to the town still assembled in town-meeting; whereupon the minds of the people appeared to be quieted.

The Council was adjourned to the next morning to see the minutes made by the Secretary of this day's proceedings set in order as well as to do some other business that had been assigned over to that time.

The Secretary in his draft expressed what had been said in debate in these terms: "Divers gentlemen of the Council informed his honour the lieutenant-governor they were of opinion that it was the determination of the people to have the troops removed from the town and that this was not the sense of the inhabitants of the town of Boston only but of other towns in the neighbourhood who stood ready to come in in order to effect this purpose, be the consequence of it what it may unless they shall be withdrawn by the commanding officers, which in their opinion was the only method to prevent the effusion of blood and in all probability the destruction of His Majesty's troops who must be overpowered by numbers which would not be less than ten to one"

This form was allowed strictly to express the truth, but that it would not stand well on the Council records. One of the gentlemen of the Board prepared an amendment as in the words following: "that the people of this and some of the neighbouring towns were so exasperated and incensed on account of the inhumane and barbarous destruction of a number of the inhabitants by the troops that they apprehended imminent danger of further bloodshed unless the troops were forthwith removed from the body of the town which in their opinion was the only method to prevent it". This amendment was substituted and the minutes of the whole proceedings set in order and agreed to. *Signed,* Andrew Oliver.

Suffolk, Boston, 13 March 1770. Andrew Oliver Esq. made oath before me the subscriber, one of his Majesty's Justices for this county, that the foregoing by him subscribed was true. *Signed,* Foster Hutchinson. [C.O.5/759, fo. 114]

XXIV

Lieut.-Governor William Bull to Earl of Hillsborough (No. 23)

6 March, Charleston

My Lord, by His Majesty's packet *Sandwich* I am honoured with your lordship's letters No. 30 and 31 and a duplicate of No. 29. The letter therein enclosed to Mr Stuart, His Majesty's Superintendant for Indian Affairs, I sent to him immediately and forwarded those for His Majesty's Agent at Turks Island and to Mr Atkins at Bermuda in a few days, as opportunities soon offered.

I am to return my humble thanks to your lordship on behalf of the four poor Germans for the ready attention paid by your lordship to their case in obtaining His Majesty's order for remission of their fines. I shall be obliged to trouble your lordship with the case very lately mentioned to me of a person in gaol under sentence of death, hitherto reprieved by Lord Charles Montagu at the instance of the Court of Admiralty Sessions held under His Majesty's royal commission last May in the Council Chamber of this province, recommended to His Majesty's royal clemency. From your lordship's known humanity, attention to and punctuality in business, as no answer signifying the King's pleasure thereupon has been received, I am induced to apprehend that Lord Charles Montagu's letters on that subject must have unfortunately miscarried. Not having time before this packet sails, I shall by the next opportunity lay a full state of the matter before your lordship.

I have nothing new to add to the proceedings of the Associators. Their general committee go on in rigidly enforcing obedience to their resolutions and what they call their interpretations thereof, to the great interruption of commerce, and many of themselves are greatly hurt thereby as well as transient persons wholly unacquainted with the purport thereof before they arrived here. No violence has as yet been used against such as hesitate a compliance, though sometimes threatened; but men after a little cool reflection have chosen rather to submit than stem a torrent of popular opinion or perhaps resentment.

It would be injustice in me not to represent to your lordship the firmness with which all the members of His Majesty's Council except one, and almost all His Majesty's servants in this province, have refused to subscribe to the Articles of Association although they daily experience great losses thereby as subscribers are forbidden to purchase rice, indigo etc. from non-subscribers; but the conscious satisfaction arising from a propriety of behaviour affords a consolation superior to every inconvenience.

At present no reason can convince these Associators that their plan is founded upon mistaken principles and must fail of success, but I am persuaded within less than twelve months, if left in this way, the loud voice of distress will awake the generality of them from their dreams; but alas! then the condition of many may be perhaps irretrievable. But I hope that His Majesty's wisdom and the vigilance of his ministers, supported by the advice and authority of the Parliament, will put an end to our unhappy situation and lead us into the right way of pursuing our own true interest.

Notwithstanding my inability to make any progress in dispersing those clouds of discontent and jealousy which spread a gloom over this country, my duty to the best of Kings, whose greatest happiness is his people's welfare, and regard for the people of this province at present under my care, call upon me to exert myself in promoting the public good in such matters as the times will admit.

In this disposition I am endeavouring to sow the seeds of such future benefits to Great Britain and this province as will ripen into perfection as soon as the genial warmth of restored confidence and affection between the mother country and her colonies shall break forth upon us. And permit me, my lord, to express my most ardent prayer that the patronage of your lordship's administration may crown the happy event. Besides the articles mentioned in my letter No. 19 to your lordship, I had prevailed on the Assembly to grant a sum to defray the expense of purchasing and importing vines proper for wine to be entrusted to the management of the French colony at Hillsborough, as most experienced in such matters. I last week sent up a wagon loaded with the best vines of Portugal for that purpose, and means will be used to procure some from France. Olives shall be imported next fall, may they prove happy omens of peace! And to promote ornamental and useful learning, I have recommended to the Assembly to put the provincial grammar school on a better establishment and to build and endow a college for academical studies; and for education suitable to the condition of the poor, that they would provide schools and schoolmasters at various places in the remote settlements.

I did not forget Mr Hammerer, but he has quitted his plan of civilizing the Indians for trafficking with our back-settlers.

I have taken the liberty to enclose to your lordship a copy of the report [Vol. I, No. 162i] of the Assembly on the last article, as also relative to the building gaols and court-houses of sufficient strength and accommodations, and a gaol in Charleston, all which I had recommended to them. *Signed.* [C.O.5/393, fo. 22]

XXV

Lieut.-Governor William Bull to Earl of Hillsborough (No. 24)

7 March, Charleston

My Lord, upon receipt of your lordship's letter No. 31 enclosing His Majesty's royal Order in Council confirming the Circuit Court Act,

I immediately gave public notice of His Majesty's most gracious approbation by a proclamation. And as the benefits thereby intended are not to take effect until the court-houses and gaols are all built and as no limitation of expense or dimensions of the buildings are expressed in the Act to guide the discretion of the commissioners appointed to erect those edifices, I thought it proper, that all such difficulties and causes of delay might be obviated, to recommend the matter to the Assembly, and they have now agreed upon large, convenient and uniform plans for all those buildings. I do not think it possible that they can be carried into execution in less than twelve months and the Act consequently not operate in the administration of justice before that time.

Your lordship's direction to me to transmit by the first opportunity the names of such persons as I think properly qualified to be associate judges, to the end your lordship may receive His Majesty's commands thereupon, will put me under very great difficulty when I consider the importance of the trust reposed in them by this Act. For although two judges go the circuit together yet for the dispatch of business, which must all be over in six days at each place one judge takes care of the Crown Pleas and the other of the Common Pleas, whereby the life and property of the subject are in the hand of one judge. The shortness of the term allows little time for consideration and therefore requires more than a superficial knowledge of the law, or otherwise the decisions would be made rather according to chance than judgement, for as many judges, so many different judgements, would render the law very uncertain and might insensibly deviate from the Common Law of England.

Unhappily for this province men educated in the law-line of very moderate standing find much more profit as attorneys or counsellors than the amount of the three hundred pounds sterling salary to the associate judges; and if they are appointed as hitherto (when they had the assistance of the Chief Justice, or in his absence friends or books to refer to in difficult cases) from among the mere lay gens of this province, gentlemen whose best qualifications were their integrity and common understanding and leisure to attend the courts, though sufficient for the present service, will not be equal to the trust reposed in them by this Act. There are many who are ready to accept the office but it is your lordship's intention and my wish that the salary should be a reward for real abilities.

In obedience to your lordship's command, I shall as soon as I have made some inquiry transmit the names of four of the most proper persons I can meet with to your lordship, but upon the whole I beg leave to express my wishes to your lordship that from among the many gentlemen in London regularly bred to the law, who are arrived at a time of life when the sanguine hopes of rising to eminence or a comfortable share of practice in the profession are extinguished by a very moderate employment therein, some could not be prevailed upon to accept of such commissions in this province where their advancing age would be cherished by our mild climate, give dignity to their office, and authority to their decisions. Inland inhabitants of England, I

know, are terrified with ideas of Indians and savage beasts behind every tree in our woods, but gentlemen of a liberal education are superior to such vulgar prejudices, and though the circuits require riding four or five hundred miles through woods, yet they are well-inhabited and there are roads and accommodations for travellers, not to be expected equal to those in England but the most comfortable would always be given to the judges. Your lordship will pardon those minute circumstances but they are placed before your lordship to obviate objections which may be started perhaps by some worthy man whose abilities would do honour to the office and who might be prevailed upon to come over if the inconveniences apprehended can be removed. *Signed.*
[C.O.5/393, fo. 26]

XXVI

Lieut.-Governor Thomas Hutchinson to Earl of Hillsborough (No. 5)

12 March, Boston

My Lord, for a long time past there have been frequent quarrels between the troops and the inhabitants of the town. On the 2nd and 3rd of this month there were repeated skirmishes between small parties of the inhabitants and the troops in the streets. The soldiers were without firearms and one or two of them were much hurt. The 5th, in the evening, one of the bells of the town near my house was rung and I supposed it to be for fire, but in a few moments several of the inhabitants came running into my house and entreated me immediately to come out or the town would be all in blood, the soldiers having killed a great number of the inhabitants and the people in general being about to arm themselves. I went out without delay in order to go to the Council Chamber as the people were killed near to it in King Street, but I was soon surrounded by a great body of men, many of them armed with clubs and some few with cutlasses and all calling for their firearms. I discovered myself to them and endeavoured to prevail on them to hear me but was soon obliged for my own safety to go into a house and from thence by a private way into King Street, the people having returned there expecting me. After assuring them that a due inquiry should be made and justice done as far as was in my power and prevailing with the commanding officer of the troops in the street to retire with them to their barracks, the people dispersed. Expresses had gone out to the neighbouring towns and the inhabitants were called out of their beds, many of them armed themselves but were stopped from coming into town by advice that there was no further danger that night. A barrel of tar which was carrying to the beacon to set on fire was also sent back. Upon examination before two Justices of the Peace, Captain Preston of the 29th who had the command of the guard was committed to prison, being charged with ordering the troops to fire, as also seven or eight privates charged with firing. Four persons were killed, two more are said to be mortally wounded, divers others wounded but not so dangerous, among them is a gentleman of the town who standing at his door was shot in the arm and the bone splintered. How far the affronts and abuses offered by the inhabitants may avail to excuse this action is uncertain, but it is certain that nothing more unfortunate could have happened for a very great part of the people are in a perfect frenzy by means of it.

I summoned all the members of the Council who were near enough to meet the next morning. When I came to them, I found all the select-men of the town and great part of the Justices of the county waiting for me at the Council Chamber to represent to me their opinion of the absolute necessity, in order to prevent a further effusion of blood, that the troops should be at such distance as that there might be no intercourse between the inhabitants and them. The selectmen acquaint-ed me they had been applied to to call a town-meeting and that the inhabitants would be under no restraint whilst the troops were in the town. I let them know that I had no power to remove the troops. I then sent to desire Colonel Dalrymple and Colonel Carr to be present in Council. Soon after a message came by a large committee from the town to me, being in Council. I told the Council also that the removal of the troops was not with me and I desired them to consider whilst Colonel Dalrymple was present what answer I could give to this application of the town. The principal quarrel had been with the 29th Regiment and, upon hearing from the Council what they had to urge, Colonel Dalrymple let me know that he was willing the 29th should go into barracks at the Castle and engaged that the 14th should be so disposed in Boston as to prevent occasions of dispute between the inhabitants and the regiment. I thereupon signified to the committee of the town what Colonel Dalrymple had agreed to, repeating to them also what I had said to the selectmen that the ordering of the troops did not lie with me. Upon report made to the town, they by general vote declared they could not be satisfied unless both regiments were at the Castle. I met the Council again in the afternoon when the commanding officers of both regiments and also Captain Caldwell of H.M.S. *Rose* were present. I would have desired some other Crown officers to have been there but I knew the Council would not consent to it. The town soon sent a second committee to me with their vote, which I required the Council to give me their opinion upon. They advised me to desire Colonel Dalrymple to remove the 14th Regiment also to the barracks at the Castle, and with one voice most earnestly urged it upon me and every one of them deliberately gave his opinion at large and generally gave this reason to support it, that the people would most certainly drive out the troops and that the inhabitants of other towns would join with Boston in it, and several of the gentlemen declared that they did not judge from the general temper of the people only but they knew it to be the determination not of a mob but of the generality of the principal inhabitants, and they added that all the blood would be charged to me alone for refusing to follow their unanimous advice by desiring that the quarters of a single regiment might be changed in order to put an end to the animosities between the troops and the inhabitants, seeing that upon my joining with them in desiring it, Colonel Dalrymple would consent to it.

It now lay upon me to choose that side which had the fewest and least difficulties, and I weighed and compared them as well as the time

I had for it would permit. I knew it was most regular for me to leave this matter entire to the commanding officer. I was sensible the troops were designed, upon occasion, to be employed under the direction of the civil magistrate, and that at the Castle they would be too remote in most cases to answer that purpose; but then I considered they never had been used for that purpose and there was no probability they ever would be, because no civil magistrate could be found under whose directions they might act and they could be considered only as having a tendency to keep the inhabitants in some degree of awe and even this was every day lessening and the affronts the troops received were such that there was no avoiding quarrels and slaughter. The soldiers themselves had also in many instances been very abusive. Although I thought it not improbable, yet I was not so sanguine as all the Council and the generality of persons of good judgement are, that an open attack would be made on the troops or, if there had been, that they would soon have been overpowered; but there was a moral certainty that the people of this town would have taken to their arms and that the neighbouring towns would have joined them which would have brought on infinite confusion and, if any violence had been begun, much bloodshed, the spirit being full as high now as far as can be judged as it was at the time of the Revolution and the people four times as numerous, and it was most probable the confusion would have continued until the troops were overpowered, for Colonel Dalrymple assures me that in both regiments he could not make 600 effective men nor have been able to have brought above 400 together at one place. Before I determined, I asked the opinion of the three officers of the Crown who were present and of the Secretary and they all agreed that I should not be able to justify a refusal to comply with this advice. I thereupon acquainted the committee of the town that as the Council had unanimously advised me, I would desire Colonel Dalrymple to remove the 14th as well as the 29th to the barracks at the Castle, and he promised that upon my desiring it he would order them accordingly. A copy of my letter [Vol. II, No. XXII] which I sent the next morning by an express to General Gage I shall enclose to your lordship. It has been generally reported that the 14th Regiment is intended to be ordered to New York, if so this proceeding may possibly affect the design. I shall by the first opportunity write also to Commodore Hood. I have been very far from exaggerating facts ever since I have had the honour of transmitting accounts of them to your lordship, but I should be culpable if I should omit communicating the true state of what occurs in the province and I am sure in the present instance no just exception can be taken here to what I have related because men of every order have in the most open and strong manner declared to me that at all events the people were determined the troops should leave the town. *Signed.* [C.O.5/759, fo. 59]

XXVII

Lieut.-Col. William Dalrymple to Earl of Hillsborough

13 March, Boston
My Lord, I presume to trouble your lordship with this letter and at

the same time to forward a narrative of the late extraordinary transactions at Boston.

I shall also take the liberty of sending a state of the melancholy
oppressions done to a worthy officer. His case will I hope excite your
lordship's compassion.

I can safely assure you, my lord, that the matters set forth in both
the papers abovementioned are fairly and justly stated. *Signed.*

A Narrative of the Late Transactions at Boston. On the 3rd of March
last the commanding officer, being informed that there had been some
frays between the inhabitants of the town of Boston and some soldiers
of the 29th Regiment, in consequence of some gross abuse given by a
rope-maker to a soldier of the said regiment, thought it his duty to use
every means to put an end to the disputes.

Repeated orders were given to the troops against their quarrelling
with the inhabitants, and a letter was wrote to the lieutenant-governor
giving him information of what had passed and entreating him to direct
the civil magistrates to use their authority with the inhabitants and to
restrain them from further violences.

From the 3rd to the 5th day of the month there were frequent
complaints from the soldiers of their being knocked down and in
other ways ill-treated.

On Monday night which was the 5th about nine o'clock the alarm
bells were rung as in cases of fire, and the multitude assembled. The
supposed fire was said to be in King Street in order that the people
might be drawn hither. On examination the report of fire was found
to be groundless, and the real intention of the alarm appeared viz.
the bringing of the populace to the place of the intended action.

About this time a considerable body of the inhabitants were at the
gates of a barrack containing two companies of the 29th Regiment
whom they were abusing and inviting to come out and fight. The
soldiers were according to orders restrained and kept in their barracks
by their officers.

From thence the multitude proceeded to King Street where the
Custom-house is situated, threatening to put to death the sentry that
was posted there to protect his Majesty's treasure. On their arrival
they surrounded him and by force compelled him to retire to the
Custom-house door. Being thus environed he was obliged to call for
aid, and the captain of the day (Captain Preston of the 29th Regiment)
was informed of this situation by a townsman. The captain took a
small party of soldiers from the main-guard and proceeded to the
Custom-house to extricate the sentry.

The melancholy consequences of this matter appear at large in
Captain Preston's own narrative, supported by affidavits. Soon after
this the lieutenant-governor arrived at the Council Chamber and the
multitude were by him prevailed on to disperse.

A message was sent to the commanding officer who waited on him
immediately. Some Justices of the Peace were employed in examining
into the affair. On a warrant being issued Captain Preston surrendered

himself to the sheriff and the soldiers who composed the party before mentioned were delivered to the magistrates.

A Council was summoned to meet next morning at ten o'clock and the commanding officers of both regiments were by a message from the lieutenant-governor desired to attend it.

On their arrival at the Council Chamber, they were informed by the lieutenant-governor that the reasons for his desiring their attendance were the following.

On the first meeting of the Council, the magistrates and selectmen had waited on the lieutenant-governor and Board, and acquainted them that in consequence of the troops being quartered in Boston and of the late and former disputes, the peoples' minds were so inflamed that they could not be quieted, that unless the troops were immediately removed from the town they were determined to take up arms and compel them by force of superior numbers to quit it. They also added that the inhabitants of the adjacent towns were determined to act in concert with them and were arriving hourly in Boston for that purpose.

The Councillors then separately informed the lieutenant-governor of the absolute necessity of the removal of the troops, adding that to their knowledge there were upwards of 4000 men to take arms on a refusal, and many of those men of the first property, character and distinction in the province. They further added that the information relative to the inhabitants of the neighbouring towns, as given by the magistrates, was just, and two gentlemen of the Council who were newly arrived from the country were called upon to prove the above assertions from their own observations, and they concurred entirely with what had been affirmed.

As the late disputes had been entirely confined to the soldiers of the 29th Regiment, it was thought expedient to endeavour to quiet the people by removing that regiment some distance from among them and the commanding officers were willing to have it done until such time as General Gage's pleasure should be known.

A committee from the inhabitants of the town of Boston assembled at Faneuil Hall were then in waiting for an answer to a message delivered to the lieutenant-governor in Council, praying the removal of the troops, and were now called on and acquainted by the lieutenant-governor and Council of the measure proposed for the satisfaction of the people. The committee withdrew and the Council adjourned until the afternoon.

In the afternoon the Council again assembled. The meeting of the inhabitants being too numerous to be contained in Faneuil Hall, they made choice of a large meeting-house for their assembling.

The committee waited again on the governor and Council and reported that the answer to their former message was in no respect satisfactory and that nothing less than the immediate and total removal of the troops would satisfy the inhabitants.

The lieutenant-governor and Council were further told that the people were become very impatient, that night approached and an immediate answer was expected, that a thousand men were already arrived from the neighbourhood, and the country in general motion. After which they withdrew.

The commanding officer had during the course of the Council's sitting frequently informed them of the impossibility of his going any further lengths in the matter, that he had already in his apprehension exceeded his powers in the alteration proposed to be made in the quartering the 29th Regiment, an alteration only to be justified by the necessities of the times. He added that the information given of the intended insurrection or rebellion, to which such implicit credit was given by the Council, was in itself a sufficient reason against the removal of His Majesty's forces. To this last argument it was answered that the people knew how insufficient the force at Boston was to prevent their purposes and therefore it was of no effect.

It was answered by the Council that the arming of the people was by them admitted to be treason and that the people knew it so, but nevertheless they were determined to pursue the measures of attacking the troops and that before morning their present numbers estimated at more than 4000 would be increased to ten thousand and the most tragical issue was to be expected.

The lieutenant-governor then proceeded to lay before them the last vote of the inhabitants of the town of Boston, to ask their advice and to demand their judgement upon it.

They thereupon unanimously were of opinion that it was absolutely necessary for His Majesty's service, the good order of the town, and the peace of the province, that the troops should be immediately removed out of the town of Boston, and therefore advised the lieutenant-governor to communicate this advice of Council to Colonel Dalrymple and to desire that the troops might be sent to Castle William forthwith.

The lieutenant-governor finally agreed with the Council and communicated the vote with his desire thereon to the commanding officer who assured him of his obedience.

The committee being informed by the lieutenant-governor of this resolution, they withdrew and the Council adjourned.

If to these facts the following circumstances are added viz. the people running to the house where the artillery is kept, endeavouring to get possession of it, which however, owing to a favourable accident, they failed in the first time, taking the town arms from Faneuil Hall, and attempting to fire the beacon (a signal for bringing in the people from the country with arms) there will little doubt remain that a plan had been preconcerted for attacking the troops on that or the other succeeding nights, and of which further evidence will it is thought be procured.

Case of Captain Thomas Preston of the 29th Regiment. It is matter of too great notoriety to need any proofs that the arrival of His Majesty's troops in Boston was extremely obnoxious to its inhabitants. They have ever used all means in their power to weaken the regiments and to bring them into contempt, by promoting and aiding desertions and with impunity even where there has been the clearest evidence of the fact, and by grossly and falsely propagating untruths concerning them. On the arrival of the 64th and 65th, their ardour seemingly began to abate: it being too expensive to buy off so many, and attempts of that kind rendered too dangerous from the numbers. But the same spirit revived immediately on its being known that those regiments were ordered for Halifax, and has ever since their departure been breaking out with greater violence after their embarkation. One of their Justices, most thoroughly acquainted with the people in their intentions, on the trial of a man of the 14th Regiment, openly and publicly, in the hearing of great numbers of people and from the seat of justice, declared "that the soldiers must now take care of themselves, nor trust too much to their arms, for they were but a handful, that the inhabitants carried weapons concealed under their clothes, and would destroy them in a moment, if they pleased" This considering the malicious temper of the people was an alarming circumstance to the soldiery. Since which, several disputes have happened between the townspeople and the soldiers of both regiments, the former being encouraged thereto by the countenance of even some of the magistrates and by the protection of all the party against government. In general such disputes have been kept too secret from the officers. On the 2d instant, two of the 29th going through one Gray's rope-walk, the ropemakers insultingly asked them if they would empty a vault. This unfortunately had the desired effect by provoking the soldiers, and from words they went to blows. Both parties suffered in this affray, and finally the soldiers retired to their quarters. The officers on the first knowledge of this transaction took every precaution in their power to prevent any ill consequence. Notwithstanding which, single quarrels could not be prevented, the inhabitants constantly provoking and abusing the soldiery. The insolence as well as utter hatred of the inhabitants to the troops increased daily, insomuch that Monday and Tuesday the 5th and 6th instant were privately agreed on for a general engagement, in consequence of which several of the militia came from the country armed to join their friends, menacing to destroy any who should oppose them. This plan has since been discovered.

On Monday night about 8 o'clock, two soldiers were attacked and beat. But the party of the townspeople, in order to carry matters to the utmost length, broke into two meeting houses and rang the alarm bells, which I supposed was for fire as usual, but was soon undeceived. About 9, some of the guard came to and informed me the town inhabitants were assembling to attack the troops, and that the bells were ringing as the signal for that purpose and not for fire, and the beacon intended to be fired to bring in distant people of the country. This, as I was captain of the day, occasioned my repairing immediately to the main guard. In my way there I saw the people in great commotion and heard them use the most cruel and horrid threats against the troops. In a few minutes after I reached the guard, about 100 people passed it and went towards the Custom-house, where the King's money is lodged. They immediately surrounded the sentry posted there and with clubs and other weapons threatened to execute their vengeance on him. I was soon informed by a townsman their intention was to carry off the soldier from his post and probably murder him. On which I desired him to return for further intelligence, and he soon came back and assured me he heard the mob declare they would murder him.

This I feared might be a prelude to their plundering the King's chest. I immediately sent a non-commissioned officer and 12 men to protect both the sentry and the King's money, and very soon followed myself to prevent, if possible, all disorder, fearing lest the officer and soldiers by the insults and provocations of the rioters should be thrown off their guard and commit some rash act. They soon rushed through the people, and by charging their bayonets in half circle kept them at a little distance. Nay, so far was I from intending the death of any person that I suffered the troops to go to the spot where the unhappy affair took place without any loading in their pieces; nor did I ever give orders for loading them. This remiss conduct in me perhaps merits censure, yet it is evidence resulting from the nature of things, which is the best and surest that can be offered, that my intention was not to act offensively, but the contrary part, and that not without compulsion. The mob still increased and were more outrageous, striking their clubs or bludgeons one against another and calling out, Come on you rascals, you bloody backs, you lobster scoundrels, fire if you dare, G-d damn you, fire and be damn'd, we know you dare not, and much more such language was used. At this time I was between the soldiers and the mob parleying with, and endeavouring all in my power to persuade them to retire peaceably but to no purpose. They advanced to the points of the bayonets, struck some of them and even the muzzles of the pieces, and seemed to be endeavouring to close with the soldiers. On which some well-behaved persons asked me if the guns were charged. I replied, Yes, they then asked me if I intended to order the men to fire. I answered, No by no means, observing to them that I was advanced before the muzzles of the mens' pieces and must fall a sacrifice if they fired, that the soldiers were upon the half-cock and charged bayonets, and my giving the word fire under those circumstances would prove me to be no officer. While I was thus speaking one of the soldiers having received a severe blow with a stick, stepped a little on one side and instantly fired, on which turning to and asking him why he fired without orders, I was struck with a club on my arm which for some time deprived me of the use of it, which blow had it been placed on my head most probably would have destroyed me. On this a general attack was made on the men by a great number of heavy clubs and snowballs being thrown at them, by which all our lives were in imminent danger, some persons at the same time from behind calling out, Damn your bloods, why don't you fire. Instantly three or four of the soldiers fired, one after another, and directly after three more in the same confusion and hurry. The mob then ran away except three unhappy men who instantly expired, in which number was Mr Gray at whose rope-walk the prior quarrel took place; one more is since dead, three others are dangerously and four slightly wounded. The whole of this melancholy affair was transacted in almost 20 minutes. On my asking the soldiers why they fired without orders, they said they heard the word fire, and supposed it came from me. This might be the case, as many of the mob called out Fire, fire, but I assured the men that I gave no such order, that my words were, Don't fire, stop your firing. In short it was scarcely possible for the soldiers to know who said fire or don't fire or stop your firing. On the people's assembling again to take away the dead bodies, the soldiers supposing them coming to attack them were making ready to fire again, which I prevented by striking up their fire-locks with my hand. Immediately after a townsman came and told me that 4 or 5000 people were assembled in the next street and had sworn to take my life with every man's with me. On which I judged it unsafe to remain there any longer, and therefore sent the party and sentry to the main-guard, where the street is narrow and short, there telling them off into street-firings, divided and planted them at each end of the street to secure their rear, momently expecting an attack, as there was a constant cry of the inhabitants To arms, To arms, turn out with your guns; and the town drums beating to arms, I ordered my drum to beat to arms, and being soon after joined by the different companies of the 29th Regiment, I formed them as the guard into street-firings. The 14th Regiment also got under arms but remained at their barracks. I immediately sent a sergeant with a party to Colonel Dalrymple, the commanding officer, to acquaint him with every particular. Several officers going to join their regiment were knocked down by the mob, one very much wounded and his sword taken from him. The lieutenant-governor and Colonel Carr soon after met at the head of the 29th Regiment and agreed that the regiment should retire to their barracks and the people to their houses, but I kept the picket to strengthen the guard. It was with great difficulty that the lieutenant-governor prevailed on the people to be quiet and retire, at last they all went off, excepting about a hundred.

A Council was immediately called, on the breaking-up of which three Justices met and issued a warrant to apprehend me and eight soldiers. On hearing of this procedure, I instantly went to the sheriff and surrendered myself, though for the space of 4 hours I had it in my power to have made my escape, which I most undoubtedly should have attempted and could easily [have] executed had I been the least con-scious of any guilt. On the examination before the Justices two wit-nesses swore that I gave the men orders to fire, the one testified he was within two feet of me, the other that I swore at the men for not firing at the first word. Others swore they heard me use the word 'Fire', but whether do or do not fire, they could not say; others that they heard the word fire, but could not say if it came from me. The next day they got 5 or 6 more to swear I gave the word to fire. So bitter and inveterate are many of the malcontents here that they are industriously using every method to fish out evidence to prove it was a concerted scheme to murder the inhabitants. Others are infusing the utmost malice and revenge into the minds of the people who are to be my jurors by false publications, votes of towns, and all other artifices. That so from a settled rancour against the officers and troops in general, the suddenness of my trial after the affair, while the people's minds are all greatly inflamed, I am, though perfectly innocent, under most unhappy circumstances, having nothing in reason to expect but the loss of life in a very ignominious manner without the interposition of His Majesty's royal goodness. *Signed,* Thomas Preston, Captain, 29th Regiment. [C.O.5/759, fo. 117]

XXVIII

Commissioners for Trade and Plantations to Governor Lord Botetourt

16 March, Whitehall

My Lord, the King having been pleased to signify to us his commands by the Earl of Hillsborough that we should report our opinion upon an address and memorial presented to your lordship by the House of Burgesses of Virginia, representing the expediency of the western boundary of that colony being extended further than is limited by His Majesty's present orders to his Superintendant for Indian Affairs for the Southern District, we shall not fail to give this important business the fullest consideration and the greatest dispatch in our power; but as we observe amongst other reasons stated by the House of Burgesses for the alteration proposed, they principally urge the propriety of including within the limits of settlement those lands beyond the Kanahway which are claimed under grants heretofore made by the government of Virginia in consequence of the orders and encouragements given by His late Majesty, it is absolutely necessary before we can form any judgement upon the present proposition that we should be distinctly and fully informed of the nature and extent of those grants, and whether any or what steps have been taken or attempted to be taken for the settlement of the lands. We must therefore desire that your lordship will transmit to us as soon as may be the most exact and particular account that can be procured of this matter, and if you will be pleased to extend your enquiry and report to us all such grants as have been made of any lands beyond the line of settlement prescribed by His Majesty's proclamation of October 1763, it will be of much utility and give great facility to every consideration which may occur in respect to the future disposition of the whole of the lands ceded to His Majesty by the Indians at Fort Stanwix, which is in various lights now become an object of great attention.

The use that is to be made of this information makes it necessary that it should be as full and precise as possible, as well with respect to the situation of the lands which have been granted and the number of acres, as to the persons to whom such grants have been made and the degree of improvement that has followed as far as that can be ascertained; and from the confidence we have in your lordship's care and exactness we have no doubt that the account will be such as to afford us every light we can want. *Entry. Signatories,* Soame Jenyns, George Rice, William Fitzherbert, Lisburne. [C.O.5/1369, p. 22]

XXIX

Lieut.-Governor Thomas Hutchinson to Earl of Hillsborough (No. 6)

27 March, Boston

My Lord, the General Court has sat at Cambridge ever since the 15th but the House of Representatives would not enter upon business until yesterday when they passed certain resolves protesting against their sitting anywhere except at Boston and declaring that it was from absolute necessity they submitted to this grievance.

Although I perceive no disposition in the majority of the House to make my administration uneasy to me from any personal prejudice, yet the same principles with respect to parliamentary authority remain as prevailed in the last session and they have appointed a committee of grievances whose business probably will be a recapitulation of what they have already enumerated, unless they should be discouraged by any intelligence from England which we are every day expecting.

The effect of the late unfortunate action of the troops will long continue. The town have taken a great number of depositions which they have printed here in order to publish them in England, and the House of Representatives are preparing instructions to their agent upon the subject, and I am informed the Council intend also to furnish their agent with a state of the case. The minds of the people are so inflamed that it is much to be desired that the trial of the officer and soldiers should be deferred, but the town by their committee have taken upon them to act as prosecutors and press the court with so much earnestness that I doubt whether they will have firmness enough to resist it. The grand jury have found bills against three or four persons, one of them a waiter in the Customs, for firing guns upon the people from the Custom-house at the same time the soldiers fired in the street. They have moved to the court to be admitted to bail and if the evidence be so slight as is commonly reported it cannot be refused. The Commissioners of the Customs, except Mr Temple, have kept but little in town since the people were killed. Assurances are given by many who pretend to have great influence that the Commissioners are not in danger of any injury or insult, but so much pains has been taken to prejudice the minds of the people that both they and their families apprehend that upon any little disgust they have no security. Upon their application to me I gave an order to the commanding officer at Castle William to receive and afford the best accommodation to them and their families which they propose to make use of only in case of immediate danger. This was the only way in my power of affording them assistance for the whole government has been taught to connect together the office of the Commissioners and the duties in the Revenue Acts and there is no authority which would take any step to support or defend either one or the other. When the troops were in the town the Commissioners were sensible they could have no dependence upon them for if any riot had happened I know of no civil magistrate who would have employed the troops in suppressing it, those who from principle would have been disposed to it refusing and giving this reason, that they must immediately after have left the country. Just the same principles prevail with respect to the troops which are said to be unconstitutional and, although established by an Act of Parliament, yet it is an Act which it is said does not bind colonists.

I find, my lord, I have not strength of constitution to withstand the whole force of the other branches of government as well as the body of the people, united against the governor in every measure he can propose for suppressing those irregularities which appear to me repugnant to the fundamental principles of government and tending to a separation of the colonies from the kingdom, and must humbly pray that a person

of superior powers of body and mind may be appointed to the administration of the government of the province. I shall faithfully endeavour
to support such a person according to the best of my abilities and I
think it not improbable that I may be capable of doing His Majesty
greater service in the province even in a private station than I am at
present. *Signed*. [C.O.5/759, fo. 143]

XXX

Governor Guy Carleton to Earl of Hillsborough (No. 28)

28 March, Quebec

My Lord, herewith enclosed, I transmit to your lordship an Ordinance
[Vol. I, No. 221ii], just published, to correct the ill consequences of the
clause therein repealed and to put an end to the improper and oppressive
use made thereof in some part of this province, a measure become so
necessary to the ease and happiness of the people and in the end to the
King's interests that it would have been highly injudicious to have
either delayed or suspended their relief any longer.

Your lordship has been already informed that the Protestants who
have settled or rather sojourned here since the Conquest are composed
only of traders, disbanded soldiers and officers, the latter, one or two
excepted, below the rank of captain. Of those in the Commission of
the Peace, such as prospered in business could not give up their time
to sit as judges, and when several from accidents and ill-judged under-
takings became bankrupts, they naturally sought to repair their broken
fortunes at the expense of the people. Hence a variety of schemes to
increase the business and their own emoluments: bailiffs of their own
creation, mostly French soldiers, either disbanded or deserters,
dispersed through the parishes with blank citations, catching at every
little feud or dissension among the people, exciting them on to their
ruin, and in a manner forcing them to litigate what, if left to themselves,
might have been easily accommodated, putting them to extravagant
costs for the recovery of very small sums; their lands, at a time there is
the greatest scarcity of money and consequently but few purchasers,
exposed to hasty sales for payment of the most trifling debts, and the
money arising from these sales consumed in exorbitant fees, while the
creditors reap little benefit from the destruction of their unfortunate
debtors. This, my lord, is but a very faint sketch of the distresses of
the Canadians and the cause of much reproach to our national justice
and the King's government.

In my last tour through the country, the outcry of the people was
general. The enclosed copy of a letter [Vol. I, No. 221iii] I received at
my return to this place, from a very sensible old captain of the militia,
is exactly the language of all I met in this progress, and some recent
instances could be brought of their resistance to officers of justice,
acting illegally indeed, a strong symptom among many others of their
patience being near exhausted.

But among other reasons besides the foregoing (which I am apt
to believe your lordship will however think fully sufficient) that
might be alleged for the expediency of reducing the Justices of the

Peace to nearly the same power they have in England, and of reviving part of the ancient mode of administering justice in this province, there was one which had due weight, and that was the confusion arising from so many different jurisdictions, all acting upon different ideas and notions to the great perplexity of the honest part of His Majesty's new subjects, and of which the cunning and ill-designing among them did not neglect to make their advantage. And if your lordship only considers that the new residents here since the Conquest came not only from all parts of the King's extensive dominions but from all parts of the world beside, there is no great reason to wonder at that variety of sentiment in regard to what is right or wrong, and that in general being men of no great learning or extraordinary abilities, they should conform their notions of justice to what they had formerly seen practised rather than to the present circumstances of things in this province.

By the present plan, it is intended that the King's judges, paid by the Crown, may in future chiefly if not altogether take cognizance of matters of property, which of course will produce a greater uniformity in the administration of justice, and as these gentlemen enjoy salaries it will be more incumbent upon them in point of interest as well as for their honour and reputation to give satisfaction to the public than it ever can be upon those who for their daily subsistence depend merely upon the emolument of office, which it will consequently ever be their interest to enhance.

This new disposition will indeed occasion some additional expense to government until a provincial revenue can be settled, as another judge must of course be appointed, and that on account of the circuits they are henceforward to take within their respective districts, both for the sake of administering justice and to see that nothing detrimental to the King's interests is carrying on among the people, I have thought proper to make an addition of fifty pounds a year to each of those already established. *Signed.* [C.O.42/30, fo. 7]

XXXI

Lieut.-General Thomas Gage to Earl of Hillsborough (No. 41)

10 April, New York

My Lord, your lordship will have received by the way of Boston much earlier intelligence than it has been in my power to transmit of an unhappy quarrel between the people of that town and the soldiers, in which several of the former were killed and wounded. But I take the first opportunity to send your lordship the best account I have been able to procure of this unfortunate accident as well as to represent the critical situation of the troops and the hatred of the people towards them.

The occasion which brought the regiments to Boston rendered them obnoxious to the people, and they may have increased the odium themselves as the disorders of that place have mostly sprung from disputes with Great Britain. The officers and soldiers are Britons and the people found no advocates amongst them. It was natural for them without examining into the merits of a political dispute to take the part of their country, which probably they have often done with more zeal than discretion, considering the circumstances of the place they were in, for in matters of dispute with the mother country or relative thereto government is at end in Boston and in the hands of the people who have only to assemble to execute any designs. No person dares to oppose them or call them to account, the whole authority of government, the governor excepted, and magistracy supporting them. The people prejudiced against the troops laid every snare to entrap and distress them, and frequent complaints have been made that the soldiers were daily insulted and the people encouraged to insult them even by magistrates, that no satisfaction could be obtained, but the soldiers if found in fault punished with the rigour of the law. Such proceedings could not fail to irritate but the troops were restrained by their discipline, and though accidental quarrels happened matters were prevented going to extremities.

In my letter to your lordship No. 40 I mentioned a misunderstanding between the inhabitants and soldiers in this town, soon after which advice was transmitted from Boston that the people there had quarrelled with the troops and lay in wait for them in the streets to knock them down, insomuch that it was unsafe for officers or soldiers to appear in the streets after dark. A particular quarrel happened at a rope-walk with a few soldiers of the 29th Regiment. The provocation was given by the ropemakers though it may be imagined in the course of it that there were faults on both sides. This quarrel it is supposed excited the people to concert a general rising on the night of the 5th of March. They began by falling upon a few soldiers in a lane contiguous to a barrack of the 29th Regiment, which brought some officers of the said regiment out of their quarters, who found some of their men greatly hurt but carried all the soldiers to their barrack. The mob followed, menacing and brandishing their clubs over the officers' heads to the barrack-door, the officers endeavouring to pacify them and desiring them to retire. Part of the mob broke into a meeting-house and rang the fire-bell, which appears to have been the alarm concerted, for numerous bodies immediately assembled in the streets, armed, some with muskets but most with clubs, bludgeons and suchlike weapons.

Many people came out of their houses supposing a fire in the town, and several officers on the same supposition were repairing to their posts, but meeting with mobs were reviled, attacked, and those who could not escape knocked down and treated with great inhumanity. Different mobs paraded through the streets passing the several barracks and provoking the soldiers to come out: one body went to the main guard where every provocation was given without effect, for the guard remained quiet. From thence the mob proceeded to a centinel posted upon the Custom-house at a small distance from the guard and attacked him. He defended himself as well as he could, calling out for help, and people ran to the guard to give information of his danger. Captain Preston of the 29th Regiment being captain of the day, his duty upon the alarm carried him to the main guard, and hearing the centinel was in danger of being murdered, he detached a sergeant and twelve men to relieve him, and soon after followed himself to prevent any rash act on the part of the troops. This party as well as the centinel was immediately attacked, some throwing bricks, stones, pieces of ice and snowballs at them, whilst others advanced up to their bayonets and endeavoured to close with them to use their bludgeons and clubs, calling to them to fire if they dared and provoking them to it by the most opprobrious language. Captain Preston stood between the soldiers and the mob, parleying with the latter and using every conciliating method to persuade them to retire peaceably. Some amongst them asked him if he intended to order the men to fire, he replied by no means, and observed he stood between the troops and them. All he could say had no effect, and one of the soldiers receiving a violent blow instantly fired. Captain Preston turned round to see who fired and received a blow upon his arm which was aimed at his head, and the mob at first seeing no execution done and imagining the soldier had only fired powder to frighten grew more bold and attacked with greater violence, continually striking at the soldiers and pelting them and calling out to them to fire. The soldiers at length perceiving their lives in danger and hearing the word Fire all round them, three or four of them fired, one after another, and again three more in the same hurry and confusion. Four or five persons were unfortunately killed and more wounded. Captain Preston and the party were soon afterwards delivered into the hands of the magistrates who committed them to prison.

The misunderstanding between the people and the troops in this place was contrived by one party, not only to wound their adversaries, who had voted to supply the troops according to Act of Parliament, through the sides of the soldiers by making them and their measures odious to the people, but also to have a pretence to desire the removal of the troops, which I am assured was mentioned if not moved at the time in the Council. This plan of getting the troops removed by quarrelling with them was soon transmitted to Boston, where they immediately put it in execution by endeavours to bring on a general quarrel between them and the townspeople. We fortunately found not only magistrates but many people of consequence in this place who discovered the designs of the adverse party and exerted themselves in keeping the people quiet and preventing mischief, without whose assistance I am confident something very disagreeable must have happened here, notwithstanding the uncommon pains taken with the soldiers. And had the magistrates and those who have influence over the populace in Boston taken as much trouble to appease and restrain as they have on too many occasions to enflame and excite the people to tumults and mischief I am as confident that no blood would have been shed in that place. But it appears unfortunately that their schemes were not to be brought about through peace and tranquillity but by promoting disorders.

Some have swore that Captain Preston gave orders to fire, others who were near that the soldiers fired without orders upon the provocation they received. None can deny the attack made upon the troops but differ in the degree of violence in the attack.

I hope and believe that I have given your lordship in general a true relation of this unhappy affair, and sorry I am to say there is too much reason to apprehend neither Captain Preston or the soldiers can have a fair and impartial trial for their lives. The utmost malice and malevolence has been shown already in endeavours to bring on the trials whilst the people are heated by resentment and the thirst of revenge and attempts have been made to overawe the judges. The inveteracy of the people against the Commissioners has also appeared in this affair, for there is information that the grand jury took pains to bring them in as conspiring with the army to massacre, as they term it, the inhabitants; and an officer of the Customs belonging to Gaspee with a gentleman of his acquaintance and two servants of the Board have been committed to prison where they have lain some days as accessories for firing out of the Custom-house upon the evidence of a French serving boy of 14 years of age, notwithstanding the officer, by name Manwaring, was apprehended by a warrant from a popular justice and dismissed upon the detection of the villainy of the boy.

Lieutenant-Governor Hutchinson and Lieutenant-Colonel Dalrymple having acquainted His Majesty's ministers with the reasons for removing the troops from Boston to the island of Castle William, it is needless for me to trouble your lordship with a repetition of them. His Majesty alone can judge whether the lieutenant-colonel who acted contrary to his own opinion should have refused to comply with the desires of every part of the civil government in that respect as well as of most of the officers of the Crown, in order to avoid greater evils than they should suffer from the absence of the troops.

Conceiving the troops to be of no use at the island, I proposed to the lieutenant-governor to remove them out of the province, and one of them immediately. The last measure I shall be obliged to take shortly or run the risk of some contagious disorders getting amongst the men from their being so much crowded in small rooms. Not finding the proposal agreeable, I have consented to let both regiments remain till the arrival of the February mail from England, though I can't perceive any services hopeful from them unless it is to serve in the last extremity as an asylum to which the officers of the Crown might fly for the security of their persons. But if there are any reasons to apprehend dangers of the kind, I am ignorant of them. It has indeed been proved that they were of no other use in the town of Boston, for the people were as lawless and licentious after the troops arrived as they were before. The troops could not act by military authority, and no person in civil authority would ask their aid. They were there contrary to the wishes of the Council, Assembly, magistrates and people, and seemed only offered to abuse and ruin. And the soldiers were either to suffer ill usage and even assaults upon their persons till their lives were in danger, or by resisting and defending themselves to run almost a certainty of suffering by the law. *Signed.* [C.O.5/88, fo. 55]

XXXII

Governor John Wentworth to Earl of Hillsborough (No. 30)

12 April, New Hampshire
May it please your lordship, being now confined to my room by a

violent rheumatic complaint, I can only exert strength and overcome the pain just to inform your lordship that the General Assembly of this province are sitting and almost finished their business, having concluded on a Supply Bill which I believe will prove equal to the common establishment of the government.

There have been but few other Acts prepared and those of little consequence. As soon as the Assembly rises and the whole business recorded and transcribed, I will embrace the earliest opportunity to transmit them to your lordship with such explanatory reasons as may induce my assent to them for His Majesty's service. The Assembly have resolved to forward their dormant petition for relief from the Revenue Act which has laid on their table neglected for two years. It is much more moderate than any other that has been sent and the agent is directed not to present it if the repeal of the Acts or its own contents should render it inexpedient.

I wish it was in my power to represent to your lordship that this province was in equal quiet and moderation as they enjoyed at the time of my last dispatches. The death of five men killed by the troops at Boston in March last has spread a flame like wildfire through all the continent. It is impossible to describe to your lordship the unhappy effect it has produced. Upon this event the Assembly were prevailed on to forward their petition which would otherwise have slept forever. All the people will not be persuaded but that the Commissioners of the Customs and the Revenue Acts are exerted to absorb the property and destroy the lives of the people. Reason has no effect against such prejudices and in short this part of the continent resembles a troubled ocean. I never saw such an exasperated spirit in this province.

The cry of blood re-echoed from one to the other seems to infuriate them. Hence a town-meeting at Exeter in this province voted economy, non-importation and frugality nearly like the Boston town-meetings, from whom it is more than probable they had pressing invitations but till this unhappy event would not enter into them. The town of New Ipswich are of still less importance, being a new and thin-settled township who trade at Boston solely, and receive their orders, being indebted and engaged there. Two of the Commissioners of the Customs have been here near three weeks. Many attempts were made to lead this people into some violent measures against them but I have prevailed to preserve peace and by no means to molest them; they have resided here without the least insult or molestation and will be in the greatest personal safety as long as they choose to remain here.

Upon the arrival of McMasters, one of the Boston importers, the people assembled and voted not to buy or encourage his sales; because of the great scarcity of cash and his underselling the inhabitants might be led into indiscreet purchases and the town impoverished by a man who paid no taxes. All violence to him or to any other was expressly disavowed. A committee were desired to confer with him, and he readily agreed with them and still resides here without any interruption and has sold most of his goods. Notwithstanding the present agitations, public peace and good order is fully maintained nor do I apprehend an appearance of any riotous mobs breaking out. An inflammatory publication was posted up some days since: on notice to the selectmen, they went in a body with a constable, took it down and publicly destroyed it, whence such writings are suppressed.

I hope soon to be able to get into the country where I expect a more speedy recovery and that I shall then transmit the public business of this province completed. In the meantime, permit me to assure your lordship that I shall continue to exert my utmost fidelity and diligence in His Majesty's service.

By the death of Theodore Atkinson Jnr. Esq., there is another vacancy in His Majesty's Council to which I beg leave to recommend Paul Wentworth Esq. of Portsmouth in this province, now in London, being a gentleman of large property, influence, ability and loyalty, and every way qualified and disposed eminently to promote His Majesty's service in that place. *Signed.* [C.O.5/937, fo. 11]

XXXIII

Earl of Hillsborough to Major-General Thomas Gage (No. 27)

14 April, Whitehall

Sir, by the New York mail which arrived here the 2nd instant, I received your dispatch [Vol. I, No. 139] No. 40 and have laid it before the King.

His Majesty approves your sending the 16th Regiment to Pensacola and the other arrangements which are to be made in consequence thereof.

Whether the military force now to be sent to West Florida is or is not to continue there will depend upon future circumstances and events and upon the conduct and measures of the Court of Spain in respect to Louisiana, but whatever may be the final determination on this point it seems highly necessary that the forces should have better lodgement at Pensacola than the miserable huts now there will afford them, and therefore the King approves of your having sent orders to stop any farther proceeding upon the barracks at St Augustine and is well pleased to find that the contract for that work is in such terms as to admit of the wood-work being applied to the same use at Pensacola.

I am sorry to find that you are confirmed in your opinion of the causes of the commotion amongst the savages and that there is so much reason to apprehend that an Indian war may be the consequence. The alternative to which we are reduced is certainly a disagreeable one. The uniting the savages in one common interest is a measure which abstractedly considered appears to be founded in principles of justice and humanity; but if such union is to be accompanied with the hazard of their turning their arms against us and thereby endangering the tranquillity of our frontiers, good policy certainly points out a different system of conduct towards them, and self-preservation will justify what humanity might otherwise condemn.

After you had so strongly urged to Sir William Johnson how much it was his particular business to lay before the King's ministers the critical situation in which the affairs of his department stood (which you will observe from my last dispatch to you corresponds exactly with my own expectations) I cannot but express to you that I was much surprised not to have received any letter from him by the last packet, without which it is impossible for me to form a judgement of what instructions ought to be given, nor can I take upon myself to advise His Majesty to authorise the incurring any expense beyond what the ordinary establishment for Indian services will admit of without being able to show from the report of the proper officer that it is absolutely necessary and unavoidable.

It has given the King great concern to find that any of his subjects in New York could have entertained so wicked and malevolent a design as that of creating a quarrel between the inhabitants of New York and the soldiers, which had it not been checked by measures of the greatest temper and prudence might have led to consequences of a very alarming nature.

His Majesty attributes the prevention of those evils to your prudence and discretion, and trusts that the agreement you have made with the lieut.-governor in respect to quartering the troops, of which agreement I have received a copy from him, will have the good effect to prevent all such disagreeable discussion on the subject as may serve for a handle to create further disturbances.

The indictment found and presented by the grand jury at Boston, of which you enclose to me a copy [Vol. I, No. 139ii], shows equally the malice and weakness of those who seek to disturb the peace and tranquillity of that colony; and though it is a proceeding which in almost every light in which it can be viewed exposes itself to contempt rather than notice, yet His Majesty from his royal inclination to give every countenance and support to an officer of your rank and merit has commanded me to refer it to his Attorney- and Solicitor-General for their opinion what steps it may be proper to take to defend you against any consequences that may follow from it. *Draft*. [C.O.5/88, fo. 48]

XXXIV

Earl of Hillsborough to Lieut.-Governor Cadwallader Colden (No. 38)

14 April, Whitehall

Sir, I have received and laid before the King your letter [Vol. II, No. XX] of the 21st February, No. 9, together with the attested copy of the Act to which you have thought fit to give your assent, declaring the Judges of the Supreme Court incapable of sitting in the Assembly, and also the copy of an agreement entered into with Major-General Gage for the application of the money given by the General Assembly for providing necessaries for the King's troops.

In my letter [Vol. II, No. XV] No 37, I transmitted to you an Order of His Majesty in Council disallowing the Act for emitting £120,000 in paper bills of credit, and I now enclose to you a further Order in Council [Vol. I, No. 203] disallowing the Act for explaining the duty of the loan offices as being consequential of and dependent upon the other law.

It gives me great concern after having in my last letter signified to you His Majesty's displeasure on account of your having assented to the paper currency Bill without a suspending clause to be again under the necessity of taking notice of a fresh instance of disobedience to His Majesty's instructions in the like assent given to the Bill for disqualifying the judges from sitting in the Assembly, a bill which is not only of a new and extraordinary nature in every construction of those descriptive words but is evidently founded on reasoning and precedents not applicable to the state of New York.

What measures His Majesty may think fit to pursue when this Act comes before him in his Privy Council I will not presume to say, but I have thought it my duty to lose no time in receiving the King's commands to lay it before the Lords of Trade in order that they may make such report thereupon as they shall think fit, and I shall be very glad if your reasoning upon the Act shall furnish their lordships with any arguments to extenuate the impropriety of your conduct in a case of so much importance to the King's government.

After the experience we have had of the little utility on the one hand and the dangerous use that has been made on the other of meetings of commissioners from the several colonies to consider of matters in which they have a separate and distinct interest, I have at least great doubts of the propriety of giving encouragement to such a congress for the purposes of regulating the Indian trade; and whatever your own opinion might have been of the expediency of such a measure, it is past a doubt that you ought not to have given your assent to any law for such a purpose without His Majesty's directions.

At the same time that the King sees with just displeasure these instances of disobedience to his instructions, His Majesty commands me to say that as far as your conduct has been really intended and has operated to promote a good agreement between the several branches of the legislature, to encourage the friends of government, and check the promoters of discord, it will be considered with every attention due to its merit. *Draft.* [C.O.5/1101, fo. 54]

XXXV

Additional Instruction for Lord Charles Montagu[1]

14 April, St James's
Additional instruction to our trusty and well beloved Charles Greville Montagu Esq. commonly called Lord Charles Greville Montagu, our Captain-General and Governor-in-Chief of our province of South Carolina in America, or in his absence to the Lieutenant-Governor or Commander-in-Chief of our said province for the time being. Given at our Court at St James's, the 14th day of April 1770.

Whereas it hath been represented to us that our House of Representatives or Lower House of Assembly of our province of South Carolina in America have lately assumed to themselves a power of ordering, without the concurrence of our Governor and Council, the public Treasurer of our said province to issue and advance out of the public

---

1   Enclosed in Hillsborough's letter to Bull, 14 April 1770: Vol. I, No. 268.

Treasury such sums of money and for such services as they have thought fit, and in particular that the said Lower House of Assembly did on the 8th day of December last past make an order upon the said public Treasurer to advance the sum of ten thousand five hundred pounds currency out of any money in the Treasury, to be paid into the hands of Mr Speaker, Mr Gadsden, Mr Rutlege, Mr Parson, Mr Ferguson, Mr Dart and Mr Lynch, who were to remit the same to Great Britain for the support of the just and constitutional rights and liberties of the people of Great Britain and America. And whereas it is highly just and necessary that the most effectual measures be pursued for putting a stop to such dangerous and unwarrantable practices and for guarding for the future against such unconstitutional application of our treasure, cheerfully granted to us by our subjects in our said province of South Carolina for the public uses of the said province and for the support of the government thereof, it is therefore our will and pleasure, and you are hereby directed and required upon pain of our highest displeasure and of being forthwith removed from your government, not to give your assent to any bill or bills that shall be passed by our said Lower House of Assembly, by which bill or bills any sum or sums of money whatsoever shall be appropriated to or provision made for defraying any expense incurred for services or purposes not immediately arising within or incident to our said province of South Carolina, unless upon special requisition from us, our heirs and successors, nor to any bill or bills for granting any sum or sums of money to us, our heirs and successors, in which bill or bills it shall not be provided in express words that the money so to be granted or any part thereof shall not be issued or applied to any other services than those to which it is by the said bill or bills appropriated, unless by Act or Ordinance of the General Assembly of our said province. And it is our further will and pleasure, and you are hereby directed and required upon pain of our highest displeasure as aforesaid not to give your assent to any bill or bills that shall be passed by our said Lower House of Assembly as aforesaid, by which any sum or sums of money whatever shall be granted to us, our heirs and successors, generally and without appropriation unless there be a clause or clauses inserted in the said bill or bills declaring and providing that the said money so to be granted shall remain in the Treasury subject to such appropriation as shall thereafter be made by Act or Ordinance of the General Assembly and not otherwise. And it is our further will and pleasure that you take especial care that in all and every bill and bills so to be passed by you as aforesaid for raising and granting public monies, a clause or clauses be inserted therein subjecting the public Treasurer or any other person or persons to whose custody public monies may be committed, in case he or they shall issue or pay any such money otherwise than by express order contained in some Act or Ordinance of the General Assembly, to a penalty in treble the sum so issued contrary thereto, and declaring him or them to be *ipso facto* incapable of holding the said office of Treasurer or any other office civil or military within our said province. And it is our further will and pleasure that this our additional instruction to you be communicated to our Council and Lower House of Assembly of our said province of South Carolina, and entered upon the Council Books. *Copy.* [C.O.5/393, fo. 30]

XXXVI

Earl of Hillsborough to Sir William Johnson (No. 13)

14 April, Whitehall

Sir, I have received and laid before the King your dispatch [Vol. II, No. XIII] of the 10th of February, No. 12.

The matter proposed to the confederacy of the Six Nations by the Cherokees is of great importance, and it is with concern His Majesty observes that the answer to be given to the Cherokees is made to depend upon your opinion and advice, by which the King will stand committed in measures which, if they adopt the proposition of a war against the Southern and Western Indians, are irreconcilable with the principles of humanity, and if on the contrary they tend to union of Indian interests and politics, endanger the security of His Majesty's colonies by enabling the savages to turn their arms against us.

This consequence, however, which you seem to think would follow from discouraging a war against the Southern and Western Indians, is certainly to be avoided if possible, and therefore the King however unwillingly cannot but approve of your adopting the alternative, and making the security of his subjects and the peace of the frontiers the principal object of your attention at the congress, but it would be most pleasing to His Majesty if it could be attained without encouraging the savages in their barbarous attacks on each other.

It would have been more fortunate upon every consideration that this congress could have been avoided, not only as it does in its consequences involve His Majesty as a party in a business of so disagreeable a nature but also as it will I find be attended with an expense beyond what your stated allowance will admit of.

The King however relies upon your assurances on the one hand that this expense is unavoidable, and on the other that the service shall be conducted with all the frugality and economy that is possible consistent with the public safety; and under these assurances His Majesty approves of your replying to Major-General Gage, who will have orders to defray what expense shall be absolutely necessary on this occasion.

It is to be hoped that it will not be long before those colonies whose security depends upon the goodwill and affection of the savages will see the necessity of such regulations as will be effectual to prevent those abuses which at present give so much discontent to them. In the meantime you will not fail to exert every influence in your power to prevent these abuses from having such an operation upon the minds of the Indians as to disturb that tranquillity which is so essential to their true interests. *Draft.* [C.O.5/71, Pt. 1, fo. 81]

XXXVII

Lieut.-Governor William Bull to Earl of Hillsborough (No. 26)

15 April, Charleston

My Lord, by His Majesty's packet *Le Despencer* on the 1st instant, I was honoured with your lordship's letter [Vol. II, No. XVI], No 33, and duplicate of No. 32, with letters enclosed for Governor Shirley and Governor Bruere and Mr Stuart, the Superintendant, all which are forwarded respectively.

I am to acquaint your lordship that according to the intimation in my letter No. 20, when the Tax Bill, read a second time (the method of proceeding observed here) came up to the Council, they objected to the article in the estimate which was to replace the £1,500 sterling voted the 8th of December last, and sent a message to the Assembly relative thereto. The Assembly seeing a rupture unavoidable and having fourteen bills ready, they were accordingly presented to me and received my assent on Saturday the 7th instant, and then the Assembly seemed determined to do no more business with the Council in this session, although a bill for the schools and one for the encouragement of tobacco and flour were engrossed and required only the form of comparing the engrossed bill with the original by a committee of Assembly with a committee of Council, which I regret very much though these matters doubtless will be resumed hereafter.

The Assembly met the Monday following when I was in hopes they would, from a consideration of the public utility thereof, have consented to present the Tobacco and Flour Bill for my assent; but when it was proposed from the Chair, the general voice called out No, no. They then turned their thoughts upon what steps were to be taken in regard to the Council. I was unwilling to prorogue them until I could discern, and your lordship be informed, what course the stream of their resentment would take. This appeared next day to be an address to the King to pray that a constitutional branch of legislature might be appointed by His Majesty independent of the Council, and an address to me to procure satisfaction for the insult they had received from the Council. On Wednesday morning when they had just begun the debate upon the report, I thought it necessary to put an end to the session by prorogation to prevent their carrying those resolutions into effect, especially when I considered that popular assemblies met in an ill humour, if permitted to continue long assembled, are too apt to be hurried by their heated imaginations into wanton and extraordinary resolutions from which they rarely can be brought afterwards to recede. I accordingly prorogued the General Assembly to the 5th of June in case I should receive any matters in command from His Majesty to be laid before them, and if not, I shall continue them by further prorogation to the middle of July, and endeavour then to have such business taken into consideration as is most necessary.

Although this prorogation prevented the House from concurring with the report of the committee and therefore their resolutions could not be printed by order, they are however to be printed by the direction of almost all the members as private men.

By His Majesty's packet *Eagle*, which will sail in about fourteen days, I shall transmit to the Right Honourable the Lords Commissioners for Trade and Plantations the Journals of the Council and Assembly to the end of the session, that they may be inspected if any particular information relative to their proceedings is wanted; also the Acts passed, all which I have ordered to be prepared immediately. *Signed.* PS. April 16, 1770. As the *Gazettes* dated April 5 and 12 were delivered out this morning I thought proper to transmit them[1] to your lordship as they contain the resolutions of the committee referred to in the preceding letter, the titles of the Acts, and other matters relating to our present situation. The mail will be closed this day. [C.O.5/393, fo. 39]

1   Vol. I, No. 277i, *Gazette* for 5 April only.

XXXVIII

Governor Guy Carleton to Earl of Hillsborough (No. 32)

25 April, Quebec

My Lord, from the temper and disposition of His Majesty's old subjects in this province, with which your lordship is already well-acquainted, it could not be a matter of much surprise to me that the Ordinance transmitted in my letter [Vol. II, No. XXX] No. 28 produced a stir among some of them, or that a regulation depriving so many of a most unfair means of subsistence, although raised under the specious pretext and colour of the law, should engage these to struggle for a repeal of what was likely in so great a degree to affect their private circumstances, as well as the influence and sway they had acquired in consequence of the powers they were before invested with.

Soon after the publication of the Ordinance six gentlemen, the same who certify the copy of the memorial, waited on me with said copy, whereof a copy [Vol. I, No. 290i] is herewith enclosed; they said they were chosen to present me that remonstrance, as they styled it, against the Ordinance and that as it was pretty long they would not then read it but leave the same for my consideration.

I told them very possibly the Ordinance might require amendment which time and a little experience would clearly show, that for my part I should always be obliged to any gentleman who took the trouble to set me right in any mistake I might commit or point out anything that could be of advantage to the province, but that for their own sakes I was concerned at their attempts to follow the conduct of a province which had incurred the displeasure of government at home, and whose manner of demanding redress had proved the means of preventing it in those very points wherein government wished to gratify them, had they asked in a proper way or with becoming decency, that I was really ashamed of the manner in which I was informed many of the King's old subjects had behaved, sending about hand-bills to invite the people to assemble in order to consult upon grievances, importuning, nay insulting, several of the Canadians because they would not join them, that I was not only ashamed of it but astonished they did not see how much they acted against their own interests, for if in tumultous meetings or by dint of numbers only, laws were to be made or abrogated, the lowest dregs of the people and the most ignorant among them would of course become the lawgivers of the country, and the firm refusal of the Canadians as well as of most of their own countrymen plainly showed the opinion the generality entertained of their proceedings.

They replied with temper and submission, denied their having acted with any violence, and begged I would not believe all that had been reported upon that head. However, I could not help observing to Mr Charles Grant, who has all along put himself at the head of this affair as I was well assured, and that some time before the Ordinance was near perfect he made this declaration, that as he had not been consulted, though one of the most considerable traders in the country, he was resolved to oppose it; to this he made no reply. I had been long informed that one Mr Shepherd, formerly in trade here, who owed a considerable sum to some merchants in London of the name of Grant which he had no other means of discharging than by the very beneficial employment, as he made it, of Clerk of the Peace of this district which he had enjoyed for some years, was determined to cause a bustle and pushed on this same Mr Charles Grant to take the part he has acted therein.

After considering with the greatest attention all that they have or can possibly object against this Ordinance, I cannot at least for the present discover any foundation for repealing any part thereof. That which seems to carry with it the greatest appearance of plausibility, the lands not being liable to be sold for debts under twelve pounds currency, I am well convinced can be attended with no particular inconvenience, for the produce of the smallest farms allowed by the French regulation, about sixty acres, which in my humble opinion was a very prudent and political one and ought to be kept up, besides the stock, will considerably more than pay that sum, exactly equal to nine pounds sterling; and I believe the Canadians would not very readily adopt the wise proposal these gentlemen make of saving the latter for settling new lands where they must toil like slaves for two or three years before they can introduce the plough.

Within these four or five years between three or four hundred families have been turned out of their houses, obliged to sell their lands and seek new habitations, a real loss to trade as they become a burthen to society and are years before they can be enabled to purchase our manufactures, and what is still a greater hardship upon them the lands have not been sold for a sixth or eighth of their value, so that many instances can be brought of debtors being ruined, the produce consumed in fees, and the creditor's demand remaining undischarged.

It is but a few months since sixteen debtors were released out of the gaol of Montreal at the expense of government by my orders, whose debts and gaol-fees, the latter of which were above one-half of the whole, did not amount to quite forty pounds sterling. What effect this must have upon a people to whom an arrest of the body for debt was almost entirely unknown, I humbly submit.

A trading justice was likewise a new practice, no ways likely to make the Canadians relish British government. There was not a Protestant butcher or publican that became a bankrupt who did not apply to be made a Justice. They cantoned themselves upon the country, and many of them rid the people with despotic sway, imposed fines which they turned to their own profit, and in a manner looked upon themselves as the legislators of the province.

To ease the poor people of such intolerable oppression, to render them useful to Great Britain and the society they live in, and that the only order of Canadians most likely to reap any advantage from the change of dominion might feel the full benefit of this change, were the only motives which guided my conduct upon this occasion. I shall be happy if it procures the end proposed.

Before I conclude I cannot help mentioning to your lordship that though I disapproved that mode of administering justice, and it appears to me not at all calculated for the peculiar circumstances attending this country, and though I have great reason to be dissatisfied with the conduct of some of the Justices, there are worthy men in the Commission of the Peace in both districts and particularly in that of Quebec. *Signed.* [C.O.42/30, fo. 43]

XXXIX

Lieut.-Governor Cadwallader Colden to Earl of Hillsborough (No. 10)

25 April, New York
My Lord, to have fallen under His Majesty's displeasure as I find I have by your lordship's letter [Vol. II, No. XV] of the 17th of February, No. 37, gives me the deepest concern. I have had the honour to serve the Crown in this province near 50 years and have heretofore been happy in His Majesty's approbation of my conduct. It adds greatly to my affliction that I should have forfeited it when I am so near the close of life; but I have this comfort, that however I may have erred it was not from any want or neglect of duty but from an error in judgement, thinking that giving my assent to the bill for emitting bills of credit at the time I did was greatly for His Majesty's service in preventing the tumults and disorders with which the province was at that time threatened. The Chief Justice and another gentleman eminent in the profession of the law were present when the Council unanimously advised me to give my assent to that bill and were of opinion that it contained nothing in it contrary to the Act of Parliament, and that the time allowed by the Act before it was to take place was equivalent to a suspending clause. Your lordship blames me for giving my assent when I knew that a similar bill, transmitted by Sir Henry Moore, was under consideration and before I knew the result; but, my lord, the circumstances of the province at that time would not permit delay, and I must own it was some inducement to me to give my assent, knowing that a similar bill was then under consideration and consequently that His Majesty's pleasure must be known before any part of the Act could take effect; and so it has happened. And in pursuance of your lordship's commands I immediately published His Majesty's disallowance of the Act that all persons may govern themselves accordingly.

My lord, I flatter myself you will indulge me in giving the state of the province at that time. A violent faction prevailed in opposition to government and the authority of the Parliament of Great Britain, which from many circumstances appeared to be acting in concert with a similar faction at Boston. Numerous papers were dispersed about the town exciting the people to sedition and exasperating them against the soldiers then quartered in this place. The soldiers walking peaceably in the street were several times attacked, beat and abused—this of consequence drew on their resentment, and we should have had the same mischievous effects produced here which have since happened at Boston, had not a body of the principal inhabitants assured the magistrates of their assistance in preserving the peace of the city, which with the prudent conduct of the magistrates and officers of the army prevented this wicked design. Of this I informed your lordship in my letter No. 9. The similarity of the proceedings of the factions in this place and in Boston will induce a belief that they acted in concert. But besides this, one of the judges, who is known to have connections with those who are thought to be the leaders of the faction, advised the withdrawing of the troops from this place as the only method to delay the disturbances; and one of the Council, who is known to have the same connections with the judge, strenuously insisted that the withdrawing the troops was the only method to restore peace to the place. These I think strong proofs that the views of the factions in this place and in Boston were the same. That they did not succeed here was owing to the principal inhabitants being entirely pleased with the conduct of the administration and were resolved to support it, of which I have since that time received several public acknowledgements. The giving my assent to the bill for emitting bills of credit served much to reconcile the minds of the people and to put them in good humour. Had I refused my assent to this bill and had the Assembly granted no money for the troops, as in that case they would not, the faction would have succeeded in their design to disturb the government, and it is not easy to say what might have been the consequences. Upon a review of my conduct under these circumstances, I hope, my lord, His Majesty may be graciously pleased to think more favourably of it.

The good effects of the harmony which prevailed between the several branches of the legislature in the last sessions is very evident in the good order and submission to the authority of government which has ever since subsisted in this place. Government has renewed its strength which the events of some past years had greatly weakened. A disappointed faction by publishing the most gross calumnies and impudent lies in order to asperse my character and the characters of the gentlemen joined with me in the administration have drawn upon themselves a general detestation and so far sunk their own characters in the estimation of every man of reputation that for the future they can have no general influence. And I hope from all these circumstances the administration will be made much more easy to my successor and that I shall have the pleasure to deliver the government to his lordship in good order and tranquillity.

The grand jury of this city now sitting have found an indictment against Alexander McDougall for publishing a libel against the government, which I mentioned to your lordship in my letters [Vol. II, Nos. IV, XX] No. 8 and 9. It is thought he cannot have his trial this term as the court will be fully employed the few days they have to sit in the trial of capital criminals.

The governments of Quebec and Pennsylvania have agreed to send commissioners to meet the commissioners of this province in order to form some plan for regulating the Indian trade, and I expect they will meet at this place the 10th of July next.

As I have had my duty constantly before my eyes and have pursued it sincerely to the best of my ability, the thoughts of closing my life under His Majesty's displeasure give me great pain and that by any error I may have forfeited your lordship's regard. *Signed.* [C.O.5/1101, fo. 56]

XL

Earl of Hillsborough to Lieut.-Governor Thomas Hutchinson (No 36)

26 April, Whitehall

Sir, your dispatch [Vol. II, No. XXVI] of the 12th of March, No. 5, was delivered to me by Mr Robinson who arrived here on Saturday last, and I lost no time in laying it before the King.

The transactions at Boston on the 5th and 6th of March are indeed of a very melancholy and alarming nature, and in whatever light they are viewed they give His Majesty the greatest concern.

It is now under consideration what measures it may be proper to pursue in consequence of this event; in the meantime His Majesty does not entertain a doubt of your making a prudent and proper use of the powers placed in your hands for the due execution of justice and the support of the dignity of government; but in so very extraordinary a case as that of Captain Preston and the soldiers appears to be, I am commanded by the King to signify his pleasure to you that if upon their trial they should be convicted and condemned, you do respite the execution until His Majesty's pleasure shall be known, transmitting to me in order to be laid before His Majesty copies of all the proceedings on such trial to the end that His Majesty may give such further directions as justice and the nature of the case shall appear to require.

As the present state of the town of Boston and the frenzy of its inhabitants afford but too just ground to apprehend that they may be induced to commit further violence, the King has thought fit that His Majesty's commands should be signified to Major-General Gage and to Commodore Hood that they do give every assistance in their power which you and the other civil officers and magistrates at Boston shall require to enable you to preserve the public peace and support the legal authority of government; and His Majesty trusts that by availing yourself in a prudent and constitutional manner of the assistance these gentlemen will be able to afford you, all obstruction to justice and the execution of the laws may be prevented until further measures shall be fallen upon for restoring a due influence to the King's government and security to His Majesty's subjects in the province of Massachusetts Bay.

Major-General Gage and Sir Francis Bernard having informed me that indictments have been preferred and found against them in the Superior Court of your province, on the ground of their representations of the state of public affairs there in their letters to His Majesty's ministers, I am commanded by the King, before whom copies of these indictments have been laid, to signify to you His Majesty's pleasure that you should direct the Attorney-General to enter a *noli prosequi* in the King's name in every suit that may be commenced on any indictment of such a nature either against them or any officer of the Crown whatever. *Draft.* [C.O.5/759, fo. 133]

XLI

Talk from Escotchaby or the Young Lieutenant of the Lower Creeks to John Stuart[1]

26 April, Creek Nation

Last fall my young people made great complaints to me about the white people settling on the line and over it and building cowpens. I told them that I believed it to be lies, and to satisfy them said I would go and see whether it was so or not that there might be a stop put to it before any mischief happened; and on my way towards Little River within 20 miles of it I heard a great many guns fired round about me, and thinking that there might be some Indians hunting in that part, to my great surprise I came on a camp of white hunters. They had killed a good many deer, and I took from them three deerskins and some meat, and at the same time the white people's cattle were 20 miles from the said settlement; and immediately I desired the white people to gather their cattle near the settlement for fear of my young people who were hunting and might kill some of them which would breed mischief, and I then spoke more in behalf of the white people than of my own colour. And at the same time some of the white rogues stole two of my horses in return for the trouble I took in their behalf. I remained there some time in hopes of recovering my horses, but I could hear nothing of them. I then came down to Mr Galphin's and applied to him for his assistance in recovering them, but although he used every means in his power he could not hear of them. I then returned towards home and on my journey camped hard by the place where I lost my horses, and hearing that the people kept store there and sold goods very cheap, being in want of a little powder, I sent in my son with five raw deerskins to buy it and desired him to enquire of the white people about my horses. But as soon as my son came to the house one of the white men came out of it and endeavoured to take away his gun from him and tried to throw him down. Another white man then came out and assisted my son in recovering his gun and told him to go off as fast as possible; he then run with haste away but the white people pursued him near two miles,

1   Enclosed in Stuart's letter to Hillsborough, 8 June 1770: Vol. I, No. 393.

throwing juncks of wood at him and at last fired at him which frightened him so much that he dropped his bundle of skins. He at last reached the camp with much difficulty and acquainted me with the treatment he had met with. The next day there were three other fellows who went to fire on the settlement, but when I heard it I put a stop to it till such time as I could acquaint you. It is very lucky my son is not killed.

If you do not put a stop to those outstores that are established on Little River and Ogeechie, it will shortly bring on a war, for the Indians finding out the stores and hearing that goods are sold so cheap are encouraged to come down if [sic, ? where] they are sure to be killed. So you must stop all the outstores from having any dealings with the Indians or else you may depend it will bring on a war upon your country and it will not be in my power to stop the young people except you stop all the stores on the frontier settlements and on Little River, which will be the first place where any mischief will happen. There is a wagon road that goes through our land from Savannah by which the outstores are supplied with goods and rum to trade with the Indians on Little River. This wagon we intend to lay wait for and break and take all that is in it as a free prize, as it goes through our land. Last fall you acquainted us that you intended to stop all the outstores, which we were very glad to hear but where there was one then there are three now. Except those stores are broke up it will bring on a war, for before I could leave the place where my son was shot at I lost two more horses. *Copy.* [C.O.5/71, Pt. 2, fo. 5]

XLII

John Stuart to Earl of Hillsborough (No. 22)

2 May, Charleston

My Lord, upon the 10th of last month I met all the principal chiefs of the Cherokee nation at the Congarees in this province, and I have the honour of submitting to your lordship minutes [Vol. I, No. 320i] of the conferences at said meeting; by which the difficulty of obtaining from them a more extended boundary on the side of Virginia will fully appear to your lordship. And I humbly offer it as my opinion that if their apprehensions on account of their lands are removed and the traders to their nation can be laid under proper regulations, there will not be the least danger of a rupture with them. I have furnished my Lord Botetourt with a copy of the minutes, and hope soon to be honoured with your lordship's orders respecting the pretensions of Virginia, that the Indians may be put out of suspense.

Since my letter No. 17 I have not had any intelligence of the Creeks that merits your lordship's attention. Some emissaries from the Shawnese and Delawares were sometime ago amongst the Cherokees and are now in the Creek nation to sound the disposition of said Indians towards a confederacy with them and the Western Indians, upon the principle of defending their lands from our encroachments; but I have not learned that any attention has been paid them by either. Indeed the principal warriors of the Cherokees refused to confer with them upon the subject.

On the 17th ultimate at my return to this place, I had the honour of receiving your lordship's letter [Vol. I, No. 132] of 17 February No. 14, and by the same conveyance I received His Majesty's warrants for my admission as a member of the several Councils within my district. I have the most grateful sense of the great honour conferred upon me by this mark of royal favour.

It is a very long time since I have received any intelligence from West Florida. I have now the honour of laying before your lordship the last accounts I have had from thence, contained in a letter [Vol. I, No. 320ii] from Monsieur de la Gautrais, late commissary in the eastern part of the Choctaw nation, to Mr Charles Stuart, my deputy for that part of the district. The accounts contained in it seem to justify the opinion that the irregularities of the Indians contiguous to West Florida proceeded from the machinations of the Spaniards. As a packet is hourly expected from Pensacola I hope to be enabled to write a more ample and satisfactory account of affairs in that quarter. Generals Gage and Haldimand have been pleased to write me that they had received from Mr O'Reilly the strongest assurances of his inclinations to maintain a good correspondence with His Majesty's subjects in that part of his dominions and to keep the Indians in proper subjection, and we have since heard of his having returned to the Havana with all the troops except about 600 men.

I beg leave to lay before your lordship copies [Vol. I, No. 320v-vi] of Lieut.-Governor Browne's letter to me and my answer relative to his appointment and the pay of Mr Westrop as my deputy in West Florida, in which my reason for not paying said gentleman are assigned, and I humbly hope they are such as will meet with your lordship's approbation. No other correspondence ever passed between Mr Browne and me upon that subject and I further must represent to your lordship that I never received a letter from Mr Westrop and that no part of my instructions to my deputy were carried into execution by him, although General Haldimand opened and communicated them to Governor Browne, being directed on His Majesty's service; by which means the officers employed in the regulation of the Indian trade in that part of my district continued to act many months longer than was intended.
Signed. [C.O.5/71, Pt. 1, fo. 105]

XLIII

Commissioners for Trade and Plantations to the King

4 May, Whitehall
May it please Your Majesty, in obedience to Your Majesty's commands signified to us by the Earl of Hillsborough, one of Your Majesty's Principal Secretaries of State, we have taken into our consideration a memorial [Vol. I, No. 240i] delivered to Lord Weymouth on the 29th of March last by the French Ambassador, complaining of several obstructions which the subjects of France have met with in carrying on the concurrent fishery on the coast of Newfoundland and of certain new pretensions set up by English fishermen contrary to the spirit of treaty; whereupon we humbly beg leave to represent to Your Majesty.

That, as the French Ambassador has in his observations upon the several heads of complaint referred to orders given and declarations made by the late and present Commanders-in-chief of Your Majesty's ships and vessels in those seas, and by the officers employed under them, we thought fit to refer this memorial to Captains Byron and Pallisser, whose report and observations [Vol. I, No. 323i-ii] thereupon we humbly beg leave to annex.

From the facts stated in this report, from the observations made by Captain Pallisser, and from what we find upon our own books relative to former proceedings in consequence of disputes which have arisen between British and French fishermen, it appears to us,

First, that the regulations contained in Your Majesty's instructions respecting the concurrent fishery upon the coast of Newfoundland between Bonavista and Point Riche (which instructions are founded on the stipulations of the Treaties of Utrecht and Paris, and the propriety of them at all times admitted by the Court of France) have been observed on the part of Your Majesty's officers with the greatest exactness and with the most scrupulous attention to the rights of the subjects of France.

2dly. That although it may be doubtful upon a construction of the words of the Treaty of Utrecht whether the subjects of France have a right to resort to every part of the harbour of Bonavista, yet in fact the exercise of this right never has been refused as no vessel of that nation has ever yet attempted to establish a fishery in that harbour, and that there is no foundation for what is asserted of the menaces used by Lieutenant Parker in respect of French vessels that should resort thither.

3dly. That the utmost endeavours have been used, under repeated instructions from Your Majesty, to prevent those sedentary establishments referred to in the 2nd article of complaint, which we conceive are not warranted by law and are equally prejudicial to the fishery of both nations.

4thly. That no direct or particular order has ever been given to prevent the French fishermen from carrying on their business on Sundays and holidays, the only case in which they could possibly be affected by any general order for the observation of the Lord's Day being that of the order stated by Captain Byron to have been given at the harbour of Green's Pond, and

Lastly, that the single instance in which there could have been the least foundation for the complaint contained in the fourth article of the memorial is that of the orders given by Captain Pallisser in August 1768 in the case of the pretensions set up by Captain Hamont, which orders appears to us to have been founded upon considerations of reciprocal utility and convenience, and to conform with the greatest exactness to those laws and rules which the French have thought fit themselves to prescribe for their fishery on the coast of Newfoundland.

With regard to the claim set up by the Court of France to the amount of the sale of a whale found dead upon the coast of Newfoundland by a French fisherman, as we are not acquainted with the particulars of this case nor with the promises said to have been made last year, upon which the claim appears to be founded, we are not able to report any opinion upon it; but we beg leave humbly to observe that the greatest caution ought to be used in any discussion of this nature to avoid giving the least colour to claims that are not warranted by treaty.

Upon the whole, when we consider the equity of the instructions already given by Your Majesty for regulating the concurrent fishery on the coast of Newfoundland, the great care that has been taken to secure and preserve the just rights of France in the provisions of them, the justice and moderation with which they have been executed, and the beneficial consequences that have followed from them to the subjects of that nation in the great improvement and extension of their fishery, we cannot but be equally surprised and concerned that the Court of France should upon no other ground than the vague reports of matters equally frivolous in their nature and false in their foundation, made by fishermen who seek for subject of cavil and dispute merely for their own personal interest, attempt to revive the discussion of new claims and pretensions in a matter so amicably settled and which ever has been and ever ought to be an object of the greatest national jealousy in this kingdom.

It is not for us to suppose that the bounties given by the Court of France to vessels that should resort to new harbours could have any other intention than to extend and improve their fishery as allowed by treaty; but it is evident that the effect of these bounties has been to aggravate those subjects of contention to which the concurrent fishery is in its nature but too liable, and indeed we cannot but concur in opinion with Captains Byron and Pallisser that they have been principally the foundation of the claims and disputes now in question. Therefore we are not without hope that the Court of France will be induced to desist from a regulation which in the opinion of the most sober even of their own fishermen could have no other consequence than what we have stated, and that they will rest satisfied of the uprightness of Your Majesty's intentions in the instructions which have been already given, and with the great advantages they derive from the stipulations of those treaties upon which they are founded. *Signed,* Greville, Soame Jenyns, William Fitzherbert, W. Northey. [C.O. 194/29, fo. 13]

XLIV

Governor James Wright to Earl of Hillsborough (No. 43)

10 May, Savannah

My Lord, your lordship's letter [Vol. I, No. 122] of the 17th of February, No. 29, I had the honour to receive, and with respect to the letter from the Speaker of the House of Burgesses of Virginia enclosing the resolves of that House I have the pleasure to acquaint your lordship that no farther notice has been taken of that letter or the resolves than what I wrote your lordship in mine, No. 37, and our session being at length over, I shall in my next give your lordship an account of the proceedings.

What I wrote your lordship in my letter No. 37 relative to the resolutions for non-importation was literally fact, and what was called the resolves of the merchants and of the planters and inhabitants in general was published in the next *Gazette* that came out, which I transmitted for your lordship's better information, but if your lordship will be pleased to recollect I then mentioned that I believed "as much or more was meant here for show and to save or keep up appearances than in reality, some few excepted, and that I was persuaded that numbers disapproved and were against it". And, my lord, I was presently acquainted that although these resolves seemed to be agreed to yet they were not signed at that meeting, but that there was to be another call or general meeting when the resolutions were to be signed.

I well knew, my lord, that if I appeared openly to oppose this measure or even to reason on the matter and endeavour to convince them of the impropriety of it and to prevail on them to desist, that considering the then temper of the times I should probably have done more harm than good. I therefore determined to take every opportunity I might have of talking the matter over in a private way with individuals, which I did and soon had reason to believe there would be such a division that the resolutions would not be signed at all or only by a few and have no kind of effect, as I wrote your lordship in my letter of the 8th of November last, No. 38, and every attempt since made to get them signed has proved abortive, as I wrote your lordship in mine [Vol. I, No. 156] of the 1 of March, No. 41. *Signed.* [C.O.5/660, fo. 96]

XLV

Governor James Wright to Earl of Hillsborough (No. 44)

11 May, Savannah

My Lord, I am now to give your lordship some account of the proceedings of the Lower House of Assembly during the late session. I wrote your lordship at our first meeting that I believed the business would be gone through with good humour and dispatch. The first I cannot object to, the other was not only my own opinion but the opinion of everyone of the Council, and to my knowledge the opinion of a great many of the Assembly. And yet, my lord, it has proved otherwise for out of 25 which the Assembly consists of there is 14 new members, many of them totally unacquainted with business, and 3 of whom proved to be men of turbulent spirits, great liberty boys, and very loquacious with a degree of plausibility, but I may venture to say men of bad hearts, and such men your lordship well knows are capable not only of protracting business but embarrassing and doing a great deal of mischief, especially amongst weak and rather ignorant people and where there are not many capable of answering, clearing up, and removing difficulties or objections started. There was some necessary adjournments, and a considerable part of the time that they sat to do business I am informed was spent in mischievous and unnecessary altercation promoted by those three members on purpose to endeavour to perplex matters and interrupt the harmony that appeared to subsist, and which really did and now does subsist amongst us. And notwithstanding the strong expressions in their address of the necessity of a bill for regulating Indian affairs, yet my lord many real difficulties arose, there being such a variety of matters to provide for and many objections were started and made by the above persons, so that this bill after taking up much time was at length laid aside for the present.

The framing of a proper bill is really a difficult matter and if one had been settled and agreed upon, yet it could not have operated effectually without the concurrence of the neighbouring provinces.

This is doubtless, my lord, a matter of great importance but as I sometime ago wrote my sentiments fully on this subject I shall forbear saying more but that I am still clearly of the same opinion.

The Negro Bill, my lord, after it was gone through and settled by the Lower House was passed and sent up to the Council as an Upper House without the suspending clause as directed by His Majesty's royal instruction. The Council added the suspending clause by way of amendment, which produced a conference of a committee of both Houses, and on a report being made to the Lower House they refused to agree to the amendment of the Upper House, and thus the matter rested for some time. I desired the Council not to reject the bill, for as it was a matter of very great consequence to the province in general I would talk with the Speaker and some of the members and try whether they might not yet be prevailed upon to agree to the amendment of the Upper House, and at length a free conference of both Houses was brought about and the Assembly agreed to the amendment and the suspending clause was accordingly inserted, but the following resolve entered the 14th of March vizt. "Resolved nem.con. that this House agrees to the suspending clause solely from the necessity of the case and not from any conviction that such a clause ought to be inserted in any bill whatsoever, that this House looks upon suspending clauses to be of such pernicious consequences that it almost tends to annihilate the rights of an Assembly and may prevent the execution of any Act, though ever so immediately necessary and beneficial to the province".

The present ideas of liberty in America, your lordship well knows, are high, and such a watchful eye is kept to prevent what they call extending the power of the Crown to abridge or restrain them in their rights etc. that in short they are mistrustful and jealous of every appearance, and I'm told it was urged, and seems to be their general opinion and voice, that they have a right to pass whatever bills they think proper without any saving or suspending clause or restraint and more especially such a bill as this in which no matter of prerogative etc. is mentioned or can be concerned, and that the governor may assent or not as he sees fit and finally the Crown repeal or disallow, and that this is the only restraint or power they ought to be under.

On the 16th November, my lord, I received the enclosed address No. 1 to which I gave the answer No. 2, and on the 27th of November I laid the matter before the Council for their opinion which I received as per No. 3 and sent the same down to the Assembly. And on the 31 [sic] of February I received a second Address from the Assembly, No. 4, to which I returned the answer, No. 5, and on the 12th of March I received the Address from the Council, No. 6, which with my answer

[Vol. I, No. 343i-iv] I sent down to the Assembly and after some altercation in the Lower House they on the 23rd of March entered the following resolution vizt. "Resolved nem.con. that it is the opinion of this committee that the address of the Council of the 12th instant presented to His Excellency the Governor and published in the Gazette of this province is an unjust reflection and an unprovoked insult offered to the dignity of this House". And they also resolved that there should be a clause in the Tax Bill to exempt the 4 southern parishes from paying tax, they not being represented in the House, and thus this matter rests, my lord, and I am humbly to request that I may receive His Majesty's royal instructions thereupon.

As to the silk culture, they desired to defer answering my message till the Tax Bill was taken under consideration, and then they were at a loss what to recommend. They were clearly of opinion (and I think properly so) that the province cannot at present afford to give any bounty or premium, but could not resolve on any particular matter which might encourage the culture. Nor can I, my lord, say anything more on the subject than I have in my former letters.

During this session I have assented to 18 bills and ordinances and rejected 2, and upon the whole, my lord, everything has been done that I could have wished except the bill for regulating Indian affairs, and we parted on good terms. And I cannot but think that this Assembly, some few excepted, and the people in general in this province, have as little design to thwart measures of government and are as well if not better disposed, or at least more moderate, than any upon the continent. And as a proof of which, no further notice has been taken of the Virginia resolutions than barely reading 'em and entering 'em on their journals, and no resolutions for non-importation have yet been signed, though proposed and attempted to be done several times. And we had no illuminations or rejoicings on the day of Wilkes's discharge. But, my lord, there always will be in every province and in every Assembly some bad men. I thought it but justice to the people in general to mention these matters which appear in their favour, and yet, my lord, I do not mean that I would be answerable for their conduct.

As soon as the bills that I have assented to can be copied I shall transmit them to your lordship with my remarks on such as may require any, also a copy of one of the bills that I rejected with an address of both Houses to me thereupon. The other bill that I rejected was a Road Bill. *Signed.* PS. I omitted in the original letter to mention that in mine of the 26th of December 1768, No. 27, to which I beg leave to refer, I wrote to your lordship on the very point taken up by the Assembly relative to issuing writs to elect members for the 4 southern parishes but never was honoured with any answer thereto. [C.O.5/660, fo. 98]

XLVI

Lieut.-General Thomas Gage to Earl of Hillsborough (No. 44)

14 May, New York
My Lord, Count O'Reily has transmitted me a letter received by him

from Mons. Rocheblave who commands the Spanish post of St Genevieve opposite the Ilinois, with a letter wrote by order of Lieutenant-Colonel Wilkins to said Mons. Rocheblave, and his answer thereto. I perceive from the correspondence of the two commanders there has been an altercation, rather warm, between them on account of a British subject put in jail at St Genevieve, as Mons. Rocheblave alleges for theft, but no judgement can be formed of the merits of the dispute from these letters. Count O'Reily has not applied to me by way of complaint but through a desire that these small accidents may be checked in their beginnings; and to show the pains he has taken to oblige the subjects of our respective Sovereigns to live resiprocally in peace and good harmony, has furnished me with a copy of the instructions [Vol. I, No. 347i] he has given to the commanders of all the posts within his government, which I have the honour to transmit to your lordship.

I shall enquire into the cause of this dispute by the first opportunity and desire Lieutenant-Colonel Wilkins may give no just cause of complaint, intending at the same time to direct him to support the rights of His Majesty and protect his subjects with firmness, but to make his representations with politeness and to avoid any hot expressions that might be construed into rudeness.

My last dispatch from the Ilinois is of the 5th December, which informs me that the Indians of the Ouabache had plundered a trader's store at St Vincent, in which some of the French settlers had openly assisted and shared the spoils; and that there is such a nest of villains at the post and at St Joseph's as will grow in a little time too formidable to be easily eradicated, and perhaps produce consequences of the most serious nature.

The French settlers on the Spanish side of the Mississippi were a good deal alarmed at the news of the arrival of the Spanish troops and the severities afterwards exercised at New Orleans. Many of them have refused the oath of allegiance tendered to them who consequently will be obliged to remove unless they change their resolutions.

When His Majesty's commands were received to send a reinforcement of troops to West Florida and to strengthen the forts, Brigadier-General Haldimand was directed to leave St Augustine and repair to Pensacola to make preparations for the reception of the 16th Regiment and to settle some plan of fortifying the forts in the best manner their construction would admit of. He was to sail accordingly from St Augustine on the 14th April, and I am to hope with the materials he carried with him and those sent from hence with the artificers who preceded the regiment, he will be able to put the men under cover.

With regard to the forts in West Florida, that of Pensacola is no more than a stockade and will serve only to secure the inhabitants and their effects against the Indians. It must cost very considerable sums and require years to fortify it in such a manner as to render it capable of resisting an attack from regular troops; and all that can be done with it at present is to replace with good pickets such of them as are bad. The fort of Mobile is of brick, in very bad condition, which may be repaired and put in order. And for the better defence of the province, Brigadier

Haldimand proposes to visit the Island of St Rose and a place called the Red-Cliff in order to examine whether batteries could not be raised there that would defend the harbour of Pensacola.

Governor Grant appears to be a good deal disappointed that so many troops are sent to Pensacola and a stop put to the building of barracks at St Augustine, having assured himself that two regiments at least would have been posted there. And Lieutenant-Governor Durnford is equally jealous of the preference he thinks has been given to East Florida, and hopes the barracks will be put up at Pensacola in lieu of the miserable huts in which the soldiers are quartered. It is not necessary to say more on this head as I have by your lordship's desire taken the liberty to give an opinion in a former letter concerning the stations of the troops in the Southern District in the way I conceive the most beneficial to the general service, and I shall wait His Majesty's commands before I proceed further either in posting the troops or erecting the barracks.

The Indians had given an alarm to West Florida by plundering a trader who had seated himself at the Natches, but the apprehensions of further disturbances were subsided. Frequent complaints have been made against the trader for distributing rum in very large quantities amongst all the neighbouring nations so as to prejudice the other traders and put them in a danger from drunken Indians. It is even supposed the savages were excited to this act by some of the traders.

Nothing has yet transpired relative to the conferences that were to be held between the Six Nations and other Northern Indians, and no advice of moment has been received from the Indian forts since the winter. A number of artificers were sent to Niagara early in the spring to complete two redoubts for the better defence of that place, though it is to be hoped we may hear of no disturbance from that quarter. And as most of the vessels are rotting very fast, from their having been built in a hurry with green wood, I have directed timber to be cut at a proper time and laid up to season for the building a vessel for Lake Ontario and another for Lake Champlain.

Mr Stuart has finished his congress with the Cherokees to his satisfaction, who appear determined to continue the war with the western nations and may possibly give so much employment to those upon the Ouabache as to prevent their disturbing us at the Ilinois. They complained of the behaviour of the traders and of disorders committed in their country by a number of vagabonds who steal their horses and insult them. The new boundary-line proposed by Virginia was by no means agreeable to them, for they declared positively the line must run by Chiswell's Mine, and they would seize all the cattle and horses found straggling beyond it; that they had hitherto restrained their young men from plundering, but the daily encroachments of the white people and their killing the deer were become insufferable. I am given to understand the pretensions of Virginia to the line they are desirous to obtain is founded upon the cession made by the Six Nations at Fort Stanwix, in whom the people of that province would suppose an absolute right to dispose of the lands without considering any claim of the Cherokees to them. *Signed.* [C.O.5/88, fo. 76]

XLVII

Lieut.-Governor Cadwallader Colden to Earl of Hillsborough (No. 11)

16 May, New York

My Lord, by the repeal of the Act for emitting £120,000 in bills of credit, one thousand pounds granted out of that fund by the Assembly in their last session for supplying His Majesty's troops quartered in this place with necessaries is become deficient. I have no hope given me that the Assembly will at this time supply that deficiency and therefore I think it is prudent to delay calling the Assembly till after the arrival of Lord Dunmore who must certainly have more influence than in my present situation I can have. The grant of money for the troops is unpopular. We have two parties in violent opposition to each other: one is careful to preserve their popularity in order to secure their seats in the Assembly, and the other takes every method to gain popularity in hopes of a dissolution of the Assembly on the arrival of a new governor.

The merchants in this place and in Philadelphia have under consideration whether to import goods from Great Britain or not. I am told the majority both in this place and at Philadelphia are for importing and that they will come to a determination in a few days. The party in opposition to the present administration join with the people of Boston in measures to prevent importation, and for that purpose stole late in the night last week a procession of the mob to expose a Boston importer who happened to come to this place. The magistrates knew nothing of the design till it was too late, otherwise I believe it would have been prevented. Though the parties are much exasperated against each other, I hope the public peace will be preserved and the issue will be favourable to the government. *Signed.* [C.O.5/1101, fo. 61]

XLVIII

Lieut.-Governor Thomas Hutchinson to Earl of Hillsborough (No. 12)

18 May, Boston

My Lord, I shall cover a printed copy of the instructions [Vol. I, No. 349ii] of the town of Boston to their Representatives and a written copy of an address [Vol. I, No. 349i] to me from the Corporation of Harvard College with my answer to it. The instructions appear to be the ravings of men in a political frenzy. I need not point out to your lordship the insinuations contained in them of the necessity of the people's preparing to defend themselves and their rights not by arguments and reasoning only but by arms and open resistance. I am very sensible that the authors of this and the like publications expect to obtain their ends by intimidating and they have more sense than to think we are capable of any long defence against the power of Great Britain, but the body of the people are deluded by them and made to believe they are really in earnest and the same flame is raised as if they really were so, and I think it must be in consequence of such an opinion that applications have been made to me from different quarters to put the militia upon a more respectable footing. The town also press their Representatives to endeavour it and not very obscurely intimate for what reason.

Hitherto we have gone no farther than to disown the authority of Parliament but now even the King is allowed little or no share in the government of the province except the appointing a governor who is not to be directed by His Majesty nor subject to his instructions.

This publication is not indeed the act of the province but it is the act of a town whose influence extends to every other town in the province and it is extremely probable that many other towns will follow the example of Boston and give instructions of the same tenor to their Representatives.

The address from the College is caused by the awe which the Corporation are under, most of the members being persons at other times well disposed to government.

There has been some delay in sending back the goods imported from England and I am informed the owner of the ship which carries them, free of freight, would willingly be excused and that some other active merchants are also afraid of consequences, but the lower class of people who were called in as servants in order to intimidate such as refused to join in the combination are now become masters and at a meeting lately called determined that the goods already arrived and those expected should all be sent back.

None of the importers can be prevailed upon to bring an action against the committees who apply to them to send back their goods. It is said they voluntarily agree to do it at the desire of the committee, but could there be a fair trial, this desire would appear to be as compulsory as the desire of a highwayman to a traveller to deliver his purse and it is the fear of danger to their persons and property upon their refusal which causes a compliance.

The opinion which prevails, but which I would still hope is ill-founded, that nothing will be done in Parliament to suppress these combinations, and the speeches said to be made in Parliament affirming them to be legal, and letters received by the heads of the combiners from persons of character in England exhorting to perseverance, all conspire to keep up the spirit here in the body of the people and to encourage the Council to persist in their refusal to co-operate with me in any measures for suppressing it. I will neglect nothing which is in my power but this is very little more by the constitution than a mere negative, a power of refusing my consent to elections and other acts of government. *Signed.* [C.O.5/759, fo. 194]

XLIX

Deputy Governor John Penn to Earl of Hillsborough (No. 21, duplicate)

19 May, Philadelphia

My Lord, by one of the late packets I was honoured with your lordship's letter [Vol. I, No. 40] No. 21 enclosing the King's most gracious speech to his Parliament and the addresses of both Houses with His Majesty's gracious answer, and also the duplicate thereof by another packet.

Your lordship mentioned the not receiving the originals of my letters, Nos. 17, 18, 19 and 20; the three former were forwarded by the ship *Hercules*, Captain Scott, by the way of Liverpool, and the latter by the *Britannia*, Captain Jefferies, to London; and hope they have long since got safe to hand.

I confess I ought to have mentioned to your lordship in my letter No. 17 the concurrence of the merchants of this place with those of the other colonies in their Association against importations from Great Britain, but as that circumstance happened above three months before it really did not occur to me at the time I wrote that letter.

The reason given by the merchants here for delaying to adopt the measure so long was because they judged any such rash and untimely resolutions, instead of answering the purpose intended by them, would rather irritate the government against them and be the means of frustrating the design of the petitions which have been sent by the Assembly of this province to the King and the Parliament, and therefore they thought it most advisable to decline entering into any agreement proposed to them till they should know the success of those petitions. But afterwards, on hearing they were not likely to have the desired effect, they immediately joined heartily in the general Association.

The ships lately arrived here from England have brought accounts that the House of Commons have agreed to pass a bill for the repeal of the duties on paper, glass and painters colours, but that the duty on tea is to be continued. On receiving this news the merchants here had a general meeting a few days ago to consult on the best plan of conduct now to be pursued by them. But I understand they did little more at this conference than agree to wait till the 5th of June before any steps should be taken in order to make themselves acquainted with the sentiments of the merchants of the neighbouring colonies, that they may act in concert with them in framing such resolutions as shall be judged most expedient, and I am fully of opinion that their determination will then be to prolong their former agreement of non-importation from Great Britain till the duty on tea shall be repealed. *Signed*. [C.O.5/1283, fo. 3]

L

Lieut.-Governor Thomas Hutchinson to Earl of Hillsborough (No. 15)

27 May, Boston

My Lord, upon advice from Philadelphia that the merchants there were disposed to break up their association except so far as relates to importing tea, near 50 merchants of this town met together and declared their willingness to join with the Philadelphians. This alarmed the heads of the combination here and, at a meeting of the populace called the same day in the afternoon, it was voted strictly to adhere to the non-importation until the whole of the duties in the late Act shall be taken off.

I find many of the merchants are very much dissatisfied that their trade should be regulated by people not concerned in trade and without property, but their timidity is such that a meeting of such great numbers of people in opposition to them immediately discourages them from pursuing what seemed to be their determination. There are three or four principal merchants who are very free in expressing to me their disapprobation of the present measures, but they cannot be prevailed with to join with the rest who are of the same sentiment. It is thought their additional weight upon the late occasion would have turned the scale.

I have acquainted Governor Penn with the state of things here, to prevent the merchants there from being imposed upon by false accounts in private letters and in print, and I have desired a correspondence with him and shall desire the like from Mr Colden, that every circumstance in either of the governments favourable to the bringing to an end these most illegal and destructive combinations may be improved to that purpose, though after all we shall be in continual danger of the revival of them until the just and necessary provision is made by Parliament for suppressing them. *Signed*. [C.O.5/759, fo. 211]

LI

Lieut.-Governor William Bull to Earl of Hillsborough (No. 29)

7 June, Charleston

My Lord, in the latter end of April we had the pleasure of Governor Tryon's company here for a few days, during which His Excellency's attention to the duties of his public office always appropriated some hours, in the midst of our hospitable endeavours to entertain him, to discourse with me upon such matters as he thought might promote the service of his province, and in particular with regard to our boundary line. I was very happy in a concurrence of sentiments with His Excellency upon the urgent necessity of a continuation thereof from the place where the commissioners left off near Wateree or Catabaw River in 1764, but I could by no means agree to his proposal that this continuation should be by a direct west course from that line, but that the line proposed in a report made by a committee of His Majesty's Council in this province, transmitted last year to your Lordship and Mr Garth by Lord Charles Montagu, appeared to me to be very reasonable, and as that matter was now lying before the King we must wait for the royal pleasure upon the arguments adduced by the two provinces in support of their respective pretensions. As I have formerly troubled your lordship upon the necessity of continuing the boundary till it intersects the north line constituting the limits between His Majesty's subjects and the Cherokees, I shall not presume to add anything further on that subject as I am satisfied all the dispatch will be given thereto that His Majesty's more important affairs can admit.

As I took the liberty of mentioning in my last letter my intention to make a tour through some of our western settlements, I shall now do myself the honour to represent to your lordship the extent of my tour, about three hundred and fifty miles, with such observations relative to the condition and prosperity of the province as occur to me. As I presume your lordship has a map I shall mark my movements upon that. I went in a chariot to prove the practicability of the roads and proceeded near the banks of Santee River. At Beaver Creek I reviewed the militia of Congaree, Amelia and Orangeburgh Townships, where seven hundred and fifty-six rank and file appeared, and though awkward in their exercise they were willing to be improved. I then crossed above the conflux of Broad and Congaree Rivers and reviewed the militia between those rivers which, though by return amount to 2,005 men, made a very slender appeareance as to numbers and men. The colonel excused the former on account of the apprehensions of having their horses stolen away if they were all absent from home and the busy time of approaching harvest, and I confess the characters of some and dress of all gave me a lively idea of the founders of ancient Rome. I thence crossed the country to Cambden, a village settled upon private land a little above Fredericksburg Township on Wateree River. Here I reviewed the militia lying upon Wateree, between Broad River and the sources of Black River up to the boundary line; the returns amount to two thousand two hundred and ten men. There were one thousand three hundred and sixty rank and file under arms; every man came on horseback. The officers were more orderly and civilised than the last preceding. I took some pains to instruct them in the use and manner of platoon firing with which they were well pleased, and the officers agreed to meet and improve in their learning the military exercises. In my return I reviewed a small battalion of militia at Monks Corner. I am sorry to inform your lordship that the spirit of the militia is at a very low ebb even in those parts of the province where it is most necessary, near the sea coast, against the invasion of foreign and the insurrection of our domestic enemy. Though every man is expert in the use of a gun as an individual, I endeavoured to make them sensible that it is discipline alone and exercising in a body that can enable them to oppose or make them formidable to an enemy. Though I did not go much further west than the Congarees it may be proper to mention that the returns of militia lying above Congaree and between Saludy and Savannah Rivers amount to one thousand two hundred and sixty-five men, so that upon our north-west frontiers we have five thousand four hundred and eighty men, exclusive of the numerous settlements on the branches of Peedee towards the boundary line. Having thus passed the undisciplined militia in review before your lordship, give me leave, my lord, to open the more pleasing scene of agriculture in those parts. The face of the country is very different from the flat sandy soil which generally prevails within fifty or sixty miles of the sea coast; as we leave that, the lands swell into hills, increasing as we go further back. Here we meet with variety of gravel, rock, chalk, slate with appearances of iron and copper mines, though the most valuable mines to a commercial people lie within the reach of the farmer's plough. Fields of wheat, oats, barley, rye, indian corn, indigo, hemp, tobacco and madder lately, are cultivated here. I visited with great satisfaction the vineyard of the poor German at Broad River, whom I mentioned to your lordship in my letter No. 19, where I saw 1,600 vines neatly planted, clear from weeds and well enclosed. That your lordship may see what industry and perseverance can perform when assisted by a fertile soil and a benign climate, I must take the liberty to acquaint your lordship that this man began his experiment with vines eight years ago with only five cuttings, that he has distributed cuttings to ten of his neighbours, some of whom have now five hundred vines. I cannot omit here to acquaint your lordship that I have received accounts from the French Protestants of New Bordeaux in Hillsborough that most of the vines I sent there last spring, mentioned in my letter No. 23 to your lordship, have taken root, and the French and Germans may now contend for the honour of first introducing wine into this province.

The country being well watered affords many conveniences for mills, which are erected only for the necessary purpose of sawing and grinding grain. The facilitating the carriage of produce to the market is of great consequence to the planter, as it in some degree draws his land nearer the metropolis. There is now in contemplation the cutting a canal of communication from the head of Cooper River to Santee, through which the valuable articles raised upon the wide spreading branches of Santee may be conveyed at the small expense of water-carriage to Charleston. At present there are computed to be three thousand wagons come to Charleston in a year loaded with deerskins, indigo, flour, biscuit, hemp and tobacco, which calculation is not far from the truth as precise accounts are taken of the numbers which pass over ferries.

Sensible that every trespass on your lordship's public hours is a trespass upon the public welfare, I have endeavoured to present to your lordship's view a prospect of our province in miniature though I fear your lordship will think I am so pleased with the subject that I forget myself. I confess, my lord, I am pleased with it, as it opens a view of great growing prosperity to this province, and on such grounds as will nourish no seeds of jealousy and rivalship but will tend always to keep up a correspondence and commerce with our mother country. And I must request your lordship will do me the justice to believe that in all I may seem to have painted in too florid colours, I have borrowed none from imagination to adorn this subject. I have most literally adhered to truth, which I always observe when I write to your lordship. *Signed*. PS. Rather than give your lordship the trouble of another letter, I beg leave to mention that I have prorogued the General Assembly till the 23rd July next at which time, if I can discern a probability of doing business, I shall permit them to sit. [C.O.5/393, fo. 64]

LII

Earl of Hillsborough to Lieut.-Governor Thomas Hutchinson (No. 37)

12 June, Whitehall
Sir, since my letter [Vol. II, No. XL] to you of the 26th April, No. 36, I have received your dispatches [Vol. II, No. XXIX; Vol. I, No. 280] Nos. 6, 7 and a separate letter [Vol. I, No. 283] of the 21st April, and have laid them before the King.

What passed on occasion of the unhappy event of the 5th March and the state of the province since that period, as described in your two last letters, clearly point out that every measure that can be taken for the support of its civil government will be ineffectual until that government has in itself that vigour and activity which is essential to all civil constitutions.

The consideration of what may be properly done to give it that vigour and activity has opened a large field of discussion, and many doubts and questions have occurred upon which it will be necessary to have the advice and opinion of His Majesty's law servants before any final resolution can be taken; in the meantime the King has approved of such a number of his troops being continued in the island of Castle William as can be conveniently accommodated in that island, and I have signified His Majesty's commands to Lieutenant-General Gage that he should put the Castle into such a state as may make it respectable as a place of strength and security in any exigency.

I am very much concerned, though not surprised, to find that the hopes held out and entertained by many persons of a discontinuance of the combinations against importing goods from Great Britain have proved delusive, more especially as I have reason to believe that those hopes did in a great degree prevent those measures being taken in Parliament for restraining such combinations which I find by your letter of the 21st of April you fully expected. *Draft.* [C.O.5/759, fo. 156]

LIII

Earl of Hillsborough to Lieut.-Governor Cadwallader Colden (No. 39)

12 June, Whitehall

Sir, I have received and laid before the King your letter [Vol. II, No. XXXIX] No. 10 in which you endeavour to justify your conduct in having given your assent to the Paper Currency Bill by arguments drawn from the then state of the colony, and as I have reason to believe from what you allege that you erred from real good intention I have not failed to represent your conduct in that light to His Majesty.

There certainly may be circumstances and situations in which a governor will find it necessary sometimes to depart from the strict letter of his instructions, but then the motives for such deviations ought to be stated in the fullest manner and no circumstance omitted that can either tend to his own justification or give information to government of the true state of the colony. I mention this in order to introduce the remark that there are some facts and observations relative to the state of New York in the letter to which this is in answer that were not stated in your former correspondence, but more particularly that of one of the judges and a member of the Council advising and strenuously insisting that the King's troops should be withdrawn from the colony, a fact which whether it respects the measure itself or the persons who advised and supported it is of great importance to His Majesty's service and ought to have been stated in the fullest and most explicit manner and names not concealed, for as all public measures depend in a great degree as to their effect upon a knowledge of the true character of men in public situations, it would be very difficult to judge of the propriety of those measures without some knowledge of the principles by which the conduct of such men is influenced and the degree of trust and confidence each man is entitled to.

Enclosed I send you an Order of His Majesty in Council [Vol. I, No. 382] containing a disallowance of the Act passed at New York in January last declaring certain persons therein mentioned incapable of being members of the General Assembly of that colony, upon which Order you will not fail to take such steps as have been usual and are necessary for carrying His Majesty's commands into execution. I likewise enclose to you an Act [10 Geo. III c. 35] passed in the last session of Parliament entitled "An Act to enable the Governor, Council, and Assembly of His Majesty's Colony of New York to pass an Act of Assembly for creating and issuing upon loan paper bills of credit to a certain amount, and to make the same a legal tender in payments into the Loan Offices and Treasury of the said colony" and I make no doubt that if the legislature of New York shall think fit to pass such a law as the Parliament has authorized it will be approved by His Majesty. *Draft.* [C.O.5/1101, fo. 59]

LIV

Charles Stuart to John Stuart[1]

12 June, Pensacola

Sir, I wrote you some time ago a few lines by Mr McGillivray enclosing returns of presents and provisions issued in 1769, the duplicates of which I now send you. I am extremely sorry that the short notice I had of his intentions of calling at Georgia put it out of my power to be more full at that time, and I have not had any other opportunity since, till now, and as this packet has been daily expected for several months and nothing very extraordinary happening in your department, I did not think the expense of an express by land necessary, otherwise would not have hesitated at sending one.

Agreeable to your instructions I have done all I could to establish a peace between the Choctaws and Creeks, and have so far succeeded as to bring both to agree to it, some few fellows excepted on both sides who, not having done any feats during the war, think to gain reputation and the name of warrior by not consenting to make peace. After repeated promises and tokens of friendship interchanged on both sides through me, and when I thought peace firmly established, and the Choctaws so confident of it that they buried all their war-sticks or clubs and ventured out carelessly to hunt, the Creeks fell upon a party of them upon the Chickesaw path and killed four and took a wench prisoner, niece to Mingo Touma Chito, Great Medal Chief of the Little Mucklasses, who was the person employed to settle the peace. This misfortune has rubbed up old sores and leaves them in doubt what to do. I have prevailed with them to wait till such time as I can learn from the Creeks the cause of this breach of faith, and they consent to forgive this last injury, being tired of the war, if the Creeks will give up the wench. I expect here this day or tomorrow Emistisiguo who will I hope put all to rights, although the Choctaws say there is not

---

1   Enclosed in John Stuart's letter to Hillsborough, 16 July 1770: Vol. I, No. 505.

much faith to be put in the Creeks. I have not learnt what town it was that did this deed but I suspect the Tuckabatchies and I fear some white people may be concerned who do not desire to see them at peace.

I herewith send you some talks which have passed upon the occasion, and I make no doubt but I shall soon bring the whole to an amicable conclusion on their parts. How far it may tend to the tranquillity of this province seems a doubt to the inhabitants, but I am clearly of opinion that they are often more to blame than the Indians, and while they continue to deal with them for rum they must expect bad consequences, and such is the profuse quantities now given that nothing is otherwise bought of Indians than with it, except by the traders in the nations and they dispose of as much of it as they can with safety to themselves; but possibly now a stop may be put to it as the legislature have passed an Indian Act for that and other purposes, a copy of which I will endeavour to send you, but I believe they will find it harder to put into execution than they imagine.

When Lieut.-Governor Durnford arrived here I laid before him part of my instructions from you respecting the line between your and his department, setting forth the necessity I was under of keeping my own side and of his defraying all expenses on his. He took the advice of his Council upon the occasion, and it was agreed that as the situation in which the province then was with respect to money and Indian presents was confined, I should act for both till such time as matters were represented at home and some provision obtained, which I undertook.

There happened sometime ago a small skirmish at the Natchez between some traders and some Choctaws. The cause was rum I believe principally, but the Indians say it was owing to some promises made the Indians by one Bradley (a merchant residing at Natchez) by order of Lieutenant-Governor Browne to let them have presents, and being disappointed fell upon Mr Bradley's store and plundered him of his rum, shutting him up; but getting some assistance, they pursued the Indians, came upon their camp and fired upon them, which they returned and fled, leaving part of the rum. Several I hear on both sides were wounded but none killed. The headmen say they are sorry for it but as none were killed and the white people as much to blame as them they hope it will be overlooked. They sent me down a horse and some skins of the leaders of the party who did the fact as an atonement and make many fair promises. They also sent a horse and some skins requesting the forgiveness of Cholkto-Oulacta, Small Medal Chief in the Six Towns, who some years ago headed a party who killed a white man by mistake in the night.

I consulted with the general and governor who were then at Mobile, who agreed with me that as we were mediating a peace for them it might be attended with good effects if all former faults were forgiven, as they promised so fair to behave well in future, and to give satisfaction for the smallest as well as the greatest crimes; and this article they agreed to in the nation at a general meeting, and I have the vanity to flatter myself that if any disturbance ever happen here with Indians it will be owing to those concerned in the trade rather than to the Indians.

You will see by some of the talks from the Creeks that some Shawnese have been there. What their real meaning is I cannot tell but I think we should be very watchful of their motions nor trust too much to their flattery.

The main subject of their talks now is a congress, but of this I can say no more than acquaint you of it, and that they are always reproaching me with a breach of our promise. The lieut-governor is extremely desirous of one and says he expects one soon. If such a thing should take place I am of opinion that it should not be till next year, in the month of May, as I can keep them in temper I believe till then, and it will be a saving as it is their planting season and not so many will attend as at any other season.

There was 9 hundredweight of the gunpowder lost on the passage to Pensacola which article I most want, but I will make a shift till I hear from you.

There are in store a number of old articles much damaged which I will send you a list of and endeavour to exchange them for gunpowder and provisions.

With respect to the Spaniards I do not think they ever will hurt us much with the Indians, although I am credibly informed that they have bestowed medals on two of the Indians residing near the lakes, one Gaspart a Choctaw fellow, and one Le Blanc a Pascagoula fellow, who live together; they also have Spanish colours. I sent to know whether they chose to remain Spaniards or to return to me. They answered if I would forgive them they would deliver up medals and colours, but that I must also give them English ones in lieu. I sent for them again but they are not yet come.

I should be glad, sir, that you would give me some instructions with respect to commissions and marks of distinction for Indians. The governors also are furnished with medals, and if the Indians are to receive honours or commissions from so many it will cause such a jealousy as may be prejudicial, and I am well convinced of this by what little I have already seen owing to Governor Browne's bestowing a medal on a most worthless fellow without knowing his character, and only for some information he gave him, which would have been better paid with a keg of rum.

The Chickesaws are much harrassed by the Northern Indians and complain much for want of ammunition. I was very kind to Pai-Mattaha and party, gave him a salute from the fort which pleased him much. He wants a commissary again and the lieut.-governor promised to write home about one, also for one to the Choctaws. Pai Mingo Euleuroy has brought in 4 scalps and 5 prisoners from the northward, and I expect him down. If commissaries are not appointed again some regulation must be made to prevent transient persons from going without leave into the Indian nations and holding meetings or propagating reports among them. I here, sir, allude to such merchants as supply Indian traders etc. who in some measure pay little or no regard to any regulations, nor do they care what happens if they answer their own purpose. There is now in the nation two of them, Mr Alexander McIntosh and Mr Strothers who, taking the advantage of the times, there being no regulations yet in force, when they heard that the Assembly were framing laws, went off to the Chickesaws, and I am told stayed five days in the Choctaws. As I was apprised in some measure of their design I took upon me to give Mr McIntosh a nominal commission as commissary, having in person settled the point with him at Mobile, with orders to prevent them from calling any meeting or holding any talks with the Indians.

As this step does not appear to me to have any evil consequences depending, I flatter myself you will not be displeased at it. Governor Durnford has promised him the preference in case of commissaries being again appointed. He is very deserving.

I wish something could be properly settled about an armourer. I have hitherto obeyed your directions concerning him but Governor Durnford is of opinion that some part of the charge should fall on you as Indians come down in your department as well as in his and want their guns mended.

What colours I have in store are good for nothing nor do the Indians now care much for the suits of clothes you sent me, of which a good many suits remain.

General Haldimand and I propose visiting the lakes. I am sorry the poor people thereabouts are so much harrassed with Indians so as that most of them have been obliged to abandon their settlements. I believe this is in a great measure owing to some wicked persons in Orleans who trade privately with our Indians and are jealous of the poor settlers interfering.

I am informed by Governor Durnford that the Creeks say they get rum enough from the Havana. I can hardly think so but I will try and find it out. I am also informed that they have robbed some white hunters in their lands, this I think we cannot find fault with; and there has been two white men found dead and scalped on the Creek path to this place but no certainty by whom, I suspect the Choctaws and will find it out.

I have nothing more material to acquaint you of, but as the packet is now established opportunities will be more frequent and you may depend on hearing by every one that I know of. *Copy.* [C.O.5/71, Pt. 2, fo. 25]

LV

Lieut.-Governor Elias Durnford to Earl of Hillsborough

13 June, Pensacola

My Lord, in my letter [Vol. I, No. 415] to your lordship relative to the seizure of the sloop *Brittain* and of Captain Jackson's sailing to La Vera Cruz to represent this affair to the Viceroy of Mexico, I could not write publicly what I ought to communicate to your lordship in a private manner on this subject. I had for some time wished for an errand to send to that place in order to gain some information of the strength, situation and numbers of the troops and fortifications of that place and New Spain; but none happened until this, which I thought it my duty not to let slip. I was very desirous of opening a communication by means of the contraband trade which is carried on to the Spanish Main as a more certain means of obtaining the wished state [Vol. I, No. 417i] of their force, which I beg leave to enclose for your lordship's perusal. Whenever I may be able to get any other information on this head I shall not fail sending it to your lordship. *Signed.* [C.O.5/587, p. 357]

LVI

Lieut.-Governor Thomas Hutchinson to Earl of Hillsborough (No. 17, duplicate)

16 June, Boston

My Lord, I shall transmit herewith to your lordship certain resolves [Vol. I, No. 428i] of the House of Representatives which they have not communicated to me but chose rather to send them to the Council, but the principal view in passing them, I imagine, is in order to vindicate themselves and to keep up the spirit of opposition through the province and by doing it in this way they expect no answer will be given to them. They have also sent an extraordinary message to me in which they desire a recess unless I will carry them to Boston. It is the influence of Boston which causes the unconstitutional refusal of the House to do business at Cambridge. I shall not remove them there until I receive your lordship's further directions unless I should find myself under a greater necessity of doing it than I am at present.

The council also have officiously inserted themselves and sent me an address or message [Vol. I, No. 428ii] which I shall likewise transmit with my answer to it. This measure was strongly opposed and dis-approved of by some who were this year newly admitted into the Council but it was carried by force of a particular connection which for several years past has been very unfavourable to the prerogative.

I intend to keep the Court sitting some days longer in hopes of receiving further advices from England which may enable me to make a better judgement in what manner to treat them than I am able to make at present. The leaders of the House seem to have no fear of consequences. By a general confusion they make themselves of more importance. They are in no danger of punishment, personally. If the public suffers, the chief of them have so small an interest in the public that they do not think it worth regarding. The House in general I would hope do not act from perverseness and without regard to the public interest, but they are misled and, like the bulk of the people they represent, imagine they are supporting their rights without seeing that they are subverting the constitution and that they act from prin-ciples which are repugnant to a state of government.

One of the reasons given by your lordship for the removal of the Court from Boston, viz. to show resentment against the disorderly behaviour of the inhabitants, hath acquired more weight as the disorders have increased and I see no prospect of the interposition of authority to restore order there.

Mr Colden writes to me from New York in answer to a letter I lately wrote that their case as to the combinations is very similar to ours, but he adds that although the merchants there cannot agree to import openly they will generally import privately and that no attempt will be made to obstruct it. It is not yet certain that our merchants will do so but the number in favour of it is much increased. *Signed.* [C.O.5/759, fo. 224]

LVII

Charles Stuart to John Stuart[1]

17 June, Pensacola

Sir, in my last, per packet *Dilligence,* I acquainted you that Emistisiguo was here, but her sailing so soon put it out of my power to give you any account of the cause of his coming.

The Governor assembled his Council; the General and most of the officers were present.

He began his discourse with the usual compliments and ceremonies and repeated what he had seen and heard from you before, all which he said he well remembered and held the talk fast and always would do so, but it was no wonder if red men forgot talks if white people did; for the talk was that white people should not hunt in their lands which were now full of them, that he was sorry for it as he did not want to spoil the talk nor hurt white men, but the talk was to take away their goods if they were found hunting and not to hunt them, that he had once in company with Sempoyaffé done so. He talked a good deal on this subject on account of a Shawnese fellow that was with him who had robbed a white man in their hunting grounds lately, who speaks good English and whose father had a commission from Oglethorpe. He also talked about our encroachments upon their hunting grounds, that he had heard some people had fires on their side the line, and desired they might not be allowed as that might spoil the talk. He also said that there were several white men who took goods from this place and traded in the woods to the great prejudice of their traders who could not pay their debts, and desired they should be stopped as they may also spoil the talk, for they may be robbed as it was the talk that nobody should trade in the woods. He said he did not know who killed the two white men but would endeavour to find it out and would let us know. These men it seems were killed on the path between Pensacola and their nation, they were not scalped nor do we know who they were, but it was rumoured at Mobile that two scalps had been carried into the Choctaws that were not red men's, but I have no further accounts of it.

He then observed that sometime ago some Northward Indians had been in their nation and had brought bad talks, that he did not harken to them, that they were levelled at the Choctaws but that he told them that the Great Beloved Man of Charleston at Augusta last year (meaning you) told him to bury the hatchet, that he had done so and would not take it up, and that you told them to make peace with the Choctaws which they did and sent the talks to me at Mobile, and that he hoped all was straight and white now as he wanted nothing so much as peace.

1   Enclosed in John Stuart's letter to Hillsborough, 2 December 1770: Vol. I, No. 763.

He again repeated that part of trading in the woods and asked if Indians might keep store and sell goods as several of them had goods from Augusta. He concluded with saying he had always held the English fast by the hand since they first came here and would never let them go, and whatever bad talks he might hear against the white people he would immediately send and let us know.

His honour answered all his talks much to his satisfaction and very pertinently assured him he would abide by former talks and would not allow any person to do otherwise, thanked him for his talk and recommended to him to remember it and to make his people do so too. He hinted that his limits were very confined but that he must make the most of it till he thought proper to grant him more, to which his honour received no answer.

I then gave him a talk from the Choctaws confirming the peace, with three strings of white beads, one from the Six Towns, one from the East party, and one from the West party, accompanied with pipes and tobacco, all which he received with great joy, and it was observed that he had not till then been seen to smile. I told him that I was authorised by the whole Choctaw nation to tell the Creeks that now they looked upon the path to be quite white and straight, and on their part they could not see the least black spot and that I hoped it was so with the Creeks, that I had made every Choctaw throw away his war-stick and even the flints they had in their guns when at war, and had given them new ones to kill deer which they said they would now do without fear.

He said he was very glad to hear my talk, that he always thought me his friend, that you told him so, that he now sees what you told him is true, that you would make peace between them, that he did not think you would have been able to do it, but great men can do what they please, that he is sure you are his friend as none but a friend makes peace between two people, that now he will carry my talk into his nation and make his people glad, that as a proof of their being at peace with the Choctaws he had returned a woman that some of the Abekoutchies had taken since the peace talks began and that he imagined she was by this time in the Choctaw nation. He then delivered me two white strings and some tobacco to be sent to the Choctaws as the last token of friendship to wipe away all bad talks, that one wing [*sic*:? string] and tobacco was from the Mortar, the other from himself, and desired I would tell the Choctaws that all was white now and desired that I would tell them to send a headman into their towns and he would see that they were now his friends, all which I promised to do and parted for the present.

In the evening I took him by himself and questioned him about those Indians that were in the nation, what brought them there and what they intended, how long they stayed, and what they said. He answered that their talks were bad, that he did not listen to them nor would have anything to say to them, that they said they had lost a great chief to the Northward (meaning I suppose Pondiac for he seemed to say so when I mentioned his name) and that they were come to take up the hatchet against the Choctaws and join them, but that he nor his people would not listen to it, that he made them send peace talks to the Choctaws, which I had received. He said after I had pressed him very hard that they were to return again in about two moons with more talks and long strings, but let the talks be what they would he would let us know.

This, sir, is all I could get out of him and he seemed a good deal upon his guard, nor would he mention anything they said concerning the white people. He was well pleased with the marks of friendship shown him, had considerable presents made him and great respect shown him by the General. He went away very much pleased and told me he would send his son to see me.

You will by this, sir, be able to judge of the report you have from the Northward. I have given you all I could gather as near as I possibly can and I make no doubt but you will think it necessary to watch their motions. I shall do all I can to get intelligence and will if possible endeavour to be in the nation at the time of their return. The method in which he expressed the time was when the moon is gone and another gone and another as far gone as this is, that then they are to be in the nation. I hope you will receive this time enough to be able to take what steps in it you may see proper, but you may rest assured that nothing shall be wanting on my part to come at the bottom of it and to let you have the earliest notice of it.

I have mentioned my ideas to the General who thinks we should be very watchful and careful how we treat those people for fear of the worst. He tells me he writes you by this opportunity and he has been extremely civil to Emistisiguo as has also Governor Durnford.

I shall be very glad to hear from you as soon as possible and please be particular as to commissions to Indians, for Governor Durnford has given one to a fellow that came down with Emistisiguo without acquainting me. I did intend to mention him to you for a gorget as a friend of Emistisiguo's, but this prevented my giving him any hopes or promise.

I have no more to add but to repeat that you may depend on my utmost attention in this and every other matter entrusted to me, and that I shall not take any step of moment without the approbation and consent of the Governor and Council and the General. This goes by the way of St Augustine and I would have sent you a duplicate by land but that another vessel sails for the same place in a few days. *Copy.* [C.O.5/72, fo. 85]

LVIII

State of the Disorders, Confusion, and Misgovernment which have lately prevailed and do still continue to prevail in His Majesty's province of the Massachusetts Bay in America[1]

21 June
The King having thought fit to command that a state of the disorders, confusion and misgovernment which have of late prevailed in the

---

1   Enclosed in John Pownall's letter to Clerk of Council, 21 June 1770: Vol. I, No. 432.

province of Massachusetts Bay should be laid before his Privy Council for their advice to His Majesty thereupon, the papers herein referred to are submitted as containing all the material facts which show the distracted situation of that province.

From these papers it will appear that notwithstanding the colonies in America, by the nature and principles of the constitution of this kingdom, are and have by law been expressly declared to be subordinate unto and dependent upon the imperial Crown and Parliament of Great Britain, and that it hath also been enacted and declared that the King's Majesty by and with the advice and consent of the Lords Spiritual and Temporal and Commons of Great Britain in Parliament assembled had, hath, and of right ought to have full power and authority to make laws of sufficient force and validity to bind the colonies and people of America in all cases whatsoever; yet nevertheless a variety of illegal, violent and unwarrantable acts and proceedings, tending to question and deny that right and authority, to subvert the constitution, and to oppress the subject, have been committed and done within the province of Massachusetts Bay; and that the General Court in their corporate capacity have not only pursued no measures nor provided any means for suppressing the same and punishing the offenders as it was their duty to have done, but that the Council acting in their separate capacity as a board of advice have in all cases where the authority of the supreme legislature was in question shown a backwardness to concur in such measures as were judged necessary for the preservation of the public peace, and that the House of Representatives have countenanced and encouraged such violent and illegal acts by adopting the same opinions and declaring the same principles upon which they were grounded.

A narrative of the material transactions in the government of Massachusetts Bay since the repeal of the Stamp Act will justify the above observation, and the papers themselves from which it is drawn will support the charge it contains.

The success which had attended the flagitious publications in the Boston newspapers on the subject of the Stamp Act in exciting the popular tumults which followed the promulgation of that law was too obvious to escape the attention of those who wished to see the same opposition given to the subsequent Revenue Laws; and therefore when it became known that such laws were proposed, or at least so soon as they were published and the concomitant establishment of Commissioners of the Customs for America had taken place, the press again teemed with publications of the most daring nature denying the authority of the supreme legislature and tending to excite the people to an opposition to its laws.

The effect of these publications and the general disposition of the people to adopt the principles they held out were apparent, not only in unwarrantable attempts to evade the payment of duties imposed by Act of Parliament, but also in the rescue by force of seizures made in consequence thereof and in the grossest ill-treatment of the Revenue Officers and of all those who gave them countenance and support, several instances of which in the years 1766, 1767 and 1768 will be found in the papers referred to, in some of which instances the cases appear to have been attended with very aggravating circumstances of the most daring insult and violence.

Whilst the spirit of opposition to the authority of government and to the laws of this kingdom was confined to libels in the newspapers and to acts of violence and disorder committed by individuals, there was reason to hope that by a due exertion of the constitutional powers granted by the charter such unwarrantable proceedings might have been suppressed and the authors brought to due punishment; but it is represented that those cases in which the Governor thought he could not act without the advice of the Council were not only deliberated upon in a manner that apparently showed they were not disposed to concur in any measures that might be effectual for that purpose, but that those persons from whom the remedy was to be expected were deeply infected with those principles from the adoption of which these disorders had arisen.

Upon the election of the Council in May 1766, the Lieut.-Governor, the Secretary, the Judges of the Superior Court, and the Attorney-General, all of which except the Attorney-General are stated to have been usually elected members of that Board, were excluded apparently, as the Governor represents, for no other reason but to mark a disrespect to the Crown officers, for the men themselves were of unexceptionable characters. But no argument of justice to them or respect to government could prevail; on the contrary the Lieut.-Governor was soon after excluded from being present at the meetings of the Council notwithstanding his claim to such privilege had both reason and usage to support it.

In the interval of the adjournment of the General Court in 1766 a transport with two companies of artillery was driven by distress of weather into the port of Boston, and upon application made to the Governor by the commanding officer that these companies might be quartered pursuant to the Act of Parliament, the Governor with the advice of the Council ordered the commissary to furnish them with the articles required by the said Act. When the Assembly met, this matter was moved in the House and it appearing that the Act of Parliament above referred to had with some other Acts of Parliament been printed by order of the Governor and Council, a message was sent to the Council desiring to be informed by what authority the said Act or Acts had been so published, and whether they knew of any Act requiring the registry of ordinances which the legislature there had not consented to. The Council having in answer to this message referred the House to the Governor for the information they desired, the answer was voted to be not satisfactory and a committee was appointed to take the matter into consideration during the recess.

Upon the meeting of the Assembly on the 28th of January 1767 a message was sent to the Governor, desiring to be informed whether any provision had been made at the expense of that government for the King's troops lately arrived in the harbour of Boston. In answer to which the Governor sent them the copy of the minute of Council by which provision was made for the artillery companies pursuant to Act of Parliament, and also an account of the expense that had been incurred. In reply to which they charged this measure upon the Governor as a violation of the charter which was (they say) the more grievous to them as it was justified upon the authority of an Act of Parliament which was as great a grievance as the Stamp Act, which took away the unalienable right of freedom from all taxation but such as they should voluntarily consent to and grant.

The next important matter taken up by the Assembly that manifested a spirit of opposition to the authority of Parliament was that of the circular letter of the 11th of February 1768 to the other colonies inviting them to concur in petitions for redress in the case of the Revenue Laws, in which letter they did at least draw into question if not openly deny the authority of Parliament to enact laws binding upon the colonies in all cases whatever, asserting that the Acts imposing duties upon the people of that province with the sole and express purpose of raising a revenue were infringments of their natural and constitutional rights.

The same doctrine and principles were also held forth in other letters written by order of the Assembly at the same time to such persons of rank in this kingdom as they conceived concurred with them in opinion, and also in a letter to their agent, in which letter a variety of other Acts of Parliament and measures of government founded thereon are stated to be grievous and oppressive and a violation of their charter-rights.

The publication of these letters which the House ordered to be printed with their Journals and the atrocious publications in the newspapers which continued without any control could not fail of having a very mischievous effect.

On the 18th of March, the anniversary of the repeal of the Stamp Act, some disorders were committed and the Governor was induced from many concurrent circumstances to suspect that further and greater violences were intended, upon which he thought fit to ask the opinion of the Council whether they would at that time advise him to take any measures for securing the peace of the town, and what those measures should be. To which they replied that as they apprehended there was no danger of any disturbance they did not think any measures necessary to be taken for that purpose; but upon the Governor's laying before them a letter from the Commissioners of the Customs expressing their apprehensions that insults would be offered to them and one of their officers having made oath before the Council of his having been threatened with mischief, they adjourned the consideration of what might be proper to be done to a later hour, when no disturbances being reported to them they declared their adherence to their former opinion. Upon which the Governor thought fit to acquaint the Commissioners that he could give them no protection.

In the beginning of March 1768, subscriptions were made and associations entered into for the non-importation of goods from Great Britain, but this last measure was at that time defeated by the merchants in other colonies refusing to concur in it.

The exclusion of the Lieut.-Governor and other officers of government from the Council at the general election in 1766 has already been mentioned. The same disrespect was shown to them in 1767 and repeated upon the meeting of the General Court in 1768, and whilst the conduct of the Assembly was actuated by such principles and such a disposition in which it is represented that the Council had upon many occasions manifested a strong inclination to concur, there was little room to hope that the disorders in that government would abate. On the contrary it appears that in consequence of the seizure of a vessel in the harbour of Boston for running uncustomed goods, a mob was assembled on the 10th of June 1768 and that the Collector of the Customs, the Comptroller and other officers and persons who were assisting in the said seizure, were violently assaulted by the said mob, their lives endangered and the houses of several of them attacked and attempted to be forced; and that this riot was followed by papers stuck upon Liberty Tree, containing an invitation to the people to rise and clear the country of the Commissioners and their officers, one of which is said to have been devoted to death.

On the 11th of June 1768 the Governor recommended the state of the town under these violences and disorders to the consideration of the Council who advised that such of the members of the Board who were Justices of the Peace should make inquiry into the particular facts and report the same to the Governor in Council, that so they might take proper measures upon this interesting occasion. The Governor observes however in his letter giving an account of this transaction that there appeared a disposition in the Council to meddle with it as little as possible. On the 13th of June 1768 the Governor communicated to the Council a letter from the Commissioners of the Customs, complaining that no notice had been taken of the late disturbances in the town of Boston whereby they were so immediately affected. Whereupon the Governor at the desire of the Board wrote an answer to the said letter and informed them that the Board being under no apprehensions of fresh disturbances when they met last, they had postponed the consideration of the business to that morning. This being done the Governor stated his apprehensions that there would be fresh disturbances and urged the consideration of measures for the prevention thereof. But the Council thinking that there was no immediate danger of such disturbances advised that the matter should be referred to the consideration of the General Court.

In consequence of this resolution of the Council and upon the Governor's acquainting the Commissioners that he could give them no protection and that Boston was no place of safety for them, they went on board His Majesty's ship *Romney* and obtained an order from the Governor for their admission into Castle William.

What is here stated with regard to the proceedings of the Council is taken from their Journals, but as many things are related by Governor Bernard to have passed at the meeting on the 13th of June 1768 which are not stated upon the Journals, it may not be improper to refer to the Governor's letter to Lord Hillsborough on that subject, dated the 14th of June 1768.

In this letter mention is made that on the 13th of June notice was given by a paper fixed on a tree called Liberty Tree for all those who in this time of oppression and distraction wish well to the town and province to assemble at that tree upon the next day; and the Governor relates in another letter, dated the 16 of June, that in consequence of this notice there was a tumultuous meeting of the people at the said tree, from which they adjourned to the town-hall where it was objected they were not a legal meeting, whereupon they adjourned to the afternoon that in the meantime the selectmen might call a town-meeting to legalise the assembly.

In the afternoon they met in a meeting-house, the town-hall being not large enough for the company, and Mr Otis was chosen moderator.

The Governor, in his letter to Lord Hillsborough giving an account of this transaction, relates that at this meeting many wild and violent proposals were made but were warded off. Among these were that every captain of a man-of-war that came into the harbour should be under the command of the General Court. Another was that if any person should promote or assist the bringing troops there, he should be deemed a disturber of the peace and a traitor to his country. But nothing was done finally except the passing a petition to the Governor and appointing a committee of 21 persons to present it to him, and also a committee to prepare instructions for their Representatives and a letter to Mr Deberdt as their agent, after which they adjourned to the next day.

In the petition and in the instructions which in consequence of these resolutions were agreed upon and afterwards published in the Boston newspapers, it is asserted as a fundamental principle of the constitution "that no man shall be governed by laws or taxed but by himself or representative legally and fairly chosen and to which he does not give his own consent; that laws and taxes are imposed upon them to which they have not only given their assent but against which they have firmly remonstrated as violations of their constitution and as meant only to support swarms of officers and pensioners in idleness and luxury".

They say that to contend with their parent-state is a dreadful extremity but that they cannot bear the reflection of tamely submitting without one struggle, and apprehend that it is in the option and power of the Governor to prevent them effecting too much and save them the reproaches and shame of attempting too little; that as the Board of Customs have thought fit, of their own motion, to relinquish the exercise of their commission, and as they cannot but hope that being convinced of the impropriety and injustice of such an establishment, and of the inevitable destruction which would ensue from the exercise of their office, they will never re-assume it, they flatter themselves the Governor will redress the other grievance by immediately ordering the *Romney* man-of-war to remove from the harbour;

That they would maintain their loyalty to the King, a reverence and due subordination to the British Parliament as the supreme legislative in all cases of necessity for the preservation of the whole empire, but at the same time to assert and vindicate their dear and invaluable rights and liberties at the utmost hazard of their lives and fortunes.

They then state the case of impressing as a grievance contrary to an express Act of Parliament, desire their Representatives will pursue measures for their redress and for preventing impresses of all kinds, and to promote Parliamentary enquiry whether the Commissioners of the Customs or any other persons whatever have really written or solicited for troops and for what end, and that they would forward if they thought expedient resolutions that every such person who shall solicit or promote the importation of troops at this time is an enemy to that town and province and a disturber of the peace.

Whether proceedings and resolutions of this nature in a town-meeting, legal only to the purposes of election of officers and the management of the prudential affairs of the town, are or are not criminal, or if criminal what is the degree of the guilt, must be submitted; but it is necessary to observe that they were followed the next day by a concurrent vote of the Council and Assembly that inquiry should be made into the grounds and reason for the present apprehensions of the people that measures have been and are now taking for the execution of the late Revenue Acts of Parliament by a naval and military force.

In this situation the disorders and confusions which had prevailed in the town of Boston remained unnoticed until the 22nd of July when the Governor moved the Council to take into consideration some measures for restoring vigour and firmness to government. Whereupon it was agreed to take up this consideration on the 27th and to summon such members as were within such a distance as to be able to give their attendance.

At this meeting the Governor recapitulated what had passed relative to the riot on the 10th of June 1768 and desired the opinion of the Council what might be done to punish the perpetrators of those outrages, to preserve the peace of the town and to give such protection to the Commissioners of the Customs as that they might return in safety to Boston.

The Governor further stated that the proposition made at a former meeting, that this business should be taken up by the General Court at large, had produced no effect, and that all the disorders complained of and objects recommended to consideration remained unredressed or unprovided for, that no measures had been fallen upon to enable the Commissioners of the Customs to return in safety, to punish the raisers and perpetrators of the riots and tumults, or to preserve the peace of the town and to support the authority of government, that this neglect would certainly be taken notice of at home, and therefore he required them to give him their full, free and true advice, according to the duty of their office and the terms of their oath to perform the same, that he had received advice from General Gage that the troops at Halifax were ordered to be in readiness in case he (the Governor) should require their assistance, in return to which he had informed the General that he would communicate this to the Council and if they advised him to require those troops he should do so, and if they should not advise him to require them he should not, being determined in such a business to do nothing without the advice of the Council, and therefore he desired their advice whether he should, according to General Gage's offer require troops from Halifax to support the execution of the civil power.

On the 29th of July 1768 the Council made a reply to what had been laid before them and proposed by the Governor, in which they stated that the disorders which happened on the 10th June 1768 arose from the violent and unprecedented manner in which the officers of the Customs had made seizure of the sloop *Liberty.*

They reminded him of the order that had been made on the 11th of June for the Justices to inquire into the facts relative to the riot that had been committed; they alleged that the matter as it stood referred to a committee of the General Court included a consideration of measures necessary to be pursued for the prevention of the like disturbances for the future, that the bringing that consideration to a report and issue was prevented by what passed in consequence of the orders from home, by which the Assembly was threatened with a dissolution and was finally defeated by the prorogation and dissolution that followed in consequence thereof; that they are now ready upon the first call since that dissolution to do everything in their power to prevent future disturbances; that with regard to the Commissioners of the Customs, their quitting the town was a mere voluntary act of their own, no insult having been offered to them nor any attack upon their persons or houses; that the posting men-of-war in the harbour was an imputation on the loyalty of the town and a discouragement to its trade; that if the Commissioners had procured those ships or had endeavoured to procure troops to be sent thither it could not be thought strange that the province entertained no affection for them, that they detested and abhorred the riots and disorders which had been committed, and therefore advised the Governor to direct the Attorney-General to prosecute all persons guilty thereof or that any ways aided or abetted the same, and to issue a proclamation for preventing, suppressing and punishing all tumults and unlawful assemblies; that with regard to the offer made by General Gage, they were of opinion the civil power did not need the support of troops and that it was not for His Majesty's service or the peace of the province that any troops should be required; and that if any persons have made application to General Gage for troops, they deemed them in the highest degree unfriendly to the peace and good order of the government as well as to His Majesty's service and the British interest in America.

The foregoing account of what passed in Council on the 27 and 29 of July 1768 is taken from the Journal of their proceedings, but it is submitted whether it may not be advisable on this occasion to refer to the Journals themselves and to the account given by Governor Bernard of these proceedings in his letter to Lord Hillsborough of the 30th of July 1768, where many things are stated that do not appear upon the Journals and many remarks are made upon the manner in which the Council attempt to justify their conduct in the case of the riots and disturbances in the month of June 1768.

The General Court having been dissolved in August 1768 in consequence of the Assembly's refusal to rescind the resolution that gave birth to the circular letter of the 11th of March, it is necessary to state many facts and events of a very extraordinary nature subsequent thereto.

Notice has been already taken in a former part of this paper of the attempt made in March 1768 to set on foot associations and subscriptions for not importing goods from Great Britain and of the causes of the

failure of that attempt. This unwarrantable measure was howeve
again tried with better success in the beginning of August, when mos
of the merchants of the town of Boston entered into and subscribed a
agreement that they would not send for or import any kind of goods o
merchandise from Great Britain, some few articles of necessity ex
cepted, from the first of January 1769 to the 1st January 1770 and tha
they would not import any tea, paper, glass or painters colours unti
the Act imposing duties on those articles should be repealed.

On the 5th of September 1768 there appeared in the *Boston Gazett*
a paper containing certain queries calculated to possess the people wit
an opinion that the measures of Parliament with respect to Americ
and those which Government had pursued for the support of them wer
of such a nature as that the political union between Great Britain an
the colonies was thereby dissolved, and therefore that it was necessar
that a convention should be held in order to agree upon a plan for th
government of that colony in particular.

The Governor, alarmed at the dangerous doctrines held out in thi
paper and for the consequences which might follow therefrom if th
troops which General Gage had informed him were by the King'
command coming from Halifax should arrive without the people'
having any intimation of them, thought fit to give out that he had privat
advice that such an event might be expected.

In consequence of this intelligence being made public, severa
private meetings (as the Governor represents) were held by the in
habitants of Boston, in one of which it was the general opinion that the
should raise the country and oppose the troops; that it was reporte
and believed that a resolution was come to in the other meeting t
surprise and take the Castle; and that an empty turpentine barrel wa
put upon the pole of a beacon that had been lately erected without hi
consent; that the Council, alarmed by these reports and appearance
desired a meeting might be summoned, which was accordingly done
at which meeting orders were given for taking down the barrel fixe
upon the beacon.

On the 12th of September the freeholders and other inhabitants c
the town of Boston assembled in town-meeting at Faneuil Hall, an
after a prayer upon the occasion by the Rev. Doctor Cooper, Mr Oti
was unanimously chosen moderator, and a petition of the inhabitant
praying that the town might be legally convened in order to inquir
of the Governor the grounds and reasons of sundry declarations mad
by him that three regiments might be daily expected there, and als
to consider of the most wise, constitutional, loyal and salutary measure
to be adopted on such an occasion, having been read, a committee wa
appointed to make the inquiry requested and a petition to the Governo
was framed, praying him to issue precepts for convening a Genera
Assembly with all speed.

At the same time a committee was appointed to take the state c
public affairs into consideration and report the measures they apprehen
the most salutary to be taken in the present emergency.

On the next day to which the meeting was adjourned, the committe
reported the following declaration and resolves.

Whereas it is the first principle in civil society, founded in nature and reason, that no law of the society can be binding on any individual without his consent given by himself in person or by his representative of his own free election.

And whereas in and by an Act of the British Parliament passed in the first year of the reign of King William and Queen Mary of glorious and blessed memory entitled an Act declaring the rights and liberties of the subject and settling the succession of the Crown, the preamble of which Act is in these words vizt. "Whereas the late King James the second by the assistance of divers evil counsellors, judges and ministers employed by him, did endeavour to subvert and extirpate the Protestant Religion and the laws and liberties of this kingdom", it is expressly among other things declared that the levying money for the use of the Crown by pretence of prerogative without grant of Parliament for a longer time or in other manner than the same is granted is illegal.

And whereas in the third year of the reign of the same King William and Queen Mary, their Majesties were graciously pleased by their royal charter to give and grant to the inhabitants of this His Majesty's province all the territory therein described to be holden in free and common socage, and also to ordain and grant to the said inhabitants certain rights, liberties and privileges therein expressly mentioned, among which it is granted, established and ordained that all and every the subjects of them, their heirs and successors, which shall go to inhabit within the said province and territory and every of their children which shall happen to be born there or on the seas in going thither or returning from thence, shall have and enjoy all liberties and immunities of free and natural subjects within any of the dominions of them, their heirs and successors, to all intents, purposes and constructions whatever as if they and every of them were born within the realm of England.

And whereas by the aforesaid Act of Parliament made in the first year of the said King William and Queen Mary all and singular the premises contained therein are claimed, demanded and insisted upon as the undoubted rights and liberties of the subjects born within the realm.

And whereas the freeholders and other inhabitants of this town, the metropolis of the province in said charter mentioned, do hold all the rights and liberties therein contained to be sacred and inviolable, at the same time publicly and solemnly acknowledging their firm and unshaken allegiance to their alone rightful Sovereign King George the Third, the lawful successor of the said King William and Queen Mary to the British throne. Therefore,

Resolved, that the said freeholders and other inhabitants of the town of Boston will at the utmost peril of their lives and fortunes take all legal and constitutional measures to defend and maintain the person, family, crown and dignity of our said Sovereign Lord George the Third and all and singular the rights, liberties, privileges and immunities granted in the said royal charter, as well those which are declared to be belonging to us as British subjects by birthright as all others therein specially mentioned. And whereas by the said royal charter it is specially granted to the Great and General Court or Assembly therein constituted to impose and levy proportionable and reasonable assessments, rates and taxes upon the estates and persons of all and every the proprietors and inhabitants of the said province or territory for the service of the King in the necessary defence and support of his government of the province and the protection and preservation of his subjects therein. Therefore,

Voted, as the opinion of this town, that the levying money within this province for the use and service of the Crown in other manner than the same is granted by the Great and General Court or Assembly of this province is in violation of the said royal charter, and the same is also in violation of the undoubted natural rights of subjects declared in the aforesaid Act of Parliament freely to give and grant their own money for the service of the Crown with their own consent in person or by representatives of their own free election.

And whereas in the aforesaid Act of Parliament it is declared that the raising and keeping a standing army within the kingdom in time of peace, unless it be with the consent of Parliament, is against law, it is the opinion of this town that the said declaration is founded in the indefeasible right of the subjects to be consulted and to give their free consent in person or by representatives of their own free election to the raising and keeping a standing army among them, and the inhabitants of this town, being free subjects, have the same right derived from nature and confirmed by the British constitution as well as the said royal charter, and therefore the raising or keeping a standing army without their consent in person or by representatives of their own free election would be an infringement of their natural, constitutional and charter rights, and the employing such army for the enforcing of laws made without the consent of the people in person or by their representatives would be a grievance.

This report was unanimously accepted and recorded, and the following votes were also unanimously passed, after which the meeting was dissolved, vizt.

Whereas by an Act of Parliament of the first of King William and Queen Mary it is declared that for the redress of all grievances and for amending, strengthening and preserving the laws, Parliaments ought to be held frequently, and in so much as it is the opinion of this town that the people labour under many intolerable grievances which unless speedily redressed threaten the total destruction of our invaluable [sic], natural, constitutional and charter rights.

And furthermore, as his Excellency the Governor has declared himself unable at the request of this town to call a General Court, which is the Assembly of the states of this province, for the redress of such grievances:

Voted, that this town will now make choice of a suitable number of persons to act for them as a committee in convention with such as may be sent to join them from the several towns in this province in order that such measures may be consulted and advised as His Majesty's service and the peace and safety of his subjects in the province may require.

Whereupon the Hon. James Otis Esq., Hon. Thomas Cushing Esq.,

Mr Samuel Adams and John Hancock Esq. were appointed a committee for the said purpose, the town hereafter to take into consideration what recompense shall be made them for the services they may perform.

Voted, that the selectmen be directed to write to the selectmen of the several towns within this province, informing them of the foregoing vote and to propose that a convention be held, if they shall think proper, at Faneuil Hall in this town on Thursday the 22nd of September instant at 10 o'clock before noon. Upon a motion made and seconded, the following vote was passed by a very great majority vizt.

Whereas by an Act of Parliament of the first of King William and Queen Mary it is declared that the subjects being Protestants may have arms for their defence, it is the opinion of this town that the said declaration is founded in nature, reason and sound policy, and is well adapted for the necessary defence of the community.

And forasmuch as by a good and wholesome law of this province every listed soldier and other householder (except troopers who by law are otherwise to be provided) shall be always provided with a well-fixed firelock-musket, accoutrements and ammunition, as is in said law particularly mentioned, to the satisfaction of the commission officers of the company; and as there is at this time a prevailing apprehension in the minds of many of an approaching war with France, in order that the inhabitants of this town may be prepared in case of sudden danger, Voted that those of the said inhabitants who may at present be unprovided be and hereby are requested duly to observe the said law at this time.

The Hon. Thomas Cushing Esq. communicated to the town a letter lately received from a committee of merchants in the City of New York, acquainting him with their agreement relative to a non-importation of British goods, whereupon the town by a vote expressed their high satisfaction therein.

The town taking into serious consideration the present aspect of their public affairs, and being of opinion that it greatly behoves a people professing godliness to address the Supreme Ruler of the World on all important occasions for that wisdom which is profitable to direct.

Voted unanimously, that the selectmen be a committee to wait on the several ministers of the Gospel within this town, desiring that the next Tuesday may be set apart as a day of fasting and prayer.

Ordered that the votes and proceedings of the town in their present meeting be published in the several newspapers. The town voted their thanks to the moderator for his good services and then the meeting was dissolved.

The following is a copy of the circular letter written by the selectmen of Boston and directed to the selectmen of the several towns within that province agreeable to the above votes.

Boston, September 14, 1768.

Gentlemen, you are already too well acquainted with the melancholy and very alarming circumstances to which this province as well as America in general is now reduced. Taxes equally detrimental to the commercial interest of the parent country and her colonies are imposed on the people without their consent: taxes designed for the support of the civil government and the colonies in a manner clearly unconstitutional and contrary to that in which till of late government has been supported by the free gift of the people in the American Assemblies or Parliaments, as also for the maintenance of a large standing army, not for the defence of the newly acquired territories but for the old colonies and in a time of peace. The decent, humble and truly loyal applications and petitions from the Representatives of this province for the redress of these heavy and very threatening grievances have hitherto been ineffectual, being assured from authentic intelligence that they have not yet reached the royal ear. The only effect of transmitting these applications hitherto perceivable has been a mandate from one of His Majesty's Secretaries of State to the Governor of this province to dissolve the General Assembly, merely because the late House of Representatives refused to rescind a resolution of a former House which implied nothing more than a right in the American subjects to unite in humble and dutiful petitions to their gracious Sovereign when they found themselves aggrieved. This is a right naturally inherent in every man and expressly recognised at the Glorious Revolution as the birthright of an Englishman.

This dissolution you are sensible has taken place, the Governor has publicly and repeatedly declared that he cannot call another Assembly, and the Secretary of State for the American Department in one of his letters communicated to the late House has been pleased to say that "proper care will be taken for the support of the dignity of Government", the meaning of which is too plain to be misunderstood.

The concern and perplexity into which these things have thrown the people have been greatly aggravated by a late declaration of his Excellency Governor Bernard that one or more regiments may soon be expected in this province.

The design of these troops is in everyone's apprehension nothing short of enforcing by military power the execution of Acts of Parliament, in the forming of which the colonies have not and cannot have any constitutional influence. This is one of the greatest distresses to which a free people can be reduced.

The town which we have the honour to serve have taken these things at their late meeting into their most serious consideration, and as there is in the minds of many a prevailing apprehension of an approaching war with France, they have passed the several votes which we transmit to you, desiring that they may be immediately laid before the town, whose prudentials are in your care, at a legal meeting for their candid and particular attention.

Deprived of the councils of a General Assembly in this dark and difficult season, the loyal people of this province will, we are persuaded, immediately perceive the propriety and utility of the proposed committee of convention; and the sound and wholesome advice that may be expected from a number of gentlemen chosen by themselves, and in whom they may repose the greatest confidence, must tend to the real service of our most gracious Sovereign and the welfare of his subjects in this province, and may happily prevent any sudden and unconnected measures which in their present anxiety and even agony of mind they may be in danger of falling into.

As it is of importance that the convention should meet as soon as may be, so early a day as the 22nd of this instant September has been proposed for that purpose, and it is hoped the remotest towns will by that time, or as soon after as conveniently may be, return their respective committees.

Not doubting but that you are equally concerned with us and our fellow citizens for the preservation of our invaluable [sic] rights and for the general happiness of our country, and that you are disposed with equal ardour to exert yourselves in every constitutional way for so glorious a purpose.

The foregoing account of the proceedings of the town-meeting was printed by their direction in the *Boston Gazette* of the 19th of September, but as there are many circumstances relative to what passed at this meeting related in Governor Bernard's letter to Lord Hillsborough of the 16th of that month, which appeared to be very material for consideration, it is presumed that letter will be referred to.

It may be proper here to repeat what has been before said in respect to the proceedings of a former town-meeting, that is to say, that whether they are or are not criminal or if so what is the degree of guilt, must be submitted; but it is also here as in the former case necessary to observe that no steps whatever were taken to suppress so extraordinary a proceeding, nor does it appear to have been taken any notice of by the Council or by any of the civil magistrates of the colony.

On the 22nd of September 1768 a number of persons, upwards of 70, being committees from 66 towns and districts assembled in convention at Faneuil Hall to consult and advise the most effectual measures as might promote the peace and good order of His Majesty's subjects in that government at this very dark and distressing time.

The first step taken in this extraordinary convention was the choosing a chairman and a clerk, and the objects of this choice were the late Speaker and the Clerk of the Assembly; after which they agreed upon a petition to the Governor, praying that he would summon the constitutional Assembly of the province in order to consider of measures for preventing an unconstitutional encroachment of military power on the civil establishment for promoting the prosperity of the King's government and the peace, good order and due submission of His Majesty's subjects.

The Governor, however, thought fit to refuse the receiving of this petition, assigning for reason that such a reception would be to admit this convention to be a legal assembly, which he could by no means allow, and therefore he admonished them by message to break up instantly and separate themselves before they did any business, in order to avoid the consequences of the high offence they were committing.

In answer to this message they endeavoured to justify themselves by stating the grounds on which they assembled, and by openly disclaiming all pretence to any authoritative or governmental acts, but the Governor refused to receive any paper from them, and after having sat for three days, they adjourned to the third of October when they broke up, finishing their proceedings with the publication of a paper which they styled The result of the conference and consultation of the Committees chosen by a number of Towns and Districts and convened at Boston on the 22nd of September 1768.

On the 19th of September the Governor communicated to the Council the letters which he had received from Gen. Gage and the Earl of Hillsborough, informing him of the orders that had been given for sending to Boston two regiments from Halifax and two from Ireland, and moved the Board to give him their advice in what manner provision should be made for their reception and accommodation.

As the answer given to the Governor by the Council on this occasion and what passed in consequence thereof, as well as upon the arrival of the troops, in respect to the quartering of them in the town of Boston, are very material to the consideration of the state of the government of Massachusetts Bay and to the conduct of the Council as a board of advice and consultation, and as the subject-matter of these transactions cannot be related abstractedly without a hazard of misleading, it is submitted whether it may not be most advisable to refer, not only to the Journals of the Council but also to the Governor's letters to the Secretary of State upon the subject, in which are related the many difficulties that were created to obstruct the King's service on this occasion, the pretences that were used to evade and defeat the operation of the Act of Parliament for quartering His Majesty's troops in America, and to bring reproach upon and excite opposition to the measures His Majesty had been graciously pleased to pursue for supporting the civil magistrates and enabling them to execute the law.

It was not, however, in this business alone that the Council are said to have obstructed the measures of government; they are stated by Governor Bernard to have shown upon every other occasion where they were consulted by him upon matters relative to the state of the colony, in cases where the authority of Parliament was in question, a resolution to persevere in a conduct that could have no other effect than to increase the disorders and ill-humours that prevailed and to defeat every step that could be taken for restoring peace and good order in the town of Boston. It would be drawing out this paper to too great a length to enumerate all the instances of this disposition which are stated: they are fully set forth in the Governor's letters to the Secretary of State, and it is to this disposition in the Council that he attributes that weakness in the government which rendered ineffectual every measure that had been directed or proposed for remedying the disorders which had so long existed in that province, and for supporting His Majesty's authority and that of the supreme legislature.

There is one fact, however, stated in the account of the transactions of this time which is too material to be passed over in the consideration of the state of the province, as it relates to the conduct of the Council, which is the pretence they are said to have set up of acting as a Council of State without the intervention of and separate from the Governor, and their presuming to publish the minutes of their proceedings and their resolutions in some instances before they were communicated to him.

It must, however, be observed that the Council have in three letters to Lord Hillsborough, two of the 15th of April and one of the 12th of June 1769, thought fit to give an explanatory detail of their conduct in the cases in which they are charged by the Governor with neglect of duty and want of zeal for the support of government, to which letters it may be also proper to refer. But whatever was the cause to which the weakness of government in that province is to be attributed, the fact is that all the unwarrantable proceedings stated in the foregoing sheets were committed and done with entire impunity; and though repeated orders were given to the Governor to pursue every measure for bringing the offenders to justice and for making inquiry into the grounds and causes of the disorders and distractions, and every support given that was required to enable the officers of the Crown and the civil magistrates to perform their duty, yet these orders had no effect; and therefore it was thought fit in the beginning of the year 1769 to submit the state of the colony to the consideration of Parliament.

The result of this measure will appear in the joint resolutions of both Houses of Parliament and in their address to the King in February 1769.

The censure of the proceedings in the province of Massachusetts Bay and of the conduct of the Council and other civil magistrates, expressed by both Houses of Parliament in their resolutions, and their approbation of the measure of sending troops thither to support and protect the magistrates and the officers of the Revenue were very far from producing the good effect that might reasonably have been hoped for. A disposition to deny the authority and resist the laws of the supreme legislature continued still to prevail, not only in flagitious publications in the daily newspapers but also in a variety of violent and unwarrantable resolutions and proceedings of those merchants and others who had subscribed to the agreements for non-importation of goods from Great Britain.

Meetings of the Associators are represented to have been held in as regular a manner as any other meeting authorized by the constitution. Committees were appointed to examine the cargoes of all vessels arriving from Great Britain and regular votes and resolutions of censure were passed in these meetings upon all such as refused to concur in these unlawful associations; their names were published in the public newspapers as enemies to their country; and the mandates and decrees of those committees met with a respect and obedience denied to the constitutional authority of government.

In some cases goods imported from Great Britain were locked up in warehouses under the care of these committees in order to prevent their being sold, and in one or two instances they were re-shipped to Great Britain.

It is not necessary to relate all the unwarrantable and violent proceedings of these Associators. The nature and effect of them can only be judged of by reading the proceedings themselves which are here referred to.

On the 31st of May 1769, the General Court met at the Court-house at Boston pursuant to His Majesty's writs, and the first step the Assembly took before they proceeded on any other business was to send a message to the Governor asserting that the having ships in the harbour and troops in the town of Boston was inconsistent with their dignity and freedom, and therefore that they had a right to expect that he would give orders for the removal of the forces by sea and land from that port and from the gates of the city during the session of the Assembly; and at the same time the House came to several resolutions to the same effect as the declarations contained in their message to the Governor.

The Governor having in reply to their message acquainted them that he had no authority over His Majesty's ships in that port or his troops in that town nor could give any orders for the removal of them, they then proceeded to the election of Councillors, in which election not only the Lieut.-Governor and other officers of government were excluded but also several other gentlemen who had been of the former Council and who (the Governor represents) showed a disposition to support the King's government, to acknowledge the authority of Parliament and to preserve the people from democratical despotism, and were otherwise distinguished by their integrity and ability.

On the 13th of June the Assembly sent an answer to the Governor's message of the 31st of May in which he told them he had no authority over the King's ships or troops.

In this answer they assert that by the principles of the constitution the Governor of that colony has the absolute military command, that the sending a military force there to enforce the execution of the laws is inconsistent with the nature of government and the spirit of a free constitution, that the unwillingness of a people in general that a law should be executed was a strong presumption of its being an unjust law, that it could not be their law as the people must consent to laws before they can be obliged in conscience to obey them.

Several other messages passed between the Governor and Assembly upon the subject of the troops but they are little more than a repetition of the matter that has been already stated, and the altercation ended on the 21st of June with a resolution of the Assembly "That the British Constitution admits of no military force within the realm but for the purposes of offensive and defensive war, and therefore that the sending and continuing a military force within this colony for the express purpose of aiding and assisting the civil government is an infraction of the natural and constitutional rights of the people, a breach of the privilege of the General Assembly, inconsistent with that freedom with which this House as one branch of the same hath a right and ought to debate, consult and determine, and manifestly tends to the subversion of that happy form of government which we have hitherto enjoyed".

Whilst the General Court was sitting, intelligence was received of the resolutions of Parliament respecting the disorders within the province of Massachusetts Bay, and authenticated copies of such of the correspondence with the Governor as had been laid before Parliament had been transmitted from thence. Upon which the Assembly did on the 7th of July come to several resolutions, asserting that the sole right of imposing taxes upon the inhabitants of that colony was legally and constitutionally vested in the House of Representatives lawfully convened according to the ancient and established practice with the consent of the Council and of His Majesty the King of Great Britain or of his Governor for the time being; that the convention in September 1768 was a measure of necessity, nor could it possibly be illegal as they positively disclaimed all governmental acts; that the establishment of a standing army in that colony in time of peace without the consent of the General Assembly was an infringement of the natural rights of the people and a violation of their charter; that the sending an armed force into the colony under pretence of assisting the civil authority was an attempt to establish such a standing army without their consent and was highly dangerous, unprecedented and unconstitutional; that too many persons in power at home do avow most rancorous enmity against the free part of the British Constitution and are indefatigable in their endeavours to render the monarchy absolute and the administration arbitrary in every part of the British empire; that the extension of the power of the Courts of Admiralty was highly dangerous and alarming, that all trials for treason, misprision of treason, or for any felony or crime whatever, committed or done in that colony ought of right to be had and conducted within the courts of the colony, and that the seizing any person or persons residing in that colony suspected of any crime whatsoever committed therein and sending such person or persons to places beyond the sea to be tried is highly derogatory of the rights of British subjects, as thereby the inestimable privilege of being tried by a jury from the vicinage as well as the liberty of summoning and producing witnesses on such trial will be taken away from the party accused.

These are some of the principal declarations contained in the resolves of the Assembly, but they do also contain a variety of other assertions of a very dangerous and malignant nature, tending to inflame the minds of the people against the King's government and against the Governor and Commander-in-chief; and Sir Francis Bernard having in repeated messages recommended to them to make provision for the expenses that had been incurred in quartering the King's troops, the session ended with an answer to these messages in which they arraign in the strongest terms the justice of the supreme legislature in passing the Revenue Laws and more especially that for quartering the King's troops, and declare their resolution never to make provision for the services pointed out in the Governor's messages.

The General Court having in consequence of these proceedings been prorogued by the Governor to the 10th of January 1770, nothing of any great moment occurred in the colony excepting a continuance of very violent and unwarrantable measures for supporting the Associations for non-importation of goods from Great Britain until the unhappy quarrel between the townspeople of Boston and the soldiery on the 5th of March, from the accounts of which as well as from the frequent attacks that had at different times been made upon the troops, there is much reason to apprehend that there was a premeditated design to seek occasion by such quarrels for forcing the regiments to leave the town.

Since this event every endeavour has been exerted by the people of Boston to accelerate the trial of Captain Preston and the soldiers who surrendered themselves up to justice, and to involve the Commissioners of the Customs and their officers in the guilt of aiding and abetting the soldiers in (what is called) the massacre of the people. And though the courts of justice have endeavoured to withstand the attempts that have been made to influence their proceedings, yet there are but too many symptoms of their being awed and terrified by the violences of the people.

The firmness of the Lieutenant-Governor in negativing in one or two instances the elections of persons who have been most forward in opposition to the authority of the Parliament seems in some degree to have checked the dangerous spirit which hath prevailed, yet there is great reason to believe that he has only the shadow of power, not being able to act without the Council who will not consent to any proposal for discountenancing the usurpation of the powers of government by the town of Boston. And the people being now possessed of an opinion that they have many advocates in Parliament who justify them in all they have done, the state of the colony is more desperate than ever. But this will be better explained by the instructions from the town of Boston to their Representatives on the 15th of last month, and by the Assembly's answer to the Lieutenant-Governor's message of the 7th of April and his reply thereto. *Entry.* [C.O.5/765, p. 116; with Appendix at pp. 160–167 listing sources on which this report is based]

LIX

Petition of House of Burgesses of Virginia to the King

[27 June]

May it please your most excellent Majesty graciously to permit your ever dutiful and loyal subjects, the Burgesses of Virginia now met in General Assembly, to approach your royal presence and with all humility renew their most earnest entreaties that your Majesty in your great goodness would be pleased to extend your fatherly protection to them and all their fellow subjects in America.

Having, sire, upon former and recent occasions humbly submitted to your royal wisdon our just claims to be free and exempt from all taxes imposed on us without our own consent for the purpose of raising and establishing a revenue in America, we should not now presume to recall your Majesty's gracious attention to the same subject had we not the most convincing testimony that the sentiments and dispositions of your Majesty's ministry confirmed by the voice of Parliament still continue extremely unfavourable and alarming to your Majesty's American subjects, a reflection to us at this time the more irksome and grievous as we had from the late agreeable prospect flattered ourselves that a broad and permanent foundation would soon have been laid for restoring and perpetuating that pleasing harmony which once so happily united the interests and affections of all your majesty's subjects both British and American.

Words, most gracious Sovereign, cannot sufficiently express the exceeding great concern and deep affliction with which our minds have been agitated and tortured upon finding almost a fixed and determined resolution in the Parliament of Great Britain to continue the several Acts imposing duties for the sole purpose of raising a revenue in America, exposing the persons and estates of your Majesty's affectionate subjects to the arbitrary decisions of distant Courts of Admiralty and thereby depriving them of the inestimable right and privilege of being tried by their peers alone according to the long established and well known laws of the land. From these baneful sources have already been derived much disquietude and unhappiness which are not likely to abate under the continuance of measures apparently tending to deprive the colonists of everything dear and valuable to them.

A partial suspension of duties, and these such only as were imposed on British manufactures, cannot, great sir, remove the too well grounded fears and apprehensions of your Majesty's loyal subjects whilst impositions are continued on the same articles of foreign fabric and entirely retained upon tea for the avowed purpose of establishing a precedent against us.

We therefore judging it at all times an indispensable duty we owe to your Majesty, to our country, ourselves and posterity, humbly to lay our grievances before the common father of all his people, do now, impressed with the highest sense of duty and affection, prostrate ourselves at the foot of your throne, most humbly beseeching and imploring your Majesty graciously to interpose your royal influence and authority to procure a total repeal of those disagreeable Acts of Parliament and to secure to us the free and uninterrupted enjoyment of all those rights and privileges which from the laws of nature, of community in general, and in a most especial manner from the principles of the British Constitution particularly recognized and confirmed to this colony by repeated and express stipulations we presume not to claim but in common with all the rest of your Majesty's subjects under the same or like circumstances.

That your Majesty and your royal descendants may long and gloriously reign in the hearts of a free and happy people is the constant and fervent prayer of your Majesty's truly devoted, most dutiful, loyal and affectionate subjects, the Burgesses and Representatives of the People of Virginia. *Signed,* Peyton Randolph, Speaker. [C.O.5/1348, fo. 139]

LX

Deputy Governor Robert Eden to Earl of Hillsborough (No. 6)

[Undated ? June]

My Lord, I have the honour of enclosing to your lordship the pamphlet [Vol. I, No. 447i] containing the proceedings of the committee which sent home the brigantine, as also two *Gazettes* [Vol. I, No. 447ii-iii] containing the different opinions of some members of the committee with respect to their proceedings, which have not met with the general approbation the sanguine ones expected. From what I can observe I do not imagine that the taking off the duties on glass, paper, and colours will put an end to the Association while the duty on tea continues, although there are some here desirous of ending it and associating not to import tea, amongst whom I have heard is Mr West, principal author of this pamphlet. The general voice is that it will stand as a precedent for laying duties in America on some future occasion. I have endeavoured to convince the reasonable people that the Act laying the threepence on tea can only serve as a precedent for any future Act that may operate in the same manner it does, which is as a relief, the 25 per cent drawback exceeding the duty, tea being now much cheaper than it was before that was laid on; and that we ought not at any rate to complain of an Act that was beneficial to us, as this is. But this argument has not the weight I could wish. I am pretty certain that the laying sixpence in England or keeping back the sevenpence-halfpenny and taking off the threepence here would answer the wishes of the Americans entirely.

Your lordship's letter [Vol. I, No. 130] (No. 17) gave me the greatest satisfaction as it confirmed to my conduct the approbation of His Majesty and his ministers, which your lordship may be assured I shall use my utmost endeavours to merit a continuance of. By the first vessel from this port I will send your lordship the Votes and Proceedings since the year 1763 with the copies of the laws since then enacted.

Our General Assembly at present stands prorogued to the 7th August. Without particular orders I shall hardly meet them then, the middle of September being a more convenient season, at which time we must meet that the Inspection Law may not expire.

By a vessel which left Lisbon the 25th April, we learn that the packet from London thither in six days brought an account of the Parliament being up and a partial repeal of the Revenue Act, the duty on tea still remaining.

The Assembly of this province will be dissolved of course at the end of the next sessions. *Signed.* NB. Your lordship will be pleased to let one of your clerks number this as by absence of my secretary I am unable to get at the book in which my letters to your lordship are entered and numbered before the post goes out. [C.O.5/1283, fo. 30]

LXI

Governor Guy Carleton to Commissioners of Customs at Boston[1]

4 July, Quebec

Sirs, my letter [Vol. I, No. 457vi] of the 25th of October last complained to your Board that Mr Ainslie, the Collector of this port, and Mr Hooton, your Inspector, had in the course of last autumn greatly increased the fees of the officers of the Customs established here, more particularly those of the Collector, without the knowledge of the King's government in this province; it also informed you that I had given orders to the Custom-house officer not to receive any additional fees until approved of by the Governor and Council. In return, your secretary in his letter [Vol. I, No. 457viii] of the 14th of last May informs me by order that your Board has been under a long adjournment which prevented your answering my several letters but that at their first meeting you will

1   Enclosed in Carleton's letter to Hillsborough, 5 July 1770: Vol. I, No. 457.

take under consideration the points I have laid before you and communicate to me your sentiments thereon; in the meanwhile that you had directed the officers of the Customs to receive fees agreeable to a list which the Collector and Comptroller of Halifax certify, the 23rd of December last, to be taken by the officers of the Customs of that port.

With all deference due to gentlemen at the head of a Department which requires so much good sense, moderation and discretion, while disobedience seems to be the raging vice of the times, I humbly conceive my complaints on this point merited some consideration before you decided so roundly against us, and I flattered myself, considering the experiences you have had at Boston, that your Board would accordingly have taken them under consideration before you directed the officers under your comptrol to throw off all subordination and to act in open and avowed disobedience to the King's government in the province where they reside. Even supposing I was in an error, you surely must know it is the King's interests you strike at by such directions and not mine, I am only his servant raised in authority by his will and removed at his pleasure, but his government in whatever hands entrusted should still remain uninjured. To put a speedy stop to this dangerous beginning, I must explain to you very clearly that in my judgement neither the officers of the Customs nor your Board have any power to increase the established fees of office in this province, nor to expound Acts of Parliament on that head, nor will I suffer any such precedent until I know the King's pleasure thereon; I have therefore acquainted the officers of the Customs that I expect they will strictly comply with those orders of not increasing their fees until approved by Governor and Council, as Mr Ainslie has at large informed you.

In less than twelve months I see here three lists of fees and, though very different one from the other, all pleading the authority of the same Act of Parliament. In the second the Collector has taken very great care of himself indeed, little troubling himself how ruinous it may prove to the people, and this he calls the Halifax list. Your secretary sends me a third list [Vol. I, No. 457ix], heavier than the first, but not quite so exorbitant as the second; this is also the Halifax list. Had the Act of the 5th of his present Majesty named the port of Halifax, and did it now remain to be carried into execution, I should write to the King's governor of that province to learn of him what fees were legally established at that port the 29th of September 1764, taking especial care no more were introduced into this poor province, and not content myself with an account certified last December of what the officers of the Customs are now pleased to take there. But this is not the case, the Act of Parliament does not name Halifax but the nearest port, which is New York for some hundred miles; and agreeable thereto Mr Stuart, who had then the same direction of the Customs your Board has now, brought the list of fees taken at New York and they were received in this province in obedience to the supreme power and much to the satisfaction of the officers of the Customs, for these fees then were, or were understood to be, the most lucrative. The Act was then carried into execution, and such it shall remain till I am better informed or till it be changed by lawful authority.

According to Mr Ainslie's doctrine, which you support, the King's subjects in this distressed province are forever to be at the discretion of a Collector, for I presume the Collectors of New York and Halifax have as much right to increase the fees of office without permitting their respective governments to interfere or take cognizance thereof, and as their fees augment, he may take his choice of either port, informing us New York is nearest by land, Halifax by water; in time it may suit his purpose to demand the fees of Newfoundland and still agreeable to said Act.

You may rest assured, gentlemen, that as no man or number of men in this province dare oppose any Act of Parliament or interrupt an officer of the Customs in an honest and faithful discharge of his duty, so whenever these attempt the same uncontrolled freedom they have already done of laying new burthens upon the people for their own profit and by their own power, or should they attempt to have fair traders condemned who never meaned to trade illicitly, because they have fallen into inaccuracies the officers themselves have artfully occasioned, lying in wait until a rich prize shall enter their decoy, you may I say be assured that on all such occasions they shall find me firm in their way; and if a remedy cannot be procured on this continent I will bring the case before those who I am confident will pronounce righteous judgement.

And in all this, gentlemen, I think I only comply with the will of the King our master, who requires of me that to the utmost of my power I should protect his subjects within my government from oppression and wrong, that I do not suffer Acts of Parliament to be confounded with the mercenary iniquity of men in office, and that I put it out of the power of artful turbulent spirits to deceive the people by showing the supreme power to the multitude through such filthy mediums. The people here are not misled by the factious but are informed of their Sovereign's gracious intentions and taught to apply to his government with decency and respect for the performance of this indispensable part of their duty and not to have recourse to tumults and rioting.

I hope you will excuse my troubling you with so long a letter, but I think 'tis necessary you should clearly and fully understand the principles which govern this province, and if I might presume to offer my advice to gentlemen of your abilities I would respectfully recommend to you the sending to the Lords of His Majesty's Treasury, as I shall, copies of our correspondence, that if I misjudge what is best for the King's interests I may be better informed by his confidential servants or receive His Majesty's commands which, as in duty I am bound, I shall obey, before you again attempt to introduce here a contempt of the orders of government, an indecency not common in this province. I am the more emboldened to propose this method as I think it more decent than the former, and seeing we serve the same master I wish much we should unite in good humour cordially to promote his interests.

PS. Since my writing the above, I find Mr Ainslie who has been very violent upon the occasion threatens all the officers who cheerfully complied with my order with his indignation, in which he feeds himself with the vain hopes, as I am persuaded he will find them, of being assisted by you. In a letter to Mr Lock, a copy whereof is enclosed, he accuses Mr Scott of refusing to do the official business although well known to be a diligent officer, and that his willingness to submit to my order and disinclination to enter into the mercenary views of his colleague, can be the only reason for casting upon him such a reproach, when at the very time and ever since his arrival Mr Ainslie has not signed a single clearance, and that it is Mr Mellish, his deputy, clerk, and tidewaiter, who transacts all the Custom-house business except what regards the fees, and that Mr Ainslie indeed pays the greatest attention to. Finding himself all alone and that his orders and threats are to no purpose, Mr Ainslie has at length, though with reluctance, obeyed as you will see by the enclosed copy of his letter [Vol. I, No. 457 xiv] of the 23rd June 1770, which for that purpose I enclose. G. C. *Copy*. [C.O.42/30, fo. 105]

LXII

Order in Council

6 July, St James's
    Present, The King's Most Excellent Majesty.
    Whereas there was this day read at the Board a report from the Right Honourable the Lords of the Committee of Council for Plantation Affairs, dated the fourth of this instant in the words following, vizt.
    "Your Majesty having been pleased by your Order in Council of the 22nd of last month to refer unto this Committee a State [Vol. II, No. LVIII] of the Disorders, Confusion and Misgovernment which have lately prevailed and do still continue to prevail in Your Majesty's province of the Massachusetts Bay in America, the Lords of the Committee in obedience to Your Majesty's said Order of reference have taken the state of the said province into mature consideration and having carefully perused the papers referred to and examined witnesses well-informed of the transactions there for some time past, do agree humbly to report to Your Majesty that the instances in which those disorders do more particularly appear are,
    First, the encouragement given to, and the impunity with which, seditious and libellous publications have been put forth in that province, having a tendency and apparently manifesting a design to excite the people to acts of violence and opposition to the laws and to the authority of Parliament.
    Second, goods liable to duties have been forcibly landed without payment of those duties, and lawful seizures have been rescued by force of arms, and the officers of the Revenue insulted, abused and violently treated in the execution of their duty.
    Third, the illegal and unwarrantable acts and proceedings of the inhabitants of Boston in the town-meetings of the 13th of June and 12th of September 1768, and the convention of committees from other towns in the province, which was held at Boston on the 22nd of the said month.

Fourth, the Association and combination not to import goods from Great Britain, entered into by the merchants and others of Boston, on the 1st of August 1768, and the various resolutions and proceedings of the said Associators and their committees in consequence thereof.

Fifth, the declarations and doctrines inculcated by the House of Representatives in repeated resolutions and messages to the Governor and Lieutenant-Governor of that province, and by the town of Boston in the instructions to their Representatives on the 15 of May 1770.

Sixth, the disposition of the Council to adopt those principles and to countenance such illegal acts and proceedings, evidently manifested in their backwardness to concur with the Governor in such measures as were necessary to restrain and suppress them; and their taking upon them to meet and act as a Council of State without a summons from the Governor or without his being present, and causing their resolutions to be printed and published.

Having thus laid before Your Majesty several instances of the disorders which have prevailed in Your Majesty's province of the Massachusetts Bay, the Lords of the Committee take leave to observe to Your Majesty that as the declarations contained in the Assembly's answer to the Lieutenant-Governor's message of the 7th of April 1770 may encourage the people of that province to commit further violence, and as the instructions from the town of Boston to their Representatives on the 15th of May 1770 show an evident disposition to support by force the unconstitutional doctrines which have been inculcated, the Committee are humbly of opinion that the rendezvous of Your Majesty's ships stationed in North America should be in the harbour of Boston and the fortress which commands the harbour be put into a respectable state of defence and garrisoned by Your Majesty's regular troops.

These precautions the Committee recommend as the means to check further violences and prevent illicit trade, and to defend and support the officers of the Revenue in the execution of their duty and the magistrates in the enforcement of the law.

But the Committee are of opinion that the weakness of the magistracy and the inefficacy of law may be most effectually redressed by the interposition of the wisdom and authority of the legislature; wherefore the Committee humbly submit to Your Majesty that it may be advisable for Your Majesty to recommend the consideration of the state of the province of Massachusetts Bay to Parliament".

His Majesty taking the said report into consideration was pleased with the advice of his Privy Council to approve thereof, and hath this day ordered the Lords Commissioners of the Admiralty, the Master-General and Principal Officers of the Ordnance, and His Majesty's Secretary at War, to give such directions therein as to them might respectively appertain. And His Majesty doth hereby order that the Right Honourable the Earl of Hillsborough, one of His Majesty's Principal Secretaries of State, do likewise give such directions herein as to him may appertain. *Signed*, W. Blair. [C.O.5/26, fo. 119]

LXIII

Earl of Hillsborough to Lieut.-Governor Thomas Hutchinson (No. 38)

6 July, Whitehall

Sir, since my letter [Vol. II, No. LII, 12 June 1770] to you of the 14th of last month I have received your dispatches [Vol. I, Nos. 302, 322, 346, 349, 355, 359] numbered from 9 to 14, and have laid them before the King.

These dispatches do all of them, except the last, relate only to the disorders and disobedience which continue to prevail in the province under your government and your inability in the present state of it to prevent or check the abuses or punish the offences which are every day committed.

As it is now but too plain that the lenity and forbearance of Parliament have had no other effect than to aggravate the evil and to encourage a still further opposition to the supreme legislative authority, and that measures are now carried to such a length as to menace the supporting by force the unjustifiable acts which have been committed and the unwarrantable doctrines which have been inculcated, I received the King's commands to lay before His Majesty in Council a State [Vol. II, No. LVIII] of the Disorders, Confusion and Misgovernment which have for some time past and do still continue to prevail in the province of Massachusetts Bay.

This State has been accordingly referred to a Committee of the Privy Council for Plantation Affairs who having made their report to the King, His Majesty has been pleased to approve thereof, and enclosed I send you a copy of the Order in Council [Vol. II, No. LXII] thereupon which you are at liberty to make such use of as you think will best promote His Majesty's service without making it public or communicating it by message or speech to the General Court. This Order will inform you of the measures which the King means to pursue, and I am to acquaint you in consequence thereof that it is His Majesty's pleasure that the company in the pay of the province now doing duty in Castle William be withdrawn, and that the possession of the fort be delivered to such officer as Lieut.-General Gage shall direct to take the command of it, and therefore you will not fail, so soon as General Gage shall have communicated to you the orders given by him for this purpose, to take the proper steps for the execution of that part of this service which depends upon you.

The settlement of the country to the eastward of the River Sagadahock by persons under colour of grants from the General Court, which by the express terms of the charter are of "no force, validity or effect until approved by the Crown" is a matter of great importance in various lights, but in none more so than in that of the encouragement it has given to the waste and destruction of that timber, the preservation and supply of which is become a matter of the most serious consideration in respect to the naval strength of this kingdom.

You say in your letter No. 14 that no restraint to these illegal settlements is to be expected or obtained unless by an interposition of royal authority, but how that authority can be exerted so as to operate as a remedy to a mischief of this magnitude I am not able to perceive. On the contrary it appears to me that the remedy ought properly, and can only effectually, come from the province within whose jurisdiction the lands lie, and that the neglecting to exert every legal means to prosecute such trespasses and prevent such unwarrantable intrusions will be justly imputed as a default for which the province will stand responsible.

What you suggest of the propriety of a proposal to the province to quit their claim to all the lands east of Penobscot and to take as a compensation the absolute property of the lands between that river and Kenebec, deserves consideration; but I very much fear that any accommodation of this kind will in the present state of the province and temper of the people be very difficult to be obtained. If, however, you think that such a measure might be effected and that there is no other possible remedy, I shall be very glad to receive your further sentiments upon it and to be furnished with every fact and material argument that can be produced to support the proposition.

I think it proper to acquaint you that I have been informed that Col. Goldthwait has been removed from his office of truckmaster by the Assembly, who have elected a man exceptionable in himself and more so from his connections with the opposers of government. It is said that you have consented to the election of this person but I hope such consent, if it should have been given, will not have the consequence to remove Col. Goldthwait from the command of Fort Pownall, as it is of great importance that it should not be in the possession of such as countenance an opposition to the authority of the King's government.

The King entirely approves of your having summoned the General Court to meet at Cambridge, but in case the meeting there should be attended with any such inconvenience as may make it advisable to hold it in some other place, His Majesty is pleased to leave it to your discretion to remove it to any other town in the province except Boston. *Draft.* [C.O.5/759, fo. 206]

LXIV

Lieut.-General Thomas Gage to Earl of Hillsborough (No. 47)

7 July, New York

My Lord, the anulling the Act, passed by the legislature of this province in their last sessions, for emitting bills of credit has caused a deficiency in the funds appropriated to the supply of the King's troops quartered here. Lieutenant-Governor Colden has given me notice of it by letter, of which I transmit a copy [Vol. I, No. 476i], wherein he gives me small encouragement to hope that the Assembly at their next meeting will make good any deficiencies. And indeed the supposition of the contrary is so very strong that nobody will advance the smallest sum to supply the troops with fuel. We know by experience what is paid by the Crown will never be refunded, but in order to prevail with the Assembly to pay the arrears that will arise from the deficiency of the funds provided, and that the troops may be supplied with firing, the officers for the present find their men with that article at the regulated allowance, and will present memorials to the governor to be repaid at the next sessions of the Assembly. This method is the only one that can be tried to throw the expense upon the province which they ought to defray, though the prospect of its succeeding is at present indifferent. Your lordship will however think it reasonable that the King's Barrack-Master General should repay the officers if the province refuses. He has always supplied the regiments at Boston for the like reason, and if any troops are to continue at Castle William the barracks there must be repaired before winter. A fever prevails in the regiment now quartered there, and it is well that the 29th Regiment was removed from the island before the hot weather began.

The Creeks and Choctaws being mutually tired of the war they have waged against each other for some years past are both desirous of peace, which is now negotiating through the mediation of Mr Stuart. The first overtures were made through his influence, and it is presumed will induce both those nations to look upon the English in a respectable and friendly light and be the means of cementing the union that has subsisted a long time, though too often interrupted by little accidents chiefly from the behaviour of our frontier people. The back inhabitants of Georgia have endangered the public tranquillity lately by a very unwarrantable and licentious conduct towards the Creeks, but Mr Stuart says the temper of that nation in general is very pacific and friendly, and Governor Wright is taking steps to punish some of the ringleaders in the riot.

The Creeks have made another visit to the Havana by means of the Spanish boats who fish upon the coasts of the peninsula of Florida. Mr Stuart complains of this fishery as it serves to keep up an intercourse between the Spaniards and the Indians which might be of bad consequence in case of a rupture with Spain. Governor Grant on the other hand thinks the fishery is beneficial, as it affords opportunities to our merchants of trading with the Havana.

Lieutenant-Governor Durnford is of opinion that the fort of Mobile is in so ruinous a state as not to be repaired under the expense of four or five thousand pounds, and therefore recommends the materials of the fort to be used (allowing the officers' square to stand for the detachment necessary for the town of Mobile) for the building of barracks, one to be erected on the Bay of Mobile for such a number of troops as shall be proper to defend the country about Mobile, and another within the stockaded fort of Pensacola, and that the remainder of the materials should be expended in making batteries and barracks on the Red Cliffs at the entrance of the Bay of Pensacola, building the barracks in general in such manner as to render all attempts from Indians fruitless. The lieutenant-governor proposes these measures as the best, unless strong forts were to be built, but nothing will be undertaken in consequence of the King's orders for the better defence of the province till the arrival of Brigadier-General Haldimand whose opinion concerning the best method of defending it, I observe in his last letters from St Augustine, agrees with the ideas of Mr Durnford. The engineer appointed for the province has left it, but Mr Durnford who is an engineer in the King's service will give all the assistance in his power.

Sir William Johnson has not yet held the congress so long in agitation though I expect the receipt of your lordship's last letter to him will bring it on; but he complains greatly of the want of Indian goods which at present are difficult to be had, and nothing of moment can be transacted with Indians without them. All was quiet on the Lakes as far as the Detroit on the 17th May; and no advices being received from the westward gives reason to hope no disturbance has been given in those quarters. The only report from the Detroit regards the bad condition of the vessels on Lake Erie, though I trust they may serve the next year, that there may be time sufficient to prepare well-seasoned timber before it becomes absolutely requisite to construct a new vessel for that lake.

The letter from your lordship to Lieutenant-Governor Hutchinson sent under my cover has been received by that gentleman, and I transmit your lordship extracts of two letters [Vol. I, No. 476ii] I have since received from him and of one [Vol. I, No. 476iii] from Lieutenant-Colonel Dalrymple. The event so much feared by the lieutenant-governor, and which he asks my opinion how to prevent, is too likely to happen; but I don't know on what foundation he has adopted the sentiment that troops might be of service, though no magistrate would interpose. When the troops first arrived indeed at Boston, the people were kept in some awe by them, but they soon discovered that troops were bound by constitutional laws and could only act under the authority and by the orders of the civil magistrates who were all of their side, and they recommenced their riots, though two or three regiments were in the town, with the same unbridled licentiousness as before. I have reminded Mr Hutchinson of this circumstance and told him I knew nothing could resist force but force, and I should be prepared to give him every aid and assistance he should require from me as well as to obey any commands the King shall judge it expedient to send me in the present posture of affairs. I have also hinted to him, should not measures more efficacious be adopted, the putting the prisoners on board one of His Majesty's ships of war, or the confining them at Castle William. The regiment quartered upon the island might ferry over in the night a strong detachment, who might march to Boston and receive the prisoners, and escort them to the Castle after their condemnation. Most people are of opinion they will be condemned, justly or unjustly, for that no jury will be found in Boston who will dare, though inclined to it, to give any other verdict. *Signed.* [C.O.5/88, fo. 109]

LXV

Lieut.-Governor Cadwallader Colden to Earl of Hillsborough (No. 12)

7 July, New York

My Lord, it gives me the greatest concern to learn from your lordship's letter [Vol. II, No. XXXIV] of the 14th of April, No. 38, that I had incurred His Majesty's displeasure by giving my assent to a bill for disqualifying the judges from sitting in Assembly. However necessary it appeared to me for preserving a good agreement between the branches of the legislature at a time when assiduous endeavours were making to produce discord, I should not have done it without a suspending clause till His Majesty's pleasure be known, had I not been confident that there would be no session of Assembly before there had been sufficient time to have His Majesty's pleasure known in this place, and that in the meantime it could produce no effect. For this purpose I transmitted an attested copy of the bill by the first opportunity before it could be engrossed as usual and the seal affixed. Had your lordship known in what manner some of the judges at several times have made use of their influence in elections, not for His Majesty's service but with interested views, and afterwards in supporting a party in the House, you would not wonder that the Assembly have it so much at heart to exclude them. I apprehend that unless the Assembly be gratified in this point it will remain a perpetual bone of contention between them and the governor. In my humble opinion the judges can be of more real use to the Crown by being disinterested in all party disputes, without which they cannot gain or preserve the general esteem of the people or their sentiments have that weight on the minds of the people which otherwise a judge of sufficient ability and known integrity must always have.

I had not the least suspicion of any prejudice to His Majesty's service from the meeting of commissioners of the neighbouring colonies for regulating the commerce with the Indians. The trade with the Indians from this province, Pennsylvania and Quebec is so much intermixed that no plan can be effectual without their mutual consent. Colonel Carleton embraced the proposal heartily and desired the meeting to be at New York. Pennsylvania seems more cool. I have since that time received a letter from Colonel Carleton signifying that the commissioners from Quebec cannot attend in the summer months, though we chose that time from an opinion that it would be most convenient for them, as travelling in the winter from Quebec is very difficult and often dangerous. I now suspect that the commissioners will not meet, or if they do they will not agree on any plan by reason of the different interests of the several colonies. Sir William Johnson is likewise of this opinion.

My lord, I flatter myself that from the good effects of the measures which the administration of government in this province has adopted that they will receive His Majesty's approbation and will excuse what otherwise might have been partly blamed. The principal inhabitants are now heartily united in favour of government with a resolution to suppress all riots and tumultuous meetings, and I am persuaded that if the same measures be pursued this province will be in tranquillity and good order.

Soon after it was known that the Parliament had repealed the duties on paper, glass etc., the merchants in this place wrote to Philadelphia that they might unitedly agree to a general importation of everything except tea. They at first received a favourable answer and their agreement to the proposal was not doubted; but soon after a letter was received at Philadelphia from a gentleman in England on whom the Quakers in that place repose the greatest confidence, advising them to persist in non-importation till every internal taxation was taken off. This changed the measures of Philadelphia, but the principal inhabitants of this place continue resolved to show their gratitude for the regard the Parliament has in removing the grievances they complained of. As there still remains a restless faction who from popular arguments, rancours and invectives, are endeavouring to excite riots and opposition among the lower class of people, a number of gentlemen went round the town to take the sentiments of individuals. I am told that 1,180, among which are the principal inhabitants, declared for importation, about 300 were neutral or unwilling to declare their sentiments, and a few of any distinction declared in opposition to it. I am informed likewise that the merchants of this place resolve to acquaint the merchants of Boston and Philadelphia with their inclinations to import. Having removed from the city to my house in the country, after the Earl of Dunmore's furniture arrived, that the governor's house may be fitted up for his reception, I am not sufficiently informed of the final resolution of the merchants but I believe they are resolved to import. Of this your lordship will be informed with certainty from the merchants in London, their correspondents. The packet's being ready to sail next morning obliges me to close my letter before I receive a perfect information of the resolution of the merchants.

The disorders in North America began while the administration of government was in my hands, while no governor in any of the colonies had sufficient authority to suppress them. I am happy that now while the administration is again in my hands the people of this province set an example to the other colonies of returning to their duty. All men of property are so sensible of their danger from riots and tumults that they will not rashly be induced to enter into combinations which may promote disorder for the future but will endeavour to promote a due subordination to legal authority.

From the different political and religious principles of the inhabitants, opposite parties have at all times and will exist in this province, which at different times have taken their denomination from some distinguished person or family which has appeared at their head; but you may be assured, my lord, that it is not in the power of any one family to distress the government while the administration is conducted with prudence, which often requires a compliance with popular humours.

I am so far advanced in years that it is most desirable to retire with the reputation of having gained, and if at the same time I can gain His Majesty's approbation I shall be very happy, for I have had His Majesty's service sincerely at heart. If I shall be so happy, I make no doubt of preserving your lordship's regard and am with the greatest respect and submission, my lord, your most obedient and faithful servant. *Signed*. PS. The Secretary informs that he sends by this packet all the minutes of Council to the 6th of June last which had not been formerly sent. [C.O.5/1101, fo. 78]

LXVI

Address of Council of West Florida to Earl of Hillsborough[1]

[9 July]
May it please your Lordship, we His Majesty's most dutiful and loyal

---

1   Enclosed in Durnford's letter to Hillsborough, 9 July 1770: Vol. I, No. 482.

subjects, the members of his Council for the province of West Florida, beg leave through your lordship to return His Majesty our most humble and sincere thanks for the additional force which he has been graciously pleased to order for our protection, and at the same time to assure your lordship that the inhabitants of this colony must ever retain a most lively sense of the gratitude which they owe to your lordship for the attention you have been pleased to show to their representations and the influence you have exerted in their favour.

The addition of one regiment to the few troops lately left for the protection of this frontier province and the removal again of the headquarters hither have given to this town and its neighbourhood such an appearance of strength in the eyes of the savages as will we trust secure us in future from their barbarities, but it is with much concern we acquaint your lordship that facts have evinced the justice of our apprehensions from the first removal of the troops from the forts on the River Mississippi where since that event so many ravages have been committed by the Indians that scarce any settlement hath escaped feeling the effects of their insolence, which nothing can prevent but the appearance of a military force there.

The importance of His Majesty's territory upon the River Mississippi, considered both with regard to the extreme fertility of the land and its advantageous situation for securing to Great Britain the extensive deerskin and fur-trade which has been long carried on by the French, are such as we humbly conceive cannot be too earnestly recommended to government. Many persons of character and fortune from the back parts of Virginia and other Northern Colonies where the lands are worn out or are remote from water-carriage have lately viewed that part of the province and have given the strongest assurances that numerous families of skill and abilities in planting would immediately remove thither, could they have proper assurances of protection from government, in so much that his honour the lieutenant-governor, at the request of a gentleman of some consequence lately deputed by his neighbours in the back parts of Virginia upon that errand, hath been pleased to order in Council that a large tract of land be reserved upon that river sufficient for the settlement of two thousand inhabitants which the petitioner engages to settle in one year provided he can depend upon protection, and this we presume would not be long requisite as such numbers soon after their establishment might be able to defend themselves.

With regard to our commercial interest, we humbly conceive the re-establishment of Fort Bute would have the most salutary effects in securing to His Majesty's subjects, who would be thereby induced to settle in that neighbourhood, the very extensive trade of deerskins and furs hitherto carried on by the French whose prohibition from further traffic must necessarily cause a large consumption of British manufactures, were traders secure in their lives and property.

We beg leave to represent to your lordship that a congress hath been long expected by the Indians, it having been promised to them by the late Governor Johnstone and the Superintendent of Indian Affairs at the expiration of three years from the last that was held. They continually reproach us with this breach of promise which prevents the Creeks from enlarging His Majesty's territory near the town of Pensacola, where it is evidently too much confined, and serves them for an excuse for the many infractions of treaty they have lately been guilty of.

When the last General Assembly for this province met, upon being acquainted by his honour the lieutenant-governor that His Majesty had been pleased to entrust the regulation of the Indian trade to the legislature of each province, we did our utmost to frame such a bill as might answer the purposes of that lucrative and extensive branch of commerce, as well as of equity towards the Indians; but we are sorry to observe that all our efforts must remain ineffectual for want of means to put the law in execution, which can only be compassed by commissaries resident upon the spot who might in a great measure prevent the Indians from their present frequent custom of visiting Pensacola and Mobile upon frivolous pretences merely to obtain presents, check the lawless behaviour of the hireling traders, and if not totally prevent any improper connections being formed between different tribes of Indians, at least be the cause of procuring the earliest intelligence of their intentions towards us, should they be inclined to act violently. The Indians best disposed to our interest complain of the want of such persons and are themselves sensible that it would be of general advantage to have them resident amongst them, but as this is an expense which we are wholly incapable of defraying we must humbly entreat your lordship to use your influence in procuring a sum sufficient for that purpose to be added to the usual supplies for this province. And we must in this place observe to your lordship that there is the most urgent necessity that a boundary line should be drawn between this and the neighbouring colonies that each trader may be restricted to the laws which may prevail in the territory he trades in; otherwise no regulations can be effectual.

We most earnestly request that your lordship will be pleased to use your good offices to procure for the inhabitants of the town of Pensacola a sum sufficient for building a church, for want of which His Majesty's most gracious intentions in appointing a clergyman of the established Church are in a great measure defeated, as not one-third of the people can be held in the largest house that can be had here. As we have the firmest reliance upon your lordship's disposition to render services to these countries under your immediate protection, so we flatter ourselves that these, our most urgent wants, will not be disregarded, and we can truly assure your lordship that we have suppressed many of less weight rather than be thought importunate with His Majesty or troublesome to your lordship. *Signed*, William Clifton, James Bruce, David Hodge, James Jones, William Godley, Phillips Comyn. [C.O.5/587, p. 377]

LXVII

Lieut.-General Thomas Gage to Earl of Hillsborough (No. 48)

10 July, New York

My Lord, overtures have been making for some weeks past by the traders of this city and those of Boston and Philadelphia to break their association against importing, but without determining anything. At length the merchants of New York resolved to import, and application was made to me to use my influence with Mr Colden, the postmaster, to detain the packet two or three days, that time might be given them to write for goods. I was glad to give every assistance in promoting so desirable a measure, and the packet that was to have sailed on the 8th inst. is detained till tomorrow.

They agree to import everything but tea, though glass, painter's colours etc. are not to be imported till after Christmas, when the Act for laying duties on those articles expires. *Signed.* [C.O.5/88, fo. 120]

LXVIII

Lieut.-Governor Cadwallader Colden to Earl of Hillsborough (No. 13)

10 July, New York

My Lord, the faction in opposition to importation from Great Britain having last week attempted by every method in their power by riots, clamour and threats to deter the merchants in this place from agreeing to import without the concurrence of Philadelphia and Boston, the merchants were desirous to know the sense of the inhabitants with certainty in a matter of so great consequence and after my last of the 7th instant was wrote desired to have the packet detained a few days which was accordingly done to the Wednesday following. Persons on both sides of the question were appointed to go from house to house to collect the sentiments of the inhabitants. I am informed that a great majority declared for importing and consequently I make no doubt the merchants send their orders for importing by this packet. This is of so great importance that I think it my duty to give your lordship the earliest notice of it. It must be agreeable to you as it will give a favourable impression to His Majesty of his subjects in this province. It gives me great pleasure to have it accomplished while the administration is in the hands of, my lord, your most obedient and faithful servant. *Signed.* PS. I enclose your lordship a printed advertisement [Vol. I, No. 486i] which has just come to my hands. [C.O.5/1101, fo. 80]

LXIX

Alexander Colden to Anthony Todd[1]

11 July, G.P.O. New York

Sir, a day or two before the *Duke of Cumberland* packet boat sailed, the principal and most numerous of the merchants of this city had a meeting and came to a resolution that proper persons should go through the several wards of the city with two subscriptions, the one for non-importation, the other for importation, in order to collect the sentiments not only of the merchants but of the mechanics and every inhabitant relative to importing goods from Great Britain as formerly.

At that time it plainly appeared by the lists a great majority was for

---

1   Enclosed in Todd's letter to John Pownall, 3 September 1770: Vol. I, No. 585.

importing, upon which the committee of merchants dispatched expresses to Philadelphia and Boston, informing the merchants at these places the sentiments of this city. At this time it was known the generality of the merchants of Philadelphia inclined to break through the non-importation agreement, but before the express reached Philadelphia a letter was published in the Philadelphia papers from a gentleman in London on whose opinion and advice it's said the Quakers and those in their interest entirely rely, the purport of which letter was advising the Philadelphians by all means to abide by their non-importation agreement as the only means of obtaining full redress from the grievances they complained of. This made the Philadelphians change their sentiments and resolve to abide by their agreement. You will see the committee of merchants at New York, Letters to the Merchants at Philadelphia and Boston, published in the papers and also the above letter from London and the merchants' answers to our committee's letter. The answers from Philadelphia and Boston did not discourage the principal and most thinking merchants amongst us from pursuing their scheme, not doubting they should soon bring about a general consent in this city to break through the non-importation agreement, being sensible many families must starve if an importation of goods from Great Britain did not soon take place, for many could not subsist their families, especially the mechanics, unless we imported sundries of which we at present stand in absolute need of and can't get elsewhere. This would have been effected some weeks ago had it not been for the opposition of a small, inconsiderable, noisy, blustering faction whose whole aim is to keep the country in confusion in order to answer their purposes and keep up a popularity which by vile means they have obtained among the lower class of the mechanics and inhabitants, well knowing should an importation take place they would lose that popularity, be disregarded by every honest man and well-wisher to his country, and sink into their former state of being despised and perhaps treated (as they justly deserve) as enemies to their country. Notwithstanding the principal gentlemen and merchants have been at great pains to show the unreasonableness of abiding by the non-importation agreement (after the legislature of Great Britain had been graciously pleased to repeal the Act relative to laying duties on sundry articles, except that on tea, and how much it would redound to the honour of this province immediately to show their gratitude for this favour by ordering all kinds of goods from home on which there was no duty to be paid in America) things remained in a fluctuating state till last Friday evening, the night before the mail by the Halifax packet was to be closed, a number of merchants met at a tavern and then agreed at all events to send their orders by the packet to send them goods as usual, except tea. The faction being informed of this resolution published an inflammatory anonymous advertisement the next morning desiring all the inhabitants to meet that day at 12 o'clock at the City-hall where the faction and their cabal, such as they were, met accordingly: amongst the number and the principal of them was one Isaac Sears (who you will find often mentioned of late in our papers), Captain McDougald, the American Wilkes, and some others of the same kidney. Every merchant of any note met at the same time at the coffee-house, and a number of other gentlemen.. The cabal at the City-hall proposed an opposition to importation and as I have been informed (whether true or not I don't presume to say but do not doubt it) Isaac Sears publicly declared if any merchant or number of merchants presumed to break through the non-importation agreement till the several provinces had agreed to do the same, he would lose his life in the attempt, or the goods imported should be burnt as soon as landed, and strenuously advised that every measure in the power of that faction should be attempted to frustrate the resolutions taken or to be took by the gentlemen and merchants for bringing about an importation.

The merchants met at the coffee-house resolved to use their best endeavours to bring it to pass, and resolved that persons of note should again be sent through the several wards to take the sense of all the inhabitants on this subject in general, and made not the least doubt but by far the greatest number would be for importation. This being agreed to only about 1 o'clock last Saturday, and the mail was to close at twelve that night, it would be impracticable to know the result time enough to send the necessary order to their correspondents for goods by this packet, which they were very desirous to do as early as possible; wherefore they appointed a committee of their body to wait on me desiring me to detain the packet for two or three days, which I told them I could not possibly do without breaking through my instructions. They then sent to the lieut.-governor who was out of town at his country-seat about 17 miles off and sent some of the committee to the General requesting the packet might be detained. Upon their application to the lieut.-governor and to General Gage, they wrote me the following letters.

July 7th 1770

Sir,
It is for His Majesty's service that the packet be detained till Wednesday next which you are desired to do accordingly.

Cadwallader Colden

To Alex. Colden Esq.,
Agents for the Packets.

New York, July 7th 1770

Sir,
Application having been made to me that the packet might be detained for two or three days in order to give time to the merchants of this place to make out orders to their correspondents at home for such British merchandise as they shall severally want, being on the point of breaking the non-importation agreement, I am therefore to desire that you will detain her accordingly.

I am etc.
Thos. Gage.

Alex. Colden Esq.,
Agent for the Packets.

Upon receipt of these letters, joined with the application the merchants made to myself, I agreed to detain the packet till this day, not doubting but I should have the happiness of their lordships the Postmaster-General's approbation for so doing, and immediately advertised that the packet was detained and to sail this day. I am now closing the mail and the packet will sail as soon as the tide permits.

Mr James Parker, Secretary and Comptroller.to the General Post Office for this district, died a few days since. This must cause some new appointments in the American General Post Office; if any which may be more honourable or profitable than the one I now enjoy as Postmaster in this city, I hope you will not forget me. *Copy.* [C.O.5/1101, fo. 85]

LXX

John Stuart to Governor Lord Botetourt[1]

12 July, Charleston

My Lord, on the 10th current in the evening I was honoured with your excellency's letter [Vol. I, No. 505v] of 21st ultimate, desiring me immediately to enter upon a treaty with the Cherokees in order to obtain as soon as possible for the dominion of Virginia a cession of those lands pointed out in His Majesty's instructions to me.

On the 11th in the morning I sent off an express to Mr Carson my deputy with the necessary directions of convening the Cherokee chiefs on the 5th of October at Lochaber 250 miles from Charleston and about 45 miles from Keowee in the lower Cherokee settlements.

It will be impossible to prevail with the Indians after the above-mentioned time to come to any meeting as it will interfere with their hunting which they chiefly depend upon.

I send enclosed a list of goods which I think absolutely necessary with the Charleston prices to which is added an account of the other unavoidable expenses which will attend the negotiation, the whole amounting to £20,194 2s. 6d. this currency, which at the common calculation of seven pounds for one sterling is equal to £2,884 17s. 6d. sterling.

The non-importing resolutions of the merchants and inhabitants have rendered Indian trading goods scarce. I thought myself extremely fortunate in being able to secure the goods contained in the enclosed estimate at the prices therein mentioned which are about 42 per cent. advance on the prime cost in England. I shall without loss of time hire wagons at the cheapest rate and beg your lordship will be assured that the whole shall be conducted with the strictest economy and that I will be as cautious of incurring unnecessary expenses as if I were laying out my own money.

The enclosed estimate exceeds what my idea of the expenses was when I wrote your lordship that £2,500 would be sufficient but the great delay on the part of Virginia has considerably altered circum-

1 Enclosed in Botetourt's letter to Hillsborough, 10 August 1770: Vol. I, No. 562.

stances. The Cherokees are not in the same temper they were at that time; they have since been solicited by the southern and northern tribes to enter into confederacies against our encroachments. The uneasiness they expressed at being kept in suspense with regard to your boundary line occasioned my meeting them in the spring which cost a considerable sum of money.

I think it will be necessary that your lordship empower me to draw upon London for the expense of the negotiation, except about three hundred pounds sterling which, if possible, I beg to have sent me in gold as it is extremely difficult to get cash for bills without allowing a discount of 5 to 3 per cent, which I presume would not be agreeable. Of this I beg to be informed by your lordship as soon as convenient, as I mean to be extremely punctual with the Indians.

Your lordship will be pleased to observe that the expense of marking the line after obtaining a cession of the land is not included in the estimate. The advanced season of the year will render it impossible to undertake that service before April. My deputy and interpreter with the Indians commissioned by their nation for that purpose will then attend and meet your lordship's surveyor and commissioner at any appointed place. The expense of provisions etc. attending this particular service will be defrayed by Virginia as has been done in all other provinces, an estimate of which will be better made in your lordship's province than by me.

If your lordship will be pleased to send a gentleman of your confidence to be present at and witness to the transactions of the congress it will probably give great satisfaction to your House of Burgesses as well as to me. *Copy.* [C.O.5/1348, fo. 135]

LXXI

Thomas Walpole to Earl of Hillsborough

16 July, London

My Lord, I take the liberty of troubling your lordship again by letter relative to the application I am concerned in for a grant of lands in America because I think this method the most likely to save your lordship's time and my own.

The last time I had the honour of appearing before your lordship at the Board of Trade, you was pleased to acquaint me with the difficulty of assembling a full Board without which nothing could be determined in my business, and that your lordship's Board would adjourn in a fortnight, so that unless I could prevail on the other Lords to meet within that time no report could be made to the Council.

I was then, as I still am, at a loss to express my surprise at an event which delays for an unlimited time a business which has been so long before your lordship, which you was pleased to think of much importance, and which by our agreement with the Treasury upon it has received no small encouragement.

An apprehension that your lordship is averse to the proposal would determine me not to prosecute it any further, if I was not convinced the fitness or unfitness of the grant stands entirely upon public grounds, and as the solicitors for it are desirous to meet that argument I should do them as well as your lordship injustice if I did not make use of every means in my power to induce government to come to some decision upon it.

I can add nothing to the letter addressed to your lordship in particular by Mr Wharton to prove that the principal object of government by the Treaty of Fort Stanwix was to give peace and security to the rest of the colonies, that the best means to complete this desirable end would be by settling the country ceded to His Majesty under a proper government, and that such settlement would be of the greatest utility to this country.

But, my lord, I shall beg leave to refer you to the enclosed paper [Vol. I, No. 503i] to show that the constant policy of this country has been to encourage settlements over the Allighany Mountains, that the Virginians have been availing themselves of this liberal spirit in government to their own emolument without regard to His Majesty's or the public interest, and that these lands which are now indisputably in the government are become more liable to the private depredations of the Virginians and other borderers; for grants and settlements such as are procured without the least prospect of advantage to the King and this country cannot deserve any other appellation, and unless some immediate stop is put to this growing devastation of the public stock the country will soon be garbled to the private benefit merely of a few individuals.

Permit me to say, my lord, the gentlemen with whom I have the honour to be concerned seem to have proposed the only remedy for this evil by offering to purchase the lands and obliging themselves to the settlement of the country under a legal government to be supported at their own expense, which surely is the best security that can be given of the sincerity of their intentions, and I believe the only instance for many years back of any public spirit accompanying the application for lands in America.

It will well bear the canvas against those enormous grants which have been made to others for no pecuniary consideration, or such as are perhaps now making in Virginia under the sanction of encouragement given from hence.

One other observation, my lord, occurs to me, that it has been said the settlement of these lands on the Ohio will prevent that of the Northern Colonies where large tracts of land are vacant and governments are already established. This is an objection in nature which no human policy can remedy whilst there is opportunity of settling in a more favoured climate. When this shall be full, it will extend north and south, and the variety of produce will gradually form connection to link the whole together. The sooner therefore the Middle Colonies are settled, the extremities will be benefited.

I ask pardon for detaining your lordship so long, hoping however to have shown the pressing necessity of coming to some resolution with respect to the lands situated betwixt the River Ohio and the Alleghany Mountains. A delay beyond the present season will increase the difficulties infinitely. The application I am concerned in having alarmed all those who are interested in defeating it, they may avail themselves of a long delay in a manner to oblige me and the rest of my associates to drop all further prosecution of this matter, notwithstanding our agreement with the Treasury, as that cannot be supposed to stand out against us if the circumstances of the country should vary from those under which we made our proposal whilst we have neglected nothing on our parts for carrying it into effect and are now soliciting your lordship for a speedy report upon it. *Signed.* [C.O.5/1332, fo. 194]

LXXII

Resolutions of Inhabitants of Philadelphia[1]

19 July, Philadelphia

The news being spread that the merchants of New York had departed from their non-importation agreement and had resolved to import everything except tea and such articles upon which a duty is or should hereafter be laid, the inhabitants of this city and suburbs and a great number from the county assembled at the State House, and having nominated Joseph Fox, Esquire, chairman, entered into the following resolves, vizt.

1st. That the non-importation agreement entered into by the merchants and traders of the colonies is a safe, peaceable and constitutional way of asserting our rights, and if persisted in there is reason to believe it will produce the desired effect and therefore ought to be considered as a bulwark of our liberty.

2nd. That the good effects of this measure depend upon perseverance and that the strength of the colonies consists in their union.

3rd. That a breach of the agreement at present cannot be owing to any want of real necessaries, especially in the northern colonies, and that the partial repeal [of] the American Revenue Act is no just foundation for deviating from the agreement entered into, as the claim of right to tax us without our consent is still kept up and the duty on tea retained as a test of that right.

4th. That the alteration adopted by a majority of the inhabitants of the city of New York is a sordid and wanton defection from the common cause and that by that defection they have as much as in them lies weakened the union of the colonies, wounded the public character of America, strengthened the hands of our enemies and encouraged them to prosecute their designs against our common liberty.

5th. That all the bad consequences that may ensue to the liberties of America by their defection are chargeable upon a prevailing faction at New York.

6th. That as a testimony to the world of our disapprobation of the late measure adopted by that prevailing faction, we will break off all commercial intercourse with New York so far as not to purchase of any of the inhabitants of the colony of New York any goods except alkaline

1   Enclosed in Deputy Governor Penn's letter to Hillsborough, 5 September 1770: Vol. II, No. LXXXIX.

salts, skins, furs, flax and hemp, until they return to their agreement or until the Act of the 7th of George the third is totally repealed. And we pledge ourselves each to the other that if we know of any person attempting to bring into this city or province any goods from New York except those above enumerated that we will immediately give information of them to the merchants' committee that their names may be published in the newspapers. Provided always that every inhabitant of this town and province who has effects at New York may have liberty to remove them from thence, provided it be done within six weeks from this date. *Copy.* [C.O.5/1283, fo. 11]

LXXIII

Commissioners for Trade and Plantations to Governor Lord Botetourt

20 July, Whitehall

My Lord, the enclosed papers will fully inform your lordship of an application made by several persons of wealth and consideration in this kingdom for a grant on the ground of purchase of a part of the lands ceded to His Majesty by the Six Nations of Indians and their allies and confederates at the Treaty at Fort Stanwix in 1768, and of the proceedings which have been had in the different departments of government upon that application.

Your lordship will also observe that this business is now before us for our report thereupon, but as it appears to us, abstracted from other considerations of general policy and public utility, that the colony of Virginia has such an interest in the lands in question as that it ought in justice to be acquainted with what is proposed before any final resolution is taken, and as the information relative to the acts and proceedings of the Governor and Council of Virginia, as stated in the paper [Vol. I, No. 503i] No. 9, is of a very extraordinary nature, and the facts if true have a material relation to the proposal under consideration, we thought fit to come to the resolutions contained in our minutes of the 18th instant.

These minutes will point out to your lordship very explicitly the informations we wish to receive relative to the state of the country in question before any further steps are taken; and as we conceive this to be a matter of the greatest importance we trust that the return that your lordship will be pleased to make will be as full and particular as may be, and that we shall receive every light and information from your lordship that you think may be useful and necessary in this great consideration, both at this board and in those departments of government which are finally to decide upon the proposal referred to. *Entry.* *Signatories*, Hillsborough, Edward Eliot, William Fitzherbert, Greville, Robert Spencer. [C.O.5/1369, p. 34]

LXXIV

Governor James Wright to Earl of Hillsborough (No. 46)

20 July, Savannah

My Lord, the last [Vol. I, No. 369] I had the honour to write your lordship was of the 28th of May, No. 45, by Mr. McGillivray who I took the liberty of introducing to your lordship as a gentleman perfectly well acquainted with our Indians and Indian affairs in every respect and one on whose information your lordship may entirely rely.

Since his departure I have been successful enough to put an end to all the present disputes between the Indians and the back-settlers, and those Indians who had been ill-treated by some of our lawless bad people have declared themselves entirely satisfied and reconciled. But, my lord, I have received very good intelligence that a party of the Creek chiefs are gone to Mobile to meet a party of the Choctaws in order to ratify the peace lately agreed upon between those nations. This, my lord, is a circumstance that I'm afraid will be attended with bad consequences to His Majesty's subjects here, for as the Indians will now have nothing to amuse themselves with and as they are a people who cannot rest or be satisfied long without having their hands imbued in blood, it's highly probable they will pick a quarrel with us, and in the weak and defenceless condition we are at present this very nursling province may be ruined as I suppose by far the greatest part of the plantations would be broke up and destroyed. But there is one thing, my lord, which has occurred to me that I think would be of infinite service and probably continue these southern provinces in peace with the Indians till we may be strong enough to defend ourselves, that is, my lord, if I were authorised to endeavour to prevail on some of them to take a voyage to England. I don't know, my lord, whether I might be able to prevail on them to do it or not, but I am persuaded if one head-man from the Upper Creeks and one from the Lower Creeks with their attendants, who I suppose might be to the amount of 10 or 12 in the whole, were to go the immense grandeur of everything they would see there with the innumerable crowds of people would have a much greater and better effect upon them than ten times the money it would cost the government would have if laid out in presents and sent here for them. It would be a security to us while they are gone, and when they come back the accounts they will give their countrymen will strike them with wonder and amazement and have the best effect possible. As this is a measure which will be attended with an expense, I would not presume to carry it into execution or even mention it to the Indians without orders. I know the province is not able to bear the expense, were I to propose it to the legislature. If this should be thought expedient, my lord, the next spring will be the proper time for them to embark but I presume they will require six months notice to prepare, if they should agree to go, so that there is no time to lose in notifying it to me in case the proposition is approved of.

My lord, I think it my duty to transmit the enclosed Carolina newspaper [Vol. I, No. 53liv]. Such a general illegal combination, my lord, such a declaration by the people or mob to usurp powers of that kind into their own hands, such a confederacy to destroy all true liberty and deprive a part of His Majesty's subjects of his protection and the enjoyment of the laws of their country and of their natural and real rights as British subjects, I believe was never known or heard of in any part of the British dominions till in the spring 1766, as appears by the enclosed paper [Vol. I, No. 531i] and also now, both times in Charleston, South Carolina; and all this, my lord, suffered without any the least attempt to check it, not so much as by issuing a proclamation against unlawful combinations and confederacies or showing any kind of disapprobation whatever. At least I am informed so from thence, and nothing has yet appeared in print. These things, my lord, have been in agitation some time, and I have had accounts of it and am very sensible of the bad effect it has with many people here. Can it be said, my lord, that either law or government operate in South Carolina? Can it be said that liberty or property is safe there when the very people who call themselves Sons of Liberty and protectors of the rights and liberties of the people have the insolence to resolve to deprive them of both? Pardon me, my lord, but surely these things are not to be suffered. Indeed, my lord, it's throwing too much upon a man's shoulders who endeavours to do his duty and keep things in some kind of order; they are enough to inflame a whole province where there is any tincture of the same spirit and to set them against any governor who will not suffer them to assume illegal powers etc. as far as he can prevent it, and under these difficulties and embarrassments, my lord, did I labour during the whole time of the continuance of the Stamp Act when the people in Carolina did just what they pleased and without any kind of check. These things happening, my lord, with some others and the season of the year advancing apace, I believe I shall be obliged to delay going to England till the next spring.

My lord, I sometime ago mentioned Mr Stokes, the Chief Justice, to be of the Council. This will really be necessary, my lord, for there is not a man of any knowledge in the law at the Council Board (except Mr Jones who I believe does not pretend to a great deal) and I could wish to see Mr Stokes there early in the next winter, by which time I should presume his mandamus might be here. I take him to be a gentleman of knowledge and of great probity and one who does and will discharge his duty and acquit himself on the bench with reputation.

A weak infatuated grand jury, influenced and imposed upon by two or three of their own body who were drawn in and set on by one of the three factious Assemblymen mentioned in a former letter (but who is since dead) made the enclosed strange, groundless and false presentments [Vol. I, No. 531iii], from which and the animadversions thereon your lordship will see how far people will go, even without a foundation to endeavour to slander and raise a prejudice against those who they know will do everything they possibly can to do justice and keep 'em within due bounds. *Signed.* PS. By letters from Charleston of 15 inst. just this moment received, it is confirmed that resolutions are to be entered into relative to the West India islands as mentioned in the paper [Vol. I, No. 531vi] of the 5th July. How far may not these people go, or where stop, my lord? PS. [*in duplicate*] The several papers mentioned were enclosed with the original letter, and the paper now sent is to show your lordship that they have actually compelled a Rhode Island vessel to return and would not suffer the captain to trade. [C.O.5/660, fo. 116]

LXXV

Lieut.-Governor Thomas Hutchinson to Earl of Hillsborough
(No. 20, duplicate)

26 July, Boston

My Lord, the New Yorkers having agreed to an importation of all goods except tea, which they have no occasion for from England, their Dutch trade being under no restraint, our combiners seem to be distressed. If the town was a corporation as New York is, I have no doubt the magistrates would know the minds of the inhabitants in the same way as the Mayor and Aldermen of that city discovered the minds of the people there; but the selectmen of Boston are the creatures of the populace and would be deterred from any measure contrary to the minds of the populace if they were of different sentiments themselves. It is owing to this that the lowest class of the people still have the rule in Boston, a few merchants countenancing and encouraging them. If Philadelphia should follow the example of New York, I think Boston will hold out no longer. If it should not, I doubt whether there is firmness enough in the merchants to oppose the populace. Tea will be excepted. There will not be a pound less imported but it will come from Holland instead of England.

I met the Assembly yesterday at Cambridge. I shall enclose the speech [Vol. I, No. 537i] I made to them. If they will not go to business I must prorogue them further and give myself no concern about them. Their constituents are the only sufferers and when they feel their sufferings to a little degree beyond what they do at present, I think they will in many towns express their dissatisfaction with the behaviour of their Representatives. In the meantime I shall treat them with moderation but firmness. I am very sure if the members of Boston were out of the House I should have a majority in favour of government. *Signed.* [C.O.5/759, fo. 251]

LXXVI

Earl of Hillsborough to Lieut.-General Thomas Gage (No. 32)

31 July, Whitehall

Sir, as there is not at present anything relative to His Majesty's service under your direction that requires any particular instructions, I shall confine this letter to such observations as have occurred to me upon a mature consideration of the state of the British possessions on the River Mississippi.

The commercial advantages which may be derived from these possessions and the near relation they bear to the safety and security of His Majesty's North American dominions in general render them an object deserving the most serious attention, but the great difficulty lies in suggesting any proper plan for the improvement of them to these ends that will not either be attended with an expense too heavy for the state to bear or otherwise liable to very great objections.

It is evident that unless the inhabitants of Louisiana are prevented from intruding upon the British territory and from the dangerous communication with the savages under the King's protection, which is the consequence of that intrusion, neither the commerce nor the dominion of the country will be secured, and it is at the same time but too obvious that Fort Chartres cannot from its situation have that effect. In fact that post appears to me little better than a mere mark of possession and a monument of the unhappy fate of the many brave men who have fallen a sacrifice to those fatal diseases which are the consequences of the unwholesomeness of the spot in which it is placed.

Establishments in those situations near the mouths of the Ohio and Illinois Rivers, which command these two great channels of communication, accompanied with proper restrictions both as to the times and places at which the peltry-trade should be carried on, would doubtless have the consequence at least in a great degree both to establish the dominion and secure the commerce of that vast country which lies between the Mississippi and His Majesty's American colonies on the side of the Atlantic; and if it consisted with just principles of commercial policy in reference to the true interests of this kingdom to allow in those establishments a certain degree of colonisation, the military part of them might at first be formed upon a narrower scale than would otherwise be necessary and might after some time be wholly withdrawn; but as in a consideration of this nature expense must and ought to have, from the circumstances of the state, a great weight in the scale of deliberation on the one hand, so on the other hand the seeking to avoid that expense by substituting a system erroneous in its principles and prejudicial in its consequences would be highly blameable; and though the idea of colonisation in the Illinois country is very favourable in the economical view of it, yet there are many and great objections to it, not only in a general light but also from the effect it may have in respect to that peculiar commerce which is a principal object of the measure in contemplation.

The great and solid advantages arising to the commerce and navigation of this kingdom from its North American colonies depend principally upon giving proper encouragement to the fishery, to the production of naval stores, and to the supply of the Sugar Islands with lumber and provisions.

A very great part of the sea coast and islands in North America on the side of the Atlantic (where alone these branches of commerce can be cultivated and improved) remains unsettled, and therefore in the abstract consideration of colonisation, I cannot conceive that it can ever be sound policy in this kingdom to allow settlements in places where, though the mildness of the climate and the fertility of the soil may invite colonists, yet none of the above mentioned great national objects are attainable and consequently settlement cannot be of that commercial benefit to the state which it would be of in the other places.

Many other arguments against colonies in remote situations might be drawn from the manifest difficulty that would attend the keeping such colonies in a just subordination to and dependence upon this kingdom, but I am persuaded they will occur more forcibly to you than I shall be able to state them, and therefore I will proceed to mention those objections which I think lie against colonies in the

Illinois with a view to the peltry-trade, which is the peculiar commerce of that country.

This commerce cannot (I apprehend) be useful to Great Britain otherwise than as it furnishes a material of her manufactures, but will on the contrary be prejudicial to her in proportion as other countries obtain that material from us without its coming here first; and whilst New Orleans is the only port for exportation of what goes down the Mississippi no one will believe that that town will not be the market for peltry or that those restrictions which are intended to secure the exportation of that commodity directly to Great Britain can have any effect under such circumstances.

Those who argue in support of the advantage of an exportation of peltry by the channel of the Mississippi have sometimes, in answer to this objection, urged the practicability of a passage into the ocean by the Ibberville; but as it has been represented that the bed of that canal may for a great part of the year be passed dry-shod, that it is many feet above the bed of the Mississippi, that it is only rendered navigable for boats by the waste water of that river when the floods come down, and that the passage even at such times is frequently obstructed by trees and logs which have been borne down by the torrent, it is evident that if that should be the case that river never can be used to the purposes of the commerce I am speaking of: in fact it never has been used for that purpose since we have been in possession of it.

I have indeed been informed by Captain Pittman and others who have surveyed the Ibberville that by cutting a channel of a certain depth from the Mississippi to a part of it where there is always water for canoes, and which is stated to be but a small distance, and by widening what remains of it from thence to its confluence with the River Amité (in which operation the force of the current through the supposed cut would greatly assist) the navigation might be rendered practicable. If this can be done for a small expense, so as to make a free passage from the Mississippi to the Gulf of Mexico by the Lakes, it would certainly have some weight against the difficulties and objections which I have stated, and therefore I should be glad to have your thoughts on that subject from the information which you may have received.

In the meantime, from what I have said, you will see that though I am fully aware of the propriety of some possession on the Mississippi that should have the effect to secure the commerce and mark the dominion of the country which belongs to His Majesty on the east side of it, yet nevertheless the only two methods of attaining this object are each of them accompanied with such objections as leave my judgement in a state of perplexity I am not able to get over.

Forts and military establishments at the mouths of the Ohio and Illinois Rivers, admitting that they would be effectual to the attainment of the objects in view, would yet I fear be attended with an expense to this kingdom greatly disproportionate to the advantages proposed to be gained, and those objections to civil establishments which I have above stated do weigh so strongly against that measure in the scale both of general and local policy as greatly to discourage that idea.

Under this dilemma I have taken the liberty to impart to you my thoughts upon the subject, trusting that from your knowledge of it, founded on facts and materials which I am not able to come at the possession of, you will have it in your power either to furnish me with such explanation as shall remove the difficulties and doubts I am under or to suggest some other plan not liable to the same objections.

If no such other plan can be suggested it will be of the greatest use and satisfaction to me to have your opinion as fully as possible both upon the idea of military establishments and that of colonies, and whether in case the former should be adopted some method may not be fallen upon so to regulate the peltry-trade as that the produce of the Ohio and Illinois countries may be brought to this kingdom either through the channel of Quebec or that of Pennsylvania or New York. *Draft.* [C.O.5/88, fo. 100]

LXXVII

Earl of Hillsborough to Governor Lord Botetourt (No. 35)

31 July, Whitehall
My Lord, the papers which your lordship will receive by this conveyance from the Board of Trade will fully inform your lordship of what has passed upon the application of Mr Walpole and others for a grant of lands between the Ohio and the Allegany Mountains, with the view to the forming a new government in that country; and I am to acquaint your lordship that in consequence of what is recommended by that Board in their minute of the 18th instant, I am ordered by the King to signify to you His Majesty's commands that the Governor and Council of his colony of Virginia do desist from making any further grants of lands beyond the limits described in the proclamation of the 7th of October 1763 until His Majesty's further pleasure is signified. *Draft.* [C.O.5/1348, fo. 112]

LXXVIII

Earl of Hillsborough to Lieut.-Governor Thomas Hutchinson (No. 39)

31 July, Whitehall
Sir, your dispatches [Vol. II, No. L; Vol. I, No. 392] Nos. 15 and 16 have been received and laid before the King, and I am commanded to signify to you His Majesty's approbation of your conduct not only in the measures you pursued for improving the circumstances that appeared favourable for putting an end to the Associations against importing goods from Great Britain but also in the moderation and prudence you showed in the exercise of your negative voice on the election of a new Council.

It is plain from what passed on the advices from Pennsylvania of the disposition in that province to discontinue their Associations that the more sober and considerate merchants of Boston wish to get rid of the fetters which by their own imprudence they have forged for themselves, and I have no doubt that these unwarrantable combinations to distress the British commerce in general would long ago

have been at an end had they not been encouraged by the correspondence of ill-designing men on this side the water.

I collect from many of the late transactions at Boston that great
pains are taken by some persons to excite the people to violence; and
the use which may be made by these desperate men of the distress which
the Associations have brought upon that town is a circumstance in the
present state of the province that cannot be too closely attended to.

Every letter which has been received from Boston and communicated
to me since the advice given to His Majesty by his Privy Council
respecting the state of his province of Massachusetts Bay furnishes
additional proof of the rectitude as well as the necessity of the measures
which they have recommended. The refusal of the Council and House
of Representatives to do any business unless they are assembled at
Boston is an act that appears to me irreconcilable with both the letter
and spirit of the constitution of the government of Massachusetts Bay
and is as injurious to the rights and privileges of the people they
represent, as it is inconsistent with the just authority of the Crown to
direct the governor by instruction in the exercise of those discretionary
powers vested in him by the charter and by his commission, and therefore this is a circumstance which among many others shows the necessity for an interposition of the authority of Parliament. In the meantime
my letter of the 6th instant will remove all doubt you might otherwise
have had in respect to the conduct you are to observe on this occasion
and renders any further instruction altogether unnecessary.

The gaining further time in the case of Captain Preston and the
other unhappy persons involved with him in the same misfortune is
of the greatest importance to them, and I trust that before the time of
trial comes every prejudice will give way to truth, candour and justice.
Draft. [C.O.5/759, fo. 222]

LXXIX

Emistisiguo to Charles Stuart[1]

[?July-August]
We have sent you a belt of whampum which is all one as a letter in our
way, and we look upon you to be a brother and a friend and that you
will act for us as if we were present. This black ring on the one end
resembles the whole Creek nation, and that you may present this to
the Choctaws as a true talk from us; and on the other end is the Choctaw
nation and that there is a broad path between our two nations and this
strap resembles it; and in the centre there is Emistisiguo and the other
is a Choctaw having each other by the hand as he hopes to do at Mobille,
and the white bead to the one end he reckons to be a clear path to
Cungito; and if the headmen from that town would meet him at
Mobile and take each other by the hand as they are described in this
belt and that this belt is sent by desire of the whole Tallipousses and
Abekas, and that they have sent this as a token of their sincerity, and I
hope you will be sure that the Choctaws's is real when you give them this

1   Enclosed in John Stuart's letter to Hillsborough, 2 December 1770: Vol. I, No. 763.

into their hands if they accept it, that it may be in friendship; and take great care of the belt as it is a great beloved belt and if they refuse it you will return it safe to us again, and we shall know what we have to depend upon and return you our thanks for your trouble. *Copy.* [C.O.5/72, fo. 111]

LXXX

Affidavit of John Grout[1]

9 August, City of New York

John Grout of Chester in the County of Cumberland, attorney-at-law practising in the Inferior Court of Common Pleas for the said county, came this day before me and made oath that some time in the month of May last past, Daniel Whipple Esquire, High Sheriff of the County of Cumberland, came to this deponent's house and demanded his assistance as one of a posse he intended to raise in order to retake one Joseph Wait and others who had escaped out of his custody, being rescued by a number of armed men. That the said sheriff insisting upon this deponent's attendance this deponent accordingly accompanied the said sheriff as one of the posse, which amounted to about 15 or 16 persons to the house of the said Joseph Wait and he not being at home and being informed that he was at the house of Benjamin Wait, the said sheriff with the posse proceeded towards the said house and had travelled but a little distance before this deponent discovered a body of men approaching in a riotous manner to the number of about forty persons who were armed with guns, swords, pistols and clubs, among whom were Nathan Stone, Joseph Wait, Benjamin Wait and Samuel Stone, the persons whom the sheriff wanted to retake, together with Peter Levins, David Stone, Benjamin Thurston, Samuel Gridley, David Gitchel, Jacob Gitchel, Elisha Hawley, Ebenezer Horsington, Ebenezer Horsington Jnr., Simeon Mills, Enoch Judd, Ebenezer Curtis, Solomon Emmons, John Benjamin, Andrew Norton, Jonathan Noble, John White, Samuel Whiston, Elnathan Strong, Joseph Thompson, Joseph King, Steel Smith and Aaron Bartlet, since deceased. That the said Nathan Stone marched before the persons so assembled in a riotous manner, armed with a sword. That the said sheriff in the hearing of the persons so riotously assembled made proclamation aloud in form of law for them to disperse, but without effect, soon after which the said Joseph Wait and some others of the rioters rushed upon the sheriff and his posse. That the said Joseph Wait being armed with a pistol in his left hand and a club in his right hand struck at this deponent twice with the club, which this deponent avoided by suddenly retreating, whereupon the said Joseph Wait levelled his pistol at this deponent, by which this deponent was put in fear and dread of his life. That the other rioters thereupon in general fell upon the said sheriff and his posse which they soon overpowered and forcibly and violently seized this deponent and others of the said posse and carried them to the house of the said Joseph Wait where the

---

1   Enclosed in Dunmore's letter to Hillsborough, 9 March 1771: Vol. I, No. 1047.

sheriff was informed by the said rioters that one at least of his said posse so taken they would hold prisoners until he the said sheriff, this deponent and some others should enter into bond for five hundred pound according to the best of this deponent's remembrance and belief, to be forfeited if the matters for which the said sheriff was then attempting to take them were any further prosecuted or if any of the inhabitants of Windsor should be prosecuted at the then next general sessions for any crime whatsoever, and further that the said sheriff should engage to make return upon the process against the said Nathan Stone, Joseph Wait, Benjamin Wait and Samuel Stone, that they could not be found in his bailliwick. That after detaining this deponent a prisoner in the said house for upwards of seven hours, the said sheriff and this deponent with the rest of the posse were set at liberty and suffered to depart. And this deponent further deposeth that on the fifth day of June last, while this deponent was attending the Inferior Court of Common Pleas for the said county in the business of his profession at the township of Chester in the said county, one Benjamin Thurston and one David Getchel seized this deponent, then in the house of John Chandler Esq., Clerk of the Peace for the said county, and forcibly and violently carried him away from thence, and were soon after joined by David Stone, Elisha Hawley, Enoch Judd, Ebenezer Curtis, Andrew Norton, Elnathan Strong, Joseph Thompson, Steel Smith, Nathan Stone, Joseph Wait, Benjamin Wait, Samuel Gridley, Jacob Getchel, Ebenezer Horsington, Simeon Mills, Solomen Emmons, Jonathan Noble, Samuel Whiston, Joseph King, Ebenezer Heywood, Aaron Bartlet since deceased, and some others to the number of near thirty persons who were armed with sticks and who surrounded this deponent and after pulling, shaking and twitching this deponent with the utmost cruelty, forcibly and violently hurried this deponent along with them with the utmost precipitation to Charlestown in the province of New Hampshire, obliging this deponent to walk the whole way thither, being twelve miles distant from the said township of Chester. That on the road they used this deponent with great incivility and cruelty by pulling, twitching and shaking him. That this deponent remained in the custody of the said rioters at Charlestown aforesaid about twelve hours, from whence they carried this deponent to a place called Windsor in this province, distant about twenty miles from Charlestown aforesaid. That by means of the abuses this deponent received as aforesaid, the great fatigue he underwent, and the grief and anxiety of mind and fear he laboured under, this deponent felt himself much indisposed and entreated that his ill state of health might excite compassion. Notwithstanding which the said rioters often threatened this deponent and could hardly be prevailed on to allow him to retire to sleep although he stood much in need of that refreshment. That this deponent was not suffered to write to his wife to quiet her mind as to the dreadful apprehensions she must have entertained of what had befallen him, nor to any other of his friends but with the utmost difficulty and first submitting to have his letters perused and approved of by the rioters. That the said rioters made use of the most shocking threats to this deponent in case he should attempt to escape, swearing that if this deponent was anywhere between Heaven and Hell he should be taken again. That this deponent on Sunday the tenth day of June aforesaid effected his escape, being detained six days a prisoner in the hands of the said rioters. And this deponent further deposeth that on arriving at Charlestown aforesaid the rioters in discourse said "we have now broke up the court; if we thought we had not effected it we would go back and bring away one of the judges" (or to that purpose) and more than once asked this deponent whether he thought the court would continue to sit, to which this deponent answered (being willing to prevent any violence being offered to any of the court) that he was sure they would not sit any longer. And further this deponent saieth that from Chester to Charlestown the said rioters were commanded by Joseph Wait and from thence to Windsor by Nathan Stone. And further this deponent saieth not.

Sworn before me this ninth day of August 1770, Dan. Horsmanden. *Copy.* [C.O.5/1102, fo. 111d]

LXXXI

Affidavit of Samuel Wells[1]

9 August, City of New York

Samuel Wells of Brattleborough in the County of Cumberland Esquire, one of the Judges of the Inferior Court of Common Pleas for the said county, came this day before me and made oath that some time between the fourteenth and nineteenth day of May last this deponent on his return home from a journey called upon Colonel Nathan Stone in Windsor who mounted his horse and rode with this deponent almost through town. On the road the said Stone and this deponent discoursed concerning the High Sheriff not long before coming into Windsor to serve some precepts and his being opposed and threatened. The said Stone told this deponent that he was determined that no writs or precepts that issued out of the Inferior Court or Court of General Sessions of the Peace for the said county should be served in Windsor or to that purpose, that the making a county was a sham and not a reality, that the patent or ordinance for erecting the county was a libel as it suggested that its being erected into a county was petitioned for, which he said was false, that it was never intended that those courts should act in trying causes, that there was no justice to be obtained in the county by means of the corruption of the judges, justices and other officers, that they were ruled entirely by John Grout, attorney-at-law, that he was determined to oppose their authority while he had a drop of blood in his veins, that friendship to this deponent induced him to bear this deponent company until he had passed by most of the settlements in town, and intimated that if this deponent should ride alone through town he would be in danger of being assaulted by the people and have some violence done to him. That this deponent endeavoured by many arguments to convince the said Stone of the danger of opposing the execution of the laws and exhorted him to alter his resolution and

1   Enclosed in Dunmore's letter to Hillsborough, 9 March 1771: Vol. I, No. 1047.

told him that if he and the people would for the future make no opposition to the free execution of the laws it would be the most likely method he and they could take to induce the civil authority to pass over the opposition already made in the tenderest manner, that if Mr Grout or any of the justices or officers whom he accused of bad conduct had done anything wrong the law provided a sufficient remedy and was the only way by which they could be punished, and that this deponent apprehended he had not given himself time to consider as he ought before he had formed his resolutions. To which the said Stone replied that he had formed no resolution about the matter on a sudden, that his resolution to oppose writs being executed had been fixed at least five or six months before, and that while he had life he would oppose the sheriff and that the people of that place (meaning Windsor) and some other places would join and stand by him to the last drop of their blood.

That some time after this deponent arrived at home, he was informed by Daniel Whipple, Esquire, High Sheriff of the said county, that he with the assistance of fifteen or sixteen men had made an attempt to retake the same persons in Windsor he had before taken into custody and who had escaped from him, being rescued by the said Stone and others, and the particulars of that transaction. That on the Sunday next before the sitting of the Inferior Court of Common Pleas and the Court of General Sessions of the Peace for the said county Bildad Andros Esquire came to this deponent's house and showed him the copy of a letter which he informed this deponent was wrote by Israel Curtis Esq., one of His Majesty's Justices of the Peace for the said county, residing at Windsor, to one Webb residing in Westminster, which gave reason to this deponent to suspect that he, the said Curtis, together with the said Nathan Stone and a number of others from Windsor intended to assemble in a tumultuous manner at court. This deponent therefore as soon as possible set out for Chester and upon his way thither called upon Joseph Lord Esquire, one of the Judges of the said Inferior Court, who accompanied this deponent. That they both arrived Chester the evening before the sitting of the court and communicated the copy of the said letter to Thomas Chandler Esquire, first Judge of the said Inferior Court and to some Justices of the Peace; but as the copy aforesaid was not fully expressive of the intention of the tumult, it was difficult for them to determine what measures to take. That on Tuesday the fifth day of June last, the day appointed for the meeting of the said court, the said Nathan Stone together with Joseph Wait, Benjamin Wait, Israel Curtis, Enoch Judd, Joseph King, Steel Smith, and a number of others amounting to about thirty, as this deponent believes, appeared at the place where the court were to sit in a riotous and tumultuous manner, the said Nathan Stone being armed with a sword, the said Joseph Wait with a dagger or hanger, and the rest with large staves or clubs, and as it was feared by the judges they designed mischief the said Thomas Chandler mildly demanded of the said Nathan Stone the reason of his being thus armed and desired him not to carry his sword into court (or to that purpose). The said Nathan Stone replied in a low voice so that this deponent is not able to say what was his answer. The judges soon after took their seats and the court being regularly opened according to the usual manner, the several persons aforesaid and their associates came into the court-house with their hats on and the said Nathan Stone and Joseph Wait armed as aforesaid (the said Stone carrying his sword in his hand) approached the table before the judges' seat while their party armed as aforesaid stood at a small distance in a body facing the court. Then Stone demanded of the court what business they had to sit there as a court and said that he made his demand in behalf of the public. In this he was seconded by the said Joseph Wait and the said Israel Curtis, and were answered by some of the judges that the letters patent or ordinance erecting the county and the commission of the pleas which were always read at the opening of the court showed their authority, and all who wanted satisfaction ought to have attended to the reading of them. Whereupon the said Nathan Stone, Joseph Wait and Israel Curtis by many arguments denied the authority this government had to erect the said county, which the court thought prudent to bear with and not to make much answer to, but gave them to understand they should proceed to do the business then before them. Whereupon the said Joseph Wait, who stood indicted with some others for a riot, demanded an immediate trial. That the insolent behaviour of the said Joseph Wait, Nathan Stone and Israel Curtis and the martial appearance of them and their party, armed and ranged as aforesaid being considered, the court apprehended it not prudent that the said rioters should be then put on trial as the court and jury could not be without fear if they were convicted nor safe to refuse them a trial at that time and oblige them to enter into recognizance to appear at the next term lest they should resent it by some immediate act of violence. Therefore, the court informed them they might depart without entering into any further recognizance, after which it was moved by the said Nathan Stone, Joseph Wait and Israel Curtis that John Grout, an attorney of the said court, should be disabled from practising, representing him as a bad man; upon which they were answered by the court that if Mr Grout was a bad man, it was unknown to the court, that the court entertained a contrary opinion of him; however, if they had anything to accuse him of, they might apply to the Grand Jury and the Clerk of the Peace would assist in drawing any necessary bill or they might apply to a higher court, that Mr Grout if accused of any offence had a right to a trial, that the court had not lawful authority to comply with their request and forejudge Mr Grout on a bare suggestion that he was a bad man supported by no evidence nor even the particulars of his bad conduct pointed out. The said Stone and Wait then replied they were not about accusing him in such a way as to give him a trial, neither were they obliged to do it, but that the court might depend that nothing would satisfy him and the people (as he expressed himself) but Grout's being immediately expelled the court in such manner as never to have the privilege of practising as an attorney, and then directing his speech particularly to the first judge said if it is not done we shall do something which I shall be sorry to be obliged to do, which will make your honour repent not complying with our request, or words to that purpose. He was then informed by the court that they would not comply with his demand or request, upon which the party armed with clubs as aforesaid who before stood facing the court crowded nearer in a riotous, disorderly manner and showed signs of a resolution to carry their point by force. The court finding it impossible to proceed to business in this confusion and tumult and to prevent any act of violence being committed while they were sitting as a court, immediately adjourned till the next day. Soon after which the said Stone and his party seized the said John Grout in presence of some of the judges of the said court and forcibly carried him away, and that the High Sheriff of the said county at the same time made proclamation for the said rioters to disperse but to no effect, and further this deponent saieth not.

Sworn before me this ninth day of August 1770. Dan. Horsmanden. *Copy*. [C.O.5/1102, fo. 113]

LXXXII

Sir William Johnson to Earl of Hillsborough (No. 14)

14 August, Johnson Hall

My Lord, on the 12th ult. I had the honour to write your lordship my letter [Vol. I, No. 493] No. 13, previous to my journey to hold a congress with the Northern Indians and deputies from the Southward, from whence I returned some days ago attended by so many tribes and messengers on the private business of each nation that it was not in my power earlier to transmit the proceedings, which I now have the honour to enclose [Vol. I, No. 565i].

From my last letter your lordship has been enabled to form some judgement of my embarrassment arising from the disagreeable nature of the business I had to engage in, on which account I held many conferences (too long to be inserted) with the leading men of each nation upon my arrival at the place of congress, to which the issue and determination of the Indians as contained in the papers herewith transmitted must be entirely attributed, they having at length agreed through the pains I took and the extraordinary prudence and good conduct of some of the chiefs whose abilities and influence were peculiarly exerted upon that occasion, to stop proceedings against the Southern Indians until they shall propose terms of accommodation, and to decline their intended application for our assistance and support in the war, a circumstance which gave me much uneasiness at first as I found that they came with a determined resolution to demand it in public, and that not so much from necessity as with design thereby to judge of the nature of our friendship and the regard we paid to former engagements, of which they entertain great doubts, concluding upon this to be a favourable occasion that must finally determine and direct their conduct towards us; for as strict alliances with them are considered both offensive and defensive any evasion or refusal from us would undoubtedly in their present disposition have so far increased their suspicion and resentment as to make our trade and frontiers severely feel the effects of that spirit of war which now predominates amongst them at a time when we are very ill-calculated to defend the one or the other, however matters may be misrepresented with regard to our strength or their weakness. For whilst they exist in their present state they are able to make us severely to feel their power without the possibility of their sustaining a proportionate loss even from a vigorous exertion of our abilities. So that, my lord, disagreeable as the alternative was on which the issue of the proceedings first appeared to depend, I found *that* a trifling circumstance when compared with the prospect of either drawing His Majesty contrary to the principles of humanity to be an actor in their quarrels or to see at least a temporary end put to the Indian trade and the total ruin of those settlements which industry and peace have added to the colonies. This I thought myself bound to prevent as well from humanity as duty, and I hope the measures I pursued for that purpose will be honoured with His Majesty's approbation as in so doing I carefully avoided discovering what would have been the resolutions of the Crown and so conducted it as to make the issue of the congress flow from their own resolutions on a farther and more mature consideration of the business proposed.

The number of the Indians who attended upon this occasion being [blank], the great scarcity owing to the destruction of the farmers' crops this year, and the particular obligations I was under to the steadiness and good behaviour of so many leading men amongst them, which I was under the necessity of rewarding over and beside the present, but particularly the distress they were in for clothing etc. from the total want of Indian goods, have increased the expense of this congress much beyond my inclinations; but as it was unavoidable I trust all things considered it will be found cheap, salutary and advantageous to His Majesty's interest, without a due regard to which I should not have incurred it.

The rest of the proceedings which consisted in the ratification of the Treaty at Fort Stanwix and the subject of grievances will require my saying some little upon. As to the first, your lordship will observe sufficiently from the public conferences the satisfaction expressed by the Indians at the whole of that treaty with the resolutions they have taken to render it permanent and acceptable to all their dependants. The latter are only the principal grievances which were spoken in public, besides which there were many others of an inferior nature not inserted as they would have added much to the bulk of my transactions and might be deemed unworthy the attention of government. They nevertheless gave me much trouble and occasioned great delay, which was of most concern to me as the daily maintenance of such a number of Indians amounted to a large sum, to abridge which I gave them my whole time both by day and night and thereby considerably shortened the time of our sittings. Your lordship will find that the principal grievances complained of in public regarded the conduct of our frontier inhabitants towards them and the state of the Indian trade. The first (as I have repeatedly observed) is what they have but too much reason to complain of and which they have retaliated in a very few instances, though I know the contrary is too often represented. I have on former occasions said so much of the licentious spirit of the inhabitants on the southern frontiers that I need only add that it still continues and that malevolence and disregard to all treaties is still demonstrated whensoever they fall in the way of any small parties or single Indians. Even since I began this letter I have received dispatches from Mr Croghan, my deputy now at Fort Pitt, acquainting me that a soldier had shot an Indian there and that another was killed by a Virginian two days after near to Chate River, the continuance of which proceedings will render all transactions with them abortive; and although, agreeable to their wishes, some farther directions to the governors would give pleasure to the Indians, yet I fear it is not in the present state of things in the power of our governments here to put a stop to these evils.

As to the affairs of trade I wish I could say that they had no cause of complaint, but the contrary has been too often manifested of late. Commissioners have been appointed to meet from some of the colonies, but it is not expected that any expense will be incurred adequate to the service, in which case it is much better to do nothing, and *that* it is thought will be the consequence of their meeting. But a still greater and more alarming circumstance arose from the wants and disappointments of the Indians in consequence of the non-importation agreements. Those with whom they traded embraced that opportunity of accounting for the cause of their wants as prejudice dictated, and therefore had I not fallen upon a happy mode of explanation or they been accustomed to doubt the veracity of the traders, it would have had the worst consequences. These secret negotiations which from their bulk cannot appear on the face of the proceedings are the groundwork of the whole, and the beforementioned circumstance proved no small addition to the expense as I was willing to falsify a representation of so villainous and dangerous a tendency, persuaded that in so doing I should be approved of. Another circumstance much complained of as well during the treaty as since by those Indians who accompanied me to this place is of the great cargos of rum which of late in particular was sent amongst them to their ruin as they call it. Many traders carry little or nothing else because their profits upon it are so considerable, and whatever resolutions they enter into, the Indians have not virtue enough to withstand the temptation when it comes amongst them. They therefore beg it may not be suffered to come to their castles or huntingplaces, and indeed the licentious abuse of the sale, notwithstanding its peculiar profit, is extremely hurtful to the trade in general from its effects upon the Indians, besides its giving encouragement to the meanest and most profligate traders to go amongst them, in that neither capacity or knowledge of the Indians or their language is necessary for the sale of it. But very little remedy can be expected here against the abuse of that liquor though its effects are daily manifested. Again, when Indians are assembled on public affairs, there are always traders secreted in the neighbourhood and some publicly who not only make them intoxicated during the time intended for business but afterwards get back great part of their presents in exchange for spirituous liquors of the worst kind, thereby defeating the intentions of the Crown and causing them to commit many murders and other disorders as well amongst the inhabitants as themselves. This is grievously complained of by the Indians, but I know of no penal law at present subsisting for restraining the sale of that pernicious liquor even during public business, which I humbly conceive should be recommended to the immediate attention of the American legislatures as well as some law for the more effectual apprehending and punishing offenders on the frontiers in a summary way. Another head of which your lordship may find the Indians make mention is the want of religious teachers. On this subject they greatly enlarged at several conferences I had with them and appear to consider it as so great a neglect in government that I judged it most advisable to give them better hopes and thereby put an end to their murmuring. The majority of Indians, 'tis true, do not as yet request it but even they consider our neglecting to gratify those that are so disposed as a farther instance of our indifference and disregard. I have, I believe, formerly mentioned this subject on application from some of the tribes; it is now become a matter of more serious concern from the earnestness with which the whole were about to second the desire of a few, and when so fair an opportunity is afforded I apprehend it is unnecessary to enlarge on the advantage it must be of to the state to secure those who have been already instructed in its religion and to render diffusive those religious and civil sentiments that are best calculated for its advantage and support. The Mohawks have had missionaries of the Church of England amongst them from the reign of Queen Anne till within these few years; they are now without any and from the scarcity of clergymen or some other cause, the Society cannot procure them on the salary which their small funds have limited them to, whilst at the same time the Indians find that their brothers in Canada who were our enemies are regularly supplied, and one lately appointed in Nova Scotia at the expense of government as 'tis said. I therefore cannot help at the entreaty of the Indians humbly recommending to His Majesty's consideration the affording some allowance for the Mohawk Mission which has always been under the immediate protection of the Crown, declaring it as my belief that if any farther provision could be made to employ others in so good a work it would increase their reverence for the Crown and their attachment to the British interest. The other matters spoken upon during the treaty (though they occupied a good part of my time then and occasioned several hundred Indians to follow me home) are such as I trust may be settled without any trouble to government. The messages which the Indians have resolved upon to send to the south and westward, supported by the steps I shall take, will I hope have weight and prove serviceable in a high degree, and in order to be armed against anything that may in another quarter threaten to disturb the public tranquillity, I have taken measures to be informed as early as possible with the proceedings and issues of the congress which they are about this time to hold at the Great Plains of Siota near the Ohio, where some are endeavouring to form confederacies for very bad purposes, secretly countenanced and supported by French traders, renegadoes and all those Indians who have not hitherto been heartily attached to the English but with wonderful art have for a time past endeavoured to shake the fidelity of the Six Nations through the means of some of the Seneca towns who are most dissatisfied with our conduct. I have in the course of this letter touched upon the principal subjects of both the public and private conferences at the late congress. This is as much as I could do from the variety of matters that occur upon such occasions, which however trivial in appearance demand my particular attention. Upon the whole I must observe that the Indians are at present in a state of uncertainty as to what course they shall take. The measures lately taken have strengthened the fidelity of our friends and afforded a temporary satisfaction to others, but it is on the continuance of them and the adoption of the wisest measures for their redress and satisfaction we must solely rely for the securing their fidelity, which though comparatively of little moment when weighed with the great objects of concern wherein the Crown is so deeply interested is nevertheless in a relative view, from a variety of peculiar circumstances, worthy the most serious consideration, and therefore I most humbly recommend the heads herein treated of as what may be productive of the most happy effects to this country, if by any means they can be carried into execution under the auspices of the Crown, to promote which, my lord, my whole influence and the small remainder of my health shall be most willingly devoted. I hope to be honoured with your lordship's commands on the foregoing subjects. *Signed.* [C.O.5/71, Pt. 2, fo. 93]

LXXXIII

Lieut.-General Thomas Gage to Earl of Hillsborough (No. 48, numbered by mistake)

18 August, New York

My Lord, the *Lord Hyde* packet returned to this port on 12th instant, by which opportunity I have had the honour to receive your lordship's dispatch [Vol. I, No. 399] No. 30.

The 14th Regiment continues in the barracks at Castle William, and care will be taken to make the repairs necessary for the accommodation of the regiments as well as to put them in possession of the Castle, and to strengthen that fortress in case the extremity of affairs should require it. The lieut.-governor, upon provincial considerations, has not judged it prudent hitherto to put any other garrison into the fort than the provincial company. The regiment is in the barracks on the outside of the fort, under its walls. I have begged Mr Hutchinson to concert measures with Lieut.-Col. Dalrymple for the taking possession of the Castle with the King's troops upon the first appearance of danger, and the officers commanding since the arrival of the troops at Boston have had orders which will be repeated to seize the Castle the moment it became necessary.

Your lordship having signified to me His Majesty's determination relative to the disposition of the troops in the Southern District, the materials that have been provided in this place for a pile of barracks will be sent to St Augustine as originally intended, and a detachment sent from thence to the Bahamas as soon as I can settle their transportation with the commander-in-chief of the King's ships in these seas in the manner His Majesty is pleased to direct in your lordship's letter to the Lords Commissioners of the Admiralty, of which you enclosed me a copy.

The plans and report [Vol. I, No. 570i-iv] made by the engineer who was sent to the Island of Providence, which your lordship is desirous to receive, are transmitted herewith, and I am to acquaint your lordship that a proportion of stores and ammunition have been in readiness a long time for the use of the forts in said island, but detained through the want of a conveyance. It is expected that an opportunity of forwarding them will now offer in a few days.

I had the honour in a former letter No. 47 to report to your lordship the opinion of Lieut.-Governor Durnford respecting the forts of Pensacola and Mobile, and what he conceived the best to be undertaken for the defence of West Florida. I have since received letters from Brigadier-General Haldimand, from which I transmit your lordship some extracts [Vol. I, No. 570v], in French, in which language the letters are wrote. Your lordship will observe therein that the brigadier joins in opinion with the lieutenant-governor concerning the forts and the best manner of defending the province: that nothing more can be done with the fort at Pensacola than to replace old stockades with new, and that the fort at Mobile is in so ruinous a state as not to admit of any repairs but at too great an expense, and from its situation is of little or no use. The scheme of constructing batteries to defend the harbour at Pensacola is adopted by both. And that everything that shall be undertaken may be completed in the best manner and that we may proceed in these matters upon as sure and certain foundation as possible, I mean to send the senior engineer under my command to Pensacola as well to view the province and the forts as to consider the proposals that have been made and to send in plans and estimates of such works as shall be fixed upon.

Attention will at the same time be given to the application made by Lieutenant-Governor Durnford for a supply of ordnance and stores, and to furnish him with such proportions of each as is judged necessary as far as the magazines under my care will allow of.

I have the pleasure to acquaint your lordship that the company of the 18th Regiment that went down the Ohio in March last is safe arrived at Fort Chartres. There is no account of any serious attack upon the Ilinois, but three white men have been killed at Cauho some leagues from Fort Chartres by Indians in disguise, and some few of the savages of the country have also suffered. A detachment was sent from the fort to Cauho by desire of the inhabitants who took up arms, but no discoveries have been made. The tribes most suspected of doing this mischief have sent some of their chiefs to visit the commanding officer and to declare their desires of our friendship.

A detachment of 50 men under the command of an officer named Jarnaser arrived in the spring from New Orleans, of whom thirty are posted at Misere and the rest at St Louis. He paid a visit of compliment at Fort Chartres and to assure Lieutenant-Colonel Wilkins of his intentions to keep up a good understanding with His Majesty's subjects. The French people on the Spanish side of the Mississippi were a good deal disappointed at the return of the Spaniards into Louisiana and no less alarmed at their approach to the Ilinois. Some of them came over to us and others proposed, with many more from the English settlements of Kaskaskies and Cauho, to form a new settlement at a place called Cap au Grais several leagues beyond Fort Chartres above the mouth of the Ilinois River. I have desired the commanding officer in general to suffer no vagabonds to settle in any part of the Indian country, but to try all means to send them away, either to West Florida or Fort Pitt, from whence they might be conveyed towards the coast. But if any Spanish subjects should emigrate, he is told, they would be better disposed of in these provinces than in that distant country; but if they would settle in the Ilinois, they must first take oaths of allegiance and fidelity to the King and to join his forces against all his enemies. The Board of Trade has given strong reasons against forming new settlement at such an immense distances from the sea or using endeavours to increase those we have, for the country can produce nothing that will enable the inhabitants to make returns for the manufactures carried to them, except skins and furs, and they will naturally decrease as the people increase, when necessity must force them to supply themselves with clothes and other necessaries in the best manner they shall be able. But as there are inhabitants in the Ilinois country, it may be better that they should be British than Spanish subjects. Those on the English side are become more tractable than they were, the militia turns out when ordered, and they begin to be sensible that all commerce with France is at an end and that they must depend upon the English.

There is advice from many parts that deputies from the Shawnese and Delawares have been negotiating with most of the nations upon the continent with design of engaging them to enter into a plan they have concerted to unite the Northern, Southern and Western Indians in one general confederacy. A very dangerous event if the plan succeeds, but the Indian officers think it impracticable. A meeting will be held, however, very soon at the Scioto Plains to consider of the proposal, where a very considerable number of Indians are expected to assemble. Sir William Johnson has held the congress so long talked of with the Six Nation and Northern Indians, and has no doubt used every endeavour to defeat the project. He has not had time to say more of the issue than that it had proved more favourable than he at first expected, that the proposed war was deferred till some further steps are taken with the Ouabache and other nations, and the rest of the business, notwithstanding the dissatisfaction of so many tribes on several subjects wherein they expect relief, has been satisfactorily concluded.

A quarrel has happened near Missilimakinac between the traders and Indians. A French trader was stabbed and an Indian shot, another Indian was made prisoner and brought to the fort, and afterwards released. In other respects the reports from all the posts upon the Lakes are favourable, the savages well disposed, and the trade going on.

Your lordship's sentiments in the dispute between Lieutenant McDougal and the inhabitants of the Detroit about Hog Island have been communicated to the parties, but I am informed they cannot be brought to any agreement and are preparing to lay their claims before the Council Board.

The Spanish troops continue to desert from New Orleans and report that there are not four hundred soldiers left in the province of Louisiana. The French merchants are removing out of the province to France or the French islands and the rest of the French would also remove if they could dispose of their lands and plantations. *Signed.* [C.O.5/88, fo. 122]

LXXXIV

Lieut.-Governor Cadwallader Colden to Earl of Hillsborough (No. 14)

18 August, New York

My Lord, I have the honour of your lordship's commands [Vol. II, No. LIII] of the 12th of June, No. 39, with His Majesty's disallowance of the Act declaring certain persons therein mentioned incapable of being members of the General Assembly of this colony, and I have published His Majesty's disallowance by proclamation as usual. I have communicated to the Council the Act passed in the last session of Parliament to enable the Governor, Council and Assembly of His Majesty's colony of New York to pass an Act of Assembly for creating and issuing upon loan paper bills of credit to a certain amount etc. As the colony of New York is distinguished by the favour of Parliament in this particular, I make no doubt of its being received with that dutiful gratitude which may justly be expected. The other Acts of Parliament relating to the colonies, and transmitted to me by Mr Pownall, were likewise communicated and all of them lodged in the secretary's office.

An equestrian gilt statue of the King made by direction of, and purchased by, this colony came over in one of the last ships from London. On Thursday last it was opened to view, erected on its proper pedestal in a square near the Fort, and fronting the principal street of the city. I was attended on this occasion by the gentlemen of the Council and members of Assembly then in town, the magistrates of the city, the clergy of all denominations, and a very large number of the principal inhabitants. Our loyalty, firm attachment and affection to His Majesty's person was expressed by drinking the King's health and a long continuance of his reign, under a discharge of 32 pieces of cannon, a band of music playing at the same time from the ramparts of the Fort. The General and officers of the army gave us the honour of their company on the occasion. The whole company walked in procession from the Fort round the statue while the spectators expressed their joy by loud acclamations, and the procession having returned with me to the Fort, the ceremony concluded with great cheerfulness and good humour.

I am well assured, my lord, that the merchants in this place who appeared most zealous to prevent the importation of British manufactures have notwithstanding sent themselves orders for large quantities of goods. At the same time they have thrown out the basest aspersions in the public newspapers against those who promoted the importation. I am confident the example of New York will be followed by all the neighbouring colonies, notwithstanding what appears in the American newspapers to the contrary. It gives me the greatest pleasure that the people of New York under my administration are the most forward in returning to their duty. Lord Dunmore is daily expected here. I hope to deliver up the government to him in peace and tranquillity, and with a very favourable disposition of a large majority of the people, especially of any rank, to government.

Nothing gives me more pleasure than the hope your lordship allows me to have of your retaining some regard to, my lord, your most obedient and faithful servant. *Signed*. [C.O.5/1101, fo. 89]

LXXXV

Deputy Governor Robert Eden to Earl of Hillsborough (No. 8, duplicate)

19 August, Annapolis

My Lord, I have the honour of your lordship's letter [Vol. I, No. 410] of the 12th June ult. on the subject of mine [Vol. II, No. XIX, 21 February 1770] of the 25th February respecting the proceedings of the committee on the arrival of the brigantine *Good Intent* from London.

Permit me again to observe to your lordship that Messrs. Dick and Stewart, consignees and importers of goods in this vessel, and the agents and attornies of Mr John Buchannan, merchant in London, the owner or rather the employer of the brig, by their advertisement in the *Maryland Gazette* solicited as a favour that a committee from the three counties concerned would meet at Annapolis for the very purpose of having a full and strict examination made whether the goods had been shipped contrary to, and with an intention to counteract, the General Association of the traders and other inhabitants of the province.

The determination of the committee thus convened in consequence of the solicitation thus publicly and earnestly communicated was (I believe) contrary to the expectation of the importers and agents of Mr Buchannan, and I informed your lordship of the steps I took to prevent that determination, the only steps as far as I am able to judge that I could take with propriety. The importers and agents submitted: they had their reasons, they chose rather to make an immediate sacrifice of their interest than not stand fair in the opinion of those on whose esteem their success in business depended. No complaint or application was made to myself or any other person in office of injury or for protection from the merchants or from His Majesty's Custom-house officers. No disorder or outrage was committed or even threatened. It is, my lord, my earnest desire, my determined resolution, to do my duty. It ever has been, my lord, and when I fail in it I shall have the excuse of being mistaken; but that I wish to avoid, and therefore to know how it was in my power or would have been in the power of any governor in America, whether of a royal or proprietary province, to hinder the importers of goods from re-shipping them, to prevent their acquiescence under the decision of a committee they called for themselves and appealed to. They had their motives such as were natural to men in their circumstances, such as the authority of no government could control.

Associations have been formed, committees have been appointed to examine the conduct of those who have engaged in them, and goods imported into America have been re-shipped. But, my lord, these circumstances are not peculiar to Maryland, and are therefore, your lordship must allow me to remark, no indications that the authority or vigour of government is less influential here than in the provinces to the northward or southward. They only prove, my lord, that Maryland has not been so happy as to escape the flame of discontent which has overspread the other colonies.

It is no small mortification to me that your lordship should think the measure adopted by the merchants of remitting the vessel and goods to London to have been owing to any particular want of vigour in my government. How soon there may be a similar occurrence I cannot foresee, nor consequently how soon I may again be obnoxious to the censure of not exercising the powers with which I am vested; for to myself I must take the censure of want of vigour and not seek for excuse in the incompetency of my official authorities, should the laws be violated and redress be withheld from those who are entitled to it.

Had your lordship been pleased to point out in what manner government ought to have interposed, I should more clearly see by comparing my conduct with your lordship's sentiments wherein I failed in point of duty, and be prepared to guard against the appearance of remissness upon any future similar occasion.

It is not, at least I think it is not, in my power to do more than lament that the unhappy differences subsisting between Great Britain and her colonies are not at an end, which I fear the partial repeal of the Revenue Act has not effected. That they may soon subside is, my lord, the sincere wish of your lordship's most obedient and very humble servant. *Signed.* [C.O.5/1283, fo. 62]

LXXXVI

Lieut.-Governor William Bull to Earl of Hillsborough (No. 34)

23 August, Charleston

My Lord, as soon as I had received the address of the Assembly in answer to my speech at the opening of the session on the 14th instant, I immediately communicated to them a copy of His Majesty's additional instruction [Vol. II, No. XXXV]. My regard to the royal command would have led me to open my speech with a mention of this instruction but as I understood the Assembly were determined to resume the consideration of their resolves passed last April, I thought it most prudent not to mention it in that public manner. The Assembly accordingly did resume the consideration of the resolutions and agreed to all of them with some softening except the two which proposed the addressing me for satisfaction of the Council, and that wherein they proposed addressing His Majesty to appoint a new branch of legislature independent of the Council, both which were disagreed to by the House.

I yesterday received a message from the Assembly, a copy whereof with my answer [Vol. I, No. 598i-ii] thereto I take the liberty of enclosing to your lordship. Notwithstanding this appearance of some dispute I am willing to flatter myself that all business will go on except the Tax Bill, which I presume they will clog with the article of fifteen hundred pounds sterling according to the vote of December last.

I beg leave to observe to your lordship that this unfortunate vote has embarrassed many of the moderate members. It was passed, as I had the honour to represent to your lordship in my dispatch No. 20, in a very hasty manner where there was no time to consider the propriety of the application or the mode of issuing the money. Many who wish it had never passed are nevertheless very averse to rescind or censure it, as is the common disposition of all popular assemblies: they adhere to resolutions once made, and all possible industry will be used to prepare arguments to give colour to and perseverance in inserting that article in every Tax Bill till this matter is settled, there being no other way to exonerate the individuals who received and remitted the money. They urge that as they received no private benefit but intended it for the public service, though they might be mistaken in those intentions, it will be a very hard case to be obliged to refund from their private purses. I am encouraged to mention this embarras by some favourable expressions in your lordship's letter [Vol. I, No. 408] No. 35 vizt. "His Majesty's gracious indulgence in allowing this matter to be settled upon those precedents which they themselves established and for many years adhered to". Some doubts have arisen in my mind whether I am to understand that this fifteen hundred pounds sterling, though incurred "for purposes not immediately arising within or incident to this province" may be provided for if done according to the former usages and manner prescribed by the instruction, as being previous to the instruction and within the rule of *ex post facto* regulations, or in what other manner His Majesty's gracious indulgence is to be received.

The punctuality with which I endeavour to execute the King's commands and the pleasure I have in communicating any indulgence from the royal goodness make me very cautious in forming an opinion in what manner I am to act in this particular case. I have and shall again consider it with great attention before I determine, and if I should happen to think I am warranted by the above recited expressions to settle this matter, or if on the other hand I should think myself bound by the instruction from passing any law that will settle it, I humbly request your lordship's favourable representation to His Majesty of the rectitude of my intentions in case I should in either side of the question unhappily mistake the royal will.

In the meantime I most earnestly entreat your lordship to signify as soon as possible what is my duty to do on this occasion which may reach me before Christmas. *Signed*. [C.O.5/393, fo. 83]

LXXXVII

Abstract of Letter from Charles Stuart to John Stuart[1]

26 August, Mobile

Enclosed I send you the accounts of the issues from first January to the thirty-first July last, which you will no doubt think very large, but if you will be pleased to consider the occasion the making peace has given to vast numbers coming down you will the easier account for the expense, besides the number of visitors that come with little or no cause that must receive some small gratification, but I hope the worst is passed and that I shall not in future have any such heavy charges, for many of them having no provisions at home come down with peace talks merely to get subsistence.

In my last [Vol. II, No. LVII] I mentioned Emistisiguo's being a Pensacola and that I hoped to confirm the peace with him, which I did and since when none has been hurt between them; but the Lachaway Indians, and it is supposed some of the Lower Creeks also have joined them, particularly the Eutchies, have taken the advantage of the security the Choctaws thought themselves in and have attacked them several times since, killed some and carried off some prisoners, which has occasioned new talks by the Choctaws who look upon the Upper and Lower Creeks as one and the same people and say they only lull them by their peace talks to kill them the easier, nor do they hesitate to say that we are conniving with the Creeks to kill them. And it is with some difficulty that I can convince them that these people have not as yet heard the talk properly, and Mr Struthers now carries a talk from the whole Choctaw nation to the Creeks as the last, desiring them to put a stop to the proceedings of those people as they look upon them as one and the same blood. But it is apprehended here that the peace will last no longer than it suits the Creeks as they have the upper hand, and indeed it is my opinion it will last no longer than those white people who go amongst them can find means to set them by the ears, nor indeed is there one person from the first to the last in this province but wishes sincerely to keep them at war. It is very true the Choctaws are troublesome neighbours but it is also true that the white people contribute much to make them so, by giving them rum in exchange for whatever they may have to dispose of both here and in the nation, and when the poor wretches get drunk they of course do mischief for which they are blamed by the very people who gave them liquor.

It is indeed incredible the vast quantities of liquor that has been distributed amongst Indians for these twelve months past, for I verily believe that four-fifths of what has been purchased in that time from Indians has been with rum. It is certain there is nothing the Indians like better and nothing the traders had rather give, and as no trader either in the Choctaws or Chickesaws has had a licence since July 1769 to 15 August 1770, it may easily be supposed what trade has been carried on, and now licences are taken out by the securities only and for whom they please and for whose conformity to the regulations they

1 Enclosed in John Stuart's letter to Hillsborough, 2 December 1770: Vol. I, No. 763.

are answerable. You judged right when you thought the Spaniards would not be very troublesome neighbours to us as to Indian matters, for it is really so, and now few or none of the Choctaws ever go near them, and what do are poorly received, and you may judge how the Arkansas look upon them by the enclosed speech of their headman to one of their commissaries. I also send you two letters which I received from Mr McIntosh sometime ago, and the French letters he mentions were taken from a hunting party of French inhabitants going from the Illinois to the Ouabache by a party of Chickesaws. They contained nothing material. There is one concerning a Frenchman that was taken prisoner by the Chickesaws or the Cherokees: he is not amongst the former. In my last I mentioned I would endeavour to be in the Creeks about busking-time to watch the motions of the Northward Indians who were to be there about that time as Emistisiguo said, but I was advised not to go as they might not like my going at that juncture, as they might think I went there merely to spy their actions, besides its being attended with much expense as they would in a manner force me to make them promises of presents etc. and might be the cause of bringing many here who otherwise would not think of coming; but we cannot fail of hearing of anything material that may pass.

In my last I acquainted you that it had been agreed upon between the lieut.-governor and me that I should take upon me the management of his department till such time as he should hear from home, but soon after upon a closer review of your letters I acquainted him that I wished he would put the management of his department in some other hands as I was liable to be ordered away whenever you thought proper. I also acquainted him that it would be very necessary to provide an interpreter also as mine would be obliged to follow me wherever I went. This is seems his honour has taken highly amiss and has told me that he has letters from home that mention that you do not allow enough for this province out of your fund, to which I answered that I had a sufficiency allowed me to answer any purpose of your department in this part of your district.

As the bearer goes through the Creek nation he will be able to inform you what is doing there, and he will also acquaint you how much the Indians press for a congress, of which they will expect to hear fully by Governor Chester. I shall be glad of your ideas with respect to the Arkansas and Quarpaws and do not omit mentioning the commissions and medals etc. to Indians as I am often solicited on that head.

There are about 80 Virginians and North Carolinians come to settle at Natchez. I do not know how they will agree with the Indians but at present they all seem quietly disposed. *Copy.* [C.O.5/72, fo. 89]

LXXXVIII

Governor James Grant to Earl of Hillsborough (No. 39)

1 September, St Augustine
My Lord, in my letter No. 30 I had the honour to lay before your lordship an account of the helpless and distressed state of the Greek settlement at Smyrnea, and took the liberty to observe to your lordship the

necessity there was of continuing His Majesty's most gracious bounty for the support of those adventurers.

Last year's bounty has been laid out entirely for their subsistence and has actually saved them from starving, for without that well-timed help from Government there must have been an end of that numerous promising settlement.

Dr Turnbull is diligent and assiduous: he resides constantly with his Greek colonists and does as much as a man can do to repair the first fault of exceeding the number of people to be imported, and of course the funds which his constituents had agreed to advance—in place of six thousand which was the stipulated sum, they have actually, my lord, paid £24,000 and are determined to go no farther.

The Greek settlers having been well fed last year have got into health and spirits, they work well, have cleared a great deal of ground, which the Doctor has put in very good order. The Greeks this year have raised a considerable quantity of provisions, such as indian corn, pease, potatoes and greens of all kinds, and if supported they will soon get into a comfortable state and be able to supply themselves with every necessary of life. Produce, and 'tis to be hoped useful produce to Great Britain, will of course follow.

But at present they are destitute of every convenience, they are ill-clothed, many of them almost naked, and are obliged to live in small huts put up in a hurry to shelter them from the weather upon their first arrival. Dr Turnbull has neither money nor credit to supply them with clothes and has not the necessary tools and materials to build houses for them. In that distressed situation he can only look up to His Majesty for his most gracious support by ordering the royal bounty to be continued to enable him to carry an extensive and useful undertaking into execution with success. He prayed me to lay his case before your lordship and to transmit for your lordship's consideration an indent [Vol. I, No. 584i] of such things as are absolutely necessary for the existence of the settlement.

The indent amounts to £1,000. If the bounty is continued and your lordship is pleased to order Mr Nixon, the Doctor's agent to receive that money at the Treasury, he will be very careful in the purchase and packing of the assortment, which may be sent to Charleston if no vessel offers for this port. The remaining thousand, if your lordship approves of the method, I shall continue to draw for upon the Treasury for the support of the settlement in the same manner as I drew for the bounty of last year. *Signed*. [C.O.5/551, fo. 73]

LXXXIX

Deputy Governor John Penn to Earl of Hillsborough (No. 23)

5 September, Philadelphia
My Lord, yesterday I had the honour to receive your lordship's letter [Vol. I, No. 468] of the 6th of July, No. 23.

I am now to acquaint your lordship that the merchants and a considerable number of the inhabitants of the City and County of Philadelphia met here on the 5th of June last, when the merchants almost

unanimously agreed "that there should not at that time be any alteration made in the agreement they had entered into on the 10th of March
1769". And afterwards, on receiving an account from New York that
a majority of the merchants of that city had broken their non-importation agreement by resolving to import from Great Britain everything
except tea and such articles upon which a duty is or should hereafter
be laid, our merchants and other inhabitants had another meeting in
this city on the 19th of July, when they immediately entered into several
resolves, a copy [Vol. II, No. LXXII] of which I beg leave to enclose
for your lordship's more particular information of their disposition
and sentiments; which as far as I can learn continue the same still,
though there always have been some among the dry goods merchants
here who would have imported from Great Britain all articles as formerly except those upon which any duty was laid. *Signed.* [C.O.5/1283,
fo. 9]

XC

Lieut.-General Thomas Gage to Earl of Hillsborough (No. 49)

8 September, New York

My Lord, your lordship's letter [Vol. I, No. 461] No. 31 enclosing a
copy of an Order in Council [Vol. II, No. LXII] dated on the 6th July
last has been duly received, together with dispatches for Lieutenant-
Governor Hutchinson which have been forwarded by express to Boston.

I wrote by said express to Mr Hutchinson and to Lieutenant-
Colonel Dalrymple for the carrying His Majesty's commands into
execution by putting a garrison of His Majesty's troops into Castle
William, and have detached Captain Montresor, engineer, to make
such repairs as shall be found necessary towards putting the fort into
a respectable state of defence, and to make repairs and additions to the
barracks.

The fort, abstracted from any commanding spots contiguous to it,
of which it might be proper to take possession if in danger of an attack,
may very well be defended by one regiment or by less numbers. It is
so very small that more would rather embarrass than assist its defence,
and shells would make unavoidable havoc amongst men crowded within
a small compass. The chief strength of the fort is towards the harbour,
from whence nothing is to be feared. It is weakest towards the land,
and the parapets are not proof, and the water that divides the island
from the main is so shallow that the King's ships could afford little
or no protection on that side. If therefore it should be advisable to raise
batteries or redoubts upon the island to prevent a landing from the
main or to take possession of and fortify a point of land upon the main
called Dorchester Point, which appears to be within the distance of a
point-blank shot from the fort, two regiments would undoubtedly be
necessary. I relate to your lordship what occurred to me on a short view
of the island and its fortress, but as Lieutenant-Colonel Dalrymple
and the engineer are instructed to inspect minutely into these and other
particulars I shall be better able to judge from their report what will
be most proper to be done.

Although I do not apprehend any danger, I mean to take every precaution in my power, for it is impossible to foresee, considering the anarchy that has so long subsisted in Boston and the poison that has been continually thrown into the people by numberless seditious publications, resolves, votes and instructions, how far the madness of the people may carry them.

In order to prevent all delay that can be avoided in succouring Lieutenant-Colonel Dalrymple, should he at any time be suddenly pressed, he is invested with powers in case of necessity to call for the aid of the troops in Nova Scotia. And I have ordered a detachment from the Royal Regiment of Artillery in that province consisting of one sergeant, one corporal, two gunners, one bombardier, and six matrosses, to be sent immediately to Castle William. I have recommended it at the same time to all concerned to keep their orders private and to do what is to be done quietly and with little noise or show.

In consequence of a former dispatch from your lordship I had corresponded with Lieutenant-Governor Hutchinson and Lieutenant-Colonel Dalrymple about placing a garrison of the King's regular troops in Castle William, and I have the honour to transmit your lordship the lieutenant-colonel's sentiments [Vol. I, No. 596i] upon the subject.

Sir William Johnson acquaints me that he has transmitted the proceedings of his late Indian congress to your lordship, which renders it unnecessary for me to trouble your lordship therewith. I trust he has been able to check the project of the Western Indians and to avert the danger that threatened us from their confederacies, and that he will fall on means to prevent the Indians from engaging in wars against each other.

This prospect of a general tranquillity was for a time interrupted by quarrels on the frontiers of Pennsylvania and Virginia, through the insolence and violence of some drunken Indians and the licentiousness of the white people. Some were killed on both sides but the difference was accommodated by the intervention of Mr Croghan, a deputy Indian agent, and the commander of Fort Pitt. Rum was the primary cause of the quarrel and is too often the occasion of disturbances. The Indians constantly complain that it is brought to them, though they can't refrain from drinking it and even demand it, and are angry when it is refused, and the prohibiting the traders from carrying it is as often talked of as a proper measure in the provinces without ever applying any efficacious remedy towards that or any other abuses committed by the traders or the frontier people.

The plan recommended by His Majesty to the several provinces by which they were to take the management of the Indian commerce into their own hands and to agree upon laws and regulations for the better carrying it on has not had that regard paid to it that might have been expected. They possibly choose to let the expense remain where it is, or may not agree upon a plan which must be general or it will be of no use. I can't give any reason why so necessary a business has been neglected, but no material step has been taken towards carrying the plan into execution.

The young province of West Florida has set a good example to the
rest in passing laws for regulating the Indian trade and for punishing
all persons who shall make encroachments upon the Indian lands or
otherwise infringe the treaties that are made with them. And if care
is taken to see the laws properly observed, the province will reap much
benefit thereby and avoid many quarrels with their Indian neighbours.

Mr Stuart has made application for an allowance for an officer to
reside in the remote nation of the Chikesaws, as well to keep him
informed of the transactions there as to serve as a check upon the conduct of the traders. Brigadier-General Haldimand has wrote upon the
necessity of sending an Indian officer to that nation, but Mr Stuart
objects that his fund will not allow him to provide for his salary, which
he thinks would amount to about £150 per annum, though he offers to
supply him annually with a proportion of presents and provisions out
of his fund. The Assembly of Virginia having provided the sum of
£2500 sterling to defray the expense of marking the boundaries between
their province and the lands of the Cherokees, Mr Stuart proposes to
run the line in the month of October.

Brigadier-General Carleton will have the opportunity to make
application in person to your lordship for the building a citadel at
Quebec and to state his reasons why such a measure is requisite. The
works of Quebec are bad and withal so extensive as to require a much
larger garrison for their defence than we may be able to afford. The
extent of the city was useful to the French as it gave room for all the
inhabitants of the circumjacent settlements who fled thither for protection when danger threatened, and there was no want of men to defend
the fortifications, a resource I fear we should not find if a French fleet
was coming up the river. Till something shall finally be determined on
this head the brigadier thinks it best, and I join in opinion with him,
to postpone the repairs that were proposed to be made to the present
works as well as to delay the building of the barrack. I thought it proper
during the absence of the brigadier that in case of accidents some officer
should be invested with the chief command of the troops in the province, and I have appointed the senior officer, Lieutenant-Colonel
Prevost, to take the command of them. *Signed.* [C.O.5/88, fo. 146]

XCI

Lieut.-Governor William Bull to Earl of Hillsborough (No. 35)

3 September, Charleston

My Lord, I have the honour to transmit to your lordship copies of a
second message from the Assembly to me with my answer thereto and
of several resolutions of the Assembly relative to the King's last
additional instruction, with a message to me signifying their having
concurred thereto [Vol. I, No. 598i-iv]. The language of these resolutions leaves me no room to explain their meaning. They are the result
not of precipitate warmth but of three weeks deliberation. I shall only
beg leave to inform your lordship by what I can discern that the two
grand points, of their right to issue monies by their order on the Treasurer in the manner by them practiced, and of the application thereof

to such purposes as they think proper, whether local or not, seem to be what they will very tenaciously adhere to.

The terms made use of in claiming rights in direct contradiction to the King's instructions as well as the disrespectful expressions regarding His Majesty's ministers might well have justified my immediately dissolving or proroguing the General Assembly. But when I consider that such a measure would only cover for a time but not extinguish the flame which would certainly break out with more violence at their next meeting and that whatever inconveniences must attend this interruption to public business would by a dissolution be only protracted, I thought it most advisable for His Majesty's service on all accounts to permit the Assembly to show the whole of their claims and arguments in support thereof by their agent according to their last resolution, to the end that the matter might be fully discussed and finally settled and they be disarmed in future of every plausible complaint that they were debarred from approaching the throne to undeceive our most gracious Sovereign and thereby avert the King's displeasure from his dutiful and loyal subjects, the Commons House of Assembly of this province.

As there seems no disposition in the Assembly to do business until this matter is settled I have prorogued them to the sixteenth day of January, by which time I hope to be honoured with His Majesty's royal will and pleasure, if not complete, yet so far as to give me some light to guide my steps thereupon in the meantime.

Although I am sensible the wisdom of His Majesty's councils does not proceed upon a bare representation of facts laid before His Majesty by any of his governors, but that such representation is referred for further examination, and that the best evidence is required and arguments advanced thereupon before any measure is formed, it nevertheless becomes my duty to explain the matter more fully as it is my ambition to stand clear in the opinion of His Majesty and of your lordship from having been deceived myself or having intentionally deceived His Majesty in anything related in my letter No. 20 in which I humbly apprehend there will appear no essential variation from truth. I might hope for some allowance if the greatest exactness should not have been observed when it is considered that in the hurry of writing then to avail myself of the conveyance by that ship I was obliged to trust only to memory in what I mentioned relative to the power and proceedings of the Assembly.

The importance of clearing up the matter from the Journals of the Assembly, which is evidence of the best authority in this case, I trust will plead my excuse to your lordship for being so tedious in stating and so particular in searching precedents of the several modes of advancing monies out of our Treasury: first by resolution concurred to by Governor, Council and Assembly, almost equivalent to an ordinance, secondly by orders in the Assembly to the Treasurer to advance money upon requisition of the Governor, of an inferior degree of validity, and lastly of orders from the Assembly alone, in which last it is submitted to consideration how far a few instances of orders that may have passed *sub silentio* from the notoriety or reasonableness of the service are sufficient to establish a parliamentary right, and whether the orders of the 2nd August 1765 for issuing six hundred pounds sterling and that of the 8th December last for fifteen hundred pounds sterling are within that predicament. I have taken the liberty to enclose a list [Vol. I, No. 598v] of the dates of several precedents from the Journals of the Assembly of each mode, which with the following account of the gradual growth of the power of the Commons House of Assembly may serve as a kind of clue to conduct such of His Majesty's servants as may be employed in that service with somewhat less trouble through a labyrinth of Journals for thirty years past, from which Journals, not the bare representations of governors, such arguments, inferences and proofs may be drawn as must establish or refute the resolutions especially the words "false, partial and insidious" charged in the sixth.

I proceed now with your lordship's permission to give a summary history of the alteration in the manner of granting money to His Majesty and the gradual increase of the power of the Assembly. I shall beg leave to take up the account where the Right Honourable the Lords Commissioners for Trade and Plantations left off, only reciting that till 1736 the estimate annexed to the Tax Bill was founded upon the salaries for the established officers and the accounts of public creditors, which were then examined and settled by a committee of Council and a committee of Assembly jointly. In the end of the year 1736 a new Assembly was convened in which a spirit began to appear that laid claim to the same exclusive right in the Assembly of framing, altering and amending money bills which is exercised by the House of Commons in Great Britain. The public accounts were audited by a committee of petitions and accounts, appointed by the Assembly only. In the beginning of the year 1739 a difference arose between the Council and Assembly upon one expression in the estimate vizt. the word honourable placed before the name of Mr Pinckney who was Speaker of the Assembly and omitted before the name of Mr Hammerton who was Secretary of the province and one of His Majesty's Council. This merely jocular beginning brought on very serious consequences. The Assembly began now to make a thorough examination into their parliamentary rights and came to the strongest resolutions asserting their exclusive right to frame, alter and amend money bills, founded on the rights of Englishmen and supported by arguments in a long report. The Council also by resolutions asserted an equal right founded on the royal instruction for that purpose. No business was done, the Tax Bill dropped, and their triennial term expiring, a new Assembly was convened. The Council and Assembly both resumed their resolutions of right to frame money bills, but as we were on the eve of a war with Spain it was considered that in case of a breach between the two Houses no supplies would be raised, which might be productive of consequences very dangerous to the safety of the province, an expedient was agreed upon to carry on business with a *salvo jure* to their respective rights, by which the Council when any amendment appeared necessary were to propose it on a separate schedule and send it with the money bill to the Assembly, where if approved the amendment was made. Business proceeded with great harmony under this salutary

expedient, renewed in succeeding Assemblies. About the year 174
the formality of renewal was omitted but the utility of it continued th
practice by tacit consent to this time, though it has sometimes bee
interrupted and the right contested as accidents kindled jealousies o
particular advantages were expected from raising differences betwee
the Houses, in which the Council after some struggle have yielded th
point and acquiesced for the sake of public peace and public credi
The Assembly thus coming off victorious soon felt their strength t
consist in holding the purse-strings of the people. In the year 175
there was a very long struggle between the Council and Assembly
Charles Crockatt Esquire who in 1749 had been by Act of Assembl
appointed agent (under which Act the correspondence was as usua
carried on by a majority of a committee of Council and a majority of
committee of Assembly, and the Act being expired, Mr Crockat b
consent of all parties continued to be corresponded with as agent) b
letter signified that his private affairs were become incompatible wit
his duty as agent and desired leave to resign. The Council thought i
reasonable towards Mr Crockat and just to the province to accept c
his resignation, and did this with the more readiness as Mr Pinckney
a member of Council and well acquainted with the interests of thi
province, was then in London and would have discharged that dut
with great advantage to this province. But the Assembly where M
Pinckney had some enemies, Mr Crockat many friends, resolved tha
Mr Crockat should continue agent and corresponded with him sepa
ately; and in the next Tax Bill inserted an article of fourteen hundre
pounds currency for his salary. To this the Council objected and afte
several fruitless expostulatory messages rejected the Tax Bill, whic
was repeated I think thrice in that year 1756. The Council remainin
thus firm, the Assembly made an appeal to the people by printing
report of their committee upon this dispute which had a tendency t
excite the resentment of the people against the Council, charging the
with being the cause of the decay of public credit and of whateve
injuries were sustained by the poor creditors of the public. The Counc
then thought themselves under the necessity of waiving the propriet
of conduct in submitting the matter first to the royal view and followin
the Assembly to the same tribunal, and printed a report made by the
committee upon this subject. These reports are very long and contai
all the arguments that can be adduced on either side. Governe
Lyttleton soon after arriving in June 1756, the Council willing t
smooth the way to his administration dropped the dispute and passe
the Tax Bill with the exceptionable fourteen hundred pounds. An
at that critical juncture, it being thought prudent to keep the Assemb
in good humour in hopes of the better success in the royal requisitio
for aid to carry on the war in America and the subject being at this tir
almost exhausted, it has been seldom moved since. In October 176
the Assembly having omitted to insert the arrears due to Governe
Boone in the estimate, some messages passed between the Council an
Assembly, the Tax Bill was rejected, but at the next session was passe
for the sake of public peace without that article, and Governor Boone
arrears were not provided for till Lord Charles Montagu brought

requisition from the King to the Assembly to provide for them.

I have thus, my lord, without loss of time endeavoured to state the whole matter as it appears to me from the most exact examination I have been able to make in so short time and amidst the interruptions of other business that must be attended to. I humbly request your lordship to believe that however deficient my judgement or researches may prove I have only truth in view, submitting the rest to the royal wisdom, without any design by forced constructions to aggravate matters or a wish to excite the royal displeasure or to disturb those streams of paternal goodness which have so often most graciously distributed protection and happiness to this province whose welfare under the royal auspices and commands I am by duty bound, engaged by interest, and animated by affection to promote. *Signed.* [C.O.5/393, fo. 95]

XCII

Lieut.-Governor Thomas Hutchinson to General Gage (Secret)[1]

11 September, Boston

Sir, I wished to have Captain Preston's trial come on and I proposed, if the jury should give in their verdict guilty, that the counsel should move in arrest of judgement and that the court should continue the motion until the next term. In the meantime I would have transmitted a state of the evidence to my Lord Hillsborough and there would have been time to obtain a pardon which might be sent to you by the first packet in the most secret manner and he be enabled to plead it upon his appearance in court and be immediately discharged. This would have been the most likely way to keep the people quiet, whereas if there should be sentence against him and a respite, or if a new trial should be ordered, in either case there might be danger of violence. But the court suddenly put off part of their business to the latter part of October, and if such a motion should have been made in arrest of judgement they could not without the people's suspecting the design have continued the consideration longer than to that time. I therefore chose not to have the trial now. We are inevitably straitened in point of time for the next term being the 2nd Tuesday in March we can scarce hope after October for a return from England in season. I am informed depositions have been taken and sent to England by your order, and that one or more persons who were present at the action have been examined before a Committee of Council in England. If the case should appear to His Majesty so favourable as to merit a pardon and it may regularly be granted, it will be most safe that it should be sent by the first packet or first opportunity here or to New York and it may be kept secret and used only in case of necessity or of a pardon sent after the state of the evidence transmitted not arriving in time. Having thus stated the case to you, I will do the same to my Lord Hillsborough that such proceedings may be had as shall be judged proper and I hope you will write to his lordship upon the subject.

1   Enclosed in Hutchinson's letter to Hillsborough, 13 September 1770: Vol. I, No. 601.

I have taken great pains in this most unfortunate affair which has been attended with infinite difficulties occasioned by the inflamed spirit of the people. *Copy*. [C.O.5/759, fo. 285]

XCIII

Lieut.-Governor Thomas Hutchinson to Earl of Hillsborough (*No. 24, duplicate*)

12 September, Boston

My Lord, the 8th, in the evening, I received by express from General Gage your lordship's letter [Vol. II, No. LXIII] of the 6 of July, accompanied with an Order of His Majesty in Council of the same date [Vol. II, No. LXII]. At the same time Lieutenant-Colonel Dalrymple received from General Gage orders for his government upon my putting him into possession of Castle William. I sent to Colonel Dalrymple and desired him to come to my house in the country the next morning, being Sunday, where we determined upon the proper steps to be taken the day after, when I gave an order for the withdraw of the garrison in the pay of the province and for placing a detachment of the regular forces in their stead. As soon as I had done this, I met the Council and directed that His Majesty's Order in Council should be read to them and acquainted them with the signification of His Majesty's pleasure in your lordship's letter for the immediate change of the garrison. It occasioned great surprise and concern but nobody suggested I could refuse obedience to the Order. I told the Council I intended to prorogue the Court a fortnight farther but, if they desired me to meet at the time it now stands prorogued, I would do it. They unanimously expressed their desire and I intend to meet the Court the 26th of this month at Cambridge.

As soon as I had dismissed the Council I went to the Castle and committed the custody and government thereof to Colonel Dalrymple by virtue of the power given me by my commission and the royal charter, having settled a form of words in which it was done to prevent cavils. I shall enclose to your lordship copies of two letters [Vol. I, No. 600i-ii] I have wrote to General Gage upon this matter of form, and I humbly beg your lordship's consideration and instruction upon the subject. I could not help grieving for the garrison. As it is a very unusual thing to discharge officers or men, they being a set of orderly and well-behaved persons, they considered their places as a sort of freehold, some of them having been there 20 or 30 and one of the officers near 50 years. I wish it was in my power to make provision for some who stand in most need. Your lordship will perceive that I have mentioned this to General Gage. I am not yet able to make a judgement of the effect of these measures upon the minds of the people. I hear of some who are under much concern and others greatly enraged, for the people have been used to consider the Castle as the property of the province, because built with the province money, although given for the King's use and by the charter in the most express terms the governor has the full direction of everything relative to it, even to the total demolition of it. The Castle being the safest place, a large proportion of the public powder has always been kept there, but not destined to the immediate service of the Castle, and all warlike stores have been lodged there, the greatest part of the small arms having been purchased for particular expeditions, and such as remained have been collected and deposited there.

I told the Council they need give themselves no concern, whatever interest the province could have or whatever constitutional or equitable claim it could have to an equivalent, all would remain entire notwithstanding the change made in the garrison, and I am taking an exact inventory of the whole. I shall make use of His Majesty's Order, as your lordship directs, without suffering any copies to be taken or communicating it by message or speech to the General Court. I must beg leave to refer an answer to what relates to the Eastern Country until another opportunity, only observing at present that I may perhaps have expressed myself somewhat improperly, but I intended no more by the royal authority than a royal requisition to the Assembly to do their duty in prosecuting all trespasses upon their lands. I will also enclose a petition [Vol. I, No. 600iii] which has no date but was offered me since the prorogation of the General Court. I never had a thought of superseding Colonel Goldthwait; on the contrary have assured him of all the support in my power. The officer I accepted in his stead to manage the truck-trade is a person of no consequence. My refusing him would have only led them to a more exceptionable person and a string of negatives in an office which was sunk almost to nothing, and would have been ill-judged at that time. There is scarcely £500 a year negotiated and the officer himself has not to this day acted in the office but, I am informed, remains in a remote part of the province, and the Act for carrying on the trade expired the 1 of July.

I shall conform to His Majesty's pleasure signified to me by your lordship concerning the place of holding the General Court. *Signed.* [C.O.5/759, fo. 275]

XCIV

Petition of Inhabitants of Orange County[1]

[22 September]
To Martin Howard, Chief Justice, and Maurice Moore and Richard Henderson, Associate Judges.

The humble petition of the Inhabitants of Orange County humbly sheweth,

That as it is a maxim in our laws that no law, statute or custom which are against God's law or principles of nature can be of any validity but are all null.

If therefore laws themselves when against reason and justice are null and void, much more the practice used by men in the law which is contrary to the law as well as reason, justice and equity, ought to be condemned. And surely it is against justice, reason and equity to exact

1   Enclosed in Tryon's letter to Hillsborough, 20 October 1770: Vol. I, No. 680.

taxes and extort fees that are unlawful from the poor industrious farmers. Yet these are but a few of a great many more evils of that nature
which has been of a long time our sad case and condition and to such a
degree general among so many of the men of the law that we quite
despaired of any redress being to be had that way. But as you, the Governor, King's Attorney-General and other gentlemen of the law, pledged
to us your words, your honours, your oaths, that we could and should be
redressed by the law, it would be tedious as well as unnecessary to
recite the world of fatigue, expense and trouble that we have been at
to obtain redress in that way, but in vain for, though so many of the
officers as has been convicted, yet we can obtain none of our money
back but instead of refunding they still continue to take the same fees,
James Walton and John Butler excepted. And notwithstanding the
wheels in this work run so heavy, we having so many of the court party
against us, yet we might nevertheless a'gained our point could we have
obtained jurors of unprejudiced men; for though the law empowers the
justices of the inferior courts to appoint the juries yet it was to the end
they might be chosen of unprejudiced men. This was the spirit, end
and design of the law. But it has so happened that too many of our
justices are parties concerned, some of them being insolvent high
sheriffs themselves and others insolvent sheriffs' securities. Yet under
all this disadvantage as we laboured against this very unfair dealing,
the goodness of our cause and uprightness of our intentions gained
ground with such justices as was not parties concerned, and for some
courts past a few of the jurors was unprejudiced men; but at our last
inferior court, Tyree Harris and Thomas Lloyd took a most notorious
and barefaced advantage of choosing the juries on the first day of the
court contrary to the known and usual custom and have made up the
jury mostly of men well known to be prejudiced in favour of extortionate
officers and of such officers themselves. Tyree Harris at whose instance
we suppose it was done was High Sheriff himself for the years 1766 and
1767, whose accounts are yet unsettled and likely he may be sued by the
Treasurer as well as the vestry to this court. Besides almost, nay we
believe every, under-sheriff he had is indictable for their extortions and
exactions of taxes, and most of them have already been found guilty
and though they attempt to make you believe the charge against them,
for exacting 4d., 6d. and a shilling extraordinary from ignorant men,
women, and in remote neighbourhoods, to be a false charge, yet it is
not only notoriously known to be the truth by hundreds of people from
whom and among whom they exacted it, but at the same time they
exacted 4d. more from every man in the county in the very same tax,
and though this was what we had some item of from the very beginning,
yet we could never come at the certainty thereof till now. We think it
can be proved beyond all doubt, and this is a very particular matter of
great weight and moment as it was one immediate cause of the rise of
the mob and for which reason we suppose the most strenuous methods
has been used to hinder it from coming to light. In the next place
Thomas Lloyd may also be said to be a party concerned, as he is one of
the insolvent sheriffs' securities and likewise the justice who committed
H. Husband without a warrant, proof of any crime and without a

mittimus; besides all this he has been vestryman and churchwarden frequently these ten years past and more, during which time the vestry accounts are unsettled and unregularly kept and large balances behind, Thomas Hart being the only sheriff that ever settled, which was for 1762, the particulars of whose accounts is also kept from the eyes of the public, all which is contrary to law and for which neglect the church-wardens and clerks are indictable.

Mr Chief Justice, you at our last court seemed to be somewhat prejudiced against us in a speech that you made in which you signified your jealousy that we acted through malice, ambition etc. but concluding that if what we did was from motives to promote justice, detect extortion etc. for the public good that you wished us all the success imaginable and heartily concurred with us in our undertaking. Oh that you might be sincere and could but a 'known our hearts. However, be that as it will your speech could not but afford us consolation and encouragement to persevere, for we could lay our hands on our hearts and call God to witness in ourselves that this was our whole sole end and purpose and that too out of pure necessity to keep ourselves and innocent helpless neighbours from utter ruin, our whole properties having become quite unsecure as well as our characters. As the two persons who was indicted last court for perjury by reason they had indicted and witnessed against extortioners are two honest innocent men, yea we need say no more but that we know these two men are honest men of good characters and innocent of that charge, whereas on the contrary to pick the whole county there cannot be found men of much worse characters than many or most of those who have sworn against them. As for the objection that some pretend to make (to wit) that it is hard to find jurymen but what is prejudiced to one side or t'other, this objection has not the least foundation in truth or reason, absolutely no more than if a gang of horse thieves had been numerous and formidable enough to have engaged the same attention and concern of the public, for these extortioners and exactors of taxes are certainly more dangerous than those thieves; and in the next place they and all who espouse their cause knowingly are as to numbers inconsiderably small, only that they have the handling the law chiefly in their own hands. Our late elections helps to prove this division, we carried our election for vestrymen twenty-five to one. The consequence of not bringing these men subject to law is wooden shoes and uncombed hair. What sense or reason is there in saying any are prejudiced to our side, for what is it we have done? We have laboured honestly for our own bread and studied to defraud no man, nor live on the spoils of other men's labours nor snatched the bread out of other men's hands. Our only crime with which they can charge us is virtue in the very highest degree, namely to risk our all to save our country from rapine and slavery in our detecting of practices which the law itself allows to be worse than open robbery. It is not one in a hundred or a thousand of us who have broke one law in this our struggle for only common justice which it is even a shame for any government or any set of men in the law once to have denied us of, whereas them who has acted the most legally are the most torn to pieces by the law through malicious prosecutions carried on against them.

To sum up the whole matter of our petition in a few words, it is namely these, that we may obtain unprejudiced juries, that all extortionate officers, lawyers and clerks may be brought to fair trials, that the collectors of public money may be called to proper settlements of their accounts, namely the sheriffs for the years 1764, 1765, 1766 and 1767, to which time the taxes was generally collected (a small part of the last year excepted) the refusing to settle for which or give us any satisfaction occasioned the past disturbances. If we cannot obtain this, that we may have some security for our properties more than the bare humour of officers. We can see plainly that we shall not be able to live under such oppressions and to what extremities this must drive us you can as well judge of as we can ourselves, we having no other determination but to be redressed and that to be in a legal and lawful way. As we are serious and in good earnest and the cause respects the whole body of the people, it would be loss of time to enter into arguments on particular points, for though there is but a few men who have the gift or art of reasoning yet every man has a feeling and knows when he has justice done him as well as the most learned.

Therefore that justice, which every man will be ashamed to own that ever he denied us of when in his power to grant, is the prayer of our petition and your petitioners as in duty bound shall ever pray. Signed by 174 subscribers. *Copy.* [C.O.5/314, fo. 22]

XCV

Governor Peter Chester to Earl of Hillsborough (No. 3)

26 September, Pensacola

My Lord, I have the honour to transmit to your lordship herein closed the copy of a letter [Vol. I, No. 618i] that I lately received from one John McIntire, together with a copy of the deposition [Vol. I, No. 618ii] of Daniel Huay, both relative to a settlement now forming at the Natches within this province. Upon my receipt of these papers I laid them before His Majesty's Council who were of opinion that the new settlers therein mentioned should have every encouragement, countenance and protection that government could afford them, and advised me to make a requisition of General Haldimand by letter written in Council for a party of His Majesty's troops immediately to be sent up the Mississippi for their protection, together with a few barrels of corn, a small quantity of powder and shot, and a little salt, under the charge of the deputy surveyor of the province who should be directed to lay out a township and settle them in a compact body. The making of an application to General Haldimand of this sort of public letter, I did not think so eligible a step until I had in a private character consulted him upon the propriety of this measure (being as yet a stranger in the province) and whether it was in his power to comply with the public requisition if made to him. For I was fearful that if such demand was made upon my first coming into the province, and refused, it might by some evil-minded people be construed as the forerunner of some future breach between the civil and military commanders, which has already proved so very disadvantageous to the settlement of this province; not that it could have had that effect as the General and myself are upon the best terms, and I have always found him very ready and willing to communicate his opinion to me and give me every information relative to the province that is in his power, but I chose to avoid every appearance that could have a tendency to create even a suspicion. Upon mentioning this matter to the General, he told me as I imagined that it would not have been in his power to have complied with my request consistent with his orders, one regiment being thought proper to be fixed at Pensacola; and that he could not risk the detaching of any troops without special directions for that purpose from Lieutenant-General Gage. My next step before I could determine upon this business was to consult Mr Charles Stuart, the deputy superintendant of Indian affairs for this department, and to procure every other information in my power whether such a settlement would give any umbrage to the tribes of Indians in those parts, and finding from my enquiries that the lands at Natches are not claimed by any of the Indian nations contiguous to the Mississippi, they were formerly the property of a tribe of that name which the French almost extirpated, and the remaining few do not exceed one hundred men who are about one-half incorporated with the nation of Creeks and the other half with the Cherokees, and now so intermarried and connected with those nations that they will not choose to return to the Natches again, and that the Indian tribes contiguous to the Mississippi could not be in the least displeased at this measure. In consequence of these representations and after having collected every information in my power relative to the propriety of giving of encouragement to settlers in that part of the province, I thought proper to comply with the earnest request and advice of Council in giving these people encouragement and supplying them with a few necessaries to prevent their starving during the winter: the expense attending it will by the estimate made by the Council be inconsiderable. And I have accordingly given directions for a few barrels of corn, a little powder and shot, and some salt to be sent up to them, which with their own hunting will greatly help to enable them to subsist until they can raise corn for themselves. The deputy surveyor of the province will have the charge of these necessaries and directions to lay out a township conformable to His Majesty's instructions, and to settle them in a compact body. I have also directed that a message or talk from me be sent into the Indian nations that lie contiguous to this proposed settlement, informing them that I am acquainted with the arrival of these people, recommending harmony among them and that they will live as brothers together. I have also received information that there is a large party consisting of a considerable number of families now on their way through the back-country to the Mississippi, who it is natural to suppose will apply for lands when they arrive, and for the like protection and a little support at their first establishment, until they can raise a crop. For they cannot bring provisions with them at a vast distance through the interior part of the country to support them a long time. During their route they subsist chiefly on venison, buffalo and game which they kill, so that when they first arrive on the Mississippi they are with their wives and children destitute of almost everything, and without a little assistance from hence of powder, shot, salt and corn, which it will be unavoidable to give them, they will be driven to the greatest distress during the winter. I know that the contingent fund was not originally intended to be applied in purchasing necessaries for the support of new settlers; yet such are the distressed circumstances of these poor people now there (as represented to me) that it would be want of humanity to deny them some support, and I suppose those that are on their route and expected, when they arrive, will be much in the same situation. As I shall take care that the expenses to be incurred shall be very moderate, I hope your lordship will excuse my appropriating a small part of the contingent fund for this purpose. If I was authorised to give proper encouragement for the settling of that part of this province which adjoins to the River Mississippi, it is my opinion that it would in a few years be filled with a number of useful inhabitants. The colonists settled on the back-parts of many of the other provinces find their lands either so barren or are obliged to pay such high prices for them to the different proprietors that many of them have been waiting with impatience for an opportunity of removing: some have been buoyed up with the hopes of new government to be established in the interior country and directed their affairs accordingly. But as they will now find that His Majesty has not thought proper to allow of settlements beyond the jurisdiction of his provinces, they will naturally flock to the Mississippi, some down the Ohio and others by sea, the soil and climate of that country having the highest character through the whole continent.

Your lordship may enquire what advantages are likely to result to the mother country in forming these settlements so far back, what measures are to be pursued, and what expenses will necessarily be incurred to give the encouragement that is required. By the best information I can collect the climate on the banks of the Mississippi is healthy, the lands exceeding fertile and produce great quantities of timber fit for ship-building and making of different kinds of lumber. No soil is more proper for the cultivation of rice, indigo, hemp and corn. The navigation for vessels is very easy and practicable down the Mississippi so that the produce of the country may with great facility be exported to Great Britain by which the inhabitants would be enabled to take in return the manufactures of the mother country to supply their own consumption and the Indian trade. So also may corn, provisions and lumber be supplied to our islands in the West Indies for their rum, sugar and molasses. The navigation up the Mississippi in large vessels was formerly thought impracticable; His Majesty's sloop *Nautillus* and two other large vessels that I have heard of, one of two hundred and fifty tons burden, have been up to Fort Bute or Manchac, which is about sixty-five leagues from the Ballise or mouth of the Mississippi. This passage may with a fair wind I am told be performed in about ten days, but take chances in general or upon an average in about one month. Here might be a port established and the inhabitants at the Natches and up the river as high as the Illinois might be supplied from hence in large batteaus, and all the returns of the upper country shipped from hence, which would prevent our traders from carrying their peltry to Orleans, that having been the case, and so secure in a great measure the whole trade not only of the Mississippi but of the Missouri and all the upper country. Thus shall we answer the original intentions of government in colonizing vizt. by improving and extending the commerce, navigation and manufactures of the mother country. Should this proposal be thought an object worthy of attention, protection must be given to the first settlers and their lives and properties secured from the outrages that may be committed by the nations of Indians that surround them in the re-establishing of the posts on the Mississippi at Fort Bute and the Natches or at such places as may be thought most convenient for the protection of the settlers and Indian commerce. These posts I am informed were abandoned in consequence of a report made by the Right Honourable the Lords Commissioners for Trade and Plantations, dated the 7th of March 1768, wherein they represent to His Majesty "that it will be in the highest degree expedient to reduce all such posts in the interior country as are not immediately subservient to the protection of the Indian commerce and to the defeating of French and Spanish machinations among the Indians, all which although in some degree useful for these purposes cannot be maintained but at an expense disproportioned to the degree of their utility". Their lordships confine their report to the protection of Indian commerce as it was not at that time imagined that settlements of any importance would be formed upon the Mississippi; for their lordships were of opinion that if it was thought expedient to settle new colonies in the interior country, they would not recommend any reduction of the military expense. Notwithstanding the King has some time since thought proper to entrust the regulation of the Indian trade to his colonies, I do not hear that any law has yet been passed for that purpose in either of the provinces except West Florida. This law passed in May last so that the effects expected from it cannot as yet be seen, but I should conceive it very difficult to punish defaulters in an unsettled country when the traders who commit these abuses are the only British subjects that reside in the Indian country or at such places as the trade is allowed to be carried on; and if it should hereafter be thought proper to confine the Indian trade of those tribes contiguous to the Mississippi to certain places, proper magistrates may be appointed to see the laws regularly carried into execution and to reform those abuses that have been too frequent and must affect the commercial advantages to be expected therefrom, and perhaps in future tend to prevent the involving us in the great expense of an Indian war. But without protection we cannot expect that any settlers of property will fix themselves in the interior country who would be fit persons to be appointed in the Commission of the Peace. The re-establishing of these posts would also be a great inducement to many of the French inhabitants settled on the Mississippi, disgusted with the treatment they have received from the Spaniards, to come over to our side of the river, and although they cannot be invited by me yet if they come into the province, take the oaths of allegiance and demand my protection, I cannot refuse it them; and I think they should be allowed the same liberty of exercising the Catholic religion that I am directed by His Majesty's instructions to give the Spanish inhabitants here agreeable to the Treaty of Paris.

If Great Britain should at any time declare war against Spain the communication with the Mississippi by the Ballise would be impracticable while they kept possession of New Orleans; but I am informed that the communication with the Mississippi by the Lakes Maurepas and Ponchartrain into the River Ibberville is very practicable for small vessels carrying about two hundred barrels of provisions, provided the Ibberville was cleared of the logs etc. that now stop the passage, and it is said that a canal may be cut to let the waters of the Mississippi into the Ibberville from a point above Fort Bute on which the Mississippi strikes with great violence. And I am informed by a person that has lately arrived from thence that the waters of the Mississippi, when it is low, are higher than those of the Lakes, but these are facts I shall endeavour to know more accurately as I propose going up to Fort Bute if possible before winter with Lieutenant-Governor Durnford, in order to view the spot and take the level of the waters. I shall not fail upon my return of transmitting to your lordship as satisfactory an account of our proceedings as lies in my power. Should this cut be found practicable or a carrying-place be established there, the troops may be supplied with provisions through this province without going round by sea and then up the Mississippi for a few years to come, and after that I should suppose at a small expense by the inhabitants settled round them, who will in so fertile a soil very soon raise much more than is sufficient for their own consumption. The maintaining of these posts and supporting the troops that garrison them will be the chief expense that will attend the encouragement desired. It will require another regiment to be sent into this province, part of which may be stationed at these posts on the Mississippi, and the remaining part at Mobile or in such parts of the province where they will be most useful. As it is thought proper to keep one regiment at Pensacola it will be necessary more troops should be sent here to supply the place of part of the 31st Regiment who expect to go home in the spring. These troops, with such an addition to the contingent fund as might enable me for one or two years to assist the infant settlers, who first come destitute, with a very few necessaries to prevent their being driven into great distress and to give premiums or bounties on such kinds of their produce as your lordship may think expedient, should be sufficient to answer the end designed. There may be some of the present settlers at the Natches mentioned in the enclosed deposition that probably are outlaws, and others of them who either could not subsist upon the barren lands on the back-parts of the provinces from whence they came, or could not afford to pay the proprietors such sums as they demanded, and were therefore induced to emigrate into a country of whose fertility of soil and temperature of climate they had received such favourable accounts in order to better their circumstances. The most of them have little or no property, but such people can labour and will make very good *first settlers*. If they are fixed in townships and have protection they may very shortly draw off many hundreds of those persons, out of the reach of law, that have infested the back-parts of the Carolinas, Virginia and Pennsylvania for some years past, who might when settled in a compact body be brought into some order and regularity by a few good magistrates among them. At the first, it is very probable that the magistrates themselves would stand in need of troops to assist the civil power in the execution of the law until the refractory had been severely punished, but in a short time by prudent management, as they would have property of their own, I think that they might be brought into order and decorum, and that their children would become useful members of the community. These sort of people, however insignificant they may appear, are the only persons we can expect that will first attempt to settle an uninhabited country, surrounded on all sides by numerous tribes of savages. But if government should think proper to give encouragement to such settlers, and townships were laid out for them properly protected, it seems reasonable to imagine that from the fertility of the soil and temperature of the climate in these parts, together with the natural disposition for emigration that prevails in all the old colonies, they would draw numbers of their inhabitants to this part of the province, among whom we are then to expect some people of *real property* who will have it in their power to make useful improvements by the assistance of those who had sat down before them, and would not themselves become the first adventurers nor trust their property until they see that protection and encouragement will be given to them.

The settling the interior parts of a province and neglecting the sea coasts I know is bad policy where it can be avoided, but such is our situation that the lands near to the sea are barren and not proper for cultivation, those above Mobile are more fertile but in the summer season very unhealthy. These circumstances joined to the unhappy divisions and the distracted state this colony was in soon after its first establishment has prevented our being little more at this day than the garrison-town of Pensacola, and I do not see any probability of our being in a more flourishing state unless some methods can be fallen upon to draw inhabitants among us and for government to give them encouragement and protection, although it is my opinion that these inhabitants might be more serviceable could they be prevailed upon to settle (if there was lands proper for cultivation) near the sea rather than on the Mississippi. But new settlements cannot be forced contrary to men's inclinations, such adventurers must at first be encouraged in infant colonies where they are willing to sit down, and thereafter some of them if they find it for their advantage may be prevailed upon to remove lower down and nearer to the sea coasts.

East Florida has had much more countenance and encouragement than this province (perhaps we have not hitherto deserved it) and I am told they are in a very flourishing condition; but we remain here, instead of improving, in much the same situation we were in some years ago. I do however flatter myself, as we have great tracts of very excellent lands, that if protection and encouragement is given to us and your lordship would deign to adopt and patronise this infant child, that measures might be pursued to place us in a more respectable situation. I shall endeavour to make myself acquainted with every part of the province and then shall be better enabled to judge what methods are most proper to be taken in order to effect this end, and I shall not fail from time to time to furnish your lordship with my sentiments and observations thereupon. *Signed.* [C.O.5/588, p. 9]

XCVI

Governor William Franklin to Earl of Hillsborough (No. 23)

29 September, Perth Amboy

My Lord, I am honoured with your lordship's dispatches [Vol. I, Nos. 404, 467] of June 12th and July 6th. The royal disallowance of the Paper Money and Secaucus Acts I have communicated to the Council and Assembly who are now sitting at this place. The members of the Assembly I find are greatly displeased at the former Act not being confirmed as they thought they had obviated every objection and fully complied with His Majesty's directions contained in the Order of Council of the 26th of May 1769. It was never imagined here that so extensive a construction would be put upon the Act of Parliament for restraining paper currencies in America as that the money should not even be a tender to the loan-offices that issued it. If this had been known here the Assembly would not have attempted to pass an Act for striking paper money for it would have been the heighth of absurdity to expect that any persons would mortgage their estates to the loan-office for money which they could not afterwards oblige the office to receive again in discharge of their mortgages. What, they say, makes their case harder is that the two proprietary governments of Pennsylvania and Maryland have had for some years past and at this very time a consider-able sum of paper money circulating, which though not a legal tender in common payments between man and man is nevertheless a tender to the Treasuries from whence it issued, that the Acts passed in those provinces for this purpose, though transmitted regularly from time to time to His Majesty, have never been disallowed. But what gives me particular concern is that I am not without apprehension that a party among them will take advantage of the ill humour occasioned by their disappointment in this respect and prevail on the Assembly not to grant any money for the support of the King's troops stationed in this province; which would in all probability have been the case last year if expectations had not been given them of a paper currency to enable them to do it in a manner easy and agreeable to the people. As it is now only the beginning of the session it is impossible to say what will be the event but His Majesty may rely upon my doing all in my power to bring them to a better temper and a proper sense of their duty. *Signed.*
PS. Enclosed is a copy of my speech [Vol. I, No. 632i] at the opening of the session [C.O.5/990, fo. 83]

XCVII

Richard Henderson to Governor William Tryon[1]

29 September, Granville

Sir, with the deepest concern for my country I have lately been witness to a scene which not only threatened the peace and well being of this province for the future but was in itself the most horrid and audacious insult to government perpetrated with such circumstances of cruelty and madness as (I believe) scarcely has been equalled at any time.

However flattering your Excellency's prospects may have been with respect to the people called Regulators, their late conduct too sufficiently evinces that a wise, mild and benevolent administration comes very far short of bringing them to a sense of their duty. They are abandoned to every principle of virtue and desperately engaged not only in the most shocking barbarities but a total subversion of the constitution.

On Monday last being the second day of Hillsborough Superior Court, early in the morning the town was filled with a great number of these people, shouting, hallooing and making a considerable tumult in the streets. At about 11 o'clock the court was opened and immediately the house filled as close as one man could stand by another, some with clubs, others with whips and switches, few or none without some weapon. When the house had become so crowded that no more could well get in, one of them (whose name I think is called Fields) came forward and told me he had something to say before I proceeded to business. The accounts I had previously received, together with the manner and appearance of these men and the abruptness of their address, rendered my situation extremely uneasy. Upon my informing Fields that he might speak on, he proceeded to let me know that he spoke for the whole body of the people called Regulators, that they understood I would not try their causes, and that their determination was to have them tried for they had come down to see justice done and justice they would have, and if I would proceed to try those causes it might prevent much mischief. They also charged the court with injustice at the preceding term and objected to the jurors appointed by the inferior court and said they would have them altered and others appointed in their room, with many other things too tedious to mention here. Thus I found myself under a necessity of attempting to soften and turn away the fury of this mad people in the best manner in my power and as much as could well be pacify their rage and at the same time preserve the little remaining dignity of the court. The consequence of which was that after spending upwards of half an hour in this disagreeable situation the mob cried out "Retire, Retire, and let the court go on". Upon which most of the Regulators went out and seemed to be in consultation in a party by themselves. The little hopes of peace derived from this piece of behaviour were very transient for in a few

---

1   Enclosed in Tryon's letter to Hillsborough, 20 October 1770: Vol. I, No. 680.

minutes Mr Williams, an attorney of that court, was coming in and had advanced near the door when they fell on him in a most furious manner with clubs and sticks of enormous size and 'twas with great difficulty he saved his life by taking shelter in a neighbouring store house. Mr Fanning was next the object of their fury: him they seized and took with a degree of violence not to be described from off the bench where he had retired for protection and assistance, and with hideous shouts of barbarian cruelty dragged him by the heels out of doors while others engaged in dealing out blows with such violence that I made no doubt his life would instantly become a sacrifice to their rage and madness. However, Mr Fanning by a manly exertion miraculously broke holt and fortunately jumped into a door that saved him from immediate dissolution. During this uproar several of them told me with oaths of great bitterness that my turn should be next. I will not deny but in this frightful affair my thoughts were much engaged on my own protection, but it was not long before James Hunter and some other of their chieftains came and told me not to be uneasy for that no man should hurt me on proviso I would sit and hold court to the end of the term. I took advantage of this proposal and made no scruple at promising what was not in my intention to perform, for the terms they would admit me to hold court on were that no lawyer, the King's Attorney excepted, should be admitted into court and that they would stay and see justice impartially done.

It would be impertinent to trouble your Excellency with many circumstances that occurred in this barbarous riot. Messrs Thomas Hart, Alexander Martin, Michael Holt, John Litterell (Clerk of the Crown) and many others were severely whipped. Colonel Gray, Major Lloyd, Mr Francis Nash, John Cooke, Tyree Harris and sundry other persons timeously made their escape or would have shared the same fate. In about four or five hours their rage seemed to subside a little and they permitted me to adjourn court and conducted me with great parade to my lodgings. Colonel Fanning whom they had made a prisoner of was in the evening permitted to return to his own house, on his word of honour to surrender himself the next day.

At about ten o'clock that evening, took an opportunity of making my escape by a back way and left poor Colonel Fanning and the little borough in a wretched situation.

Thus far may it please your Excellency with respect to what came within my own knowledge. Since my departure many different and authentic accounts say that the mob, not contented with the cruel abuse they had already given Mr Fanning, in which one of his eyes was almost beaten out, did the next day actually determine to put him immediately to death, but some of them a little more humane than the rest interfered and saved his life. They turned him out in the street and spared his life on no other condition than that of his taking the road and continuing to run until he should get out of their sight. They soon after to consummate their wicked designs broke and entered his mansion house, destroyed every article of furniture and with axes and other instruments laid the fabric level with its foundation, broke and entered his cellar and destroyed the contents. His papers were carried into the streets by armfuls and destroyed, his wearing apparel shared the same fate. I much fear his office will be their next object. Have not yet heard where Colonel Fanning has taken shelter, the last advice was that he was a mile or two from town on horseback but the person by whom this came says that the insurgents have scouting parties constantly traversing the several roads and woods about town, and should he unfortunately fall into their hands the consequence perhaps will be fatal. The merchants and inhabitants were chiefly run out into the country and expect their stores and houses without distinction will be pillaged and laid waste. The number of insurgents that appeared when the riot first began was I think about one hundred and fifty, though they constantly increased for two days and kept a number with firearms at about a mile distance from town ready to fall on whenever they were called for. This account is contradicted by some and believed by others. Certain it is that a large number of men constantly lay near the town, whether they had arms or not is not yet sufficiently determined.

As the burden of conducting Hillsborough Superior Court fell on my shoulders alone, the task was extremely hard and critical. I made every effort in my power consistent with my office and the duty the public is entitled to claim to preserve peace and good order, but as all attempts of that kind were quite ineffectual, thought it more advisable to break up court than sit and be made a mock judge for the sport and entertainment of those abandoned wretches.

This express has been delayed two days in expectation of obtaining from Mr Fanning a more particular account of the damage done him as well as the rest of the inhabitants of that desolate borough, but as the persons whom I sent for that purpose are not yet returned, think it my duty to forward this with the utmost expedition. Should my conduct through these transactions merit your approbation, it will greatly add to the felicity of, sir, your Excellency's most obedient and obliged humble servant, Richard Henderson.

PS. My express has this instant arrived from Hillsborough with the following accounts. Colonel Fanning is alive and well as could be expected. The insurgents left the town on Wednesday night, having done very little mischief after spoiling Mr Fanning's house, except breaking the windows of most of the houses in town, among which Mr Edwards's did not escape. The merchants and others are taking possession of their shattered tenements. Mr Fanning's house is not quite down, a few timbers support the lower storey but they are cut off at the sills and a small breeze of wind will throw down the little remains. Everything else that we heard respecting Mr Fanning is true with this addition that he lost upwards of two hundred pounds in cash.

Enclosed is a petition [Vol. II, No. XCIV] presented me on Saturday by James Hunter, that being the first day of the court. The answer was deferred till Monday. Your Excellency will best judge if that paper may not be of service at a future day. There are many subscribers who are all without dispute Regulators. *Copy.* [C.O.5/314, fo. 11]

XCVIII

Earl of Hillsborough to Deputy Governor Robert Eden (No. 19)

3 October, Whitehall

Sir, the last New York packet brought me a dispatch [Vol. II, No. LX] from you without any date, which I have laid before the King.

As your letter appears to have been written before the resolution taken by the merchants of New York to break through their non-importation agreement had come to your knowledge, I am hopeful that the influence of that event will so far extend itself over the neighbouring colonies that in your next dispatch you will authorise me to expect the speedy return of the good people of Maryland to their duty and the pursuit of their own interests, and that they will resolve to be no longer guided by or made subservient to the factious purposes of the enemies of their happiness and prosperity.

In the meantime, and until this desirable event shall happen, it will be your duty to persevere in your commendable endeavours for removing the prejudices so unjustly and unfortunately entertained of the dispositions of government towards the colonies, and to watch over and guard against with your usual attention every proceeding which may have a tendency to obstruct the return of confidence and harmony between the King's subjects on both sides the water, whose interests and well being are so intimately connected and whose happiness it is so much His Majesty's royal purpose and endeavour to promote. *Draft.* [C.O.5/1283, fo. 58]

XCIX

Earl of Hillsborough to Governor Lord Botetourt (No. 37)

3 October, Whitehall

My Lord, your lordship's dispatches [Vol. I, Nos. 435, 444, 553, 562] Nos. 34, 35, 36 and 37 have been received and laid before the King, and the Journals of the Council and House of Burgesses together with the Acts passed in the last session of Assembly having been by His Majesty's command transmitted to the Board of Trade, I am persuaded their lordships will not fail to take every step that shall be proper in consequence thereof, and to lay before His Majesty such of the laws as shall appear to require the royal confirmation either from their having clauses suspending their execution or from any other circumstances that shall make such confirmation necessary.

I have long seen and lamented how greatly Assemblies in America have been influenced in their proceedings and deliberations by the private correspondence of persons here in England, who seem to have no other view but to promote distress to the mother country by all possible means, and there is little doubt that both the Association [Vol. I, No. 444ii] for non-importation and the petition [Vol. II, No. LIX] of the House of Burgesses on the subject of Revenue Laws and the regulation of the Courts of Admiralty have been encouraged by advice of this sort; but I am at a loss to guess by what species of reasoning it is that the House of Burgesses of Virginia can in these cases reconcile an implicit submission to the dictates of turbulent individuals with their own dignity and with a conduct that seems in every other respect to have no other object than the public welfare.

I am convinced upon the fullest consideration that the extension of the boundary line as proposed in the address of the House of Burgesses to you in December last would never have been consented to by the Cherokees or, if their consent could have been obtained, that settlement so far to the westward would not only have been inconsistent with the true principles of policy but would also have been the ground of continual jealousy and dispute, and therefore it was very pleasing to me to find that the House had receded from its claim and closed with the proposal contained in my letter to you of the 13th of May 1769.

It would have been very fortunate if this service could have been completed for the sum originally estimated and that your lordship had not been under the necessity of adopting so unusual a measure as that of drawing upon His Majesty's quitrents for the sum of £400 which Mr Stuart thought fit to add to his estimate. The King however acquiesces in the motives which have induced your lordship to take this step, fully confiding that proper care will be taken that it shall not be drawn into precedent.

I am very happy that the answer I gave to General Mackay on the subject of his recommendation of Mr Wormly is approved by your lordship. I agree with you in opinion that his distant residence from the seat of government is a good ground of objection to his being of the Council, and I shall not fail to communicate to the Board of Trade what your lordship proposes in regard to Mr Diggs; but I do not apprehend that an appointment of that gentleman can take place until a vacancy happens, when I have no doubt that your recommendation will have its due weight. *Draft*. [C.O.5/1348, fo. 140]

C

Earl of Hillsborough to Lieut.-Governor Thomas Hutchinson (No. 42)

3 October, Whitehall

Sir, since my letters [Vol. I, No. 558] to you of the 4th of August, duplicates of which were transmitted to you by Mr Pownall on the 5th of September, I have received and laid before the King your dispatches [Vol. I, Nos. 500, 537, 559, 563], Nos. 19, 20, 21 and 22.

The great candour and moderation with which you stated the situation of the colony in your speech to the Assembly on the 25th of July and the manner in which you urged to them the propriety of proceeding to the dispatch of the public business are very much to be commended, and with men really disposed to promote the public welfare could not have failed of producing the effect you hoped for. It is however but too apparent from the violence and indecency of their answer that they have other objects in view and really mean to promote distress to the mother country at the expense of the interests of their constituents.

If neither the authority of Parliament nor the decision of the Privy Council in matters relative to the government and constitution of that colony are to be admitted, those ideas of their becoming independent which have been treated as chimerical will indeed be realised; and it is become highly proper that no more time should be lost in deliberation upon those measures that are essentially necessary to prevent such an independence taking effect; and I am persuaded that all those who wish well to the community and who do not mean to concur in the dangerous design of a few desperate men will see the necessity of such a further explanation and reform of the constitution of the Massachusetts Bay as shall have the effect to restore the dignity of the King's government and the authority of the supreme legislature. In the meantime it is certainly advisable to avoid as much as possible entering into arguments with them on the ground of such pretensions as are held forth in their answer to your speech; but some reply to that answer was clearly unavoidable, and the prudence and spirit with which that reply is drawn are equally approved by the King.

As no steps have yet been taken in respect to the arrangements mentioned to you in my letter of the 14th April last, there will be the less difficulty in complying with what you suggest in your letter No. 22 in consequence of Mr Rogers's death, which is the more to be lamented if it should have been occasioned as you seem to think by the illiberal and violent attacks made upon him in consequence of his refusing to concur in those measures which have been so disgraceful to the town of Boston. *Draft.* [C.O.5/759, fo. 263]

CI

Lieut. Governor Cadwallader Colden to Earl of Hillsborough (No. 17)

5 October, New York

My Lord, as this most probably is the last opportunity by which I can have the honour of writing to your lordship while the administration of government is in my hands, I think it incumbent on me to give you some account of the persons who are most attached to government in opposition to the party who continue to declare openly against the authority of the Parliament of Great Britain.

In my preceding letters I informed your lordship of the steps that had been taken to introduce a general importation of goods from Great Britain and of the opposition which had been made to it by that party who have in every other instance endeavoured to embarrass the measures of government. It gave me particular satisfaction to find this party entirely defeated last week in a violent struggle to turn out such of the elective magistrates of this city as had distinguished themselves any way in favour of government.

I believe your lordship will be pleased to know that the members of His Majesty's Council, with a single exception, and the Representatives of this city in General Assembly have zealously exerted themselves for a dissolution of the non-importation agreement in New York, which must have a general good effect in all the North American colonies. Mr Ludlow, whom I appointed one of the puisne judges of the Supreme Court in the room of Mr Smith, deceased, was very useful. He has many friends among the merchants, and they were the foremost in declaring for importation. He has at all times been a friend to government, is a man of genius and of application, and I doubt not will distinguish himself in his station.

No particular person has been more distinguished on this occasion than Mr Banyar, deputy secretary of the province. He took great pains to excite and preserve a proper spirit in others. He has likewise been very useful to me in every part of my administration. Permit me, my lord, to mention him as one every way deserving your lordship's attention in case anything may offer in his favour. I have been conversant fifty years in the public affairs of this government and I can truly say that he has in his office exceeded all that have been in it during that time both in ability and diligence. He has faithfully discharged every confidence placed in him by government and has so well established the opinion of his integrity and honour for upwards of twenty years past that every governor in that time has placed a particular confidence in his advice, Sir Henry Moore only excepted. Perhaps, my lord, you may expect that I mention the persons who have opposed the salutary measures of government. Though every man conversant in public affairs be well assured in his own mind who are the leaders and conductors of the opposition to government, yet as they do not appear publicly but work by their tools of inferior rank, no legal evidence I can produce against them. I must therefore beg to be excused from naming any person.

As now all kind of rioting is greatly discouraged I hope to deliver up the administration not only in tranquillity but with a prevailing disposition in the people to support government. I flatter myself that I shall retain some degree of your lordship's esteem and regard. I have the honour to be with the greatest respect, my lord, your most obedient and faithful servant. *Signed*. [C.O.5/1101, fo. 97]

CII

George Washington to Governor Lord Botetourt[1]

5 October, Mount Vernon

My Lord, being fully convinced of your lordship's inclination to render every just and reasonable service to the people you govern and to any society or body of them that shall ask it, and being in a more particular manner encouraged by a letter which I have just received from Mr Blair (Clerk of the Council) to believe that your Excellency is desirous of knowing how far the grant of lands solicited by Mr Walpole and others will affect the interest of this country in general or any set of men in particular, I shall take the liberty (being tolerably well acquainted with the situation of the frontiers of this dominion) to inform your lordship that the bounds of that grant, if obtained upon the extensive plan prayed for, will comprehend at least four-fifths of the land for which this colony hath lately voted £2,500 sterling for the purchase and survey of; and must destroy the well-grounded hopes of those (if no reservation is made in their favour) who have had the strongest

---

1 Enclosed in Nelson's letter to Hillsborough, 18 October 1770: Vol. I, No. 674.

assurances which government could give them of enjoying some of those lands, the securing of which hath cost this country much blood and treasure.

By the extracts which your Excellency did me the honour to enclose, I perceive that the petitioners require to begin on the south side of the Ohio opposite to the mouth of Scioto which is at least 70 or 75 miles below the mouth of the Great Kanhawa, the place to which the ministerial line (as it is called) from Holston's River is to run, and more than 300 from Pittsburg, and to extend from thence in a southerly direction through the pass of the Ouasioto Mountain, which by Evans's map, the best draughts of that country I have ever yet seen, and all the enquiries I have been able to make from persons who have explored those wilds, will bring them near the latitude of North Carolina. From hence they go north easterly to the fork of the Great Kanhawa (made by the junction of Green Briar and New River, on both of which waters we have many settlers on lands actually patented). From hence they proceed up Green Briar to the head of the north easterly branch thereof, thence easterly to the Allegany Mountains, thence along those mountains to the line of the Lord Fairfax, thence with his line and the lines of Maryland and Pennsylvania till the western boundary of the latter shall strike the Ohio, thence with the same to the place of beginning.

These, my lord, are the bounds of a grant under consideration, and if obtained will in my humble opinion give a fatal blow to the interests of this country, but this I have presumed to say as the sum of my thoughts as a member of the community at large.

I shall beg leave now to offer myself to your Excellency's notice as an individual in a more interested point of view and at the same time as a person who considers himself in some degree the representative of the officers and soldiers who claim a right to 200,000 acres of this very land petitioned for by Mr Walpole and others, under a solemn act of government adopted at a very alarming and important crisis to His Majesty's affairs in America. To approach your lordship in these characters, it might seem necessary to preface an apology, but I shall rely on your usual goodness and candour for the patient hearing of a few words in support of the equity of our pretensions, which cannot fail of being short as I have taken the liberty of troubling your lordship pretty fully on this head before.

The first letter I ever did myself the honour of writing to your Excellency on the subject of these lands, and to which I now beg leave to refer, contained a kind of historical account of our claim; but as no embellishment is requisite to illustrate a right when simple facts are sufficient to establish the point, I shall beg leave to give your lordship the trouble of reading the enclosed Order of Council of the 18th of February 1754 and Governor Dinwiddie's proclamation in consequence thereof; and then add that these troops not only enlisted agreeable to the terms there stipulated but behaved so much to the satisfaction of the country as to obtain the honour of its public thanks. Would it not be hard, my lord, to deprive men under these circumstances (or their successors) of the just reward of their toils? Could the act of the Governor and Council, offered to and accepted by the soldiery, be considered in any other light than as an absolute compact? And though the exigency of our affairs rendered it impracticable for us to settle this country for some years after the date of the proclamation and the policy of government forbid it for a few years longer, yet the causes being now removed and the land given to some as a recompense for their losses, and sought after by others for private emolument, have we not a title to be regarded among the first? We fain would hope so. We flatter ourselves that in this point of view your Excellency will also consider us and by your kind interposition and favourable representation of our case, His Majesty will be graciously pleased to confirm the 200,000 acres of land to us, agreeable to the terms of the proclamation. Or if it should be judged necessary to be more particular in the location of it, and your lordship will be pleased to cause the same to be signified to me, I will point out immediately thereupon the particular spots on which we would beg to have our surveys made, as part of the land prayed for in our petition of the 15th of December last, to wit, that on Sandy Creek, will not be comprehended within the line running from Holston's River to the mouth of the Great Kanhawa.

Such an act of goodness as this, my lord, would be conferring a singular favour on men who do not know who else to apply to, on men the most of whom either in their persons or fortunes have suffered in the cause of their country; and cannot fail of meeting with such acknowledgements as result from grateful minds impressed with the due sense of obligation.

PS. [Minutes of Council of Virginia, 18 February 1754, and Proclamation of 19 February 1754 quoted.] It may not be amiss to add by way of remark that the complement of men adjudged necessary (sufficient) for this service (though the event proved them otherwise) were actually raised in consequence of this proclamation; that they marched over the Alleghany Mountains through almost inaccessible passes and built a fort on the waters of Monongahela, which they were obliged afterwards to surrender to the superior force of the French and their Indian allies; but they conducted themselves in that enterprise in such a manner as to receive the honour of their country's thanks, as may appear by the Journals of the House of Burgesses in the session following; and that many of them continued in the service till the total demolition of Fort Duquesne and establishment of an English garrison in its place. G. W. *Copy.* [C.O.5/1348, fo. 177]

CIII

Lieut.-General Thomas Gage to John Stuart[1]

16 October, New York

Sir, I am obliged to you for your favour of the 6 August and glad to find the Creeks so sensible of the obligations they owe you for mediating the peace between them and the Choctaws.

The congress held at Siota by the Shawnese and Western nations

---

1 Enclosed in John Stuart's letter to Hillsborough, 28 November 1770: Vol. I, No. 755.

has had more effect than our Indian officers thought possible to be brought about. The spies sent thither inform that all the Western tribes over the Lakes and about Lake Michigan as well as the Oubache Indians had unanimously agreed to make peace with the Cherokees and other Southern nations. You see that the Shawnese deputies have not worked in vain, and hope the Creeks will be less reserved when you next talk to them upon the business of those deputies in their nation and that Emistisiguo will tell you the drift of their negotiations as he has promised to do. The scheme of the Shawnese to form a confederacy of all the Western and Southern nations is a notable piece of policy, for nothing less would enable them to withstand the Six Nations and their allies against whom they have been much exasperated on account of the boundary treaty held at Fort Stanwix. You must have observed that the Cherokees likewise are concerned in that treaty and would have felt it, had the boundaries granted been claimed in their full extent; and the not permitting the Virginians to extend their line in the manner they designed, partly under the sanction of that treaty, already appears to be a judicious and fortunate measure. They would have been hurt at it undoubtedly and been easily induced to have joined this confederacy, which I hope you will have influence enough to prevent. At the congress of the Six Nations and Northern Indians, war was strongly proposed and that hostilities should be commenced by immediately striking the Western Indians, chiefly the tribes of the Oubache, but Sir William Johnson had influence enough to persuade them to try first what messages would do. I am informed that messengers are sent to those nations to see if persuasion will bring them to their senses, though I apprehend they will be talked to in a very haughty style.

Since the commencement of the congress at Siota most of the nations who go to Fort Pitt are observed to behave civilly but appear reserved and sulky and are counselling and continually sending belts from one nation to another, and reports go that some Frenchman has promised to engage the Illinois, Mississippi and Arkanza Indians to join the league.

It appears that the fomentors of this league, of which the Shawnese seem to have been the principal, are trying to draw all the nations they can into it to make themselves as formidable as possible, for they perceive the Six Nations etc. are with us; all the Ohio Indians are the most exasperated as they are the greatest sufferers, and have no patience in seeing our frontier people settling upon the lands near them.

I have given you a sketch of the state of our Indian affairs in this quarter and trust your influence with the nations in your district will enable you to defeat the machinations of the Shawnese, whose deputies will not fail to use every endeavour to draw them into the combination they have been forming. PS. Some of the Cherokee deputies who attended the Northern congress have been waiting several weeks an opportunity to get from hence to Charleston. They will inform you what passed there, and I am informed they have engaged for their nation with the Six Nations and Northern Indians. *Copy.* [C.O.5/72, fo. 41]

CIV

President William Nelson to Earl of Hillsborough (No. 2)

18 October, Virginia

My Lord, on the 15th inst. I did myself the honour of writing [Vol. I, No. 668] to your lordship to acquaint you with the melancholy event of the death of Lord Botetourt, which had thrown His Majesty's faithful subjects of this colony into the deepest affliction. At the same time I sent a copy of the proceedings in Council to show your lordship by what means the administration of the government had fallen into my hands.

On the evening of that day your lordship's letter[1] of the 20th of July to the governor was delivered to me, and as it contains matter of great variety and importance it hath been read in Council and together with the several papers enclosed in it hath been maturely considered, and I now trouble your lordship with their's, as well as my own opinion upon the subject of them.

I must first acknowledge the propriety and justice of your lordship and my Lords Commissioners of the Treasury in delaying to report in favour of Mr Walpole and his associates for so large a grant of lands on the back of this colony until the country shall be made acquainted with it, and their reasons if they had any in objection to it should be heard; and our thanks are particularly due to your lordship for affording the Governor and Council an opportunity of defending themselves against the indecent, illiberal and unwarrantable charges contained in a letter [Vol. I, No. 503i] of the 9th of July 1770 to Mr Walpole, referring first to your lordship's consideration what degree of credibility an anonymous writer who thus stabs in the dark is entitled to, though by the great commendation he gives of the *generous* proposal of Mr Walpole and his associates to government for the purchase of the lands they want, it is probable he is one of that respectable body.

The charges in this letter are that the Governor and Council of Virginia have made large and immoderate grants of lands to the westward of the Allegany Mountains, that many such grants (of which a list [Vol. I, No. 674iii] is annexed to the letter) are made to the members of Council themselves, who by selling those lands to others make large profits, and that this practice hath been carried on and encouraged by them notwithstanding His Majesty's instructions that no larger quantity shall be granted to any one person than 1000 acres. The truth of fact is that this instruction was not given till 1763 and that all these grants so loudly complained of were made long before the existence of that instruction and in the era when it was thought good policy to settle those lands as fast as possible, and that the granting them to men of the first consequence who were likeliest and best able to procure large bodies of people to settle on them was the most probable means of effecting the end proposed. As to the grantees making large profits by the sale of them to others, I am confident the fact is otherwise since the stated price for such lands (except

1 Letter acknowledged was from Commissioners for Trade and Plantations, Vol. II, No. LXXIII.

in very few cases) hath been £3 Virginia currency per 100 acres, a price very little higher than it would cost any man who should incline to take up singly 3, 4, or 400 acres. It is very fortunate for me that whilst I am writing upon this subject I do not find my name in any of these grants though I have been 25 years a member of the Board, and am therefore no otherwise concerned than to vindicate the honour of the Governor and the gentlemen of the Council, especially of those whose names are made use of in some of those grants. I claim no merit from this circumstance as I do not think their conduct at all unwarrantable, which I hope to show in the sequel of this letter. My reason for declining such engagements proceeded from an opinion that little if any profit would arise from them, but some trouble; and the experience I have had now shows that I was right in that opinion. For I have good cause to know that those gentlemen of the Council who did engage in those grants have not received one shilling of advantage from them nor do I believe they ever will. It is true that some of the grantees residing on the frontiers, men of activity and strength of constitution, who have had all the trouble, expense and fatigue of surveying the lands and of procuring others to purchase and settle on them, I presume, have made some advantages by reserving some to themselves and by the sale of other parts; and this they seem to have deserved for their labour. In order to show your lordship how groundless the charge is that the Governor and Council have acted unwarrantably in the making unreasonable grants of lands, the enclosed paper [Vol. I, No. 674i] No. 1 contains the proceedings relative to the grants to the Ohio Company, by which it appears that by application to his late Majesty, he was pleased to order his then Governor and Council to grant them 200,000 acres upon the terms expressed in the said paper, and your lordship will observe that though some of the grantees were of the Council, yet many of them were also resident in Great Britain. The next grant in order of time on or near the Ohio was by proclamation [Vol. I, No. 674ii] from Lieut.-Governor Dinwiddie, promising 200,000 acres of land to be given and divided among such as would voluntarily enter into His Majesty's service for the defence of the frontiers, at that time violently attacked by the French and Indians, and those lands the officers and soldiers who served are at this instant surveying, in order to obtain patents for them; and their right seems to be a good one as many of them sealed the contract with their blood, whose shares will be apportioned among their surviving wives, children and other legal representatives. Thus far the Governor and Council I hope have done right. Indeed this last grant was so much approved of by his late Majesty that he soon after adopted and enlarged the plan by offering by his royal proclamation large quantities of land to the officers and soldiers who should enter into his service on this continent, the quantity not fixed, but 5,000 acres to a colonel and so less to the other officers according to their rank, and even to the common soldiers. To satisfy the regiments raised in this colony upon that promise, I presume 200,000 acres will be required. Besides these, we have been told (though we have never had an authentic copy of the treaty at Fort Stanwyx) that the Indians made it an express condition in the deed of cession to

His Majesty that 100,000 acres of it should be granted to Col. Croghan, deputy of Sir William Johnson, and a like quantity to the Pennsylvania traders as a recompense to them for the injuries and damages they sustained from the Indians during the late war. All these amounting to 800,000 acres are to the northward, and I presume near the lands which these new adventurers want, and I presume the Governor and Council to be blameless in all these. In all the other grants listed at the end of this anonymous letter No. 9, I do not find that any steps have been taken towards surveying and seating them; of course they are or will become lapsed except in the two to John Lewis and others for 800,000 acres and to James Patton and others for 100,000 acres. On those lands which are located from Green Briar River to the branches of the Holston River, and will be within the limits of the land now purchasing by His Majesty for the Cherokees, there are many hundred families settled (I ought here to observe that the Assembly of Virginia have given £2,500 sterling for the purchase of those lands) and those are the people, my lord, who were so greatly distressed by His Majesty's proclamation of 1763 requiring them to abandon all the lands on the watercourses running to the westward or into the Mississippi. This proclamation they refused to comply with; nay, they said they could not do it, for having expended their little all under the grants from this government, they had no other place to retire to, and have hitherto chose to rely on a kind providence, exposed as they have been to the resentment of the Indians; and this is the reason that I find that very little if any quitrents have been received for His Majesty's use from that quarter for some time past, for they say that as His Majesty hath been pleased to withdraw his protection from them since 1763 they think themselves not bound to pay quitrents. However, as this boundary with the Cherokees will be completed in the spring I have no doubt but regular government will take place there as it is in other parts of this dominion, and that the quitrents will be there properly collected. I entreat your lordship to let me know His Majesty's pleasure with respect to those lands, whether he is pleased to permit them to be granted or not; for, notwithstanding the assertions in the paper No. 9, we have not granted one acre in those parts since the proclamation, nor shall we until set at liberty to do it, though many applications have been made for that purpose without success. The people are still continuing to settle those lands under the equitable right they derive from the grant to John Lewis and others. James Patton's grant is also pretty full of inhabitants, and his family receive some advantage from it, and truly think they ought since the old man paid his scalp as the price of it, he being murdered by the Indians on the way as he was escorting ammunition for the defence of the settlers on Green Briar. I can only say on the subject of those two grants and all the other large ones, that they were made at a time when the policy of the day was to make large grants to persons who were likeliest to procure people to inhabit and to cultivate the lands, which ends have been nearly attained in both these instances. The late war and the prohibition by proclamation have been the causes that those lands have not been more fully peopled, which I have reasons to think will be effected soon after leave is given to grant patents for such parts as are settled. Those 1,700,000 acres which I have taken notice of in all, I suppose will take place of all new adventurers. We do not presume to say to whom our gracious Sovereign shall grant his vacant lands, nor do I set myself as an opponent to Mr Walpole and his associates. All that I can, consistently with my duty, hope for is that all prior rights whether equitable or legal may be preserved and protected. By equitable, I mean all those who have had grants but have been prevented from complying with the strict terms of them by the war or any other unavoidable impediment; by legal, I mean all those for which patents have been obtained.

If we take a comparative view of the merit of those new adventurers with that of the people who have run great hazards during the course of the war, many of whom lost their lives and fortunes in the prosecution of those settlements, others had their wives, children and other dearest relatives carried into a barbarous captivity, many of whom still languish in that distressful situation, it will not be difficult to determine on which side the weight prevails.

As to the garbling the lands which the letter No. 9 twice mentions, I beg your lordship to consider that the proposal of Mr Walpole and his associates of paying quitrents only for the cultivable lands amounts to a great deal more in its consequences. For, under that description, who can suppose that they intend to include and pay quitrents for sterile mountains or rocky lands? whereas we have a law of this country which the surveyors are obliged to conform to, requiring that the breadth of every survey of land shall be at least one-third of the length, and this was enacted on purpose to prevent the practice of garbling as it is called, that is that the patentees shall be obliged to take some indifferent land with the good.

Permit me here to observe that the 20 years indulgence these gentlemen desire before they shall be obliged to pay quitrents is more than ever hath been allowed, even by the law of 1754 which was passed by a recommendation from his late Majesty; and the merit they make of purchasing these lands is not considerable when we reflect that the price of 5s. 0d. sterling for 50 acres which every man pays before he can obtain a patent (except in particular exemptions as above) amounts on so great a quantity to as much or more; and as His Majesty and his late royal grandfather have been graciously pleased to permit the money arising from the sale of the rights to be applied to the fund for the support of government and the contingent charges thereof, that fund will sustain a heavy loss if it should be withdrawn at this time.

With respect to the establishment of a new colony on the back of Virginia, it is a subject of too great political importance for me to presume to give an opinion upon. However, permit me, my lord, to observe that when that part of the country shall become sufficiently populated, it may be a wise and prudent measure. But the argument that the settlement of those parts will be a good barrier and defence to the frontiers of Virginia appears to me from experience to be rather specious than solid; for the greatest difficulty and expense of defending our frontiers in the last war proceeded from the vast distance and extent of them. If you increase that distance and extent the difficulty and expense of defending will be proportionably increased, and the people as settled there sparsedly were incapable of defending themselves and often called for assistance from the interior and more populous parts of the country.

At all events I trust that these gentlemen if they succeed in their scheme will not be permitted to oppose their power and strength to the feeble resistance of the poor settlers who have borne the heat and burden of the day, and that these will not share the fate of the unfortunate Naboth whose vineyard became a tempting object to a rich and powerful man.

It will certainly be proper before any grant is made to Mr Walpole and his associates to have an exact list taken of the people settled on those lands and under what rights, that they may be particularly reserved, and not to leave a door open to future contention about them, which however I have at present no possible method of obtaining nor do I think it can be done but by great length of time and at no small expense.

After I had wrote thus far and was reading it to the gentlemen of the Council for their approbation, a letter from Col. George Washington to Lord Botetourt was delivered to me, which being read and appearing to be material on the present subject, they advised me to send a copy [Vol. II, No. CII] of it to your lordship which is accordingly enclosed, No. 3. I ought to acquaint your lordship that he is the gentleman who had the honour to command the first raised troops to whom the 200,000 acres promised by Lieut.-Governor Dinwiddie's proclamation is due, and therefore he may be interested in the affair; however your lordship will judge of the solidity of his reasoning.

I omitted to mention in its proper place that unless Mr Walpole and his associates should sell out the lands in small parcels at reasonable rates they will remain long without much cultivation or settlement, since men in this quarter of the globe, where it is so easy to become absolute proprietors of land, are not fond of farming them. It is a vast encouragement to the improvement and cultivation of the lands when they can enjoy the pleasure to reflect that their posterity will receive the benefit of the labour they bestow. If these gentlemen should be left at liberty to exact what terms they please for the lands, either by the sale or letting them to farm, consider, my lord, how little ground will be left to hope for a speedy settlement or population. If they should do neither of these, but each individual should keep possession of his large share till lands should be scarce and at a high price or they should require a high rent, which may be raised from time to time, we may possibly have reason to apprehend such convulsions and insurrections as happened in the colony of New York a very few years since between the great landholders and their tenants on a subject of this nature.

Thus, my lord, have I endeavoured to give the fullest and clearest answer I could to your letter and the several papers referred to and enclosed in it. If I have done it to your lordship's satisfaction I shall be happy.

I ought to beg pardon for being so prolix, which however I could not well avoid when I observed how very desirous your lordship is of as full and particular information as possible of everything necessary to this great consideration. *Signed.* [C.O.5/1348, fo. 161]

CV

Report of Congress with Cherokees[1]

18 October, Lochaber

At a general meeting of the principal chiefs and warriors of the Cherokee nation with John Stuart Esq., Superintendent for the Southern District of North America.

Present: John Stuart Esq., Superintendent, Col. John Donelson, commissioner in behalf of the province of Virginia by appointment of his Excellency the Right Honourable Lord Botetourt, Alexander Cameron Esq., Deputy Superintendent, James Simpson Esq., Clerk of His Majesty's Honourable Council of South Carolina; Major Lacy from Virginia, Col. Gervais, Major Williamson, Capt. Colhoun, John Caldwell Esq., Capt. Winter, Christopher Peters Esq., Edward Wilkinson, John Hammerer Esq., John Purves Esq., John Bowie Esq., etc., besides a number of back-inhabitants of the province of South Carolina; and the following Indian Cherokee chiefs: Oucconnastotah, Attahkullakullah, Uka Youla, Kittagusta, Kujahetoy, Tiftoy, Tarrapin, Ecuij, Skaleloske, Chinista, Chinista of Watoga, Otacite of Highwassie, The Rat, and about a thousand Indians of the same nation; John Watts, David McDonald, John Vann, interpreters.

After the usual ceremonies of smoking the calumet of peace, the Superintendant opened the congress in the following speech.

Although it is not long since I had the pleasure of smoking with you at Congarees, I now meet you with equal pleasure as I am in hopes of being able to agree with you upon such a boundary line between your hunting grounds and the dominion of Virginia as may be agreeable to both parties. The finishing this important business to your mutual satisfaction has long been wished for by me and will give the greatest pleasure to my Lord Botetourt, His Majesty's Lieutenant and Governor of said province.

The Governor of Virginia has appointed this gentleman (Col. Donelson) to be present at our conferences and to deliver you a talk which you may consider as from my Lord Botetourt. He is now ready to speak and I beg you will be attentive to him.

Colonel Donelson speaks.

Friends and Brothers, I am sent here by the Governor of Virginia who informs you through me how much it is his sanguine desire and hope that the measures which may be entered into now by your chiefs and warriors and His Majesty's Superintendent will remove all the causes of complaints which he has been very sorry to hear of.

His Majesty has given directions to treat with you for some lands claimed by you within the limits of Virginia, and the Superintendent will point out to you the line proposed, which if you agree to, His

---

1   Enclosed in John Stuart's letter to Hillsborough, 28 November 1770: Vol. I, No. 755.

Lordship the Governor of Virginia has empowered Mr Stuart to deliver you a quantity of presents. His Lordship has directed me to give you the strongest assurances that after a boundary line shall be agreed upon, he with the other branches of the legislature of the colony will take every proper measure to prevent any encroachments on the lands you shall reserve for your own use and remove as far as possible all causes of complaint, in confirmation whereof in behalf of His Lordship I deliver you this belt of whampum.

Gives a belt of whampum.

The Superintendent speaks.

Friends and Brothers, I shall now proceed to the business that occasions this meeting. It is about two years since the treaty which I now hold in my hand was entered into by you at Hard Labour. By it the boundaries dividing your hunting grounds from the provinces of South and North Carolina and Virginia were agreed upon and fixed, and I transmitted copies of the treaties to the respective governors. The line then agreed upon respecting Virginia was to begin where that behind North Carolina ended, at the division of the two provinces, to proceed from thence in a northerly-by-east course to Colonel Chiswell's mine on the Great Conhoway, and thence to run in a straight direction to the mouth of the Conhoway where it empties itself into the Ohio. I was then in hopes we should have had no further occasion to meet and talk about lands, but it appeared that by said line the lands upon which a great number of families are settled between the Great Kanhaway and Holston's River would have been cut off from the province of Virginia and determined to belong to the Cherokees. The relief of so many families who would have been involved in the greatest difficulties and distress by said lines taking place was an object that engaged the humanity of my Lord Botetourt. His Lordship represented the matter to the King who was graciously pleased to order me to enter into a new negotiation with you for obtaining such a new boundary as may secure to the families settled between Holstein's River and the Conhoway the possession of their lands. There are many amongst you who know that said lands have been inhabited by them these twenty years. At the beginning of the war with the Northern Indians, they were driven from their habitations, but as soon as a peace was re-established, they took possession again. The line I am directed to propose for said purpose is to begin where that behind North Carolina terminates, and thence to run in a due west direction to Holstein's River where it is intersected by a line dividing the two provinces, and thence to run in a straight course to the confluence of the Conhoway with the Ohio. This line will cover the inhabitants and prevent their ruin by securing to them their possessions while it will not deprive you of one foot of your hunting ground, for you know you never hunted in the ground that is proposed to be given up to His Majesty by this line. It is not His Majesty's intention that you should injure yourselves by giving up your hunting grounds, neither is any such thing requested of you by my Lord Botetourt. But as I have brought with me a quantity of presents as a consideration for the lands contained within the abovementioned lines, I hope you will not refuse to confirm it as an acknowledgement of His Majesty's goodness to you and of your friendship for your white brethren.

A belt of white whampum.

I desire to have an answer tomorrow concerning my proposal and that you will at the same time determine upon the time of marking the line that shall be agreed upon, and the number of deputies who you propose to send for that purpose. This will be necessary that provision may be made for them and that commissioners from Virginia with my deputy may know precisely when to meet them. Your deputies will be attended by Mr Cameron and an interpreter.

Friday 19th October

The Superintendent and the chiefs and warriors being met as the day before, the congress was opened as usual.

Oucconnastotah speaks.

Father, we have done smoking, we will proceed on our talk, our thoughts are straight, and this is a clear time of the day. Now we have seen one another, you are my father, whom we have met to have a good talk, and I conclude it will be so. I live at the farthest town in the nation, and now we are met I expect we will have a good talk. I am come over great mountains to meet you, which I think little of.

Gives a string whampum.

You are sitting there, an old man as I am, to hear what passes, and I will now talk with the beloved man from Virginia.

(To Col. Donelson)

This is the first time we ever saw one another or talked together, but as the land has long been talked about, I now expect the business will be concluded. Several years ago the talk begun at Augusta and all the governors heard it. 'Tis but a little land you ask, but stop a little we will have more talk about it.

A string of white whampum.

We are all old men who are come over the mountains, there are but four of us, and we must wait a while to conclude upon it. You are like a small bird singing over one's house [*Marginal note:* esteemed a bad omen] but the business cannot be so soon determined. There are four or five old men come over the mountains, the young fellows are gone out to hunt and know nothing of this and will say why should these old men give away the land without our knowledge. There are seven towns over the hills and it is they must conclude this, and I will go and talk to the governor of Virginia about it, I will meet him and lay these beads upon the ground, and when the governor and I meet we will talk about the matter. Starnacres Place I do not think much of but my young men formerly hunted there. We will however talk more of this business hereafter.

A string of whampum.

When I go to Virginia I will eat and drink with my white brethren and I shall expect friendship and good usage from them. It is but a little spot of ground that you ask and I do not want to keep it from you and am willing your people should live upon it. I pity the white people but they do not pity me, for they will still keep up the price of goods. They are encroaching on us as far as they can, and if we go and ask them for provisions they charge us more than it is worth. As for the land below Keowee it is entirely wore out, and the Lower Towns' people are obliged to go over the hills to hunt; I will give the land as far as Starnacres but cannot give it any farther.

To the Superintendent.

Father, it is the white hunters that trouble us, let them go over the mountains and not hunt on Holston's River. But Capt. Guess comes into our grounds and hunts with fifty men and kills our deer and when we tell him of it he threatens to shoot us down.

Father, the people that live in the valley gave me a string of whampum to deliver to you and desired me to talk to you and tell you as long as they see these beads they will give a good talk and will thank me for this talk.

A string of beads.

Father, I now present you this calumet with two heads, the one looking to the other, which will put you in mind when you smoke that you are looking at your children.

Attahkullahkullah speaks.

I have thought of your proposal all night and now the day is come I will give you my talk. You are the messenger that brought the talk to which I listened very attentively, and I therefore expect you will listen as attentively to mine. We are now talking. You are the two beloved men, and here is another and we will have the talk over. It is a great while since this talk was begun, now we are come young and old to conclude it. When you all met at Augusta at the great congress, I believe you may remember what passed, and it is now continued. It seems like stepping out of the door to be at the white people's settlements. I do not know what my brothers mean: it seems like coming into our houses and encroaching on us greatly. It is long since this land was first inhabited. He that made this land gave it to the Indians to live upon but the white people's land is beyond the great water and the land on this side belongs to the red. The old warriors are all dead, there are young people grown up in their room. Yet the white people want to come into their doors, but the Great Being above is looking down to see no injustice done us. There are three Great Beings above, one who has charge of the white, one of the red, and one of the black people, who take care of their several charges, but this the white people knew before me for they had writings from above. The Great Being above is very good and provides for everybody, it is he that made fire, bread, and the rivers to run, he gave us this land, but the white people seem to want to drive us from it. You are all talking together fast, I always talk loud that everybody may hear me. I expect to live in love and unity with my white brethren, and as to anything concerning the land I can give no answer to it at present. What we say is a law to our people but it is not the case amongst the white people for the traders say different things and have different regulations. The inhabitants on this side the mountains have driven away all our deer, and we find them very scarce. When we go over the mountains to hunt we find paths trodden by the Virginia people and houses built everywhere. Our people think that these settlements were not made by orders from either you or the governor of Virginia, but that they did it of their own accord.

The Superintendent then desired to know where such settlements were.

To whom he replied there were two houses built on Holston's River last winter, and in two years more he was afraid the white people would settle quite up to their doors, and proceeds as follows.

There was a very good King over the great water when I was there, who promised me that goods should be cheap, but they are now very dear. When Mr Watts was a young man he traded cheap, but now goods are much dearer. The white people get lands that last for ever but the goods given us are soon gone. Now is the day we have appointed to conclude the talk. We never had such talks formerly but now all our talks are about lands and the white people settled thereon are deaf to us and will not hear.

A string of whampum.

Oucconnastotah speaks.

As for my elder brother, the Superintendent, I am now with him and what he says is a law to me, and it gives me great satisfaction to hear him talk. I pay great attention to him and never forget his words and always put the greatest confidence in what he says.

Gives a belt of whampum and a letter from the Governor of Virginia as also a letter from Richard Paris, all which the Superintendent ordered to be interpreted unto the Indians.

The Superintendent speaks.

Brothers, I have attended to what you have said, and in order to give you an answer I must have recourse to the beginning of our talks about land.

You have mentioned what passed at the great congress at Augusta where four governors were present. I shall now put you in mind of something that passed there that you seem to have entirely forgotten. It is true that at Augusta we talked of land, but neither the governors there present nor I were authorised to transact any business of that nature. Our meeting was for a different purpose. As you mentioned what passed at Augusta upon that subject I will repeat it to you. My memory enables me to do it clearly but I do not depend upon that entirely, I have got it in writing.

During the conferences Attahkullakulla who spoke upon the occasion complained of encroachments, and in particular of settlements being made beyond the Great Conhoway or New River, and claimed Chiswell's Mine as your boundary. Governor Fauquier endeavoured to account for the settlement of the lands between New River and Holston's River. Attahkullahkullah said that as the abovementioned country was already settled, they did not desire the inhabitants should be obliged to remove but hoped no more patents would be granted beyond the Conhoway. The next day Attahkullakulla resumed the subject and said they had considered of the matter, and gave up the land between Holston's River and the Kanhoway and would confine their claim to the lands lying to the southward and westward of Long Island in Holston's River. In a little time after said congress, His Majesty' pleasure was signified that the boundary lines should be ascertained, dividing the lands reserved by the Indians from those yielded to His Majesty in the different provinces. In consequence of this order which was the effects of the King's tenderness and paternal goodness towards you, you received those messages and talks from me concerning your boundary line which you now think were troublesome. I can affirm that in my treating with you I have been actuated by a sense of my duty to my King and a very particular regard for your interest. In every other respect I was entirely disinterested and I defy you and every other tribe of Indians on the continent to say that I ever asked or received a pound of leather or acre of land from you.

In your talks to me before we met at Hard Labour two years ago, you denied what had passed at Augusta, and peremptorily insisted upon all the lands to the southward and westward of Chiswell's Mine as your right. The Governor and Council of Virginia made no objections to your pretensions, and after my fruitless endeavours to learn their sentiments of the matter I received orders from the Earl of Shelburne to acquiesce in your demands, and a treaty was accordingly concluded for that purpose. The objections of the province of Virginia to the line agreed upon, their requisition of a more extended boundary, and the delay that was necessarily occasioned by waiting for the King's orders relative to it, I have frequently explained to you; and last April at Congarees you most earnestly insisted on having the matter finally settled and determined in October, and declared if the business was put off then you would never afterwards agree to any proposals about land and that the line running by Chiswell's Mine should for ever afterwards be looked upon as your boundary. In consequence of what then passed I was supplied with a fund by the province of Virginia for purchasing the goods which I have brought here at a great expense. I am come by your appointment, a beloved man is sent from Virginia to be present at our negotiations, I see a thousand of your people here, and now you tell me that the matter cannot yet be determined, that your young warriors are out a-hunting, and that you are determined to treat with the governor of Virginia concerning a further cession.

You may do as you please, but the goods are not to be delivered till the treaty is signed and the cession formally made. My Lord Botetourt has told you that the business is to be transacted by me and nobody else. I now tell you the same, and if the matter is not now settled I cannot tell when it will be done, for I shall not be fond of coming so far to meet you for nothing.

Gives a belt of black and white whampum.

After a good deal of debate and various proposals, the line was agreed upon as contained in the treaty.

Saturday 20th October

Present as the day before.

The Superintendent proceeded and explained the following treaty and afterwards it was signed by him and the principal chiefs. [C.O.5/72, fo. 22]

CVI

Earl of Hillsborough to Lieut.-Governor William Bull (No. 40)

19 October, Whitehall

Sir, your dispatches [Vol. I, Nos. 567, 568, 576] Nos. 32, 33 and 34 have been received and laid before the King.

The circumstances of David Pryce's case fully justify your suspension of the payment of the fine to which he became subject by the sentence of the court in which he was convicted, and the King is graciously pleased to consent to a remission of that fine as far as His Majesty's interest is concerned.

The arrival of Spanish vessels in the ports of Carolina in order to purchase provisions for the distressed inhabitants of Yucatan is an event of a very new and extraordinary nature, and as the propriety of the steps which you have thought fit to take in consequence thereof is a matter that requires very serious consideration, I am not able as yet to give you any opinion thereupon.

I am surprised that you could so far doubt of the meaning of any part of my letter [Vol. I, No. 408] No. 35 as to suppose for a moment that I could take upon myself to encourage a departure in any instance from the very positive and explicit directions contained in His Majesty's additional instruction [Vol. II, No. XXXV] of the 14 April, by which you are expressly forbid to give your assent to any Act for defraying expenses incurred for services or purposes not arising in or incident to the colony.

If however there are any persons who are really innocent sufferers in the case of the remittance to the support of the Bill of Rights, I have no doubt that His Majesty would be graciously pleased to authorise you to recommend to the Assembly to make provision by a separate special bill for their indemnification in case they should think fit to present an humble petition to His Majesty for that purpose. *Draft.* [C.O.5/393, fo. 89]

CVII

Governor James Grant to Earl of Hillsborough (No. 42)

19 October, St Augustine

My Lord, I have had the honour to receive your lordship's letter [Vol. I, No. 546] No. 31 with His Majesty's most gracious licence to me to return to Great Britain to attend my private affairs: they certainly require my presence, but not so much as the infant colony under my care, to which I am more attached than ever by the obliging manner in which your lordship was kind enough to honour me with the King's permission to leave it. I therefore shall not avail myself of the permission as I think my absence inexpedient for His Majesty's service in the present state of the colony. Our planters have raised provisions for themselves and everybody has something to send to the London market, they are all attached to their own business and think of nothing else. The country of course must continue to grow fast under your protection as we are all of the same opinion and know nothing of that spirit of dissension which rages all over America, nowhere more than in West Florida where they are miserably poor, have not a plantation in the country, and yet they are as full of faction, dispute and politics as they are at Boston or Charleston. People are accustomed to me and will go on as they have begun while I remain with them, but I am afraid of trusting them to themselves. Dissension might creep in if there was a change of measures or men, and in that case East Florida which I have taken so much pains about for seven years would dwindle down to nothing. My friends press me hard to return and probably think me at sea, as an estate which I have succeeded to by the death of a nephew is strangely circumstanced, but I have put that affair under the management of General Scot and Mr Oswald, and have determined to remain here till summer 1772. Then 'tis to be hoped His Majesty will be most graciously pleased to prolong or renew my licence.

During that intermediate space of time I shall make it my duty to put things upon such a footing as to prevent any accident happening to the prejudice of the province during my absence in England.

Upon the death of a governor of Barbados the senior Councillor, appointed by the governor till His Majesty's pleasure was known, tacitly approved of but never confirmed by the King's mandamus, assumed the government of the island, disputed by a junior Councillor who sat at the same Board by a regular appointment. The conduct of the governing Councillor was approved of and his precedency confirmed at home as his rank at the Council Board was to commence from the day he took his seat by virtue of the governor's appointment in which no alteration could be made but by His Majesty's signified disapprobation of the appointment, or by the acting Councillor being superseded by a mandamus in favour of another gentleman. If I had not been well-informed upon this point I should have troubled your lordship long ago about the Councillors in this province. Those I have named and recommended are the first people in the country, any change among them would be attended with much inconvenience. Mr John Moultry who is our first and best planter has been considered as President of the Council for seven years; if he does not succeed to the administration in my absence we shall certainly lose him. It was that feather that induced him to move into the colony, he married a woman of considerable property who would not have agreed to leave her favourite Carolina upon any other terms. Mr Moultry made the salop which I sent your lordship last year, his indigo sold for six shillings and threepence a pound, which beat me by a shilling in the pound. He has made a small cask of wine this year, has a field of sugar cane ready to cut, and is to make rum and a small quantity of sugar by way of experiment to see how the cane produces. I intend to send your lordship some of each with samples of this year's indigo and a bottle or two of the wine if I think it tolerable. Such a man's leaving the province would be a great misfortune to the country. I must therefore beg leave to recommend Mr Moultry as a proper person to be appointed lieutenant-governor.

Mr Wooldridge would not do at all. He is a mean, low, poor creature, despised by everybody; he got the mandamus when he was appointed agent to the late Mr Townshend, and in return cheated him as he does everybody he can contrive to overreach, but he was so well known here that he saw it was impossible for him to be admitted or at least continued in Council: he therefore delivered up the mandamus to me and begged leave to resign any pretensions to a seat in Council that he might be the better able to attend his duty of Provost Marshal.

Mr Jolly was agent to Lord Egmont: they have quarrelled and Jolly is gone out of the province. There was no objection to the man but he was rather in a low rank in life. His father is a tailor at Edinburgh, he had a brother a shoemaker in town, and another brother an under-overseer in the country. Those circumstances could not be known in London but they would rather have been degrading to the Council here. I therefore told Mr Jolly that I should have use for him if I called an Assembly, that his being a member of it would be of more utility to the province than he could be of by taking a seat in Council, which in fact was true for he is a sensible and an honest man. Mr Jolly did as I desired him but he kept the mandamus and has it in his power to demand a seat in Council when he pleases, to which there is no objection but what I have mentioned, and that does not regard the man, but it would be very distressing if he was to take rank of the others; they would not submit to that, for going in at a door or dancing first at a little assembly are points among the women which I cannot direct and dare not interfere in.

Dr Turnbull, the third your lordship mentions, [is] unexceptionable, but his constant residence at Smyrnea is absolutely and indispensably necessary. Without his presence the business of the settlement could not go on; he and his constituents have too much at stake to neglect the Greek colony which requires all his attention. He is not to be thought of. I only count upon him as an honorary Councillor, who I don't expect to see but once a year and that only for a day or two. When he came last from Smyrnea it was to pass some days at my plantation to see the process of making indigo, in which great improvements have been made this year by my manufacturers.

If your lordship should take any step in the arrangement of Councillors or give any directions about the person to succeed to the administration in case of my death or absence, previous to your receiving this letter, as I am not to leave the province I shall not make those orders public till I am honoured with your further commands, in hopes that an alteration may take place upon your lordship's considering the circumstances which I have taken the liberty to lay before you. *Signed*. [C.O.5/551, fo. 91]

CVIII

Governor William Tryon to Earl of Hillsborough (No. 58, duplicate)

20 October, New Bern
My Lord, I have the honour to transmit to your lordship the minutes of the Council journal, with copies of the several papers [Vol. I, No. 680i-v; Vol. II, Nos. XCIV, XCVII] referred to therein respecting the outrages and high crimes committed by the Regulators during the

last Superior Court at Hillsborough. Mr Attorney-General's opinion and advice was taken in Council on this occasion and entered on the journal. I have in pursuance of the advice of the Council sent circular letters to the commanding officers of the respective regiments of militia, and by their returns as required of the number of volunteers willing to turn out on the first call in the service of their King and Country, and also of what number of men can be ordered out upon an emergency, I shall be able to form a near guess of the strength of the government and the affections of each part. This information will likewise direct me in the choice of the number of men the approaching Assembly shall think expedient to be raised for suppressing these riots, collecting the taxes and bringing the offenders to the justice of their country. It must be by the spirited aid of the legislature only that I can expect success in my endeavours to extinguish this dangerous flame.

Enclosed, my lord, is a copy of the charter [Vol. I, No. 680vi] I granted to the inhabitants of Hillsborough on their petition for the same.

The offices Mr Heron held I have filled till further orders as set forth in the journals. *Signed.* [C.O.5/314, fo. 3]

CIX

Lieut.-Governor William Bull to Earl of Hillsborough (No. 36)

20 October, Charleston

My Lord, by His Majesty's packet *Swallow*, I was honoured with your lordship's letter [Vol. I, No. 549] No. 37 and beg leave to return the most humble thanks of the persons whose pardon was therein signified for the ready attention paid by your lordship to their unhappy cases in so readily obtaining the royal mercy.

The duplicates of my dispatches [Vol. I, No. 598] No. 35 were sent about a month ago by a merchant ship, the *Charming Sally*, Captain Forten.

I take the liberty of enclosing one of our *Gazettes* [Vol. I, No. 681i] containing the proceedings of the Assembly relative to their disputes in last August. But I transmit by this packet the Journals of the Assembly authenticated under the Great Seal of the province to the Right Honourable the Lords Commissioners for Trade and Plantations in case a reference thereto may be thought necessary when the late resolutions now before His Majesty may be taken into consideration.

Our public discontents still continue. The subscribers to non-importation alarmed at the late infamous revolt (as they term it) in New York are taking large strides to enforce the rigid observing of their resolutions by threats of vengeance against the violators of the Association, which seems to indicate some apprehensions of a like change in this town, which I am persuaded is the inclination of many; but the vigilance and industry of the leaders whose impetuosity of behaviour and reproachful language deter the moderate, the timid and the dependent, who feel their present embarrassed conditions, from stepping forth in a body to assert their own opinion and wishes and makes them sink down in acquiescence to the fashion of the times. The Associators further forbid any subscriber from using the wharves of non-subscribers for shipping or landing goods or rice. This and their refusal to purchase any rice, indigo or other plantation produce from non-subscribers subjects the latter to great inconvenience as they are thereby obliged to ship off their produce, which does not suit many especially as freight is not always to be procured against such counteracting combinations. It is true many of the subscribers must submit to fate while the rich leaders enjoy their trade in state, but they suffer by their own act and comfort themselves with the pleasing delusion that their sufferings are to be the means of bringing Parliament and people of Great Britain to comply with the claims of American immunities. On the other hand the non-subscribers suffer by restrictions imposed contrary to their consent, but they bear with patience any losses which are a test of their acknowledging and submitting to the sovereignty of the Parliament of Great Britain and humbly hope the present state of things cannot continue much longer.

I have acquainted the Right Honourable the Lords of Trade and Plantations that Mr Middleton has resigned his seat in Council and I have transmitted the names of three gentlemen according to His Majesty's seventh instruction to Lord Charles Montagu, but I take the liberty of informing your lordship that it is very difficult to prevail on gentlemen of spirit and ability to accept of a seat at that Board since the sudden suspension of Mr Wragg in 1757 without any cause known here deserving such mark of disgrace, and the present overbearing spirit of democracy in Assemblies is an additional discouragement. And I have little reason to believe that either of the two first named or even the last in the list will accept; when gentlemen are sounded on the matter they declare a dislike to it. Had I known any who would have accepted whose characters would give weight and dignity to that Board I would have mentioned such as a real acquisition to the King's service. But I hope a little time may get over this no small difficulty. If the King's service should suffer by my wanting advice of Council I must request your lordship to consider that there are now only five Councillors in this province besides Mr Stuart who is only an extra Councillor, and I assure your lordship I should have filled up the Council to the number seven according to His Majesty's eighth instruction if I could have done it with men fitly qualified for that trust. I beg your lordship's pardon for mentioning this matter with so much freedom; the delicacy of the subject restrains my enlarging upon it but I thought it my duty briefly to represent what I conceive to be the chief reasons why the salutary and gracious intentions of His Majesty in his 7th and 8th instructions are not carried into execution, and why a seat at that honourable Board which formerly was solicited is now declined. *Signed.* [C.O.5/393, fo. 119]

CX

John Wentworth to Earl of Hillsborough

22 October, Portsmouth New Hampshire
May it please your lordship, as some of the most essential affairs relating to the preservation of the King's Woods in North America

have been pending in the province of New York until this week, I have been thereby necessarily delayed transmitting your lordship a full and complete state of this important service, which yields me the honour to crave your lordship's permission thereto by this opportunity. [*Marginal note:* NB. The original letter and enclosures sent to the Board of Trade].

Having discovered that some people in the Eastern division of the late called province of Maine in the province of the Massachussets Bay were cutting wild or natural grass into hay in the interior country with intention to support their cattle, while cutting and hauling mast or white pine trees out of the King's Woods in the then ensuing winter, and that many of these people living remote from the Vice-Admiralty Courts of Boston, and induced by the great cries and oppositions for the word Liberty which then agitated that province into confusion, had resolved to cut and haul the King's timber in open defiance of the laws for its preservation, that many of them had actually got some trees into the rivers and menaced destruction to any officer who attempted to seize them or attack the trespassers on the penal statute.

It immediately appeared plain to me that an open and firm execution of the laws in this instance would finally subdue all ideas of resistance or escape and effectually preserve the mast timber; wherefore I embarked on the 27th July 1769 on board the *Beaver* sloop of war in which Commodore Hood was so good to accommodate me; the next day, arrived at Wiscasset River, and on the following day took a boat which conveyed me through many rivers to Androscoggin River where the saw-mills are. Upon my arrival I sent out, notified all the people of my business, invited them to meet me on the river near the mills where all the logs floated together. At the time appointed they all came, also a Justice of the Peace whom I requested to be with them.

I then plainly told them the information given me of their illegal intentions and menaces, read to them the Acts of Parliament for preserving pine timber, explained their great use and irresistible power and the evil consequences that must fall upon whoever attempted to oppose their effect; that I was come among them with a determined resolution to execute these Acts, and as it had been reported that they intended to resist this was the best time to put it to trial upon me; that they were then together and might see I came armed with no other power or force than the Acts of Parliament upon which alone I should rely for my personal safety that this was sufficient for me, therefore I brought with me only one assistant deputy and one servant besides the boatmen who rode us: all were unarmed which I purposely directed that all concerned might know that the laws would be protection enough for those officers that were legally executing them. After some pause an old man stepped forth and desired to be heard. He said that the people were poor, depended much upon procuring timber for their subsistence, that they had been under errors, supposing a right to the soil when actually severed [*sic, ? secured*] to them gave also a title to the timber of all kinds but that they now plainly saw to the contrary, except in such tracts as were actually improved and legally possessed as private property before the year 1690, that it.was likely some warm indiscreet men might say unadvised things about this business but that I might be assured not one man among them would oppose me or any of my deputies but readily aid us at all times and that they would attend and guard me while in that country if I suspected the least insult or disrespect.

To this speech every man with one voice assented. After some reply approving their promised intentions to regard and be obedient to the laws, I singled out one man who had been the most zealous and warm in the scheme of making their country too hot for officers (as they termed it) and required him to aid and carry me off in his canoe upon the river (my boat could not come up above the falls) and there help me seize and mark about 500 logs which belonged to him and the rest who waited on the banks of the river within 30 yards, which he directly performed, and we returned to the people in whose presence I delivered the logs into the care of the magistrate and informed them I would stay that night at the inn adjacent and in the morning consider any claims they might offer for the logs, and that they might consider whether they would abide by their present resolutions of obeying the law.

In the morning the whole party came to me and to a man expressed their fixed resolutions the same as on the preceding day, that they surrendered all claims of property in the logs I had seized which they owned to have cut upon the lesser rivers in the winter preceding more than six months since, and that they took an opportunity to cut from those places the deputy surveyor had examined after he left them and was gone to other rivers, but that they would not again trespass.

From hence I proceeded to Kennebec River and thence to Sheepscut River where I found no waste had been made but that a trade for small saplin, norway and pitch pine square timber, about 9 to 12 inches diameter, and oak, beech, maple, spruce and ash timber of all dimensions were the principal objects, which were exported to Whitby in England and to Scotland for the use of the inland navigations making in many parts of Great Britain.

Among these inhabitants and at all the saw-mills I disseminated the care and respect due to these laws and was everywhere received not only without the least opposition but with the strongest demonstrations of their obedience and disposition to do rightly.

Having thus informed them of their duty, I returned to the ship at Wiscasset and embraced the first fair wind to sail for Halifax to examine more particularly what part of that province it would be most beneficial to survey two hundred thousand acres to be reserved for woods to supply His Majesty's Navy. In this province there are extensive growths of pitch, norway, saplin and apple pine, but very few or none of white pine fit for masts above 25 inches diameter, the timber being in general too short and knotty, but of oak, ash and the abovementioned pines there are great quantities and of excellent quality for ship-building, small bowsprits, topmasts and small yards, for which last mentioned uses are here growing the finest spruce fir trees on the continent.

As such a tract must hereafter be very useful to supply His Majesty's Navy Yards in America and there being no tract or tracts in that province that ever did or would produce large white pine trees for masts,

I thought it for the King's service to discover and survey a tract well-situated and clothed with these timber trees, and to inform his Excellency the Right Honourable Lord William Campbell, Governor of the province, requesting that such tract might be reserved for His Majesty's naval service until some place could be discovered whereon mast trees did and would grow. Accordingly, I found a tract bounding on the sea coast about eighteen miles westward of Halifax, replete with every desirable advantage for this purpose, having a fine harbour and commmodious rivers intersecting and covered with endless forests of various timber.

This survey had been heretofore granted to a Mr MacNutt upon terms of improvement and population which were not complied with in any measure, nor in all probability will they ever be. I then waited on the governor and requested that this tract having reverted to the Crown by failure on the part of the grantees might not be re-granted but remain for His Majesty's naval service; to which his lordship replied he would enquire into the matter and readily carry the King's service into effect. The first fair wind I embarked and in eight days arrived in New Hampshire, having accomplished my incumbent duty at Halifax.

Soon after my arrival I received information from my assistant deputy who had discovered a trespass committed on Androscogin River not long after my departure thence, and also secured full evidence to convict the offender, James Potter. I lost no time in filing my complaint in the Court of Vice-Admiralty at Boston, and upon the process obtained a decree for £350 sterling and cost of court, £7 0s. 2d. lawful money, equal to £5 5s. 1½d. sterling; whereupon Potter alienated his real estate and not being possessed of goods and chattels, his person was taken and committed to the county gaol, of which the people were not only well satisfied but approved and were aiding, so greatly had they changed all notion of resisting.

In a few days, however, Potter by the assistance of some person from without broke gaol, which was secured by only one common padlock on the outside, and escaped without alarming the gaoler or any person in the house except a prisoner in the same room, from whom we gather that it was Potter's son who helped break the lock, but it was dark and he but little acquainted with the younger Potter, therefore could not positively swear 'twas him. That this event might still tend to benefit and strengthen the law, I caused a petition to the Justices of the Session for the county requiring payment of the execution as the escape happened through the insufficiency of the gaol, according to a law of that province providing remedy in such cases.

The court upon consideration of the petition were pleased to dismiss it without relief, alleging that the escape did not happen through the insufficiency of the gaol and that the county were unable to pay the damages (which inability is I believe but too true). The true reason was to gain time, for it can be proved beyond a doubt that the gaol was insufficient, to which end I caused a survey to be had thereof in presence of the court, whereby I have it open to pursue a recovery at the Superior Court which will be attended with almost a year's delay, but I think will not fail of success. However that may be, the prosecution and execution thus far is of the greatest advantage to the service, having confirmed an opinion in the people of all ranks that these laws are not only useful and necessary for the public good but also that the violation of them cannot escape condign punishment, and the difficulty thus brought upon that county so exasperates the people that stealing timber is now almost as popularly odious as any other theft, which sentiments I take unceasing pains to cultivate and establish as the surest and most unexceptionable means of preserving mast timber. By the enclosed copies, No. 1, 2, 3, will more fully appear that these trespassers are prosecuted to the end as directed by the law, in which I shall not fail to persist diligently.

The logs I seized on Androscoggin River beforementioned, I left there as a warning to the country, where they remained until January last when an inundation of rain and melted snow broke up the ice and carried them with many mills down the river, and they were left in the sea. The trees seized from Potter remain upon the spot where they were taken and serve to notify the people that such trespasses cannot escape. In the course of this year's duty I have sent deputies to the lower district of the aforesaid province of Maine and surveyed the rivers from Damarascotte to the River St Croix, the reputed boundary between Massachussets Bay and Nova Scotia.

Upon many of these lands are most excellent white pine for large masts. There are many scattering settlers on this extended coast and almost numberless rivers who have hitherto subsisted by cutting saplin, pitch and norway pines into deals and square timber for which they are equally good as white pine for any market, and much preferable for the Sugar Islands to which their principal export is made. They also manufacture staves and heading for the same market, which with spruce spars for topmasts, yards and small coasting vessels' masts, with some fish and train-oil, complete the cargoes obtained here for the West Indies.

The saplin, norway and pitch pine are now by far the easiest and least expensive for these people to manufacture at present, being the commonest growth on the eastern shores, and may be had with very little hauling to their mills. But the white or mast pine trees growing some little distance into the country have not yet been materially broke in upon, merely from this accidental circumstance and by no means from the virtue and forbearance of the occupiers who probably never trouble themselves about either further than compelled by fear or stimulated by interest.

It may therefore be expected that the timber now in use being consumed, the people will fall directly upon the best timber and without remorse destroy the whole they can come at, unless prevented by early precautions. The most effectual that occurs to me is discouraging any settlement in that country. The property is vested in His Majesty equally as in the province of Massachussets Bay, even in their own opinion, perhaps in right much more so. Therefore, if it should please His Majesty to refuse his concurrence to any provincial appropriation or grant of these lands and to forbid their improvement, it would effectually preserve an inestimable growth of mast timber, easily and at little expense to be had at any time for His Majesty's service.

Another very great advantage would result from this measure which, though it does not directly appertain to my office, yet so far coinciding with the public interest thereof that I beg your lordship's favour to pardon my suggesting it in a few words. The cod fishery must reap the greatest benefit herefrom, for upon this coast and in the rivers are an incredible run of young fish (during the summer) which will surely be destroyed if this coast is now settled. Already the boats have found the way thither and make great profit in taking small fish scarcely fit for a negro market, a practice which is evidently destructive of an useful branch of trade and which only wants a few more residents on this coast totally to effect. It may perhaps be said if this country was granted and settled, the laws would have their course as in other parts, to which permit me to say that the claims of private property, however groundless and upon trial vain, have been the greatest devourers of the King's timber of any that have appeared in the New England provinces, more particularly to the east of Pescataqua River; therefore it may perhaps be well not to increase them where there is most danger.

As to the laws being observed I fear from the natural difficulty and present almost impracticability of roads in that district, so extraordinarily intersected with rivers and covered with forests, they will make much havoc with the pine timber before the golden age of legality will shine upon them with power to restrain their own desires from being their sole guide.

I have now to beg leave to lay before your lordship a state of my proceedings in the province of New York. In my letter to your lordship dated July 10 1769 I there mentioned my seizing some mast trees cut against the law upon Connecticut River in the town of Windsor on the New York side. Some time afterwards I contrived to apprehend the trespassers vizt. William Deane, Willard Deane and William Deane jnr., through the agency of Benjamin Whiting Esq. who was appointed a deputy marshal for that purpose.

A considerable time necessarily elapsed in sending to New York for precepts after the trespass and trespassers were discovered, it being near three hundred miles distance thither. This time William Deane employed in collusively conveying his real estate to one John Grout, a petty fogging lawyer in that country of deservedly infamous character, and making a party of those who were interested in saw-mills and timber-land upon the said river, who from a parity of illegal interests readily joined said Deane in endeavouring in the first place to contrive the prisoners' escape; if this could not be effected, then by buying off the Crown evidences or otherwise prevailing on them not to appear, thereby to preclude my sustaining the complaint upon trial; and in case neither of these could be accomplished, then to aggravate the costs as much as possible and by conveying the goods and chattels of the defendant to throw all the costs upon the Crown.

In this scheme I do from my heart conscientiously believe that Samuel Wells Esq., one of the Judges of the Court of Common Pleas and Justice of the Peace in and for the County of Cumberland in the province of New York was the principal agent, unspeakably to the injury of His Majesty's service in this case, also tending directly to subvert and annihilate the authority and effect of all other Acts of Parliament that do or may relate to America, for it is easy to foresee that Acts of Parliament in this case being contemned and evaded by a judge of the court with impunity, all other Acts of Parliament will very soon share the same fate. The reasons to support this opinion of Mr Wells are submitted in the following narrative and enclosures. The time unavoidably delayed in procuring writs from New York and returning to Windsor had quieted the fears of the trespassers insomuch that Grout reconveyed their property to them, soon after which Mr Whiting came upon and apprehended Willard Deane and William Deane jnr., William Deane snr. evading the search.

The prisoners being somewhat turbulent and the said John Grout having often insinuated that they should never be carried to New York, Mr Whiting very prudently applied to a magistrate for aid and assistance, presenting a proclamation issued by the late Sir Henry Moore requiring all officers in that province to be aiding and assisting etc. Whereupon the magistrate commanded six men to assist by turns in securing the prisoners, with whom Mr Whiting proceeded down Connecticut River towards New York and met no interruption until his party arrived at Hinsdale where Judge Wells endeavoured artfully to mislead him by advising him to pass through the Massachussets Bay where he well knew John Grout aforesaid was prepared to rescue the prisoners and arrest the officer. This is proved by the depositions, Nos. 4, 5, 6 and 7: the first which also proves the artful and covered method Mr Wells took to set the evidences free from their attendance according to their respective subpoenas, which they would have been glad to have catched hold of to save themselves the trouble of so long a journey as to New York from their families and business, for which they could not expect any adequate payment. These suggestions are still corroborated by the deposition No. 8 in the amplest manner. Yet these plans failed them although a number of men were led on to assemble and demand the prisoners at first with much warmth, but upon a full conversation with the officer and finding him lawfully executing a precept and the whole matter explained to them, they quietly dispersed and even expressed contrition for the trouble they had given and never after molested him. In due time the trespassers arrived at New York where they were legally committed. Mr Duane, an eminent patriotic lawyer, was engaged for the trespassers. Every art was practised to delay, to prevent, to defeat the trial, and in a few days it was insinuated to great numbers of rich men in New York that the successful execution of these laws would be more injurious to landholders than the Stamp Act, which word is as infectious in America as the plague and as unaccountably seizes upon the soundest constitutions; it thus operated in this case. Almost every man that heard it became alarmed and without further inquiry took part with the prisoners, supposing if they were convicted that it would be a precedent in future and would effectually preserve all mast timber described in the statutes to the detriment of the landholders who expected great profit to result from cutting the best and indeed all timber at their saw-mills.

Mr Wells came to New York and was very active in behalf of the prisoners, representing their case as pitiable and finally making himself a party in a conveyance artfully covered and directed to operate against the just decree of law.

When these prejudices were communicated to me, I instructed the advocate in behalf of the Crown, John Tabor Kemp Esq., also Mr Whiting, not to insist upon a hearing until the prisoners and their proctor acknowledged themselves entirely ready, that there might be no room left to reflect on whatsoever decree should be given nor to complain of an untimely trial.

At length after many delays too shameful for and never necessary in the cause of truth, during which the odium against the service still continued to increase and the generally supposed interest of those who held lands clothed with timber seemed universally to absorb [*sic :* ? absolve] all knowledge of and regard to the positive statute and to combine in endeavours and wishes to save the prisoners.

However, the day of trial came when the facts complained of were indubitably proved notwithstanding the proffered but unpermitted perjury of William Deane snr. before the judge and many unavailing attempts to prevail on the Crown evidences to abscond or to disguise the facts. That honourable Judge Morris gave a full decree in favour of the Crown and the trespassers were committed as directed by the statute. Upon the trial Mr Kempe exerted himself with great diligence, skill and fidelity; and so well conducted that the odium so artfully and evilly excited before the hearing then vanished and left only remaining the adverseness of private interest still to be subdued by the laws made for and embracing the public good.

I cannot justly omit here mentioning the steady upright administration of Richard Morris Esq., Judge of the Court of Vice-Admiralty, before whom this cause was tried and adjudged. From the first filing the complaint to the execution issued upon the decree [he] hath discharged the duties of his office with honourable and distinguishable fortitude and unimpeachable ability and justice, notwithstanding the multiplied prejudices dishonourably excited as aforerecited, which might naturally be feared would injure his private interest by lessening his practise as a lawyer in other courts. In this laudable rectitude Mr Morris has still the more merit as his office is without salary and in this case without fee or reward.

It is also my duty to assure your lordship of equal alacrity in Mr Kempe, King's Advocate in said court, through whose faithful attention this prosecution hath been successfully conducted. May I further pray your lordship's patience while my zeal for His Majesty's service compels me most ardently to recommend Mr Morris as herein meriting support and encouragement from government, and that his reputation and abilities would greatly promote the execution and just effect of the laws entrusted to his administration.

But to return to the conduct of Mr Wells, immediately on the decree he went back to Connecticut River and took possession of Deane's effects who remained incarcerated at New York, supported in affluence by the liberality of those who considered his cause in some degree their's, whence the convicted trespassers lived well and at little or no expense as is proved by deposition No. 8, wherein the deponent testifies that the said Deane told him so.

Upon Mr Wells's return home he industriously propagated through the country that although Deanes had been convicted, yet having contrived to leave all the costs on the Surveyor General who would soon be sickened from more prosecutions. Herein is manifest encouragement to violate the laws, spread from the mouth of a judge whose duty would have directed him to a contrary conduct, but his saw-mills depend upon employment from the destruction of mast timber, and that employment is too profitable to be neglected, *fas aut nefas*, which is also proved by the last mentioned deposition.

Mr Whiting in the course of his duty having informed me of the dangers and discouragements the service had endured, I immediately wrote to Lieut.-Governor Colden, copy of which No. 9 is herewith transmitted and Mr Colden's answer No. 10. As soon as the return was made on the execution, vizt. Messrs. Deanes', that the goods and chattels were conveyed to Judge Wells, I immediately transmitted the enclosed memorial, No. 11, being resolved to let slip no justifiable means if possible to carry the execution into effect.

To this memorial I have received for answer the letter, No. 12, a report of Council No. 13, and depositions Nos. 14, 15, 16, 17, 18 and 19, also a bill of sale No. 20. To which I beg leave to observe first upon the report No. 13. As to the opinion of Mr Wells's fair character which he is said to sustain, it may be so in the district referred to and possibly even at New York he may be thought an useful man, but I do aver his character is by no means fair or honest in any other province where he is known; neither does he dare openly to appear in any of them lest his creditors who loudly complain of his collusions should apprehend his person. Mr Wells's character was not the object of the memorial. It was his conduct in discouraging the King's officer from doing his lawful duty; his attempt to mislead him, thereby to cause an escape of his prisoners; his endeavours to make the evidences believe that the subpoenas were not binding upon them; and afterwards taking a conveyance of the effects of trespassers whereby the penalty of the law is *ipso facto* evaded, expense thrown upon the Crown and an inlet formed to encourage total destruction of an abundant growth of masts of excellent quality and in commodious situations to be procured for His Majesty's commands, and which were actually preserved by the people with great care until Mr Wells's conduct merely invited them to hope from such means to render them their own property.

These were my complaints. I neither then or now know of any unjustifiable claims of the province of New Hampshire, neither has there been any public or private communications of them to me, whence I the rather suppose Mr Wells is obnoxious from his own conduct and not from any claims whatever. Thus far I avow that until this report of committee of Council, I never knew or suspected he was obnoxious to anybody or thing except only to the King's service as herein beforementioned.

That the parties had a right to convey their effects for support may be true, but it does not appear nor is there any proof that the amount of the sale was ever applied to support them. Had either or all the deponents upon this point testified that it was so there might have appeared some humanity, though very little decency or propriety in a judge being voluntarily a trustee for persons under criminal prosecutions on process of the Crown for goods and chattels which might probably be decreed to the King, but I cannot think it appears by any of the depositions that this sale or the produce of it was applied to the support of the prisoners. Indeed the deposition of Mr Deane, No. 15, declares his belief that it was an act of humanity in Mr Wells and that it was probable the prisoners would have suffered without it, but still cautiously avoids declaring they were actually relieved by it, which would have been more natural and to the point than the curious mode of opinion upon Mr Wells's benevolence. I think it also proves that it was a concerted plan, and Mr Duane conducted skilfully for his clients, and that through Mr Wells's humanity the laws of conveyances were twisted to defeat the operation of the laws for preserving mast timber. As to the deposition of William Deane, Willard Deane and William Deane jnr., they do not merit any notice. Undoubtedly those who had trespassed, and afterwards proffered perjury before the court or upon examination, would not be very delicate in giving any depositions that would vindicate their patron and trustee who had laboured, journeyed and studied so diligently in their behalf, as it appears by the enclosures Nos. 4, 5, 6, and 7 Mr Wells had done.

In truth, my lord, the depositions of such men in this case would not have merited my reading, much less any explanation to your lordship, had they not been transmitted to me through a channel of such respectability. Yet if they in themselves merited any credit they do not clear their friends, verily I believe nothing can of less power than what can exactly and diametrically reverse all his past conduct in this affair. Neither does the deposition, No. 16, of Ebenezer Fisher add any vindication. He was a trespasser himself though from the too contracted limitation of the statute and distance of the court had escaped the penalty, but his stolen logs still lay seized at Judge Wells's saw-mills. It is therefore to be feared his testimony, though in words may be part of the truth, were not all the truth, nor so chosen as to convey the positive actual spirit of the conversation which may be gathered from even this deposition itself, for he relates that such words did pass, but artfully is desirous of their appearing to be merely a matter of conversation in which Mr Wells would be represented as informing the officer of the law. This very caution is strong evidence that Mr Wells was unfriendly to the service and was careful enough to cover his conduct by other pretences.

The deposition No. 18, though verbally calculated in Mr Wells's vindication, yet leaves the same matter of complaint, as far as it relates to this service, for Mr Whipple testifies that Mr Wells's conversation tended to and did actually alarm the officer, Mr Whiting, which can be no otherwise accounted for than by his finding the King's service endangered by a judge of one of his courts; and this explanation is proved by many of the preceding depositions as well as by this deposition, No. 18, which says they were all amicable until Mr Wells's expressions which the officer felt to be dishonourable and detrimental to the duty of all the King's servants. As to the evasion or insinuation that it was merrily said, it is too pitiable even to animadvert upon. Such a feeble attempt to cover bad conduct is so plain an implication thereof as conveys the clearest conviction to any unprejudiced mind of the practice. No. 14 is Mr Wells's deposition in his vindication, to which I beg leave only to observe that in comparing and explaining it by the other depositions herewith, and the consequences that have undeniably resulted, the whole is unravelled and his misconduct proved by his own attested defence or deposition.

I shall not trouble your lordship more in elucidating this cobweb kind of deposition, it cannot want any comment to discover its pernicious tendency to the King's service. Some of these depositions labour hard to represent Mr Wells's exertion to disperse the people assembled to molest Mr Whiting in the execution of his office; such a fallacy properly becomes such a man after continued, repeated and various insinuations dispersed among the people wherein cruelty was falsely alleged against the officer. The service itself was said to be injurious, malicious and vexatious. It is no wonder indiscreet and unwary people were covertly led into error and madness. However, upon their being informed of the truth they quietly dispersed without Mr Wells's aid. He carefully arrived at the place after the people were gone and none remained to discover that through his address they had assembled. But Mr Wells proceeds to apprehend two of the poor men and with safety enough to them, for although prosecuted and the fact incontestable, not one word is said about any fine or punishment being laid on the rioters although tried before this zealous judge, Wells himself.

This whole business is therefore the most shallow collusion with which I never would have presumed to have burdened the files of office but that such practices if suffered to remain robed in the seat of judgement and sanctified by a continued investiture of authority will soon bring destruction on this service, reduce all Acts of Parliament to mere ciphers in America and afford triumph to those whose greatest efforts are directed for the annihilation of every law made in the Parliament of Great Britain respecting the colonies.

It now remains for me to observe that if the memorial No. 11 had been granted, the sale of the lands petitioned for might have repaid the expense which now I am compelled to transmit an account of for repayment at the Treasury of the Navy.

I reasonably expected the lands would have been granted because William Deane had no title under New York, and if the patent under New Hampshire was as insignificant as suggested by report of the committee, No. 13, there does not appear to me any reason why the premises might not have been granted, especially as the grant was prayed for in behalf of the Crown and for the signal purpose of carrying an important statute into execution, but having the honour to transmit the report as full proof that I have pursued every legal step that was possible to accomplish the service entrusted to my care it can require no other observation from me.

The various enclosures and narrative being thus most respectfully submitted to your lordship's consideration in obedience to my duty and zeal for the King's service, it results therefrom that it is my duty to represent the necessity of Mr Wells's total dismission from the King's service, which it is fully evident he has discouraged and injured although in such a clandestine manner as might perhaps elude strictly legal proofs, yet for this very reason is it more just and necessary because the more covered such practices are and may be, the more dangerous and dishonourable are they to the King's service.

The course of my duty having necessarily led me to survey the interior part of the province of New York where I found many tracts well covered with mast timber, though not of the best quality yet such as will make good masts from 25 to 32 inches diameter and the largest size bowsprits for which this timber is peculiarly adapted. The proprietors of the soil claim the whole timber as private property, alleging the country was granted to them before the year 1690 and without any reservation of pine timber vizt. to Jan Janse Bleeker and others *anno* 1683; to Philip Peterse, 1683; to Killyear Van Ranselear, 1685; to Kinderhook, 1686; Manor of Levingston, granted 1683.

These have asserted their claims and seem disposed to try their property, although I have no complaint as their conduct has by no means interrupted me nor do they attempt the least violence. Hitherto they only forbid the agents of the mast contracts to cut and procure masts on the premises. I have positively asserted the King's right to the timber and shall take the first opportunity of any trespass thereon to institute a process on the penal statute unless otherwise instructed by your lordship. The patents are passed in general terms and without any reservation of pine trees whatever, and include from fifty to two hundred and fifty thousand acres each, upon each of them some improvement but to be sure not one-tenth part of the whole cultivated or even divided among the proprietors.

I have also to represent to your lordship that a similar claim of private property has been offered to me by the proprietors of an extensive tract of land upon both sides of Kennebec River in that part of the province of Massachussets Bay formerly called the province of Maine. On this tract there is an abundant growth of the best pine timber in America and very near to long and navigable rivers. The proprietors claim under a grant of the Council of Plymouth, the enclosed pamphlet was sent me by one of them and I suppose contains their title to the premises, upon which your lordship will best judge. I find there has been a consideration of such claims by His Majesty's Attorney- and Solicitor-General dated 23rd December 1726, also another dated November 12 1718 by Richard West Esq. presented to the Lords for Trade and Plantations, of which I have not copies but have heard they were in favour of the Crown.

The proprietors inform me, and I believe, they are careful to preserve all mast timber fit for His Majesty's use, but it is my duty to observe that if they are thus preserved as private property, whenever they are wanted, the King must pay their own price, and that although now preserved we cannot expect they will be any longer than the time in which they will yield the greatest profit for any use to the proprietors.

I do not in any degree diminish my care, and cause perpetual surveys to be kept up upon the premises, which the proprietors do not obstruct or impede though many of them have threatened to prosecute in the common law for trespassers the agents of the mast contract who cut and procure masts on this claim by virtue of my licence issued in obedience to the royal commands to me signified and transmitted, together with the contract of Messrs. Durand and Bacon. Hitherto they have not instituted any process; whenever they do I shall take care that every legal step shall be pursued for the support of His Majesty's right.

The proprietors being most of them gentlemen of large property and judicious men have not offered the least violence or disrespect to the King's service in their desire to appropriate and ascertain their claim, but seem to rely much on their legal title, on the merits of which your lordship cannot fail to determine with the highest wisdom and justice whenever it may be your lordship's pleasure to consider thereon.

As most if not all the claims for private property will be determined by the event of these, permit me most respectfully to entreat your lordship that I may be particularly instructed herein, which instructions I have the greatest happiness in assuring your lordship I doubt not to carry into immediate execution, and in the meantime my utmost attention will be continued that no waste be committed on the premises.

From the nature of this service lying in various parts on long extended rivers and upon countries impervious but by water or long travel on foot through uninhabited wildernesses, which necessarily causes delays in arriving at places where a sudden inspection would be exceedingly useful to the service, and in many seasons the utter impossibility of passing but by vessels and boats, I find it absolutely essential for His Majesty's service humbly to represent the use and to request that a small schooner from 60 to 100 tons with 14 to 20 men might be stationed under my orders to carry me and my deputies to the many rivers where timber is to be preserved, by which means it would soon be impossible for any waste of mast trees to be practised with impunity.

I am the more readily and earnestly led to this solicitation as it may be done without any additional expense to government, there being always many vessels of that sort employed in His Majesty's fleets on the coasts of America, which I presume could accomplish this service by six or twelve months stations, without interrupting their present utility or requiring the least augmentation of their numbers or addition to their expense, and would be highly conducive to His Majesty's service.

Having thus laid before your lordship a particular state of the survey of His Majesty's Woods in those important instances wherein it has been materially affected, I now beg leave to assure your lordship that I have the last year been peculiarly successful in preserving mast timber, having kept up an incessant vigilance and survey through every part of the country in such a manner that I am positively certain there has been less trespasses committed through the year 1769 and to this day than has been known for any equal period the last forty years.

It also gives me the highest satisfaction that I have hitherto so successfully conducted as to obtain a decree upon every process instituted, particularly in New York as before recited, where I had to combat with the greatest abilities and interest directed immediately against the statutes and the whole service embraced by them, which we recovered fully and upon the Acts of Parliament solely, which I insisted upon to be the only plea made, and that I would never offer any other, whereby they are established in the minds of the people without leaving any disgust or ideas of injury to their operation except those excited by Mr Wells which will be obliterated by his removal from the King's service and by a steady perseverance in executing the laws with candour and firmness in the Surveyor-General's department.

Another striking evidence of the respect I have disseminated towards the laws even in the country where they were formerly most opposed has come to my knowledge since I have begun this letter. I am informed from the County of Lincoln that the Justices and very many of the inhabitants, immediately upon the rising of the court to whom I petitioned, made strict search for and retook Potter whom they have recommitted to the same gaol from whence he escaped, and further to testify their sincerity are now making close search to discover and apprehend the person who from without aided Potter's escape. This they have done voluntarily and at their own expense, and they now guard him so safely that his escape is impracticable and the whole sentence of the law will be executed upon him and every future evasion or opposition radically exterminated.

In these instances I entertained the most singular satisfaction as they not only importantly prosper and secure the preservation of the King's Woods but tend effectually to restore that just and operative veneration for the Acts of Parliament which it is the duty and interest of America to obey, though of late years have been too generally rendered fearful and odious to the people through those popular artifices which have thrown many parts of this continent into confusion and madness for some years past.

In my letters relating this service which I had the honour to lay before your lordship, dated July 10 1769, was represented the urgent necessity of an appointment or rather an enlargement of the district of the Provincial Court of Vice-Admiralty in this province to contain the province of Maine, this province and at least fifty miles to the westward of Connecticut River into the province of New York, and that William Parker Esq., the present provincial judge, may preside therein. The reasons therein humbly suggested are still confirmed and increased from my observations and experience since that time, and therefore compels me in duty and faithfulness to His Majesty's service at this time to beg your lordship's leave for thus renewing my representation that such an arrangement would eminently promote the surest preservation of mast trees in that, the best district for such purposes in His Majesty's American dominions.

I have fully considered the present laws for preservation of pine timber, and from the dilatory and illusive practices which are tried and must ever be expected from the stimulations of private interest it appears my duty to represent that whenever these Acts of Parliament may be revised it would more certainly effect their design if execution issued upon the penal statute might be extended to the real estate. At present goods and chattels only are expressed in the statutes, which are seldom perhaps never possessed to $\frac{1}{10}$th part the value as of the real estate, and may be conveyed as in the case of William Deane afore-recited; and the convicted trespasser has no more than six months residence in a comfortable gaol where he is well supported by $\frac{1}{6}$ or $\frac{1}{10}$th of the produce of his farm, mayhap by the amount of his trespass, and the law evaded notwithstanding the greatest diligence of the Surveyor-General, and what is more pernicious, even after a decree is obtained. Moreover in this country a freehold estate is the object of all partiality and desire; therefore it would much more terrify and deter them from trespasses if the consequence might divest the convicted offender proportionately of his real estate, and more especially if the Act of Parliament also declared to be void all conveyances of every sort of property after process issued from the Court of Admiralty for trespasses upon the King's Woods until the decree of the Court was satisfied.

It would also be expedient to extend the time limited for entering and sustaining complaints from six months, the present time, to twelve months, in which time the officer could be sure to discover the offences, procure evidences, and direct his informations with indubitable propriety, which cannot be done unless in the most fortunate circumstances in six months from the time the fact is committed, particularly in the province of New York where the trespass may be and usually is transacted four hundred and fifty miles from the court in which it must be tried.

I must also further request with the greatest respect your lordship will be pleased to instruct me concerning the great quantities of white pine timber which from natural decay, from high winds, from making mast-roads and many other unavoidable casualties are daily falling on the ground and are and ever were unfit for masts, yards or bowsprits, and yet would be useful for deals timber and other purposes of commerce if they might be permitted, and by their removal would greatly promote the growth of the good timber which is much endangered by their decay and prompts evil-minded persons to set fire in the woods whereby fifty cargoes of masts may be destroyed in a night and morally impossible to discover the perpetrator. If it should appear expedient to your lordship that such useless timber might be surveyed, marked and delivered to the proprietor of the soil at his expense and upon his request, I apprehend it would cause every landholder to become an interested guardian of real mast timber and encourage and advance a sound growth of timber in the best manner. And by this regulation their cultivations will not be impeded, which must otherwise suffer as they may not legally cut or destroy even this timber. It would also coincide with the Act of Parliament granting a bounty on American fir timber and deals imported into Great Britain, which must soon be frustrated entirely unless this regulation is made or some one similar, for it is an incontestable fact that all the pine timber on private property will suffice but a short time for the necessities of the Sugar Islands and of course cannot be exported to Great Britain much longer.

Having in strict obedience to the trust reposed in me by His Majesty's commission and in unalterable zeal for his service completed this full and exact state of the King's Woods and the laws relating their preservation, which has unavoidably extended to a great length, for which trespass upon your lordship's time I humbly hope forgiveness as it proceeds from the deepest fidelity in His Majesty's service to which my whole heart and unceasing diligence has been applied and with a degree of success which fully supports my assuring your lordship that the preservation of mast timber is greatly prospered and that the laws relative thereto do daily obtain reverence and respect insomuch that I dare promise absolutely to carry them into effect: more especially it cannot fail if it should seem meet to His Majesty most graciously to grant the aid herein dutifully suggested or such other as may be his royal pleasure: all which is with the utmost deference submitted, respectfully hoping for your lordship's favourable representation of my conduct and of my steady fidelity and earnest attachment to His Majesty's service, humbly praying it may happily meet His Majesty's approbation. *Entry.* [C.O.5/227, p. 310]

CXI

Governor Walter Patterson to Earl of Hillsborough (No. 1)

24 October, Charlotte Town, Island of St John

My Lord, I arrived here on the 30th of last August, since which time I have been so much employed in finishing one of the houses built here by order of Mr Franklin, in such a manner as I hope will keep out a little of the approaching cold, and in sending to different parts of the continent for provisions to maintain my family during the winter, added to this the communications to the different parts of the Island being very bad, I will be able to furnish your lordship at present with but a very imperfect description of it.

So far as I have been able under the above circumstances to see of the Island, the soil appears to be very good and easily cultivated. It is of reddish colour mixed with sand, and in most places free from stones. From this account of it your lordship, whom I know to be a perfect judge of lands, will not believe it to be so good as it really is, but I never saw finer grass in my life than grows every place where it is clear of woods. It will produce every kind of grain and vegetables common in England with little or no trouble, and such as I have seen of the latter are much better of their kinds than those at home, though raised in a very slovenly manner.

The woods on this part of the Island are of very little use except for firing, and a great part of them not even good for that. They are principally beech, maple, black and white birch, spruce and several other sorts of small firs. In other parts of the Island there are some oaks and large pine trees in plenty.

The bays and rivers abound with wild fowl such as geese, brant, ducks, and as good of their kinds as any I ever met with, both in the autumn and spring.

The woods are pretty well stocked with partridges and at some times of the year with pigeons. On the sides of the rivers and marshes there are curlews, snipes and some other birds of a smaller sort. The beasts are principally bears, foxes, otters, wild cats of a very large size, hares, martens, squirrels and mice. The bears in some parts destroy the sheep; and the mice this year are so plenty that they have in most places destroyed the little grain which was attempted to be raised. The inhabitants say their appearing in such numbers is periodical, once in every seven years. My opinion is it depends entirely upon the sort of winter we have, as I am informed the last was an uncommon one, the snow falling before the frost came on, by which means the ground was kept soft and the mice, in place of being partly destroyed by the frost as is commonly the case, bred under the snow; they are in size something between our mice and rats in England.

This side of the Island is but indifferently off for fish except in the spring, when I am told we may have a small kind of cod, mackerel, trout, bass, smelts, and several sorts of flatfish, pretty plenty. At present there are only lobsters and oysters, neither very good.

The climate since I have been here has been very fine, not much warmer than that of England, and so little rain that my labourers have been prevented working out of doors by it only three days since my arrival, and I expect we will have good weather until near the latter end of November.

The winters, I am told, are so mild in the woods that the inhabitants during that season make all the frames for their houses, saw boards, and do almost all their woodwork.

The French inhabitants have for some years past been mostly maintained by a few British subjects here, who have employed them during the summer in the fishery, and have been paid their wages in clothes, rum, flour, powder and shot. With the last articles they kill as many bears, seals and wild fowls as serve them for meat; the seal-oil they call their butter and use it as such. By this means agriculture has been so much neglected; there is not one bushel of corn raised by all the French inhabitants on the Island.

There are a few British families who have raised some, from whose accounts and from what I have seen myself I form my opinion of what may be done; and I really think this Island if well nursed in its present infant state may be made as useful to Great Britain and as plentiful within itself as any country of its size in North America; but to bring it to that we will require your lordship's countenance and influence to procure some assistance for us from our mother country.

There have arrived here this summer about one hundred and twenty families, part sent by Mr Montgomery, the Lord Advocate of Scotland, the rest by a Mr Stewart of that country. The last arrived about three weeks ago at Prince Town but very unfortunately for want of a pilot their vessel ran on shore at the entrance of the harbour and is entirely lost, and part of her cargo but no lives.

I have been obliged to give Mr Duport, our Chief Justice, leave to return to Halifax for this winter, as he had neglected to lay in provisions for himself and family during the summer: they must otherwise have been starved.

I am in daily expectations of a ship from London with passengers, and one from Ireland with Mr Desbrisay and family; though I dread the consequences if they do, as there is not a house for to put their heads into, and if they do not bring provisions to serve them until next June, they must absolutely starve, for there is not one loaf of bread nor flour to make one to be bought on the Island. *Signed.* [C.O.226/4, fo. 26]

CXII

John Stuart to Governor Lord Botetourt[1]

25 October, Lochaber

My Lord, I arrived here the 15th where I found all the Cherokee chiefs with their followers of all ages, about a thousand in number; they had arrived two days before me. I had also the pleasure of finding Col. Donelson here; he was exactly punctual to the time appointed, which I inclined to have been also but various unforeseen and unavoidable accidents rendered that impossible, although the difficulty of finding a sufficient number of wagons was what principally caused the delay on my part.

I have the honour of laying before your Excellency minutes [Vol. II, No. CV] of my proceedings with said Indians, as also a treaty [Vol. I, No. 848i] by which the boundary line dividing the lands ceded to His Majesty within the limits of the province of Virginia from the lands which they have reserved for their own use is stipulated and agreed upon. No persuasion could induce the Indians to give up Long Island on Holsten's River, and they have cut off six miles from the line pointed out by my Lord Hillsborough, as still more fully appear by the treaty and minutes; which I chose to acquiesce in rather than leave the business entirely unfinished. And here I beg leave to observe to your lordship that the bad effects of underhand machinations and private tampering with the Indians appeared throughout the whole course of the transaction. It is the first instance of any nation having shown a reluctancy to treat with me, it is the only one of my having failed in carrying a point with Cherokees. The loss however to the province is very inconsiderable; the small triangle that is cut off being of exceeding poor land except upon the banks of the river. I have travelled across it and have information from persons perfectly acquainted with that part of the country.

The Cherokees proposed to run the line after crossing Holsten's River a more westerly course than to the mouth of the Great Conhoway, to compensate for what they had cut off upon said river, which would have thrown in a great tract of country. But I declined accepting of

---

1 Enclosed in Nelson's letter to Hillsborough, 15 December 1770: Vol. I, No. 848.

it, not being authorised by my instructions to exceed the bounds pointed out in the report of the Lords Commissioners of Trade. However, as the line cannot be marked till May there will be sufficient time if your lordship thinks proper to submit the matter to His Majesty and receive his orders concerning it before it can be accomplished, and Mr Cameron who will attend said service will have instructions to execute whatever may be determined upon.

The number of Indians that attended far exceeded what I expected; indeed upon any former occasion where the most important business was transacted they never exceeded half the number, which misled me in making an estimate; and as upon such occasions the expense must depend upon contingencies which cannot be foreseen, it must of course be impossible to calculate exactly. Col. Donelson carries the state of the accounts so far as they can be made out, which I hope will give satisfaction; and upon my arrival in Charleston I shall close the account entirely, there being a very few small accounts which I am not as yet furnished with.

I beg leave to return your lordship my most sincere thanks for your candour in furnishing me with the minutes of His Majesty's Council of Virginia containing the substance of Oucconnastotah's letter and the Young Warrior's talk, the whole of which the Indians declare to be a forgery which must reflect disgrace upon the persons concerned therein. Mr Richard Paris was confronted with the Indians and they declared that the said letters as well as the grants of land obtained of them were represented as containing no more than their application to your lordship for a trade, when they signed them; and that the enclosed letter to me, written for them by Mr Jacob Hite, they understood to have been to the same purpose, and were amazed when the true contents were explained to them, to which they declared that they had been utter strangers. I shall add no more with regard to said letter and talk than that it would be ridiculous to imagine that I should oppose the establishment of a boundary which I myself had recommended.

With regard to the charge of misrepresentation contained in Col. Lewis's letter, it is of a very heavy nature and must draw my serious attention. If he can support his charge, I think, and it must be the opinion of every honest man, that I am unworthy of filling the station in which His Majesty has been graciously pleased to place me. If he cannot, and I call upon him to do it if he can, I shall expect the redress which the laws of my country entitle me to. In carrying on His Majesty's service, I am actuated by no motive but a sense of my duty, and if I can obtain the approbation of my superiors and a consciousness of having acted properly, I shall have gained my aim, for I am entirely unbiased and disinterested in every other respect.

I beg leave to return your lordship my most sincere thanks for having sent a gentleman of Col. Donelson's discernment and probity to assist me upon this occasion. He is thoroughly master of every particular relative to the negotiation of the line, and as I have an entire confidence on his honour and candour I beg leave to refer your lordship to him for every particular. *Copy.* [C.O.5/1349, fo. 20]

CXIII

Governor John Wentworth to Earl of Hillsborough (No. 34, duplicate)

28 October, New Hampshire

May it please your lordship, I have now the honour to acknowledge your lordship's letter No. 31.

It is peculiarly happy to me that I may inform your lordship of my success in removing those prejudices and bad impressions which had been artfully infused into the minds of the people upon the unhappy affair in Boston. For some time it was difficult to prevail on them from acceding to the most violent measures pursued at Boston, but having caused such a delay as to give time for reason and judgement to operate and informed them I was resolved in the first instance of violence to oppose them openly in person and call to my aid every officer in the province and that whatever ruinous or fatal consequences ensued must rest upon those whose illegal conduct compelled the event, and the principal men having resolved never to submit to popular anarchy excited an extensive zeal to discourage every indecency or unwarrantable effort to disturb the public peace; by which means the heated injurious resentments at first imbibed were quite eradicated and the people wisely concluded that as they had nothing to do in the case they would not enter into any measures relating thereto. Some little time after, an advertisement appeared inviting the Sons of Liberty to meet in the most public street in Portsmouth to read letters from the Sons of Liberty at New York and South Carolina. As this advertisement, though decently expressed, might or rather was intended to gather many people from whose inconsiderateness some very zealous conduct was hoped by those who received express directions from the Hydra-headed demagogues at Boston, I thought it prudent that the usual acting magistrates and the selectmen of the town should be prepared to come among them and legally disperse and separate them, if from their number or conduct it should be necessary; but on the day appointed there were very few convened and those were generally dissatisfied at their irregular invitation. However, the selectmen with becoming spirit and prudence warned them of the impropriety and futility of such meetings and forbid any act or thing to be done, for that the law had prescribed the method of convening the town and that all other means were disorderly and should not take place; to which the people assented with great approbation and in ten minutes the whole was finished. Those who had advertised being thus disappointed, they pursued the legal steps to convene a town-meeting, at which the first mentioned letters were read and after much debate whether to consider them or not, it was voted and a committee chosen to consider and report upon them at an adjournment for that purpose. In the meantime the town of Boston voted to exclude this province from all intercourse, wrote to Connecticut, New York and all the southern provinces, from whom this province is supplied with provisions, to engage them to exclude us also and thereby to starve and compel this province into their combinations. One of the Boston zealots was immediately dispatched hither by all means to procure the people to engage with him. He even had the insolence to bring a report for the committee to offer at the town-meeting, expressed in the most abusive scandalous terms, as might be expected from the heads and hearts that composed it. Having prevailed on the committee to accept it, he endeavoured to proselyte those he dared attempt, but many of the inhabitants finding his residence here was solely with a view to inflame and disturb the good order of the country became exasperated, and at length to such a degree that it was with the utmost difficulty I prevented their tarring and feathering him, and otherwise punishing this Son of Liberty. However, he soon found his danger and decamped precipitately for Boston. Whenever his fears will admit his heart to reflect, he will rejoice in the efficiency of the laws in New Hampshire which alone preserved him from the severest outrage of an incensed people.

Upon the town-meeting to receive the report, there appeared various reports and among others the violent composition from the other province; with which the inhabitants were so disgusted that upon a question put to dismiss the whole matter and dissolve the meeting it was carried in the affirmative, and to prevent future unnecessary meetings upon such schemes a poll was insisted on by the majority which turned out about ten to one in favour of totally dismissing the whole without any resolutions whatever; and further to convince those who were desirous to interrupt our quiet and lead us into measures not approved of, it was required of the printer not to publish any proceedings or reasons in vindication of the town and province.

From this time the province has been the object of obloquy and envy to our neighbours, and still continue to persevere in an unexceptionable reverence to the laws, which having steadily persisted in from a firm and just principle of rectitude even in times when the threatened preclusion of their provision-trade menaced them with very distressful consequences, and notwithstanding the artful solicitations to engage them, whence also it is certain the non-importation combinations in other colonies were alarmed and fundamentally disheartened. Happy herein if meeting your lordship's favour in such representation as may adduce His Majesty's gracious and condescending approbation.

I beg leave to express the most perfect gratitude for your lordship's very obliging concern for the recovery of my health which receives its greatest value from your lordship's goodness, that possesses my mind with sincerest thankfulness.

My unfeigned acknowledgements are also presented that your lordship has been pleased to receive and communicate the King's pleasure in regard to Mr Wentworth's appointment to be of the Council in the room of the late Mr Atkinson, upon whose demise I appointed Theodore Atkinson Esq. to the vacant office of province-secretary, which office he had conducted for many years and resigned from a multiplicity of business, whereupon the late demised Mr Atkinson was commissionated. I have therefore found it for His Majesty's service to reappoint Mr Atkinson, from whose age, abilities, influence, property and more than forty years experience in the affairs of this government, I am convinced he is every way qualified for this department, which is of great importance to the safety and due government of the province, and yet I am very sorry to find supported in so inadequate a manner with an annually voted salary of forty-five pounds sterling per annum, which also includes for fire, candle and office hire, and nearly the same sum for fees of office in copies, examinations and recording. However, as it is absolutely necessary that the office should be safely conducted, I beg leave to entreat your lordship would be pleased to represent this recommendation in favour of Theo. Atkinson Esq. if it may be His Majesty's pleasure to confirm him secretary of the province of New Hampshire.

I have the pleasure to acknowledge the receipt of Mr Pownall's letters [Vol. I, Nos. 275, 356] dated 14th April and 22 May enclosing the Acts of Parliament passed in the last session relating to America, and His Majesty's gracious speech to both Houses of Parliament, all of which I shall diligently and carefully consider for my guidance in His Majesty's service wherein I pray your lordship to be assured that my most earnest zeal and faithfulness is exerted, humbly relying on His Majesty's grace for approbation and acceptance. *Signed.* [C.O.5/937, fo. 25]

CXIV

Lieut.-Governor Thomas Hutchinson to Earl of Hillsborough (No. 28)

30 October, Boston

My Lord, it is with the greatest pleasure I acquaint your lordship that after a long and fair trial the jury this morning gave in their verdict in favour of Captain Preston and he is now safe at Castle William. The behaviour of the people was remarkably decent during the whole trial and in general they are satisfied with his acquittal. He is a very great sufferer in the cause of government and has conducted through the whole affair in the most discreet manner. The trial of the soldiers will not come on this fortnight. From the evidence which appeared upon Captain Preston's trial, there is room to expect that at most they can be found guilty of manslaughter only and some of the court seems to think it a justifiable homicide.

I shall send under this cover copy of the proceedings [Vol. I, No. 691iii] of Council against Mr Secretary Oliver, who has been a very faithful servant of the Crown ever since he has been in office. They do not need any remarks upon them to your lordship. If the Council had any cause of complaint it was against me, for the deposition of the Secretary was at my request and I told them so and at the same time cautioned them against this proceeding, but they would not desist.

I keep the Assembly sitting yet at Cambridge doing the common business of the province very leisurely, by which their constituents are sufferers. Nothing has passed since my last letter worth communicating to your lordship except a further altercation upon the subject of Castle William. *Signed.* P.S. As Sir F. Bernard's letters may mention Captain Preston's trial, I take the liberty to cover them that they may be delivered when your lordship shall think proper. [C.O.5/759, fo. 300]

CXV

Governor John Wentworth to Earl of Hillsborough (No. 35)

4 November, New Hampshire

May it please your lordship, I have the honour to transmit to your lordship the Journals and Acts of the General Assembly of His Majesty's province of New Hampshire, committed to the care of Mr Temple, Lieut.-Governor of this province and a Commissioner of the Customs in America, who has obliged me with an information of his voyage to England by the first ship from Boston. From his extensive experience in and attachment to the King's service in America, in which he has appeared to me both intelligent and attentive, as far as my intercourse and conversation could afford me opportunity to observe, I trust your lordship will have the fullest informations, in particular of the uninterrupted quiet and good order maintained and the due obedience to all revenue regulations that has prevailed in this province to this day.

No. 1. An Act relative to the excise, and is an exact copy of those transmitted annually since my arrival and which is equally useful now.

No. 2. An Act to authorise the Treasurer to issue an extent against the purchaser of the excise or any part thereof for the money due for the same when the time of payment is past. This Act is directed solely to the end expressed in the title, by which the many collusions and delays in paying this branch of the King's revenue into the Treasury are precluded, and is therefore very much to His Majesty's service.

No. 3 is an Act for the supply of His Majesty's Treasury, which being the same as for preceding years and the sum judged adequate to the establishments hitherto afforded for the administration of government, I have no new reasons thereon; it is therefore duly submitted.

No. 4. An Act to establish an equitable method of making rates and taxes and determining who shall be legal voters in town affairs. The method of assessing and apportioning taxes having long been the subject of complaint and the source of endless lawsuits, by which means the people were exposed to unreasonable prejudices and disquietude against all taxes whatever, and the General Assembly having much expectation that equal justice in taxation would be acquired by this Valuation Act, which also is merely a local regulation, tending to the peace of the province, and the clause relating to the voters in town affairs being also part thereof, as by these voters selectmen and assessors are chosen who issue and declare the apportionment, but more particularly as it excludes from votes those transient people of no interest or property through whose unprincipled conduct all the absurd and indecent measures of town-meetings have proceeded in other governments and could scarcely be restrained in this but are by this clause precluded, and cannot fail of beneficial consequences if it shall please His Majesty to permit the Act to continue.

No. 5. An Act to preserve the fish in Piscataqua River. The preamble of this Act very fully and with great truth recites the reasons for and utility of this law being enacted, without which the fish in this, the only river from the sea into the province, will soon be destroyed to the great loss of all and to the distress of the poor who are in part supported by ish. I have therefore assented thereto and beg leave to transmit for His Majesty's gracious approbation if it shall happily seem meet herefor.

No. 6. An Act in addition to an Act passed in the 13th year of the reign of her late Majesty Queen Anne, entitled an Act for maintenance and supply of the ministry within this province. This Act I beg leave to present to your lordship as of the greatest importance to the well-being of the established Church of England in this province, which stands in need of much assistance or it will soon be totally forgotten, although with aid and protection it might arise to greater prosperity in this than in any province in North America. The many sects and divisions into which Protestants have lately fallen in all the colonies have also taken place in New Hampshire. All of them claim exemption from parish taxes under the Toleration Act. Many enter their names in the Church of England list from all parts of the province, and neither attend nor pay any taxes, whence every necessary repair and support of the Episcopal Church hath been for some years declining even to ruin, but will be again restored to health and vigour by this Act, which will effectually remedy that covetousness which alone prevents their flying to the Church as the only establishment secure from innovation and ignorant, intruding lay teachers. I need not observe to your lordship what eminent advantage would result to the civil government from the prevalence of Episcopacy in the colonies. Permit me only to assure your lordship that I think this desirable event may be incredibly advanced, not only in this province but thereby through all the colonies of New England without the least murmur or disquiet or even without any public or private opposition whatever. I think the Act of Assembly herewith presented will be the foundation of such a plan, whence I humbly hope it may meet His Majesty's approbation. If this matter should be deemed necessary to prosecute, I can with pleasure assure your lordship it shall not fail of success if committed to my care, and that at the expense of three hundred pounds sterling per annum for eight or to be sure not exceeding ten years it may be accomplished, and at the same time an estate raised to the Church of at least two thousand per annum in fifty to one hundred different towns, which small benefices will be in the patronage of the Society for Propagating the Gospel, or else immediately in His Majesty.

No. 7. The Journals of the General Assembly which being chiefly relating to the Acts beforementioned and to the various grants for the service of the last year, I have not to trouble your lordship further thereon save only to represent that the resolve for extending the time granted for Newmarket Bridge lottery is only to complete the sum first granted, which was not nor could be done in the first time allowed; and without this necessary permission the sum already raised by the lottery and laid out toward building the said bridge would have been totally lost to the province and the river incommoded by the piers built, which must have been a nuisance unless the bridge was finished.

Among the grants made for the expenses of government is a grant to me for my charge in attending a trial of piracy at Boston, in which I am reimbursed sixty pounds proclamation money for an account of one hundred and twenty guineas, which the journey actually cost me; whereby my salary is in fact reduced to five hundred and ninety-two pound lawful money for the year 1769. However, as I am in daily hopes that His Majesty will be graciously pleased to fix and grant salaries to his governors of the provinces more competent than the small and dependent pittances usually afforded by the provincial grants, I the more readily submit to the abovementioned defalcation, against which I remonstrated to them that they might have no claim of remission from their deficiency.

I am the more encouraged in my hopes of a royal, independent establishment as I have heard the same is amply granted for New York and Massachusetts Bay, both of which provinces are much more able to support their respective civil establishments, and as this province have steadily adhered to the most perfect good conduct and testified their respect to the laws of Great Britain when all the others were thrown into confusion and combinations against the commerce of the mother country, I am yet in further reliance that His Majesty will be graciously pleased to confer equal favour herein upon this province as upon the others.

Since my last general dispatches upon the province concerns, a petition was proposed to the Governor and Council by the Rev. Doctor Eleazer Wheelock, setting forth that he had obtained more than ten thousand pounds sterling through and by the charitable contributions of many pious people in Great Britain, and that His Majesty had condescended graciously to grant two hundred pounds of said sum, the whole of which is to be applied for the support and education of Indian youth and missionaries, and for the furtherance of learning in His Majesty's Plantations in America; also further premising that he, the said Dr Wheelock, had after due enquiry determined to settle said school or college in the western part of this province and that many well-disposed persons in America had offered considerable donations for said college, but that for want of incorporation the college could not be fixed nor those benefactions received, and consequently His Majesty's royal bounty could not be applied according to his beneficient intentions. Whereupon the Council unanimously advised, and a charter of incorporation was granted by the name of Dartmouth College, with such privileges as are in the charter of New Jersey College, saving always that the governor of this province for the time being shall be the first overseer of said college whereby His Majesty may ever have due information of the application of this his royal bounty; and also a Board of Trust appointed in England for the management of the moneys there, and who have an effectual consideration of all the rules and government of the college, in which Trust are nominated and requested the Right Reverend the Lord Bishop of London, the school being in his diocese, and that the interests of the Church may be promoted by his great wisdom and piety in this seminary of education; the Right Honourable the Earl of Dartmouth; and the Honourable Sir Sydney Stafford Smythe. Already an house is built for the President, Dr Wheelock, and another for the students, with which the Indians appear highly delighted, and I verily believe will be of vast advantage not only in Christianising but also in spreading a rooted influence among all the Indian tribes within six hundred miles of Connecticut River; nor do I think it too sanguine to expect that this institution will more effectually subdue the savages and prevent their incursions than any other measure that has ever yet been attempted.

No 8 are the Naval Office duplicates completed to this quarter, which I beg leave to present for your lordship's approbation.

I have made the most diligent enquiry but cannot find any new manufacture set up nor any old one augmented in this province, which is scarcely provided with mechanics eno' for the common purposes of domestic repair.

I now most humbly beg leave to submit the whole for your lordship's consideration, hoping with the utmost deference that your lordship's favourable representation of my zeal and fidelity in my duty may happily induce His Majesty's approbation. *Signed.* [C.O.5/937, fo. 31]

CXVI

Governor William Franklin to Earl of Hillsborough (supposed to be No. 24)

5 November, Burlington

My Lord, I did myself the honour to write to your lordship on the 29th of September last [Vol. I, No. 632] informing you that I was then there holding a session of General Assembly. The session lasted till the 27th of October during which nothing of much importance happened except that the Assembly in resentment for the royal disallowance of the Paper Money Act, and as instructed by many of their constituents, did actually come to a resolution after a considerable debate "That no farther provision should be made for the supply of His Majesty's troops stationed in this colony". However, upon my talking the affair over in private with some of the leading members and representing the ill consequences that would probably ensue to the province from their refusal, I at length influenced them to resume the consideration of the matter and to grant a sum sufficient for the supply of the troops during the winter. The sum they have granted is five hundred pounds currency which, as part of the firing is already provided, I am in hopes will be enough to furnish all the necessaries required by Act of Parliament till the latter end of April next, at which time they must be called again to make a farther provision. The Assembly have now left the appointment of the barrack-masters entirely to the governor and have made the money liable to be drawn out of the Treasury by warrant from the Governor and Council, two points which before they never would accede to. The province has indeed been greatly imposed upon and defrauded by the barrack-masters nominated by the Assembly. But now that they have put a confidence in government it shall be my endeavour to convince them that it is properly placed, and for the real advantage of the public. A copy of my message [Vol. I, No. 698i] to them on this head and their answer is enclosed.

The minutes of the proceedings of the Council and Assembly and the Acts passed are now copying and shall be transmitted to your lordship by the first opportunity. *Signed.* [C.O.5/990, fo. 91]

CXVII

Lieut.-General Thomas Gage to Earl of Hillsborough (No. 51)

10 November, New York

My Lord, I had not time to answer your lordship's letter [Vol. II No. LXXVI] No. 32 by the opportunity of the last packet but have since taken the contents thereof into consideration, and in obedience to your lordship's commands I now take the liberty to trouble you with the reflections that have occurred to me and the opinions I have formed as well on the state of the British possessions upon the Mississippi as on forts and settlements in general in the interior country.

The French first adopted the plan of forts and settlements in the Indian country in the view of forming a communication between their colonies of Canada and Louisiana, of seizing the passes that command the entrance into those countries and conciliating the affections of the savages, by means of which they might prevent the King's subjects having any intercourse with the Indians, secure all the commerce to themselves, and when convenient excite the Indians to make incursions on the British provinces. The nations approved of their proceedings because they appeared to be calculated merely for their use and benefit. Priests were sent to convert them and though they made but few sincere Christians yet by rendering them little services and taking pains to please they insinuated themselves into their favour and had a great influence over their actions. The forts were small and only fortified in the Indian manner, the soldiers were few and the settlers not numerous, but being trained to Indian war were able to defend themselves, they soon learned the Indian language, hunted with the natives, and became almost one people with them. By these means the French succeeded and at a small expense; the Indians, not jealous of their power, became attached to them and averse to us.

Now the forts and settlements are in British possession, other systems are adopted and other benefits are supposed to be derived from them, for we want no communication between our provinces, we have no rivals in our trade to be kept out of the country, except the people of Louisiana are deemed such, and we have not in view the spiriting up the savages to annoy our neighbours.

The advantages we are now supposed to reap by maintaining forts are: the protection of the trade, defending the traders from the violence and insolence of the savages, and preventing frauds and imposition on the part of the traders; the keeping up of friendly intercourse with the Indians; the keeping them in awe, the forts enabling us to carry war into the heart of their country; the drawing the attacks of the savages from the settled country and saving it from incursions in time of war; the preventing their joining the French in case they make attempts to recover Canada; the supporting the old British subjects in their trade who might be drove away to favour the Canadians; and where settlements are made, the keeping the settlers in subordination to government.

Those who argue in favour of the settlements allege that they are foundations of new colonies, which would form barriers to the present frontiers, give room to the people in the lower provinces to spread, and prevent their settling together in such numbers as to encourage them to manufacture, that wine, silk and other commodities might be raised in those countries, and that the settlers could raise provisions for the garrisons and save the expense of sending it up to them.

Having enumerated every benefit I have heard of, that is supposed to accrue from forts or settlements in the interior country, I shall proceed to give your lordship my sentiments upon each article, without regard to any opinions I may have formed heretofore which a farther consideration or longer experience shall have satisfied me to be erroneous.

If the forts were marts of trade as first intended they should be, and the traders confined to trade there only, it might be truly said that they protect the trade. But experience evinced the impracticability of confining the trade to the forts. The number of posts requisite to taking all the trade would be more than could with any propriety be supported. Both Indians and traders opposed the regulation and when the officers obeyed their orders the Indians quarrelled with them, and the traders threatened prosecutions, quitted the posts privately, and passed them without calling, and some of them now ramble to the distance of 500 leagues beyond our farthest post. Except Missilimakinac, where the Indians from long custom resort to for the sake of the trade during part of the summer, it may be said no trade is carried on at any of the posts; for the few skins picked up from savages who come on business to the commanders or to get presents is no object. The traders send their canoes amongst the nations.

As the officers receive the Indians kindly, give them every satisfaction in their power if injured, make them small presents, and assist them with provision, it is certainly giving them a testimony of our regard and showing a desire to cultivate their friendship; but this is doing no more than what might be as well effected by skilful Indian officers posted judiciously amongst the nations in the manner practised in the Southern District.

Notwithstanding many instances of insolence and bad intentions in the savages, and the murders they have often committed as well on soldiers as traders, the forts may tend to keep them in some sort of awe, though by it we destroy that confidential friendship we wish to establish with the Indians. The forts are now by far more respectable than when first established by the French; the Indians look upon them as bulwarks erected in their country with a design to subject them. It is true that being deposits of military stores, they facilitate the carrying war into the heart of the country, though it may be a question whether that service is not obtained at too great an expense. The necessity of military enterprises in those distant countries can scarcely happen, with proper skill and management on our part, and even should they be judged necessary, they might be undertaken from below, from whence we should now be obliged to send reinforcements of troops and provisions in case of an attack upon any of the forts.

It is not a just idea that distant forts draw the attention of the savages from the settlements in time of war. Reasons might be given against it, but it is sufficient to say that experience has proved it groundless. Forts Pitt, Ligonier, Bedford, Littleton, and Cumberland, did not protect Pennsylvania and Virginia in the late Indian war. The savages fell upon and destroyed many settlements in both those provinces, and pushed their incursions as low as Shippensburg and Winchester. And, granting that the Indian nations would either through policy or attachment declare for the French if they made an attempt upon Canada, it is much to be doubted whether the forts would not in that case be more detrimental than useful to us. We might be necessitated to send part of our force to support the forts that could be employed to more advantage below, and, diverted from the main object, protect the shadow when we should employ all our force to defend the substance. For your lordship may be assured of the truth of this maxim, whoever commands the country below will always rule the country above. From thence the trade flows and the Indians cannot do without it. The Detroit and Missilimakinac fell with Canada, and had they not been included in that capitulation there is little reason to believe otherwise than that the savages would have delivered both into our hands in a short time.

The competition for the trade between His Majesty's old and new subjects is greatly abated and must by degrees entirely subside, for if carried to extremes it would be very prejudicial to both. And with respect to the mother country, she will gain all the peltry brought to Quebec, whether it is carried thither by Britons or Canadians. I am of opinion indeed the forts have kept the French settlers in subjection, and if the settlers can't be removed or such a government established over them as to render troops unnecessary, that forts may be said to be of use to ensure their obedience.

As to increasing the settlements to respectable provinces and colonisation in general terms in the remote countries, I conceive it altogether inconsistent with sound policy, for there is little appearance that the advantages will arise from it which nations expect when they send out colonies into foreign countries. They can give no encouragement to the fishery; though the country might afford some kind of naval stores, the distance would be too far to transport them; and for the same reason, they could not supply the Sugar Islands with lumber and provision. As for the raising of wine, silk or other commodities, the same may be said of the present colonies without planting others for the purpose at so vast a distance. But on the supposition that they would be raised, their very long transportation must probably make them too dear for any market. I do not apprehend the inhabitants could have any commodities to barter for manufactures except skins and furs, which will naturally decrease in proportion as the country increases in people and the deserts are cultivated, so that in the course of a few years necessity will force them to provide manufactures of some kind for themselves. And when all connection upheld by commerce with the mother-country shall cease, it may be suspected that an independency on her government will soon follow. The pretence of forming barriers will have no end wherever we settle, however remote there must be a frontier, and there is room enough for the colonists to spread within our present limits for a century to come. If we reflect how the people of themselves have gradually retired from the coast, we should be convinced they want no encouragement to desert the sea-coasts and go into the back-countries, where the lands are better and got upon easier terms. They are already almost out of the reach of law and government. Neither the endeavours of government or fear of Indians has kept them properly within bounds, and it is apparently most for the interests of Great Britain to confine the colonists on the side of the back-country and to direct their settlements along the sea-coasts where millions of acres are yet uncultivated. The lower provinces are still thinly inhabited and not brought to the point of perfection that has been aimed at for the mutual benefit of Great Britain and themselves. Although America may supply the mother country with many articles, few of them are yet supplied in quantities equal to her consumption. The quantity of iron transported is not great, of hemp very small, and there are many other commodities not necessary to enumerate which America has not yet been able to raise, notwithstanding the encouragement given her by bounties and premiums. The laying open new tracks of fertile territory in moderate climates might lessen her present product, for it is the passion of every man to be a landholder and the people have a natural disposition to rove in search of good lands, however distant. It may be a question likewise whether colonisations of the kind could be effected without an Indian war and fighting for every inch of ground. The Indians have long been jealous of our power and have no patience in seeing us approach their towns and settle upon their hunting-grounds. Atonements may be made for a fraud discovered in a trader and even the murder of some of the tribes, but encroachments upon their lands have often produced serious consequences. The springs of the last general war are to be discovered near the Allegany Mountains and upon the banks of the Ohio.

It is so obvious that settlers might raise provision to feed the troops cheaper than it can be transported from the country below that it is not necessary to explain it. But I must own I know no other use in settlements or can give any other reason for supporting forts than to protect the settlements and keep the settlers in subjection to government.

I conceive that to procure all the commerce it will afford, and at as little expense to ourselves as we can, is the only object we should have in view in the interior country for a century to come, and I imagine it might be effected by proper management without either forts or settlements. Our manufactures are as much desired by the Indians as their peltry is sought for by us. What was originally deemed a superfluity or a luxury to the natives is now become a necessary. They are disused to the bow and can neither hunt nor make war without firearms, powder and lead. The British provinces only can supply them with their necessaries, which they know, and for their own sakes they would protect the trade, which they actually do at present. It would remain with us to prevent the traders being guilty of frauds and impositions and to pursue the same methods to that end as are taken in the Southern District. And I must confess, though the plan pursued in that district might be improved by proper laws to support it, that I don't know a better or more economical plan for the management of the trade. There are neither forts or settlements in the Southern Department, and there are both in the Northern Department, and your lordship will be the best judge which of them has given you the least trouble, in which we have had the fewest quarrels with or complaints from the Indians.

I know of nothing so liable to bring on a serious quarrel with Indians as an invasion of their property. Let the savages enjoy their deserts in quiet, little bickerings that will unavoidably sometimes happen may soon be accommodated. And I am of opinion, independent of the motives of common justice and humanity, that the principles of interest and policy should induce us rather to protect than molest them. Were they drove from their forests, the peltry-trade would decrease, and not impossible that worse savages would take refuge in them, for they might then become the asylum of fugitive negroes and idle vagabonds escaped from justice who in time might become formidable and subsist by rapine and plundering the lower countries.

I have given your lordship my opinion concerning forts and settlements in general in the distant country, and shall now proceed to treat of the British possessions on the Mississippi and matters relative thereto, which is more particularly the subject of your lordship's letter.

Establishments at the junction of the Ilinois and Ohio Rivers with the Mississippi may be said in a general view to command two passes which might in a great degree prevent the inhabitants of Louisiana from intruding their merchandise amongst the nations in His Majesty's territories, though they could not prevent their having a correspondence with those nations or belts and messages being sent from the one to the other. But it will be proper to consider the damage we do or may sustain through the want of such establishments, and whether any emoluments would arise from them adequate to the expense of forming them and afterwards of supporting and maintaining them.

The Ilinois River is of little consequence, having no powerful nations dwelling upon it, and leads only up to a tribe of the Pouteatamies at St Joseph, a licentious people who have often done mischief but they always receive their supplies from Canada.

The Ohio leads up to the Ouabache on which river there is a good deal of trade, and some boats sent by the British traders from the Ilinois to St Vincent on the lower part of said river were plundered because those Indians, it was said, would permit none but French traders in their town. But I have not learned particularly whether the French traders who supplied them with goods were from Louisiana or Canada. I am apt to believe from the last place, because the Canadians have at all times traded in those parts and sold their goods cheaper than the people from Louisiana were able to do. I am certain the trade is now carried from Canada into the Ouabache, it goes up the Miamie River which falls into the west end of Lake Erie, and by means of a short portage gets into the Ouabache. A person is appointed to manage the portage and receives a regulated price for the transporting of goods, packs of peltry and canoes, to and fro over the portage. It may be thought that the foreign traders from the Mississippi might go higher up the Ohio and carry all the commerce of that river as far as Fort Pitt, but it never has happened or can happen whilst we are at peace with the nations on the rivers. The British traders have always dealt with them, carry them the assortments they are most accustomed to, and can afford their goods cheaper than any others.

The finest and greatest quantity of peltry to be acquired on the Mississippi is in the upper parts of the river, many leagues above Fort Chartres. The traders from the Spanish side of the Mississippi and from Canada go for it amongst the upper nations. The Canada traders push up the Renard or Fox River which falls into the *Baye des Puants* in Lake Michigan, and passing over a short carrying-place fall upon the Ouisconsin, which runs into the Mississippi. But the British traders at the Ilinois remain at Fort Chartres or its neighbourhood; they are afraid to venture up the river because the French as they allege have spirited the Indians against them. And the only peltry that I can find they have gained hitherto has been from the domestic Indians and from such savages as have been drawn to the fort by invitations, the allurement of presents, and curiosity. The idea which may in some degree be just that the more peltry would be gained in proportion as we should move higher up the river has given rise to a new proposal about posts. Instead of erecting a post at the mouth of the Ilinois River, it has been recommended to build one above it, upon a spot said to be advantageous for the trade. This is a very expensive mode of trade and I fear would cost more than the trade is worth. While the traders from the Spanish side and from Canada carry their goods amongst the nations, few will come to posts merely on the account of trade, and it is the business of the British in the Ilinois to court and insinuate themselves into the affections of the Indian tribes as the French have done. And considering the time we have been in possession of the Ilinois, if they had made proper efforts towards it instead of leaning entirely upon the support of government, and that our presents had been dealt out with as much judgement as liberality, I think some of the nations would have given them their protection.

The peltry gained by the traders from Canada, whether on the Mississippi or the Ouabache, we may be satisfied generally goes down the St Lawrence River to Quebec; it has been the usual tract of those traders from the beginning and there is no reason to suspect the contrary now. But the British traders of the Ilinois who carry their goods above three hundred miles by land before they have the convenience of water-carriage cannot afford to return the same way with the produce of their trade, and it's possible that the fear of Indians or the want of bark-canoes, not to be had to the southward, and the only craft proper for shallow waters and transporting over portages, may have prevented them from sending it to Quebec. As they do send their peltry down the river, we may conclude upon the whole they found that route the cheapest and most expeditious; they can navigate the Mississippi with the same craft they navigate the Ohio or may find means to embark their peltry in the boats returning to New Orleans. As it appears to be their interest to go down the Mississippi, I know of no means to compel them to change their route for on the supposition that the best regulations were devised and enforced to that end, the extent of woody country to guard, and the vicinity of the Spanish settlements so favourable to a collusion between the traders of both nations, would probably defeat our greatest vigilance. I may observe here that the vicinity of the settlements of the two nations will also be favourable for either to smuggle goods into the territories of the other, from whence it may be imagined that the merchandise which is sold cheapest, whether British or foreign, will predominate in that country.

The method your lordship has pointed out to lure the trade going down the Mississippi into a British port by the aid of a canal to join that river with the Ibbeville I believe to be the most effectual that can be devised, and that it would answer many desirable ends if the canal would have the effect pretended by those who argue in favour of it. They say, by cutting a channel from a point, upon which the Mississippi strikes with violence, to the Ibbeville, that the former would in a short time make itself a new bed and possibly change its course.

It is said on the other side that the practicability of the scheme is very doubtful and in all events could not succeed without a vast expense. If the cut is made only deep enough to introduce the waters when the freshes come down, it would be of no more use than the present over-flowings into the Iberville. And also that there is a heighth of land, nine miles in length, between the upper part of the Ibbeville and the River Amite and unless the canal is continued to the junction of the Amite and cut as deep as the bed of the Mississippi at low water, the waters will naturally flow back into the Mississippi in the manner they do now when the freshes subside. It is to be considered likewise that the Ibbeville with the Lakes forms one side of the Island of New Orleans, the Spaniards will naturally object to our carrying on any works on their side especially as they are works which may be prejudicial to them. And if the channel, though cut, should be narrow, they might throw more obstructions into it in a few days than could be removed in months.

I have taken pains to be informed of the possibility of making a canal that would be of real use but I have not procured anything satisfactory concerning it. Lieutenant Pitman's report ought to obtain as much credit as that of any other person, but I believe the levels have never been taken nor the soils examined nor the project in general considered upon the spot with that accuracy and intelligence that it deserves. And I am of opinion that an intelligent person skilled in works of the kind and whose report is to be depended on should examine the country and make an estimate of the expense, before anything is undertaken. If any such person can be found in West Florida, I have desired Brigadier Haldimand to send him to inspect the country and to examine into the project.

Your lordship observes that Fort Chartres appears to be little better than a mere mark of possession. I cannot assign any other use it is of farther than what has been said of other forts near to settlements, that it keeps the inhabitants in subjection. And can't help thinking it would have proved more fortunate for us had we found neither fort nor settlement in the Ilinois country. And from what I have laid before your lordship concerning the Ilinois and Ohio Rivers, I am of opinion the advantages we might propose to gain from civil and military establishments at the mouths of those rivers would be greatly disproportionate to the expenses they would be attended with.

Besides what has been related of the French settlements, they had another view in establishing the Ilinois. The country abounded in buffalos and the climate is more favourable for wheat than the lower parts of the Mississippi, and they proposed from thence to supply New Orleans with salted meat and flour which, unless procured from the British colonies, they were obliged to send from Europe. I conceive this circumstance would be of no advantage to the King's subjects, was New Orleans added to His Majesty's possessions.

I have given your lordship the best information I have been able to obtain of the forts, settlements and commerce of the interior country, and in obedience to your commands I have ventured to give my reflections and opinion thereupon. Should it be necessary to elucidate any part that may appear obscure, or if there are any particular points your lordship may wish to have farther explained, you will please to point them out, that I may give your lordship all the satisfaction in my power on these important objects. *Signed.* [C.O.5/88, fo. 164]

CXVIII

Lieutenant.-General Thomas Gage to Earl of Hillsborough (No. 52)

12 November, New York

My Lord, your lordship has been informed of a very considerable congress holding at Siota by the Indians of the Western confederacy. The spies sent thither are returned to Fort Pitt and report that all the Western tribes, even those over the Lakes and about Lake Michigan as well as the nations of the Ouabache, had unanimously agreed to make peace with the Cherokees and other Southern Indians; which the deputy Indian agent confesses he thought impossible to be accomplished and writes that the spies inform him some Frenchman had promised and engaged to bring the nations about the Ilinois, Missouri and Arkansas into the league; that the French have been very active the last spring and summer, telling the Indians the usual story of the designs of the French and Spaniards to make war upon the English who want to get possession of their country through the influence of the Six Nations, which they readily believe from seeing our settlers straggle so far in pursuit of lands.

The Indians of the several nations who came afterwards to the fort behaved orderly, but appeared more sulky and reserved than usual and were holding councils and sending belts constantly from one nation to another, the meaning of which the agent could not discover, but they told him it was only to promote peace among themselves.

The officer commanding at Fort Pitt has sent later advices than the former, in which he acquaints me there never was since he commanded there so many parties of warriors from the Six Nations passing to the Cherokee country, who demand provisions and ammunition and tell him Sir William Johnson informed them they would get everything they wanted at the fort, as formerly, and appear greatly affronted if refused their demands. They say they are not going to war against the Cherokees but against any people that nation shall desire them to strike.

How all these commotions will terminate, time only can show, but there is a great appearance of war between the nations confederated in the Northern and Southern leagues, both of which are powerful; and unless the messengers sent by the first, at the desire of Sir William Johnson, meet with success in their embassy, it is likely that hostilities will soon commence. The Western tribes are exasperated to a great degree against the Six Nations for the lands they have ceded, and their resentment created the project of confederating to be able to withstand their power. The storm would probably have burst upon ourselves if His Majesty's Indian officers had not had dexterity enough to avert it by spiriting up the Six Nations to support what they had done and to maintain their superiority over the dependent nations, and this gave rise to the Northern confederacy in opposition to the other. They are both desirious of gaining the Cherokees, who from the proceedings of Sir William Johnson's late congress on the Mohock River, appear to have engaged with the Northern nations. And in these circumstances I think it fortunate that the Virginians were not permitted to extend their boundary lines farther than the Cherokees were willing they should.

I give your lordship the state of these Indian affairs as well as I have been able to learn or comprehend them, and wish we may extricate ourselves out of the quarrel. The nations of Ohio who conceived and contrived the Western league are most affected by the cessions made to us, being nearest to our frontier, and it's not unlikely, if hostilities begin, that rage and resentment will tempt them to fall upon the people settled upon their hunting grounds.

We have just had the pleasure of hearing from Boston that Captain Preston is acquitted after a trial uncommonly long, the proceedings of which I presume will be transmitted to your lordship from Boston. Some people have since attempted to bring an appeal of murder against him, as likewise suits for damages on account of the wounded. The first was ineffectual, but he is obliged to confine himself on account of the latter. The soldiers will be tried in about fourteen days.

Captain Preston has been prosecuted with great malice and has suffered much during a long confinement in a loathsome dungeon as well as in his finances, which are greatly exhausted by the cost of his trial. And as he has not rashly or wantonly brought these misfortunes upon himself, but fallen into them unavoidably in the actual execution of his duty, your lordship will pardon me in the liberty I take to recommend his case to His Majesty's royal consideration.

Being informed the state of affairs at Boston will be laid before the Parliament the ensuing sessions, and that many printed depositions have been circulated in England by people a good deal concerned in the disturbances that have happened, I take the liberty to transmit your lordship a number of depositions [Vol. I, No. 709i-lxxiv] of the 14th and 29th Regiments, taken in Castle William and New Jersey, containing many instances of the highest provocation and severest usage given the troops, previous to the unhappy accident upon the 5th March.

The engineer employed at Castle William hopes to finish the works carrying on there and to complete the plans and sections thereof by the end of this month. *Signed.* [C.O.5/88, fo. 174]

CXIX

Governor Earl of Dunmore to Earl of Hillsborough (No. 2)

12 November, New York

My Lord, nothing of a public nature has occurred within the little time I have arrived except the addresses of congratulation on my arrival, which being full of sentiments of loyalty and affection to His Majesty's person and government I have thought proper to send copies [Vol. I, No. 710i-xiii] of them, imagining they might be acceptable. I found the Assembly prorogued to the 7th of November, and I have with the advice of Council farther prorogued it till the 11th of December then to meet to do business.

The situation of the people of this province in the counties of Cumberland and Gloucester on the borders of New Hampshire is truly lamentable; a number of disorderly people are continually committing riots; a recent tumult has obliged me to issue a proclamation for apprehending the offenders, a copy [Vol. I, No. 710xiv] of which is herewith transmitted to your lordship, but the authority of the civil magistrate will avail little when even the courts of justice are obstructed and their proceedings stopped. The rioters are instigated to commit those outrages by the people of New Hampshire, suggesting that the magistrates and courts of justice established in the said counties act without good authority, for they assert that His Majesty intends to recall his royal order, already issued, and to declare the abovesaid two counties to be within the jurisdiction of the province of New Hampshire. Your lordship will observe by the proclamation already mentioned that I have contradicted this report and affirmed the above suggestion to be false. Their only encouragement in this opinion seems to be the restrictions laid upon the governor of this province with respect to granting the lands within the said two counties; and here I cannot but observe what in truth is very obvious that such restriction obstructs the settlement of that country not only by excluding fresh people from settling there, but the frequent disorders, which it has given a sort of sanction to, entirely prevents the industrious efforts of those already settled. It therefore appears to me that it is become highly necessary that the said restriction should be taken off forthwith, that I may thereby be enabled to exert my endeavours for the full settling of that country, and then the disorders complained of will of themselves subside; but which at present cannot happen from the thinness of the inhabitants, there not being enough for the appointment of magistrates, consequently those few are but very insufficient of themselves to enforce their own authority against those daring violators of the peace, supported as they are by their whole province.

I have made it my business to enquire and to find out the opinion of people here on the scheme in agitation of establishing a colony on the Ohio. I find all who have any knowledge of such affairs concur in condemning the project. They allege among variety of reasons that a colony at such an immense distance from the settled parts of America and from the ocean can neither benefit either those settled parts or the mother country; that they must become immediately a lost people to both, and all communication of a commercial nature with them be a vain attempt from the difficulty and expense attending the transport of commodities to them, which would so enhance the price thereof as to make it utterly impossible for them to purchase such commodities, for they could not raise a produce of any kind that would answer so difficult and expensive transport back. Such colony must therefore be their own manufacturers, and the great expense of maintaining troops there for their protection be a dead weight on government without the hopes of reaping any advantage hereafter. The scheme alarms extremely all the settled parts of America, the people of property being justly apprehensive of consequences that must inevitably ensue, that such a colony will only become a drain to them (now but thinly peopled) of an infinite number of their lower class of inhabitants who the desire of novelty alone will induce to change their situation, and the withdrawing of those inhabitants will reduce the value of lands in the provinces even to nothing and make it impossible for the patentees to pay the quitrents; by which it is evident His Majesty's interest must be very much prejudiced. Add to this the great probability, I may venture to say certainty, that the attempting a settlement on the Ohio will draw on an Indian war, it being well known how ill-affected the Ohio Indians have always been to our interest, and their jealousy of such a settlement so near them must be easily foreseen. Therefore, as such a war would affect at least the nearest provinces as well as the new colony, your lordship must expect those provinces will not fail to make heavy complaints of the inattention of government to their interest. I cannot therefore but think it my duty to recommend to your lordship not to suffer this scheme to have effect, at least until your lordship shall have from the most substantial and clear proofs been made thoroughly sensible of its utility. *Signed.* PS. I have just received intelligence that the plague is actually raging on the island of Hispaniola. I have had the person who brings this advice examined before the magistrates and send to your lordship his deposition [Vol. I, No. 710xv]. And have also made all the disposition this place admits of (there being no established health-office) for preventing the approach of ships from them ports until they perform a quarantine. [C.O.5/1101, fo. 106]

CXX

Earl of Hillsborough to Governors of Quebec, New York, New Jersey, Virginia, North Carolina, Deputy Governors of Maryland and Pennsylvania (Circular)

15 November, Whitehall
Sir, the enclosed extract of a letter [Vol. II, No. LXXXII] I have very lately received from Sir William Johnson will fully inform you of the complaints made by the Six Nations of Indians and their allies and

confederates, at a congress held in July last at the German Flatts, of the abuses and violences committed by the traders and frontier inhabitants of several of His Majesty's colonies; and the enclosed extract [Vol. I, No. 565i] of the conferences will point out to you how earnest the Indians have been in those complaints and what is likely to happen if they are not redressed.

After the King had thought fit, from a regard to the claims and opinions of the colonies, to leave it to them to make such regulations concerning the Indian commerce as they judged proper, there was good reason to hope that a matter on which their interest and safety do so much depend would have been an immediate object of their serious deliberation; but as contrary to all expectation nothing effectual appears yet to have been done and as the Indians have in the strongest manner expressed their impatience under the abuses to which they are constantly exposed, the King has commanded me to signify his pleasure that you should without delay represent this matter in the strongest manner to the Council and Assembly of the colony under your government, and urge them in His Majesty's name to fall upon some means of putting Indian affairs under such regulation as may have the effect to prevent those abuses of the trade and those violences and encroachments of the frontier inhabitants which the Indians so justly complain of. *Draft*. [Words 'Council and' omitted to Deputy Governor of Pennsylvania; words from 'represent this matter' to 'in His Majesty's name to' omitted to Quebec.] [C.O.5/71, Pt. 2, fo. 83]

CXXI

Earl of Hillsborough to Governor Thomas Hutchinson (No. 43)

15 November, Whitehall

Sir, I have received and laid before the King your dispatches [Vol. I, Nos. 580, 601, 630, 660; Vol. II, No. XCIII] Nos. 23, 24, 25, 26 and 27 and I have the satisfaction to acquaint you that the attention you have shown to His Majesty's commands relative to Castle William and the prudent and cautious measures concerted between you and Col. Dalrymple for conducting that important service have met with the King's entire approbation and correspond with the spirit and intention of that order.

The resolution carried by so great a majority of the Assembly to proceed to business at Cambridge, and the representation you make of the good disposition of the Council, are proofs that the enemies of the public tranquillity are losing their influence in the General Court and induces a hope that the disorders which have so long prevailed in the colony of Massachusetts Bay are drawing to a period.

I think I may venture to assure you that since Sir Francis Bernard's correspondence, no copies of letters which have come to my office have been made public which can be productive of any inconvenience to you, and it is the resolution of the King's servants to withstand as far as in them lies all such public communication. *Draft*. [C.O.5/759, fo. 292]

CXXII

Governor Thomas Hutchinson to Earl of Hillsborough (No. 29)

20 November, Boston

My Lord, I have this day prorogued the General Court, after a session of eight weeks, to the 2nd of January. The party in opposition to government have been able to retard the business by one motion after another in favour of points which they knew could not be conceded to by me, consistent with the King's instructions. Their frequent messages I think have rather hurt than served their cause with the people. They have prevented a Riot Act which has been in force ever since the exchange of the paper for a silver currency, now more than 20 years, from being revived, and they have declined taking any measures for ejecting the intruders upon the land east of Sagadehoc.

They made a grant of £325 lawful money for the support of the lieutenant-governor as a recompense for his past services and likewise to look forward. The sum was so inconsiderable that I could not consent to it. They also made grants for £300 sterling to Mr Bollan who was chosen agent for the council the last year, and for £750 sterling to the representatives of Mr Deberdt, who has been employed by the House for several years past, to both which I declined giving my consent. The Council have renewed their choice of Mr Bollan and the House have chosen Doctor Franklin and in case of his absence or refusal, Doctor Lee. Distinct standing agents for each or either of the two branches of the legislature appear to me unnecessary, irregular and unconstitutional. I have expressed my readiness to consent to an agent chosen by the two Houses and the Council proposed to the House to join in the choice, but the House declined. As soon as the several laws can be prepared I will transmit them with remarks upon them.

I now take the liberty to forward to your lordship copy [Vol. I, No. 735i] of the inventory of the ammunition and stores at Castle William. The platforms and some of the carriages are in very bad order and it is generally agreed that great alterations are necessary in the works in order to make it defensible.

I shall likewise cover the minutes [Vol. I, No. 735ii] of the evidence upon Captain Preston's trial. The friends of government generally agree that it is not advisable for him to appear in town and that it will be best he should go to England. The trial of the soldiers was assigned for this day but there being a deficiency of jurors new *venires* are issued to the several towns which will cause a delay of some days. I am doing everything in my power to procure a fair and impartial trial. *Signed.*
[C.O.5/759, fo. 335]

CXXIII

Commissioners for Trade and Plantations to the King

23 November, Whitehall

May it please your Majesty, we have had under our consideration two Acts passed in your Majesty's colony of Virginia in December 1769 entitled "An Act for laying an additional Duty upon Slaves imported into this Colony", "An Act for the better support of the Contingent Charges of Government".

Whereupon we humbly beg leave to represent to your Majesty,

That by these two laws (the first mentioned of which has a clause suspending its execution until your Majesty's pleasure shall be known) additional duties are imposed upon the importation of negroes (to the amount of fifteen per cent upon every purchase) payable by the purchaser over and above all other duties upon slaves imported laid by former laws now in force, and that these duties which in the whole amount to twenty-five per cent upon every purchase must have the effect, and are we apprehend intended, to operate as an entire prohibition to the importation of slaves into Virginia.

The annexed report[1] made by one of His late Majesty's counsel at law to the Commissioners for Trade and Plantations in the year 1728 upon an Act passed in Virginia in that year for laying a duty of forty shillings a head upon slaves imported is most humbly submitted to your Majesty as containing the strongest arguments and reasoning not only against the policy and propriety of imposing duties upon slaves imported into the Plantations in general as a prejudice and obstruction to the commerce and manufactures of this kingdom, but in particular against the propriety of such duties in Virginia as tending to discourage the culture of tobacco and by raising its price to lessen its consumption and consequently the national revenue arising therefrom.

It is true indeed that in the year 1731 it was thought fit to allow the governors of your Majesty's colonies to consent to laws laying moderate duties upon negroes imported, provided such duties were paid by the purchaser and not by the importer; and we humbly apprehend that it was under the sanction of that permission that laws in the colony of Virginia subsequent to that period laying duties of ten per cent upon negroes imported have been suffered to pass; and therefore, though both from principle and experience we might well entertain a doubt of the propriety of the policy on which that permission was grounded and are able to show that the distinction made between duties paid by the importer and the purchaser is fallacious, and that in fact the operation of either mode is the same, yet we should not have suffered that doubt and opinion to have now opposed themselves to a practice that has without complaint from the merchants of this kingdom universally prevailed in all colonies which import slaves, had those duties in the present case been confined within the limits of moderation. But when the privilege of laying moderate duties payable by the purchaser is extended so far as to have the effect of a prohibition, the objections made to the practice in the year 1728 do stand forth in their full force and extent; for which reason and for as much as the merchants of Bristol, Liverpool and Lancaster trading to Africa have both by their representations and by memorials stated to us the prejudice which these laws will be of to trade and commerce of those ports, it becomes our duty, agreeing with them in opinion, humbly to propose that the first mentioned of these laws may be disallowed, permitting the other

1 *Calendar of State Papers, Colonial Series, America and West Indies,* 1728–1729, (London: H.M.S.O., 1937) No. 510.

which is made to continue only to October 1771 and has also reference to other matters which will require a different consideration to expire by its own limitation; and that your Majesty's governor be instructed that he do not for the future give his assent without your Majesty's permission first obtained to any law by which the duties of ten per cent upon slaves imported into that colony imposed by former laws shall be increased. *Entry. Signatories,* Hillsborough, Soame Jenyns, William Fitzherbert, Robert Spencer, Greville, William Northey. [C.O.5/1369, p. 50]

CXXIV

John Stuart to Head Warriors of Upper Creeks[1]

25 November, Charleston

Head beloved men and warriors, Mr Struthers brought your talk [Vol. I, No. 763vii] to Augusta and forwarded it to the back parts of this province where I was at that time at a meeting with the warriors of the Cherokee nation, finally settling the line between them and the province of Virginia, which business was finished to the satisfaction of the red and white people so that there will be no more talks about land between me and the Cherokees, and their line will be finally marked in next May. We had nothing but good and peaceable talks.

I am very sorry for the occasion of your talk by Mr Struthers, and it belongs to you as men of sense to try every means in your power to stop such proceedings by punishing persons guilty of murder. You know blood was formerly spilled for which no satisfaction was given, now there are two more men killed at Occoni. I am pleased to observe that you have not forgotten the talks and agreements entered into at Augusta; by your repeating them I conclude you mean to fulfil them, and you say the Occoni murder was under the consideration of the Oakfuskee warriors who I hope will do justice.

I believe what you say, that the headmen throughout your nation disapprove of such acts of violence, but that is not enough. You must exert yourselves and put the murderers to death. If I or my son was to kill any of you either would be tried and condemned to die, and you know that both Governor Grant and Governor Wright gave you immediate satisfaction by putting persons to death who killed some of your people.

Brothers, you must be sensible of the instances that I have given you of my friendship upon many occasions, and thereby be convinced of the good intentions of your white brethren. We were sorry to see you and the Choctaws spilling each other's blood but did not choose to interfere in your quarrel till I was strongly solicited by you both to use my endeavour to make peace between you. I did accordingly at your request send my talk to the Choctaws who I found equally desirous of a reconciliation; but the path was no sooner made straight and washed white than parties of your nation made it bloody again.

---

1   Enclosed in John Stuart's letter to Hillsborough, 2 December 1770: Vol. I, No. 763.

The pains I have taken to prevent bloodshed must convince you and all the nations of red men that your white brethren have never acted as instruments of dissension between the red people, but on the contrary wish to see their children grow up and their people increase; but you must not blame me for declining to interfere any more in your quarrel if the agreement and peace lately concluded at Pensacola be not observed by both parties.

I have nothing more at present to say to you about land. When the line behind West Florida shall have been marked by you and that behind East Florida by the Cowetas, then all messages about land will cease.

My friends, the talks sent into your nation by the Shawnese and other Western tribes you ought to have communicated to me. I know very distinctly what passed at the great meeting in Scioto, the Shawnese town, but I hope to hear and see that all Indian nations will behave like wise men. But if the Shawnese and nations to the westward choose to behave themselves like bad men, that should not induce you to be mad also. When you tell me that you hold me fast and have a dependence on the friendship and assistance of your white brethren, I am inclined to believe you, but then I am at a loss to find out why you have kept the business of the Shawnese messengers a secret from me. I hope for an answer to this part of my talk particularly, and that you will candidly impart what you know of this matter. This talk will be delivered you by Mr Joseph Cornal who will send me your answer as soon as possible. *Copy.* [C.O.5/72, fo. 105]

CXXV

John Stuart to Earl of Hillsborough

28 November, Charleston

My Lord, I have the honour of submitting to your lordship a journal of my proceedings [Vol. II, No. CV] with the chiefs of the Cherokee nation at a congress held at Lochaber on the frontier of this province, 260 miles distant from hence the 18th of October last.

Every step that could be thought of was taken by a set of self-interested men in the province of Virginia to embarrass me in the settlement of a boundary line. Emissaries were sent into the nation to practice upon the Indians and prevail upon them to refuse treating with me. The Young Warrior, Saluij, was decoyed into Virginia and a talk put into his mouth as will appear by the minutes of Council of which my Lord Botetourt was pleased to send me a copy [Vol. I, No. 755iv]. Forged letters were sent to Lord Botetourt and the Indians were brought to sign them under pretence that they were directed to the Governor of Virginia and the Superintendent requesting a trade from that province. The persons employed to transact this business were not unattentive to their own interest: in the same fraudulent manner they obtained for themselves titles to great tracts of land beyond the established boundary. These were Jacob Hite and Richard Pears, formerly an Indian trader. The former wrote the letters, conveyances of land etc. and carried off the Young Warrior Saluij who died on his return home; the latter speaking their language remained to manage matters with those Indians.

I had information of their practices, which they knew; for which reason Mr Peares did not choose to appear at the congress without my permission, which he applied for as he said in order to justify his conduct. After the treaty was signed I sent for him and he came. I confronted him with the Indians in presence of Colonel Donelson, and they declared with great indignation their utter ignorance of the letters and talk referred to in the minutes of the Council of Virginia, as well as of the titles of land obtained from them, persisting that they understood them to be letters soliciting a trade as abovementioned.

I cannot here suppress an incident that gave me great pleasure as it showed the temper of the nation more than anything the chiefs could have said. I appeared a little warm at the second day's conference. After signing the treaty the principal chiefs with all the leading men came to me, attended by all the young people, and told that their young men thought I had taken great offence at what they had said and would not be convinced without hearing me declare to the contrary, which I very readily did.

Your lordship will be pleased to observe that I did not obtain the whole extent of country contained within the lines pointed in my instructions, the reason of which upon examination appears to be that they understood Long Island in Holsten's River would by the line proposed be given up to Virginia, to which no consideration would make them consent, an application having formerly been made to them by a trading company in said province for leave to build a trading house and establish a factory on said island, which they refused, and has impressed them with an idea that there is an intention of building a fort there; but the difference is not very considerable in point of possession, the land within this small triangle which is cut off being very poor.

The Indians offered by way of compensation for the land they refused to grant to run the line a more western course to the Ohio, which would have given a good territory upon that river; but I declined accepting it, not being within the limits of my instructions, and if I had been certain that your lordship would have forgiven it, I should not have done it as the precedent would possibly have exposed me to future solicitations.

I am extremely happy in having accomplished this important piece of service. The assiduity with which the Shawnese messengers were running through the Southern nations and endeavouring to ingratiate themselves with them and the hints I had of their attempting to draw them into a confederacy on the principle of defending their lands against encroachments, suggested to me the expediency of removing from the Cherokees all cause of complaint and jealousy on that head as soon as possible, and a late letter from his Excellency General Gage, of which I have the honour to enclose a copy [Vol. II, No. CIII] justifies my opinion. *Signed.* [C.O.5/72, fo. 20]

CXXVI

Petition of Charles Garth to the King[1]

29 November, Piccadilly

The humble petition of Charles Garth Esq., agent of your Majesty's colony of South Carolina, most humbly sheweth,

That your petitioner has received the commands of the Commons House of Assembly in your Majesty's province of South Carolina to express the grief and concern the House feels, under an apprehension of having incurred your royal displeasure manifested in a late additional instruction of the 14th April last to their Governor, which they most humbly conceive would not have taken place had they known of the representation transmitted in time to have been heard and to have vindicated the proceedings of the House before your Majesty's ministers, previous to the issuing of such instruction, and therefore to implore your Majesty's reconsideration of the said instruction.

The Commons House of Assembly as yet know not the nature of the representation which has been made to your Majesty, the lieutenant-governor looking upon himself as restrained from communicating to the House even such representations as he thinks fit to make to your Majesty's ministers of the proceedings of the House; but as by the said instruction it appears that the House has been represented to have lately assumed a power which it is said is become necessary to put a stop to, and therefore among other directions directing and requiring of the Governor that "his assent be not given to any Money Bill in which there is not an express provision that the money granted or any part thereof shall not be issued or applied to any other services than those to which it is by the said bill appropriated unless by Act or Ordinance of General Assembly", your petitioner humbly entreats to submit to your Majesty that the power which has been exercised must have been misapprehended, being far different from such power as is implied in the instruction. The order of the House of the eighth of December last, followed by an immediate resolution of providing for replacing the sum, is to all intents and purposes a vote of credit, by no means frustrating the intention of the legislature by an alteration of the appropriation of any moneys granted for particular services, is not a simple issue of any such money but borrowing a sum of the public, and there being commonly considerable sums in the Treasury which arise from surpluses of various taxes and duties, the balances of the funds are subject to disposal and appropriation different from that directed in the particular laws whereby the whole may have been raised to make good to your Majesty certain specific grants for specific purposes; hence the public Treasurer (in fact a debtor to) has been frequently considered and made a creditor of the public upon occasions that will not admit of the delay attending the raising money by regular legislation; and in the particular instance in question the public Treasurer having advanced the money mentioned in the said order and

1   Enclosed in Order of Council, 9 December 1770: Vol. I, No. 804.

in pursuance thereof and of the resolution to repay the same did in his account charge it to the public, making himself their creditor and not to any particular fund, whose name as a creditor for that sum was in consequence inserted in the schedule to the Tax Bill. From this state of the case it is submitted to your Majesty how far the power which has been exercised by the House can be construed an issue or application of appropriated money, which the House has scarce in any instance attempted by its single authority; upon any other foundation the clauses and provisions in the said instruction relating to the appropriation of such money as shall be granted by the House cannot be necessary, for every law which gives and grants to your Majesty will necessarily and sufficiently secure the appropriation of the sum granted.

The power of borrowing upon the public faith and credit solemnly pledged by a resolution to make good and repay the money borrowed is indeed of a most important concern to the province, instrumental in its exercise to avert dangers which at times may suddenly threaten the public safety, and on less momentous occasions to be salutarily exerted for the public benefit; so it is also a power not, as hath been represented, lately assumed but exercised as an ancient right and supported by usage. Your petitioner conceives he can point to many and various instances of the exercise of this power as well with as without a requisition, and for any purposes whether local or provincial or not as the House has thought expedient for the public service. Instances occur in the Journals of the proceedings of the Commons House of Assembly for years back, and having received the sanction of all or sundry of your Majesty's Governors for the time being, are in favour of a very different implication to that which has been represented to your Majesty from the exercise of the power being either recent, dangerous or unwarrantable. These instances your petitioner conceives will, when looked into and examined, militate for a continued exercise thereof, abstracted from that claim and right which it receives from ancient and modern usage, without any interposition hitherto on the part of your Majesty or your royal predecessors. Your petitioner most humbly begs leave further to submit to consideration the last clause in the said instruction, its operation retrospectively in the punishment of a public officer for an innocent act, antecedent to the issuing of the instruction, done in pursuance of the duty of office upon the public faith and credit solemnly pledged, founded in usage and practice, and at the time unquestioned and uncontroverted. The Commons House of Assembly must subject the public Treasurer to the penalty of treble the sum borrowed and incapacity of office or trust when in pursuance of their order and subsequent resolution he had become the public creditor. And with regard to its operation as a provision in future, your petitioner conceives many and innumerable evils might arise to the province and to your Majesty's service should difficulties and impediments ever stand in the way of a public vote of credit; but upon this occasion your petitioner must entreat permission of your Majesty to assert that the Commons House of Assembly have ever deemed and do deem it to be a first and essential privilege of the House to originate and prepare without any dictate or direction soever all money bills for the concurrence and assent of the Governor and Council.

Your petitioner therefore most humbly prays your Majesty to take the premises into your royal consideration, humbly hoping that your Majesty will be graciously pleased to withdraw the said additional instruction, which now puts a full stop to the payment of the public debts and the necessary provision for the expenses of government; and that your Majesty will see cause to enjoin a communication for the future of all such representations as may be intended to be sent from your Majesty's Governors relating to the proceedings of the House, in order that it may be prepared to answer and to vindicate their actions and proceedings, thereby to prevent censure and avert the royal displeasure. And your petitioner will ever pray etc. *Copy.* [C.O.5/380, fo. 5]

CXXVII

Board of Ordnance to Earl of Hillsborough

30 November, Ordnance Office

My Lord, we are honoured with your letter [Vol. I, No. 748] of the 26th inst. on the subject of Newfoundland, in which your lordship is pleased to signify that if upon full consideration of the nature and purpose of so extensive a plan of fortification and of the different objects for which it is represented to be necessary, we shall be of opinion that it would be of advantage to begin immediately with the fortified battery for defending the entrance of the harbour and to build barracks upon the spot where the fort is proposed, it is the King's pleasure that we should in such case take the proper steps for carrying those services into execution without delay, inserting in our estimate to Parliament the sum which we state in our letter to be necessary for those purposes.

On which we beg leave to represent to your lordship that we are by no means able to form any opinion upon the purposes of the intended extensive plan of fortification and the different objects for which it is represented to be necessary, being matters as we apprehend of which those concerned in the commercial and naval branches of His Majesty's service are the proper judges.

But with respect to the nature of the proposed fort and its situation, we have in all that related to our department fully stated our opinion to your lordship in our report of the 25 May 1770 as well as of the expense that would attend the works respectively.

On receipt of your lordship's letter, however, we thought it necessary to call upon Captain Debbieg in order to know from him in what time the whole or any part of the works proposed could be finished; and he has informed us that it will require three years to finish the battery or tower proposed for defending the entrance into the harbour, according to his plan, being all of masonry; two years to finish the barracks; and four years to finish the whole works if done with masonry as at first proposed, or three years including the barracks if the fort is done with earth; which several works, upon a supposition that the troops and seamen are not to be employed, he estimates as follows.

Destroying the harbour of Quiddy Viddy and indemnifying its inhabitants, £4,333 6s. 8d. Battery at the South Head, £9,221 5s. 4d. The Store House, Barracks, and Buildings within the proposed Fort, £22,666 13s. 4d. For Paving and for Wells, Drains and Boghouse, £2,200. For Building the Fort of Earth and Sod Work, Fraized and Palisadoed, with 2 small Powder Magazines etc., £27,292 7s. 11d. [*Total*] £65,713 13s 3d.

And your lordship having been pleased to refer to our opinion with regard to the propriety and utility of erecting the proposed battery at the mouth of the harbour and of building the barracks on the ground of the intended fort, we take leave to submit to your lordship that the proposed battery at the mouth of the harbour will when finished be of great utility, as we apprehend, in defending the entrance thereof, and together with the destruction of Quiddy Viddy harbour be a great means of securing that place against any small or sudden attack; but that it were much to be wished the proposed battery could be finished in a shorter space of time or that some other species of work sufficient for the purpose might be planned which might be executed in a shorter time.

In respect to the building of the barracks on the spot chosen for the chief fort, we beg leave to observe that previous to the building the said barracks a considerable excavation of earth will be necessary in order to place them so low as to be properly covered by the work afterwards intended to be thrown round them. And we also submit to your lordship that if in the present situation of things it shall be His Majesty's pleasure that the chief work should be begun and be carried on with expedition, that the erecting it of sod and earthwork would take much less time and be done at much less expense, and that such a number of His Majesty's land forces and marines as can be spared for that service and for the defence of the place may be most usefully employed in carrying on these works, which would themselves be of little use were they finished unless a proper number of troops could be allowed for their defence. We therefore beg to be honoured with His Majesty's commands in which mode the said works should be carried on, and which parts should be begun on in the ensuing season, that provision may be made accordingly.

And we also submit to your lordship whether, as this matter is not finally settled, it may not be proper to make it the subject of a subsequent and separate estimate, the annual estimate being now prepared by desire of the Treasury to be delivered on Monday next. *Signed*, H. S. Conway, Charles Frederick, W. H. Earle, Charles Cocks, A. Wilkinson. [C.O.194/29, fo. 74]

CXXVIII

Lieut.-Governor William Bull to Earl of Hillsborough

30 November, Charleston

My Lord, in obedience to your lordship's commands I have the honour to lay before your lordship a representation of the present state of religion, polity, agriculture and commerce of this province, which is humbly submitted to your lordship's candour and consideration.

South Carolina is divided into four counties, Craven County, bounded on the southwest by a northwest line from the head of Sewee River till it intersects Santee River, and then proceeds up the Congaree and Saludy Rivers to their source; Berkley County lies next, bounded to the south by a northwest line from the head of Stone River till it intersects Congaree River; Colleton County bounded by Combahee River and a northwest line from thence to the Cherokee boundary; Granville County bounded south by Savannah River. This division is of little use but to limit the jurisdiction of the Justices of Peace. The next division is into seven districts for the distribution of justice: one of Charleston where the Supreme Court sits, the other six are for the Circuit Courts at Beaufort, Orangeburgh, Ninety Six, Cambden, Cheraws and George Town. The province is subdivided into twenty-two parishes. On this division is founded the interior subordinate government of the province, as in each parish the presentation of livings is in the majority of inhabitants professing the Church of England, the election of members of Assembly, granting licence to inn-keepers by Justices of the parish, the care of the high roads under a board of commissioners in each parish, the poor rates assessed and collected by the churchwardens and select vestry annually chosen.

From hence it appears reasonable on religious and political considerations that a number of eighteen or twenty parishes with representatives to each in Assembly be established in the western parts (where the country is very populous and still increasing by new northern emigrants) so remote from the church in the parish, where by continuation of their extent unbounded to the westward they lie, that though those western settlements in a legal acceptation are within a parish whose church is situated not thirty miles from the sea, yet being a hundred or a hundred and fifty miles from the parish church must be considered as extraparochial, being destitute of all the benefits, privileges and advantages of divine worship, election of members of Assembly, ministers, vestrymen, maintaining their poor, highroads and other business of less moment.

Although by our charter indulgence was granted to all tender consciences in religious matters the Church of England is the only established church here, I mean whose clergy are maintained by public expense. A certain salary is paid out of the Treasury to each minister who officiates in a parish. The salary and surplice fees to each rector in Charleston amounts to near two hundred pounds sterling besides a good parsonage-house. There is an assistant to each rector in town with a net salary of two hundred pounds sterling but no fees or parsonage. In each country parish there is a glebe and in most a parsonage-house with a net salary of one hundred and ten pounds sterling. The fees are inconsiderable but if they behave with discretion their parishioners frequently give them presents towards their housekeeping. This method of paying clergy appears preferable to the tithes which cause so much vexation in England and the indecent and precarious method of collection by the churchwardens made in time of divine service in New England and New York.

It is worth observing that though we have benefices for twenty-four ministers we seldom have above fifteen or sixteen at a time here, although there are in England many learned and worthy clergymen who with a family pine life away upon the poor pittance of twenty or forty pounds per annum when they might so happily change their condition with a small change of climate, although I must confess the necessaries of life are dearer here than in England which in effect lessens the difference of income.

The right of presentation given by the royal charter to the Lords Proprietors was by them given up to the people here by ratifying our Church Act passed in 1706. The rector on his election is as fully seized of his living as any rector in England, and as such settled rectors have sometimes so misbehaved as to give great cause of scandal and offence to the parish, and deserved to be but could not be deprived *ab officio et beneficio* as there is no competent ecclesiastical jurisdiction for such purpose here, the rector continued to vex his flock as long as it pleased him. The people have therefore determined latterly not to elect their clergy but keep them only *quam diu se bene gesserint,* for I know no instance of any clergyman wantonly dismissed. This proceeding is founded on a clause in the Church Act empowering the church-wardens of a vacant parish to agree with any minister to officiate till a rector is elected, and they draw on the public Treasurer for his salary annually, whereas the public Treasurer pays it of course to the settled rector. The Bishop of London, in whose diocese America is held to be, formerly had his Commissary in this province for purposes of inspecting the behaviour of the clergy, but we have had none here for these fifteen or twenty years; as the Commissary receives no benefit persons to whom it has been offered refused to pay the fees which attend taking out such a commission.

There is no such thing known here as a lapse for want of presentation.

Ministers of regular Dissenting congregations are supported by rates upon the pews of their meeting-houses and interest of monies given by members thereof for such purposes, and in the settled parts of the province they find a very comfortable support.

Our toleration comprehends every denomination of Christians but the Roman Catholic, and these are subdivided *ad infinitum* in the back parts as illiterate enthusiasm or wild imagination can misinterpret the Scripture. Indeed lately the overflowings of the northern colleges send apostles to enlighten the dark regions of our western settlements where every circle of Christian knowledge grows fainter as more removed from the centre. The orderly attention paid to such preachers sufficiently shows how well disposed the people are to receive better instruction.

I am informed that between the Congarees, the Indian boundary and Saludy River where there are 1400 fencible men, there are no less than six meeting-houses built and ministers maintained by the poor inhabitants, besides the French Protestants at Hillsborough and the German Lutherans in Londonborough, and not one Church of England congregation.

From the preceding account we see the lamentable state of religion in the populous parts lying above seventy miles from the sea coast which I humbly conceive deserves some attention from political views; for though I charitably hope every sect of Christians will find their way to the Kingdom of Heaven, yet I think the Church of England best adapted to the Kingdom of England.

The legislature consists of the Governor, Council and Assembly, each vested with a negative voice. The Governor till about the year 1738 presided in Council when sitting in their legislative capacity, but at that time the Governor to comply with the royal instruction directing that freedom of debate be allowed to the Council, and as it was agreeable to the practice of the House of Lords, forebore to be present. The business was generally planned by committees of Council and Assembly jointly with great advantage and dispatch; difficulties in bills were explained or removed in conferences. But since the power of Assembly hath arisen to its present heigth and the authority and dignity of the Council sunk in proportion, that beneficial intercourse has ceased, and I don't think there has been a conference these ten or fifteen years. The Assembly pretend to justify the slight regard shown the Council by their being a dependent body, removable at pleasure, that they must obsequiously follow the dictates of an imperious Governor or be immediately suspended; whereas if, say they, the Council were constituted like the House of Lords, hereditary or even for life, the Council might more safely be confided in. It must be confessed that this argument has some weight and it is much to be wished that for the King's service and the public welfare the Council were on a more respectable footing on this account. But this alteration is attended with its disadvantages. They might by private interest, discontent or the allurement of popularity, be as much withdrawn from the guidance of reason and their own judgements and obstruct the public service as by their present supposed dependence, with which they have been so often and so injuriously accused.

The Assembly consists of forty-eight members: Charleston six, St Andrew's three, St John's three, St George Dorchester two, Christchurch two, St Thomas two, St Stephen one, St James Goose Creek three, St Mathew one, all in Berkley County; St Paul three, St Bartholomew four, St John three, in Colleton County; St Helena two, St Luke two, Prince William two, St Peter one, in Granville County; Prince Frederick one, Prince George Winyaw two, St James Santee two, St David one, St. Mark one, in Craven County. All which except St Mathew and St Mark, which are seventy miles from town, are to be considered as maritime parishes, and there are above five thousand men living westward thereof beyond a moral possibility of being represented in Assembly while elections are made at the parish church, whereby the balance of Assembly will always lie among the maritime against the interior members.

The Clerk of Assembly is appointed by royal sign manual.

Though the right of introducing bills in the Upper House is not denied 'tis seldom exercised and bills generally arise in the Assembly. The Commons House suffer no money bill to arise or be amended in the Upper House, notwithstanding the royal instruction continued to every governor from the year 1721 to the present time directing the governor to allow an equal right therein to the Council. When the bills are ready for assent, not only money bills but all bills are presented by the Speaker of the Assembly to the Governor in General Assembly in the Council Chamber for his assent, and after the Governor signs and seals each the Speaker signs his name, an unnecessary custom giving no sanction as the Governor's assent gives the full effect of a law.

Instead of prayers before they go upon business they always read the Journals of the preceding day.

The members of Assembly disdain taking any pay for their attendance though the members of North Carolina and Virginia receive eight or nine shillings sterling a day.

Of our courts of justice the *dernier resort* is that of Governor and Council pursuant to the royal instruction to receive appeals in all cases exceeding five hundred pounds sterling except in such as relate to the King's revenue. Application was made six or seven years ago to this jurisdiction, but as it had never been exercised here the Governor and Council were desirous to establish their first proceedings with circumspection and sent to the northern provinces for information but received nothing satisfactory; the appellants dropped their suit and the jurisdiction remains unexperienced.

The royal commission for holding Admiralty Sessions giving no jurisdiction for trying murders, the criminals and evidences must be sent to England. But the difficulty of sending the criminals and the reluctance with which evidences will go so far and remain so long from their private affairs will often be the cause that marine murderers will escape punishment. His Majesty's colonies in America are now so populous as to afford sufficient juries if the Statute of Henry 8 for piracy were extended and adapted to America.

The Court of Chancery is constituted by Act of Assembly in 1712, to consist of the Governor, Keeper of the Great Seal and a majority of the Council. All the various offices of the English Chancery are executed by the Secretary of the province in sealing, and the Master and Register in Chancery in other matters. The difficulty of assembling a sufficient number of the Council to make a court, and the gentlemen of the Council generally not being bred to the law, the benefit of relief in equity is not so easily attained as could be wished; and when any member happened to be of that profession his practice withdrew him from the Board as an assessor. But Mr Leigh, the King's Attorney-General, having lately declined acting either as solicitor or counsel in Chancery, the court took the opportunity to make an order that no member of that Board should hereafter practise in that court as solicitor or counsel.

The Governor alone exercises the ecclesiastical jurisdiction of Ordinary for granting marriage licences, probate of wills and granting administration of intestate's estates. The office of Register of this court is always included in the patent appointing the Secretary of the province. There seems to be some defect in the constitution of this court, for whenever a Governor may exceed the proper bounds of his jurisdiction, it might occasion some doubts how the prohibition from the Common Law courts in such cases could be enforced.

The Court of General Sessions of the Peace, Oyer, Terminer, Assize and General Gaol Delivery, by our Jury Law passed in 1731 is vested with all the powers of the King's Bench. The Judges are the Chief Justice of the province and four Associates. The Grand and Petit Jury are all drawn by ballot. Counsel are allowed to defend the cause of criminals not only in matters of law but generally. For though the Judges are considered as counsel for the prisoners, our Judges are not so skilled in law as to do them full justice therein.

The only officer in this Court is the Clerk of the Crown and Peace appointed by the King, but of small value. The expense of bringing criminals to gaol is defrayed by the public if they have not wherewithal of their own.

The Court of Common Pleas is held before the same Judges and by our law in 1736 is vested with the powers of the Common Bench in England. Juries are all drawn by ballot. The only officer is the Clerk of the Pleas appointed by the royal sign manual. About the year 1734 Mr Wright, then Chief Justice, claimed the right of appointing the clerk as is done by the Chief Justice in England; but he was obliged to yield it to that power to whose fiat he owed his own existence as Chief Justice. The profits of this office will be considerably lessened by the summary determination of causes under twenty pounds sterling and the business which used to be done in Charleston will now be done in six Circuit Courts. There are near thirty lawyers who practise both as attorneys and counsellors; about five or six carry the chief of the business, and several make from one thousand to twelve hundred pounds sterling per annum.

These are at present the only courts for criminal and civil matters in the whole province, but in a few months justice will visit the remote parts in the six Circuit Courts; and when they in the course of a few years have civilised those inhabitants and made the law more familiar to them, these benefits of distributing justice near their homes may be further extended by County Courts empowered to hold petty sessions and take cognizance of small sums.

There is no Court of Exchequer here. An attempt was made in 1733/4 to erect one. A Chief Baron and other officers were appointed, but an alarm being given through the province that the powers of that court, if once admitted, might be extended arbitrarily to the great oppression of the innocent subject, the attempt was eluded and defeated, for all the persons who were summoned to attend as jurors refused, and by the terms of our Jury Law could not be compelled to serve. People in America are very jealous of this court, and I believe the only branch of its power that would readily be admitted would be the ingrafting in one of our courts a power to find office for the King upon escheats. As many foreigners are settled in this province and die without heirs here, their lands often escheat as well as sometimes of natural-born subjects. Until such a law can be obtained here, if the instruction which restrains the Governor from disposing of escheated lands were relaxed, the Governor might be empowered to regrant lands that in law were escheated. For now there are several instances where lands that were escheated have been surveyed as vacant lands and granted by surprise, the Governor not knowing anything of the escheat; and the method of resuming lands where the King has been deceived in his grant is said to be so very circuitous in our present want of Exchequer power as to be next to impossible.

I make no mention of the Admiralty Court as our provincial laws have not attempted any regulations relating thereto.

The lowest juridical power is vested in a Justice of Peace. By our Act for trial of small and mean causes, which after long experience of its utility was amended in 1747, one Justice of Peace determines all matters of damages not exceeding twenty pounds currency equal to almost three pounds sterling.

There is a particular system of laws adapted to the condition of slaves called our Negro Act passed in 1740, calculated to punish offending and to protect abused slaves. The jurisdiction is lodged in two justices and five freeholders in capital, and one justice and three freeholders in inferior cases. The expense of these trials is defrayed by the public and in order to discourage men from screening their criminal slaves from justice a certain sum equal to the value of a new negro is allowed to the master where his slave is executed. The royal humanity has often recommended to governors that a white man who murders a negro should be punished with death. It is so in all the English colonies north of Maryland where the number of negroes is small. But in Maryland [*Marginal note*: a mistake], Virginia and all southern colonies and islands, it has been thought dangerous to the public safety to put them on a footing of equality in that respect with their masters as it might tempt slaves to make resistance and deter masters and managers from inflicting punishment with an exemplary severity, though ever so necessary.

By the happy temperament of justice and mercy in our Negro Acts and the general humanity of the masters, the state of slavery is as comfortable in this province as such a state can be; not but there are monsters of cruelty sometimes appear, who are punished and abhorred. To the mildness of law and prudent conduct of masters and patrols I attribute our not having had any insurrection since the year 1739, and that indeed took its rise from the wantonness and not oppression of our slaves, for too great a number had been very indiscreetly assembled and encamped together for several nights to do a large work on the public road with a slack inspection. But such indiscretion is now provided against by law.

Upon considering how difficult it was to procure and as difficult for every officer to hunt through our laws in order to learn his duty, I prevailed a few years ago on Mr Simpson, late Chief Justice of Georgia and then one of our Assistant Judges, to publish in one volume the paragraphs in our provincial laws and the Common and Statute Law of England extended to America, and digest them under proper heads for the use of justices, churchwardens, high road commissioners and the like, which though imperfect has been of great use in the regular execution of their respective duties.

The defence of the province as far as our own power can avail is provided for by our militia against foreign, and patrols against domestic, enemies; and a magazine of powder supplied by a powder duty paid by merchant ships. By a large accession of emigrants from the northern provinces, invited by our mild winters and fertile soil, our militia is now increased to about ten thousand men, divided into ten regiments unequal in numbers but equal in want of discipline; besides one small nominal regiment of horse and a volunteer artillery company of fifty men in Charleston, very expert in the use of cannon.

In the country almost every militia man marches on horseback, of great use for expedition and to avoid fatigue. If early intelligence of the enemy could allow time for assembling a body, they might perform good service in a short campaign, as their fighting *pro aris & focis* would animate their natural ardour at first. But troops whose obedience could not be enforced by rigid discipline would soon be tired with a camp life; when their first edge was worn out their duty would be performed with remissness or reluctance when the danger became familiar or formidable. In great danger the militia is to be reinforced with a number of trusty negroes (and we have many such) not exceeding one-third of the corps they are to join. To observe good order among the slaves one-fourth of the militia must be left at home which furnishes a constant patrol to keep all quiet there. In these times the Governor does not proclaim martial law but publishes an alarm by the advice of Council which puts the whole province under arms, and then the only martial law is the Militia Act. It is thought unlawful to march the militia out of the province. When the King's service requires such a measure troops are taken into pay.

The interior quiet of the province is provided for by small patrols drawn every two months from each company who do duty by riding along the roads and among the negro-houses in small districts in every parish once a week or as occasion requires. Though human prudence has provided these salutary laws, yet through human frailty they are neglected in these times of general tranquillity.

The approach to Charleston from sea is defended by Fort Johnson, of a very unfit construction and therefore neglected. It is mounted with a few nine-pounders on the upper works and twenty cannon, twenty-four, eighteen and twelve-pounders as a battery *en barbette a fleur d'eau*. But as ships can pass out of point blank shot it could give little annoyance to an invader. There is a shoal midway between Fort Johnson and the opposite shore where by laying stone ballast for two or three years a foundation could be made for a battery that might effectually co-operate with Fort Johnson. If the approach of the enemy could be retarded only one day, people might recover their conster-nation and prepare for defence, such as an open town can make, with a few batteries on the east side. In 1755 a resolution was formed to enclose the town and Mr De Braham, whose German credentials as engineer and specious draughts on paper recommended him to be employed in planning and superintending the carrying into execution such work at ten pounds or twenty-eight shillings and sixpence ster-ling a day to himself. But after some time spent therein it appeared that his plan would continue him long in pay and contribute little to the defence of the town; he and his plan were laid aside and nothing done but to keep up by small repairs such parts as just serve to stop the encroachment of the sea.

In 1759 by Colonel Bouquet's advice an horn-work was built to command the avenue into town, from whence lines were to be extended cross the isthmus to enclose the town on the land side, covered at each end with two redoubts; but this though well designed remains unfinished. Soon after the peace I dismounted all the cannon and housed the carriages except a few left for salutes on public days.

It is undoubtedly the duty of prudent men to prepare in the best manner for their own defence, and this spirit ought to be encouraged. Though I will not doubt but that every power will be exerted when necessary that can be expected from us, yet when I consider the extent of our town and other circumstances, in my private opinion our security against any royal armament sent to invade us must be derived from the King's protection, the vigilance of His Majesty's ministers to obtain early intelligence of, and the superiority of his fleet to defeat, any such enterprise; though our bar not admitting ships of above thirty guns is a favourable circumstance.

The civil order and quiet of the town is provided for by a company of town watch, consisting of three commission officers, three sergeants, three corporals, three drums and ninety-six privates, armed with muskets and cutlasses; and one-third mount guard every night to prevent disturbances among disorderly negroes and more disorderly sailors. The number of dwelling-houses in town taken this summer was one thousand two hundred and ninety-two, and the white inhabitants five thousand and thirty, and the black five thousand and eight hundred and thirty-one, employed as domestic servants and mechanics. Thus much for Charleston.

The shallow bar at Winyaw is the best and only defence for George Town.

But with regard to Port Royal harbour I must be allowed to enlarge. In the year 1731 by direction from the Lords of the Admiralty, Captain Gascoigne, in His Majesty's ship *Scarborough*, surveyed the bar and harbour with great accuracy and found twenty-one feet water at low tide and the flood rising about seven feet. I have been informed by several captains of His Majesty's ships that the bar is wide enough to allow a ship to turn in or out against wind. A seventy-gun ship may come over this bar and run within a mile of Beaufort Town. About a mile and half below Beaufort stands Fort Lyttelton, mounted with fifteen cannon, twenty-four, twelve and nine-pounders; it is built with tabby, a composition of oyster shells and lime like soft stone. It has barracks for one hundred men, though the provincial establishment is only one gunner. A small garrison here in time of war would secure the town of Beaufort from the insults of privateers.

About the year 1747 Captain Hamar, then stationed in a forty-gun ship at Port Royal, had orders to make a careening wharf there for the use of His Majesty's ships, which he began on a creek about three miles below Fort Lyttelton. But the proprietors of the land demanding a higher price than what Lord Anson, then at the Admiralty Board, who had seen it formerly thought it worth, and that an unfair advantage against the wants of the Crown was intended to be taken, that design was dropped. A careening wharf at this port appears to be very convenient for His Majesty's ships stationed at Virginia and south as far as the Floridas and the Bahamas, as also for the victualling or refitting any of His Majesty's ships cruising in the Gulfs of Mexico or Florida, and as from this station any squadron might easily intercept the French or Spanish ships passing from the Havana through the Gulf of Florida, as likewise for any squadron that might be designed to cover the southern provinces against any invasion. Though the bar of Port Royal lies seven or eight miles from shore, a beacon on the land and buoys on the bar would obviate that difficulty. As we are thought to be on the eve of a war I have taken the liberty of being the more copious on this subject, and if it should merit any attention I shall very readily give any further information thereupon; and I beg leave to offer a piece of land of fifty acres at a quarter of a mile above Fort Lyttelton for that service, desiring no other recompense for it than my private satisfaction at contributing a small convenience towards the public utility. A seventy-gun ship can lie very near the store at my land.

Literature is but in its infancy here. We have not one good grammar-school though foundations for several in our neighbouring parishes. All our gentlemen who have anything of a learned education have acquired it in England, and it is to be lamented they are not more numerous. The expense, the distance from parents, the danger to morals and health, are various objections against sending children to England; though there are many gentlemen well acquainted with such branches of knowledge as can be derived from the English language. We have a provincial free school, the master and usher whereof are paid by the public, but their salaries being established in the early age of the province are insufficient to engage and retain fit men. The masters when tolerably well-qualified have frequently quitted the laborious task of teaching boys for the more easy office of preaching in some country parish. It is proposed by increasing the salary and building a convenient house for boarders to put the master above the seduction of any ecclesiastical benefits here and to invite able men, perhaps ushers from some of the great schools in England.

The Charleston Library Society are incorporated by Act of Assembly and confirmed by the King. By a small annual contribution they are raising a fund for a library, and in process of time hope to be able to allow salaries for proper professors of arts and sciences. Their library already consists of near two thousand volumes, a sum is allotted for enlarging it yearly and their capital is increasing.

Of arts and sciences we have only such branches as serve the necessities, the conveniences and the comforts of man. The more refined such as serve to adorn or minister to the luxuries of life are as yet little known here. As I cannot charge it to a want of taste on one hand, neither will I attribute it to a superior degree of virtue on the other, but honestly impute it to a prudent economy, the necessary attendant on our moderate fortunes.

Our houses are plain but convenient, furniture and equipages suitable, some coaches, but chaises and Italian chairs innumerable.

There are teachers of mathematics, arithmetic, fencing, French, drawing, dancing, music and needlework, to fit men for the busy world and ladies for the domestic social duties of life.

Agriculture is in a very prosperous state. The wisdom of His Majesty's agrarian instructions in granting lands to every person who can cultivate them and only in proportion to the ability to cultivate, and the mode observed in this province of taxing all lands whether improved or not have been an happy means to prevent the engrossing large tracts, which is very prejudicial to the spirit of agriculture unless held by men of very large property and an equal share of public spirit; for by these regulations property is divided in many hands, and it will be always improved with more industry by the freeholder than the under-tenant as the fruits of his labour are wholly his own; at the same time however it nurses a spirit of liberty, independency and democracy.

The most important objects of our agriculture are rice, indigo, hemp, flour and tobacco, which are arrived to a certainty of success, vines, olives, silk, madder, are under very promising probation.

The introducing rice hath proved a very fortunate circumstance to this province as it is a grain which yields the most plentiful harvest when the ground is overflowed with water, as the experience of the Po and Ganges taught us. Many large swamps, otherwise useless and affording inaccessible shelter for deserting slaves and wild beasts, have been drained and cultivated with such banks as to keep out torrents of water in planting season, and by reservoirs supply artificial rain when wanted; thus while a nuisance is removed a great quantity of our best land has been acquired. The crop of rice is generally from one hundred and twenty to one hundred and forty thousand barrels, sufficient with what Georgia produces for the present markets.

The amount of our indigo is about five hundred thousand pounds weight a year. If the destruction made in the early planting by grasshoppers or locusts could be prevented a hundred and fifty thousand pounds more would be made with almost the same labour. The apprehension of lowering the value of these two, our principal staples, by too large quantities inclines us to introduce a variety of staples to employ our increasing hands on hemp, flour and tobacco. Hemp is considered as an inexhaustible article while the British are a trading people and is increasing every year, and as an article of export will be beneficial to navigation as its bulk will employ much tonnage. By the provincial bounty paid last year there were four hundred twenty-one thousand, nine hundred and seventy-seven pounds weight of hemp made. Notwithstanding the liberal Parliamentary premium on it, very little is exported to England. According to the present fashion of the times homespun rigging is preferred to what is much better made in England, but this branch of home-consumption will cease with our discontents, and the feelings of interest will at last open our eyes.

The Irish from Belfast have now raised flax for their own wear and barter the superfluous linen to supply their wants with their neighbours.

They have woven this year above five thousand yards of good white linen. Flour is a growing article in our exportation; above four thousand barrels are now exported when formerly we imported more. Proper mills are now daily erected in the back parts as wheat increases.

Tobacco though a bulky commodity is planted from one hundred and fifty to two hundred miles from Charleston where the emigrants from Virginia find the weed meliorate as they come south, and they cultivate it now with great spirit as they find the price profitable, notwithstanding the distance of carriage to market.

Madder, a dyeing root, grows very well here, and the present attempts give such encouragement that I hope in a year or two some parcels will be sent to England, not indeed so properly sorted at first for the market as what is imported from Holland but I am persuaded that method will soon be known.

Silk is a very flattering article as it is of great value. It is raised here of the finest sort with great ease and in great perfection. The only objection which occurs to me against its being carried to such a degree as will render it a considerable branch of commerce is as singular as it is true vizt. the great prosperity of our province. If we turn our eyes to those countries where it is made in abundance, Spain, the South of France, Italy, Turkey, China, there labour is very cheap; in our province it is very dear. When a prudent man is about planning the work of his future harvest he considers in what manner he can employ his labour to most advantage and will decline everything which may interfere with the grand resource of his revenues. Now the profits arising by silk, even if largely attempted, to a rich planter will hold a very trifling proportion to what he can make in rice, indigo or hemp, and though the care necessary in the management of silk takes up but a small part of the year, it will for the reason mentioned be attended to by the gentleman only as an amusement for his own private use and be wholly rejected by his managers, who like pack horses must trot in the beaten tract which no distant though beautiful prospect will invite them to quit. I therefore apprehend whatever is done in this article will be the work of the poorer sort who have large families of children or such who will employ their young negroes, unfit for field labour, in gathering leaves of mulberry to feed the worms, and this must withdraw their inspection from other necessary business and be some loss. This is my real opinion, though I give all public encouragement towards making a fair trial of raising it, as a means of making money. And this opinion seems well founded by experience for it was upon these principles that the French Protestants, who upon the Revocation of the Edict of Nantes, retiring into this country, made and manufactured silk here for their own use, soon laid that aside when rice was introduced; as they with the profits of rice could buy more silk than they could raise with equal labour. In some future period I think it might be carried from among the settlers near Hillsborough who pursue it with zeal among the Cherokee women who set no great value on their time.

Olives grow well in this climate. I have had some of Lucca many years in my garden and lately some from Provence. As the method of pickling them for table here is unknown they have been neglected, but I hope they will be propagated soon, and when there is plenty of trees we may soon by direction and experience acquire the manner of pickling and making oil from them, which even if coarse will be a valuable article for the woollen manufacture of England with which it is now supplied from the Archipelago.

Vines are cultivated by several of the Germans settled on Broad River and are easily propagated. I expect wine will be made by four or five persons there in two years time, which will encourage others. The like success is expected at New Bordeaux where the vegetation in their rich soil was so vigorous as to produce several branches of grapes last summer from vines with roots that came last spring from Lisbon. A little experience in the method of dressing them and of fermenting the liquor will soon discover the kind of wine most suitable to our climate.

Our back settlers have lately planted large orchards of apples, from whence cider, and peaches from whence a spirit is distilled, besides plenty for their hogs.

When the present extent of our province is all taken up by planters it will perhaps be thought proper to purchase all the lands from the Cherokee boundary westwards to Keowee, which the Indians will be more willing to consent to after a long term of tranquillity and vicinity to our settlements than they might be inclined at present to do.

The number of negroes returned in last tax is seventy-five thousand one hundred and seventy-eight. The quantity of land is two millions six hundred and seventy-eight thousand four hundred and fifty-four acres (although I am sensible several hundred thousand more have been granted, owned perhaps chiefly by non-residents) which must produce a considerable revenue to the King when duly collected; and one advantage resulting from the Circuit Courts may very probably be the more regular collection of His Majesty's rents as the courts will protect the Receiver-General's deputies in the execution of their office and some effectual method may be found out to make out the royal rent-roll.

If by a royal instruction the Governor were permitted to appoint persons at the places where the Circuit Courts are to be held, to receive proofs of family rights to land, instead of coming to Charleston, much time and money would be saved to the petitioners, many of whom come one hundred and fifty or two hundred miles. This indulgence might be put on such a footing as to guard against impositions as effectually at least as at present before the Governor in Council, who cannot so well judge of the truth of their allegations as their neighbours.

Our commerce keeps equal pace with our agriculture in improvement, and extends to almost all parts of the world consistent with the Acts of Navigation. I shall trouble your lordship with only a brief account thereof, that we employ near five hundred sail of vessels to carry off the superfluous produce and import supplies for the wants of the province. Though by the annual importation of three or four thousand negroes the balance of trade may be against us, yet we cannot be considered in debt as the negroes remain part of our stock and are the means of increasing our riches.

Interest of money is at eight per cent; if it was lowered to six there would be more adventurers in planting and commerce and the country more enriched.

The course of exchange between England and Carolina has continued for above fifty years at seven hundred pounds currency for one hundred pounds sterling, only varying as imports or exports casually fall short or exceed, a proof that our emissions of paper money on any emergencies of state have been duly sunk and that our public as well as private credit have been well supported.

As there is not a sufficiency of money, either paper or gold and silver, to serve as a medium in trade our internal commerce is carried on by credit or barter, especially between the back settlers and Charleston.

Charleston receives a considerable share of the produce from the western parts of North Carolina as their most profitable market. The settlers on the branches and waters of Savannah River send much of their produce to Savannah in Georgia as most convenient though not most profitable to them.

Our trade with the Creek and Choctaw Indians naturally decreases as the merchants in Georgia, East and West Florida, become more able to supply them. The trade of the Cherokees is not very beneficial. This nation commands the attention of government more upon political than commercial considerations, as they form a barrier against powerful incursions of Indians on the Ohio and Illinois tribes and as a counterbalance against the Creeks in case of a war with them. I cannot quit the Indians without mentioning an observation that has often raised my wonder: that in this province, settled in 1670 (since the birth of many a man now alive) then swarming with tribes of Indians, there remains now except the few Catawbas nothing of them but their names within three hundred miles of our sea coast, no traces of their emigrating or incorporating into other nations, nor any accounting for their extinction by war or pestilence equal to the effect.

Experience teaches that manufactures never thrive but in countries that are very populous and where labour is consequently at a low price. For this reason attempts to establish them here can never succeed to any degree where there is so much room to employ labour in agriculture and trade with more profit.

The manners, morals and amusements in an humbler degree are much the same in this as in the mother country. I shall only take notice of a turn which prevails more in this than any other province, which is a gratuitous execution of many branches of power under a desire of showing a public spirit and easing the public expenses. Our Assistant Judges hitherto received no emolument during the presence of the Chief Justice, nor did the various commissioners for fortifications, public buildings, stamping public orders, high roads, pilotage, streets, markets and many others, receive any pay or profit thereby. But this laudable spirit is attended with its inconveniences for when a man receives no compensation for his service there is a tenderness and reluctance shown to call him to account for his neglect of duty whereby the public often receive detriment.

Our climate affords as pleasant a winter country as any of the King's wide-extended dominions; though the genial warmth of the sun may sometimes be thought too powerful in summer, yet in winter we are often invigorated with purifying cold winds from the Cherokee Mountains, which recovers us from the languid habit acquired in the warm months of June, July, August and September; even these may be rendered tolerable with the indulgences and conveniences used in Italy and Sicily, those gardens of the ancient world.

My desire of giving your lordship a particular information of the most important matters relating to this province, perhaps too much in detail, has betrayed me into a length which needs more pardon for the trespass I have made upon your lordship's patience than I could expect but from your lordship's candour and indulgence, and which shall now restrain my pen.

Whatever imperfections may appear in the present state of the province or defects in my representation thereof, I beg leave to assure your lordship upon the whole that nature hath formed it an ample field for almost every improvement which human industry can effect and renders it an object worthy of your lordship's patronage, in which may I presume to hope your lordship will permit me to enjoy an humble share with my country. *Signed.* [C.O.5/394, fo. 5]

CXXIX

John Stuart to Earl of Hillsborough (No. 28)

2 December, Charleston

My Lord, I am to acknowledge the honour of your lordship's dispatch [Vol. I, No. 637] of 3d October, No. 19. The letters to me from West Florida, copies [Vol. I, No. 505i-iv] of which I had the honour of submitting to your lordship in mine No. 25, were received several days after I had written that of 5th July [Vol. I, No. 459]; and as I had been a long time without any advices from that quarter I embraced the earliest opportunity of laying them before your lordship.

I have since received letters from Mr Stuart, my deputy in West Florida, dated 17th June, 26th, 27th August, and 27 September, copies [Vol. II, Nos. LVII, LXXXVII; Vol. I, No. 763iii] of all which I send for your lordship's information. By them it will appear to your lordship that the Choctaws, Creeks and other neighbouring nations were then upon a friendly footing with the province of West Florida and that there was no ground for apprehending immediate danger from the disposition of those Indians when the letters referred to were written. Most of the disorders complained of arose from the barter of rum for venison, deerskins etc., but without the internal police of the provinces can fall upon means to remedy this evil, which is not peculiar to West Florida, it will not be in my power to prevent the drunken riots which give so much uneasiness.

I have in vain endeavoured to find out the murtherers of two white men, found dead on the road between the Creek nation and Pensacola; they were not scalped, which gives reason to believe that it was rather the effect of liquor or some private quarrel than any hostile disposition in the nation of the murtherers. I cannot find out who the persons murthered were, probably Virginian emigrants or hunters, both extremely obnoxious to every Indian nation to the southward: I shall continue my enquiries concerning this affair.

It gives me infinite uneasiness to think that any reasoning of mine should have laid the business of my department in an improper point of view before your lordship. I have always esteemed it my duty candidly and humbly to submit whatever appeared to me to be right, and afterwards implicitly to obey your lordship's orders thereupon. I therefore beg leave to represent to your lordship that accomplishing a peace between the Choctaws and Creeks was not the object I had principally in view in undertaking to mediate between them. Both nations with great reason considered us as the incendiaries who kindled the war; both appeared to be heartily tired of it and expressed a strong desire of peace, and both earnestly solicited my mediation to obtain their wishes. I saw a probability of their effecting a reconciliation without our interposition and that a peace would take place except prevented by our intrigues, the suspicion of which I wished to avoid. In such circumstances, my lord, our refusing to mediate would justify and confirm their suspicions, would of course tend to unite them, and draw their resentment upon us, when on the other hand by complying, I hoped to efface the bad impressions they had conceived of us and give them a proof of sincere disinterested friendship by our becoming the instruments of bringing about what would have taken place without us. Savages have minds susceptible of friendship and gratitude for benefits as well as of enmity and revenge. The peace effected between the Cherokees and Northern Indians tended more to remove the distrust and confirm the friendship of the former nation than any event that ever happened, and I hope the good effects of it will soon be apparent in their joining the Six Nations to oppose the Western confederacy. The sense the Creek nation have of our interposition and their earnest desire of establishing a peace will fully appear to your lordship by the letters and talks which I have now the honour of laying before you. I assure your lordship that every step taken by me was previously submitted to General Gage and Brigadier Haldimand, and had their approbation.

All the nations of Indians in this district have frequently solicited me to send commissaries among them to be some restraint upon the traders. These officers were recalled upon the new arrangement of Indian affairs as incident to the management of trade which reverted to the provinces, and I was in hopes of seeing the colonies join in forming some general regulation of trade before now. Commissaries appointed by me would not have answered the intention of the Indians as they would have had no jurisdiction over the traders. I acquainted General Gage with my opinion that some person in the quality of a deputy should be appointed to reside among the Chickasaws, that we might have intelligence of what passes in the remote parts of the district, and whose presence might be some restraint upon the traders. His Excellency agrees with me in opinion and by the enclosed abstract [Vol. I, No. 763v] I understand has written to your lordship on the subject. In the meantime I have sent their former commissary, Mr John McIntosh, among them who undertook to act without pay till the sense of government should be known. The additional expense of such an appointment will not exceed £150 sterling per annum.

I likewise humbly submit to your lordship that the small nations on the Mississippi ought to have a deputy residing among them. They are very remote and separated from Mobile by lakes, rivers and morasses, and their neighbourhood to New Orleans may render them a great obstacle to the navigation of the Mississippi and the settlement of the fine lands on the banks of that river. Therefore, and as General Gage is pleased to acquaint me that some Frenchmen who were at the great meeting at Scioto have offered to get the nations on the Mississippi and the Arkansas to join the general confederacy of the Western tribes, I think no time is to be lost in sending a proper person to that part of my district to counteract the machinations of His Majesty's enemies. I have accordingly appointed Lieutenant John Thomas of the Artillery to act as my deputy at Natchez until His Majesty's pleasure shall be known, and as this appointment will create an expense which cannot be covered by my ordinary estimated fund of £3,000 per annum I humbly hope provision will be made for it agreeable to the enclosed estimate [Vol. I, No. 763viii].

My attention to the settlement of the Virginia boundary line as a matter of great moment prevented my going to West Florida some time ago. That business being finished I shall prepare to go thither as soon as possible and hope to be time enough to meet the Indians at their return from hunting.

Lieutenant-Governor Durnford soon after his having been appointed wrote me from the Downs and expressed his wish that there might be a general [congress] of the nations contiguous to his province because the boundary lines with the Choctaw and Creek nations had not been clearly ascertained at the former congress held there, and that a more extended boundary would be necessary. In answer I acquainted him that I could not undertake to call such a congress without the approbation of government as it would be attended with a very considerable expense, and the boundary lines were as well ascertained as they could be except by actual survey and being marked, which could not be effected while they were at war; that we could not reasonably ask for more lands from the Choctaws, and the small nations on the Mississippi must be treated with for lands on that river, which would not be attended with much difficulty but that I found the Creeks extremely jealous with regard to land and believed a further cession could not be obtained from them without much difficulty.

In my former letters I submitted to your lordship the intelligence I had received from West Florida of the very great impatience of the Choctaws for a congress. During the last war this nation was in a manner entirely supported by the presents given by the French at annual congresses. When Eastern Louisiana was ceded to His Majesty and his troops took possession of it, those Indians were extremely poor and very bad hunters, and they expected the annual subsidy of presents from us which they were accustomed to receive from the

French. Monsieur Dabbadie met them at Mobile in congress and paid them two years arrears. Colonel Robertson, then commanding His Majesty's troops there, was present and found himself under the necessity of making some promises which they have ever since insisted upon. When Governor Johnstone and I met them they told what they expected, but we did not either confirm or renew the promise which they claimed but said we should represent the matter which we did accordingly.

I beg leave to offer it as my opinion that as all the nations have frequently received presents since the Choctaws and Chickasaws have been called to any congress, they may possibly think themselves much neglected if not soon taken notice of, and by Mr Stuart's letters they appear to be so pressing for a congress that he is apprehensive of a general dissatisfaction if they are not soon gratified.

I shall immediately write to General Gage on the above subject and draw upon him for such unavoidable expenses as may be incurred by said service, provided I can negotiate bills upon New York in West Florida; if not I shall be under the necessity of drawing upon the Lords Commissioners of His Majesty's Treasury.

When at West Florida I hope to be honoured with your lordship's instructions with regard to the measures to be pursued by me. *Signed.* PS. In the above I omitted to acquaint your lordship that the murther referred to in the Creek talks sent herewith was committed last summer at Occonni on the frontiers of Georgia in a scuffle which arose between some hunting Indians and a party of back-settlers who were in search of horses which they supposed to have been stolen. The latter were the aggressors and having the superiority beat some Indians who they met belonging to the town of Oakfuskee: some of their companions coming to their assistance in revenge killed two of the white people. [C.O.5/72, fo. 81]

CXXX

Lieut.-Governor William Bull to Earl of Hillsborough (No. 38, private)
5 December, Charleston
My Lord, the day after Captain Alexander left Charleston I was honoured with your lordship's dispatches [Vol. I, Nos. 549, 643] by the *Sandwich* packet, being a duplicate of No. 37 and originals Nos. 38 and 39, with His Majesty's free pardon to Mathew Turner of which he has had the immediate benefit.

I am now to answer your lordship's letter relative to the Associate Judges mentioned in my letter [Vol. I, No. 419] No. 30.

I have no reason to doubt of their attachment to the King's person and government but I cannot add that the three first are free from factious connections and unconstitutional prejudices. As Mr Murray is unexceptionable in his political qualifications, I shall leave him under your lordship's protection and beg leave to explain those of the other three.

Mr Pringle, the senior, is a subscriber to the American Association, and though age has cooled the small share of warmth which nature gave he can assume little merit from not appearing so active as others since his discourses countenancing unconstitutional prejudices on the bench, though spiritless, have not failed to make impressions on the Grand Juries, an audience already disposed to receive them.

Though Mr Lowndes is useful in conducting the business of the court and though he refused to subscribe as being incompatible with his office, in case any matters relative thereto might come in judgement before him, yet he maintains those arguments which deny the supreme legislative authority of taxation in the Parliament of Great Britain over the British colonies. It is further to be remembered that he and Mr Pringle were two of those judges who in 1766 made an attempt to carry on the business of the courts of justice by ordering the clerk to enter up judgement upon unstamped paper during the existence of the Stamp Act, and that upon his refusal to obey they applied to me and were backed by repeated applications of the Assembly to suspend him from his office, all which I refused to comply with. I laid the whole matter before the King and had the happiness to find my behaviour approved of by His Majesty. The two other associates are dead, but Mr Pringle and Mr Lowndes have been continued on the bench ever since.

Mr Powell is the next. He also is a subscriber and is strongly influenced by factious connections and unconstitutional prejudices which he propagates with zeal, as well as his two brethren, in his charges to the grand jury instead of discouraging them.

Your lordship will therefore wonder why I should name such persons for the office of Associate Judges. It was not from any predilection to those gentlemen but a kind of necessity for want of choice. The difficulties which I mentioned in my letter [Vol. I, No. 170] No. 24 still subsisted. There were very few who were not contaminated with these prejudices who were proper, and they averse to accept; and as these three persons had acted for some time I thought they might be permitted to keep the juridical wheels in motion until fitter men could be sent from England or be prevailed upon here, which there is more probability of when supported by a Chief Justice of spirit and knowledge how to support his own and their authority; as men of lay education feel great mortification and timidity from a sense of their being not well acquainted with their power and their duty.

I have been much distressed since I was honoured with your lordship's letter [Vol. I, No. 643] No. 39, as it leaves me no hopes of seeing our bench filled with Associate Judges bred to the law, and as I find myself under the necessity of transmitting a new list free from those essential objections to which three of the list now before your lordship are undoubtedly liable, for which reason I must beg permission to withdraw the names of Robert Pringle, Rawlins Lowndes and George Gabriel Powell. I beg leave to inform your lordship that I have attentively run over the gentlemen in town whose characters would give dignity to the office to furnish a list in lieu of that withdrawn, in which secrecy and delicacy were necessary. Some have wholly declined, others object to the fatigue of the circuits, to which three hundred pounds is not equivalent, to those who can indulge their ease and leisure at home, though it may be so to such as enjoy a robust constitution. I now present to your lordship to be added to Mr Murray the names of Wellins Calcott, George Milligen and William Henry Drayton.

Of the new list, Wellins Calcott Esquire was bred to the law; coming to America he brought with him a good character from a clergyman in London well known here, which Mr Calcott's behaviour has confirmed. It is but lately I was informed of his merit and had appointed him a Justice of Peace. He is well affected to the King's person and government and clear of unconstitutional prejudices. His age, forty-two, assumes a becoming gravity and his knowledge in the law will give him importance on the bench.

The next is George Milligen, well affected to the King's person and government and free from all unconstitutional prejudice. He has the honour of serving His Majesty at present as surgeon to the garrisons for His Majesty's forces in South Carolina at a small pay. As there are none of the King's troops now in this province the duties of judge cannot interfere; and whenever it should so happen, if His Majesty is pleased to indulge Mr Milligen in continuing his surgeoncy, the governor of the province at such time will undoubtedly take care that the King's service shall not suffer. His education renders him as capable of acquiring knowledge as others not bred to the law.

The last is William Henry Drayton Esquire who is attached to the King's person and government and free from unconstitutional prejudices. It is true he is young and not bred to the law, but his liberal education enables him to acquire some knowledge thereof with a little application. As he has the honour of being known to your lordship and is so nearly related to me, I forbear further mention of him.

Your lordship will permit me to assure you that I have always thought it my duty and made it my rule to fill up every vacant office with the most proper person I can find, though in our young country the most proper is not to be met with.

From your lordship's usual attention to the King's service I may receive His Majesty's commands time enough to issue commissions to the new judges if matters should be ripe in this province for going the circuit next April.

Now I am upon the subject of political disqualifications in judges it may not be improper to inform your lordship that Mr Middleton who lately resigned his seat in Council was the only member thereof who had signed the Association, and to add that in all contests between the Council and Assembly he was generally influenced by the popular arguments; and that William Burrows Esquire, the Master in Chancery, is highly blameable for his factious connections and unconstitutional prejudices. Had he subscribed as yielding to the necessity of the time and sat silent, I might have connived at it, but I am informed that he has been lately active in the tumults set in motion to terrify those who dared by actions to shake or disapprove the articles or acts of the Associators. If His Majesty should be pleased to dismiss such an officer from his service, and I might be allowed the liberty of recommending a proper person to fill the vacancy, I would mention John Bremar Esquire as one qualified for it. He is bred to the law and has given very sincere proofs of his attachment to the King's person and government by refusing to subscribe, and for that reason received several rude insults; and by effects of the combination suffered in his profession of the law. The office is worth about one hundred and twenty pounds sterling per annum though it depends upon the business of the court being much or little.

Mr Robert Raper, with his clerk William Hales, deserves admonition also for his behaviour. He is deputy Naval Officer and his principal resides in England. He has been very active in fomenting the popular discontents and conforming to the resolutions, though he very judiciously and casuistically distinguishes between Robert Raper the Naval Officer, who does not subscribe, from Robert Raper, attorney to the estate of Mr Colleton, who does subscribe.

Now I am upon this ungrateful subject I will beg your lordship's patience while I extend this long letter a little further to acquaint your lordship that the merchants in town, many of whom have long felt the stagnation of their trade and lament their empty stores, now resolve to disregard the Association against importation, declaring it folly in this province to stand out alone, and many planters are of the same sentiment, but several of them still suffer themselves to be deluded by a phantom of mistaken point of honour, and other merchants powerful by influence and stores filled with goods are for continuing the resolutions. Mr Myles Brewton has been an active supporter of the resolutions though he has suffered great and real loss as he made great profit by his importation of negroes, while John Edwards Hawkins in company with James Laurens and John Ward, all three charged with continuing secretly to supply their stores, are the chief in this interest from private advantages, and are supported by the noise and violent acts of some inconsiderate young men and the number of mechanics. As to Mr John Neufville, the famous chairman, he is rather a man of straw stuck up than a man of real consequence, who is pleased with the office as it flatters him with his own importance.

The first movers in the grand machine are Mr Thomas Lynch who, though a man of sense, is very obstinate in urging to extremity any opinion he has once adopted; Mr Christopher Gadsden is a violent enthusiast in the cause, he views every object of British moderation and measures with a suspicious and jaundiced eye and maintains with great vehemence the most extravagant claims of American exemptions; and Mr Mohn Mackenzie, whose education at Cambridge ought to have inspired him with more dutiful sentiments of the mother country and a more liberal interpretation of constitutional liberty, furnishes arguments that spurn at both. It would be an endless work to enumerate the subalterns of this corps; but these are the most determined leaders and are mere tribunes of the people. At public meetings, whether in taverns or under Liberty Tree, they direct the motions as they previously settle the matter.

A general meeting is summoned by these men on the 13th inst. when they hope to form some resolutions still to show a spirit of opposition to Great Britain. I expect there will be some struggle between the influence of these tribunes and those who from the feelings of interest and dictates of reason dare to differ from them and assert their own freedom in acting in their affairs as formerly.

As the clouds of popular discontent begin now to disperse in some degree several who have been injured threaten suits at law for damages as soon as a Chief Justice arrives, and those who have estates to answer damages for such injuries begin to feel some apprehensions. As soon as the 13th of this month is past, I will transmit to your lordship an account of the proceedings of that general assembly. *Signed.* [C.O.5/394, fo. 21]

CXXXI

Governor Earl of Dunmore to Earl of Hillsborough (No. 4)

6 December, New York

My Lord, I have received the duplicate of your lordship's private and confidential letter [Vol. I, No. 621], No. 41, not yet come to hand.

This city, my lord, is in the most defenceless state. The works which from time to time have been erected for its protection are so injudiciously constructed that, were they still in good repair, they would afford but little security to the place; and though there is a considerable number of cannon in a disorderly manner laying on these works, no care having been taken of them, many of them must be unfit for service and their carriages are all entirely useless.

The militia also having been for several years past without exercising would be of little use in their present state, and they are so scattered as to make it difficult to collect them on an alarm.

I assembled the Council to advise with on the necessary steps to be taken for putting the province in a condition to resist the sudden attempts of an enemy. They are of opinion that the frost being set in and the earth so hardened it would be impossible to accomplish any additional fortifications or even temporary batteries, which indeed, could we effect, we should not be able to mount cannon upon for the reasons abovementioned. But, notwithstanding this, I would not have your lordship apprehensive on our accounts. The severe weather and great quantity of ice on these coasts gives us little to fear about the approach of an enemy during the winter, and the Assembly being to meet the 11th instant, I shall recommend to them to provide everything that may be necessary for the safety of the province against the time that the season will enable us to employ them; and in the interim your lordship may depend on my taking every precaution that the circumstances of the colony under my command will admit of, although I am not inclined to believe we shall find them necessary. The spirited and vigorous measures adopted by His Majesty's ministers to vindicate the honour of the Crown will, I am persuaded, induce the Spaniards to make concessions rather than expose themselves to the merited vengeance which they will perceive so ready to fall upon them.

I am daily made acquainted (as by the enclosed deposition [Vol. I, No. 783i] your lordship will see) with fresh disorders and disturbances happening in the disputed lands between New Hampshire and this province. A number of reduced officers and soldiers of His Majesty's troops are suffering the most cruel hardships while they remain in suspense. I am therefore constrained to press your lordship to consider immediately their unhappy condition and send me forthwith instructions that may enable me to relieve them and establish order and justice among a number of His Majesty's subjects that are now in so affecting a manner without either. *Signed*. PS. In my letter [Vol. II, No. CXIX] No. 2 to your lordship, I gave an account of a report of the plague's having broke out in the island of Hispaniola, since which many vessels have arrived from that quarter who have all contradicted the said report, which we also now believe to have had no other foundation than perhaps a violent fever then raging. [C.O.5/1102, fo. 11]

CXXXII

Lieut.-General Thomas Gage to Earl of Hillsborough (No. 53)

7 December, New York

My Lord, I have had the honour to receive the duplicate of your lordship's letter [Vol. I, No. 623] No. 35 in answer to my Nos. 46, 47 and 48 [Vol. II, Nos. LXIV, LXXXIII].

The Assembly of this province is to meet in a few days, and I am sorry to find there are great doubts whether they will re-enact the repealed law concerning the emission of paper money. I perceive the only objection to it is that they are prohibited by Act of Parliament from making the paper a legal tender; they will be the only sufferers by refusing to pass the law in the shape they are allowed to do, unless a war should commence, in which case I apprehend that requisitions of troops may be made upon the province, who can only provide funds for their support by emissions of paper money. I am well informed that it is in agitation to oppose the bill unless the paper is made a legal tender, and the resolution seems to have been taken since the rumour of a war with Spain.

His Majesty's approbation of the works proposed by Brigadier-General Haldimand and Lieutenant-Governor Durnford for the better defence of West Florida has been transmitted to Pensacola, and as an engineer has also been sent from hence to assist in laying out the works I am to hope the batteries are far advanced.

I have received no accounts of any bad intentions in the Indian nations of West Florida that should occasion the apprehensions your lordship takes notice of. Misunderstandings and sometimes plundering will happen upon all our frontiers, but my letters to the 7th of October from Pensacola contain no bad reports and are rather testimonies of peace and tranquillity. Governor Chester accompanied by several gentlemen were to set out in a few days to inspect the Ibbeville and to proceed some distance up the Mississippi.

My former letters inform your lordship of the state of Castle William and the number of troops necessary for its defence, which renders it unnecessary to trouble you with any particular answer to those parts of your lordship's letter; and I have also laid before your lordship the state of the Indian confederacies as far as they were known.

Sir William Johnson is lately returned from the Seneca country, and during his residence there a party of the Six Nations who had been to the southward with design to attack the Choctaws returned with four scalps presented to them by the Cherokees, which that nation had taken from the Choctaws. The Six Nations report that there were several parties of Cherokees going out, but whether they mean to prosecute the war much further is uncertain. Sir William Johnson expects shortly to be better informed of the designs of the Indians of Sioto, and as he cannot discover any present appearances of disaffection in the Six Nations in general, whatever will be the issue of the Sioto meeting, he is certain he shall be sufficiently informed to prevent any ill designs from spreading too far.

I have been informed of some instances of the rigidity of the Spanish government at the Ilinois. Lieutenant-Colonel Wilkins writes that the people seem to be in a stupor, not knowing well how to act, but if he is not much mistaken, as soon as they come to be thoroughly awake, something desperate will be done by them. The Spanish commander, Don Pedro Piernas, with only 50 ill-appointed troops, from the nature of his absolute authority and the recent examples made at New Orleans, does at present what he pleases with them. He has put an entire stop to all communication between the two shores of the Mississippi, will not admit of debts contracted before his arrival to be paid if to be carried from the Spanish side, and no person is allowed to land from the British side without a pass from the British commander or to return without a Spanish pass. Disobedience of orders is punished by a confiscation of effects, and in order to prevent people quitting the country no person can sell or dispose of his property.

Lieutenant-Colonel Wilkins has paid a visit to Don Piernas, who resides in the uppermost settlement called Paincourt. He found the village very flourishing owing he says to its situation which affords the opportunity to intercept the trade as it comes down the river, and for the same reason he also found Cauho on the British side to surpass his conception though five miles below Paincourt. He also speaks much of the trade at the Ilinois and acquaints me that he had signed a clearance on the 25th of July last for a snow called the *Florida Packet*, Robert Roberts master, for the Port of London, with one thousand packs of peltry, the acquisition of one year only, belonging to one Mr Bradley. I wish this circumstance had been fully explained; I am left to conjecture that the snow was neither built at the Ilinois nor carried up there, but must have lain at or near New Orleans.

The company from Philadelphia failed in the Ilinois trade, and this Mr Bradley, a new trader in that country, was pillaged some months ago at the Natches by some Indians, which was supposed by some to have happened, though I don't know if justly, from his own conduct. However, from the many tricks that are played I am not ready in giving credit to all the stories and professions of the Indian traders, and I shall endeavour to find out the truth of this matter. I must confess that I have doubts about the merchandise carried up the Mississippi by Mr Bradley, whether it was British or foreign, as well as about the snow *Florida Packet* going to the Port of London with one thousand packs of peltry. If your lordship judges it of consequence enough, I apprehend the Custom-house in London might ascertain it. A clearance signed by the military commander of a fort 500 leagues from the sea must have been particularly observed by the commissioners.

The facing of the bank has preserved Fort Chartres though the torrents of the Mississippi have wore away the ground on each side of it, and it's imagined in a few years the fort will stand on a peninsula. I am sorry to add to these accounts of the Ilinois that the garrison was growing sickly, but everything was quiet and no apprehension of disturbances.

I transmit your lordship a memorial from a Swedish gentleman of the name of Nordberg, a lieutenant in the Royal American Regiment, together with a copy of a former memorial of his to Lord Halifax, and a copy of a letter from Lord Barrington to General Abercromby concerning him [Vol. I, No. 790i-iii]. This gentleman for services rendered in Sweden was patronised strongly by the late Lord Granville, and was sent over to this country I believe with assurances of his having a company in the American Regiment; but none being vacant on his arrival, General Abercromby could only give him a lieutenancy with the promise of a company on the first opportunity. The command devolved soon afterwards upon Sir Jeffrey Amherst, and by some means or other Mr Nordberg remained a lieutenant and was reduced as such at the peace. His memorial to Lord Halifax produced the King's order to reinstate him in the regiment upon the first vacancy with the notification of His Majesty's intentions to promote him to a company, which is the occasion of the memorial now presented to your lordship. *Signed.* [C.O.5/89, fo. 11]

CXXXIII

Lieut.-General Thomas Gage to Earl of Hillsborough (No. 54)

7 December, New York
My Lord, the duplicate of your lordship's letter [Vol. I, No. 624] *most secret and confidential* No. 36 has been duly received by the packet, in which your lordship is pleased to communicate the violent proceedings of the governor of Buenos Ayres against His Majesty's subjects at Port Egmont in Falkland's Islands, which unless disavowed by the Court of Spain and proper restitution made would be considered as an open act of hostility; with further information of the naval armament His Majesty had thought fit to command to be prepared in order to act as the honour and dignity of his Crown shall under future events require.

I beg leave to assure your lordship that no attention shall be wanting towards the security of the colonies within the limits of my command, and that I shall take into immediate consideration such arrangements and operations as shall appear the best for His Majesty's service in case a rupture should ensue. An express was dispatched to Fort Chartres immediately after the receipt of your lordship's letter to put the officer commanding in the Ilinois upon his guard as well as to concert measures with him for acting offensively in that quarter. A letter to the same purpose has likewise been sent to Pensacola to Brigadier-General

Haldimand, and I shall without delay direct the officer commanding in the provinces of Quebec and Nova Scotia as well as the commander upon the Lakes to be watchful against all attempts to surprise them as well as ready to resist any open attacks. *Signed.* [C.O.5/89, fo. 20]

CXXXIV

Lieut.-General Thomas Gage to Earl of Hillsborough (Private)

7 December, New York

My Lord, I have been honoured with your lordship's letter *private and secret* of the 3rd of October. The last packet carried the news of Captain Preston's trial and acquittal, and we expect an account to-morrow night of the trial of the soldiers. Captain Preston was advised to go to England to avoid further prosecutions but I have not heard of his embarking. If the letter I have written reaches Boston before he sails I shall take care to settle all matters with him as your lordship desires. Your lordship will perceive that the duplicates of your letter by the *Mercury* have been received by the packets. When the *Mercury* shall deliver the originals, No. 35 shall be destroyed and the rest numbered to correspond with the duplicates.

In my dispatches by this opportunity, I mention doubts of this Assembly passing a bill for emitting a paper currency. I believe it will depend upon peace or war, for I apprehend their design is in case of war to avail themselves of the necessities of government and procure leave to emit paper money in the shape they choose. I can assign no other reason for any demur in that business, desired generally by people of all degrees, and I never heard the objection now started till after the news arrived of the probability of a war with Spain.

The people of Boston have been cavilling and quibbling which shows they still retain a sour disposition, but I have not heard of any noise or tumults amongst them. The King's troops taking possession of the Castle has mortified them a good deal and I believe alarmed many. *Signed.* [C.O.5/89, fo. 22]

CXXXV

Commissioners for Trade and Plantations to Governor William Tryon

12 December, Whitehall

Sir, the death of our late counsel, Sir Matthew Lamb, and the long interval between that event and the appointment of Mr Jackson to that office has occasioned a delay in the examination of the laws of North Carolina passed in 1768 and 1769, which is the more to be regretted as they have reference to many important matters and fundamental constitutions of government, and more especially as those by which the courts of judicature are established and their proceedings regulated, though in general well-calculated to give stability to government and ease and satisfaction to the people, are yet in some particulars liable to material objection.

It is a requisite essential to the validity of the laws of the Plantations that they should be as nearly as may be comfortable to the laws of

England, and no deviation from this general rule is to be justified but upon some obvious apparent necessity arising out of peculiarity in situation and circumstances, and therefore we were concerned to find that the Superior Court Act had in the mode of proceeding upon attachments in civil suits extended its regulations so far as that the estate and effects of a person who never had been in the colony were made liable to an attachment at the suit of any person alleging himself to be a creditor.

We are sensible that difference of situation requires greater rigour in cases of persons absconding to avoid the payments of their just debts than would be allowed of or is necessary here; but when that rigour is extended to cases not falling within that rule of distinction and regulations are unnecessarily adopted that do not correspond with the letter and spirit of the laws of England, the interests of this kingdom become affected, and it is the duty of government here to interpose its authority.

We have no doubt that the force of this objection (in which those of this kingdom who have dealings with North Carolina in trade do concur, and upon which the agent himself is at least silent) will weigh with the legislature to amend that part of the laws to which it applies, either by an explanatory Act in their next session or by omitting the provisions objected to when the present Act comes to be revived after the expiration of the period fixed for its continuance; and we think it fit to observe that nothing less than the fullest confidence that the amendment will be made would have justified our not laying this Act (beneficial as it may be in other respects) before His Majesty for his royal disallowance.

Another part of this Act which we wish to see amended is that by which the appointment of the Clerk of the Courts is vested in the Chief Justice contrary, as we conceive, to the practice in most other colonies where such officers are appointed either by the King or by the governor; and therefore as it is our duty to take care that His Majesty's right to such appointment is not set aside, so will it become you to use your best endeavours that this clause be omitted when a new Act is passed.

With regard to the Act for the Appointment of Sheriffs, which we consider as part of the general system for the more effectual administration of justice, it certainly contains many very useful and proper regulations; but as it does not leave a discretionary power in the King's governor of nominating a sheriff, in case he should think fit to reject those recommended by the judges, it does improperly and, as we conceive, unnecessarily deviate from the rule and usage in this kingdom, and therefore unless the legislature of North Carolina think fit to remove this objection it will become proper for us to advise His Majesty to disallow the present law, for no consideration of general utility and convenience can justify an acquiescence in a regulation that does not correspond with the constitution of this kingdom in a case where there is no apparent necessity for a deviation.

The law for introducing a circulation of British copper halfpence seems to have been well-intentioned, but, besides that it is a regulation which in the nature of it ought not to have been made without the

King's consent previously obtained, and does also authorise the passing those halfpence at a rate greatly beyond their intrinsic value, the law itself is without any of those guards necessary to prevent the introduction of that base copper coin which has so fraudulently prevailed and been so much complained of in this kingdom; and therefore we have thought fit to propose that it should be disallowed, as also another Act entitled "An Act for declaring certain lots in the Town of Newbern, taken up by the Trustees for promoting the Public School in said Town, saved and improved according to law, and to empower the said Trustees to collect the Subscription due to the said School", which Act is very strongly objected to by Mr Jackson as setting aside the Statute of Limitations.

The Act for making provision for the payment of the forces raised to suppress the late insurrections on the western frontiers does certainly in every light fall under the description of those to which the 20th article of your instructions refers, and is also liable to objection as containing matters which have no proper relation each to the other. The reasons, however, which you state for having given your assent to this law are very cogent, and while we admit them as a justification of your conduct we must rely upon them as an excuse for ourselves in permitting the operation of a law which (independent of the object of it) is certainly liable to objection. *Entry. Signatories,* Hillsborough, Soame Jenyns, William Fitzherbert, W. Northey, Greville. [C.O.5/325, p. 428]

CXXXVI
Governor James Grant to Earl of Hillsborough (No. 43)

12 December, St Augustine

My Lord, I have had the honour to receive your lordship's circular letter [Vol. I, No. 621] No. 32, in answer to which it becomes my duty to lay before you what appears to me to be necessary for the safety and security of this flourishing infant colony in the event of a rupture with Spain, for if hostilities should commence, this province being the American frontier will of course become the object of His Majesty's immediate attention. West Florida, though in the proximity of New Orleans, has nothing to apprehend from that quarter: the inhabitants, full of indignation at the treatment they have met with from the Spaniards under the command and direction of General O'Reilly, would rather join any force which may be sent against that country than assist their new masters in defending themselves or in attacking their neighbours. The other American colonies have certainly nothing to apprehend from a Spanish enemy.

Their practice of fishing upon this coast, not being warranted by treaty, should and may immediately be interrupted by stationing a sloop of war and two armed vessels or cutters among the Keys of Florida, which will put a stop to their intercourse with the Indians and effectually prevent their attempting to form a settlement upon any of the Keys, to which the Spaniards seem to lay in a claim as the Governor of the Havanah has been in the constant practice of giving passports to the Florida Keys under the name of Northern Keys, of which I gave information [Vol. I, No. 829i] in April 1766 to the Lords of Trade and to General Conway, then Secretary of State.

I have hitherto been under no apprehension of any inconvenience arising from the little meetings which the Spaniards had occasionally with the Creek Indians, as I was well-informed that their sole motive for going to that expense was with a view to keep up a friendly correspondence with the savages: for by that means only their fishery can be carried on with safety, and that fishery is an object of consequence to Spain in point of subsistence to the inhabitants of Cuba, and of one species of provision for ships stationed at the Havanah and for such vessels as sail from thence to Europe.

In time of peace it was contrary to the interest of Spain to seduce our Indian neighbours. If they had persuaded them to commit hostilities against the King's Florida subjects, it could not have been kept a secret, and the discovery of such a measure must in its consequences have been attended with a stop to the fishery of which they were in quiet possession. But their views and policy will be very different in case of a war, their fishery will then of course be interrupted and their vessels frequently taken by the King's ships or private ships of war; but notwithstanding those disadvantages I am convinced that they will still endeavour to carry on the fishery and will at the same time do everything in their power to draw the Indians into a war with the King's subjects. If they should succeed in that attempt with the Creek Indians, those savages can overrun this province and Georgia, distress the frontier-settlements of South Carolina, and may be instrumental in bringing on a general Indian war all over the continent, for none of them are fond of having the English only for neighbours, but they have understanding enough to know their own interest and weakness and see clearly that nothing can be attempted with safety in their present situation, but supplies and assistance from a neighbouring enemy might alter their opinion.

Most of the materials are arrived for the construction of the new barrack, which rises fast and will be a handsome building. Two regiments stationed here will be a great security against an Indian attack upon the province, and if a greater body of troops was garrisoned here they could not be placed more conveniently for a West India expedition. The bar is absolutely an ideal difficulty, and has been complained of by the masters of packet-boats and other vessels because we have nothing to give; if we had only produce enough to send to market, all those complaints about the difficulty of navigation would soon subside. Within these two months we have not had less than forty different vessels in this port from New York and other places, and not a single accident has happened in passing or repassing the bar. If there were only a few boats, such launches as the Spaniards had, which would be a trifling expense, troops might be embarked or disembarked here more easily than in many places, at Louisbourg, and upon the coasts of Cuba and France where such a difficulty has never been mentioned or thought of, though the surf or swell is much more dangerous than this bar. But till we are provided with proper boats to carry on the service, no doubt there will be an inconvenience from delays when large vessels come upon the coast; but capital ships cannot pass the bar of Charleston, and they can ride at anchor off this place in as much safety as they can in any part of the world where there is not sufficient depth of water to bring them into a bay or harbour. Merchant vessels commanded by Messrs. Seven and Fuller received no damage when at anchor off this bar in the hardest gales of wind which we have had during the seven years that I have resided in this place. *Signed*. [C.O.5/ 552, fo. 5]

CXXXVII

Governor James Wright to Earl of Hillsborough (No. 51)

13 December, Savannah
My Lord, on the 28th of November I had the honour to receive your lordship's letter [Vol. I, No. 621] of the 28th of September, No. 33, and am extremely concerned to hear that the report of the conduct of the Governor of Buenos Ayres is confirmed but am very hopeful the Court of Madrid will find it necessary to disavow that transaction.

I have maturely considered the state of this province and beg leave to acquaint your lordship that it is in every respect weak and defence-less. There are a considerable number of people scattered over a large face of country, most of them industriously seeking a livelihood and acquiring some property, but, alas my lord, what are a few scattered militia, suppose from 2,500 to 3,000, against an invasion if any such thing was to be attempted? and of these settlers numbers would make off to the neighbouring provinces on the first appearance of danger or trouble, and many others would not obey orders, being neither in pay or subject to discipline, and if under both yet they could not be drawn down to the sea coast from their families who would probably be robbed and murdered by the Indians during their absence. So that your lordship sees what a situation we shall be in if war happens, and I presume not one half of the above number to be depended on in the whole for every place and service. But this province, my lord, though in its infancy is undoubtedly in a most flourishing state and is making vast progress. We expect the present crop of rice will amount to 25,000 barrels and when I came to the province the whole crop did not amount to 4,000 barrels. But in short as I mentioned in my last letter we have neither men nor money to do anything material in the way of war, and as I cannot, my lord, suppose that we are, or the province is, of con-sequence enough to draw the attention of the Court of Spain this way, I shall only observe on such matters as probably may happen.

Vizt. privateers and little plundering parties may land and rob or burn our towns, and we have nothing to oppose or prevent them. Fort George on Cockspur Island has been for 2 or 3 years past decaying, and by a kind of hurricane which we had last June it's so far demolished as to be of little or no use. I have always put the Assembly in mind of providing for the necessary repairs of that fort but it has been put off from time to time, and at the opening of the present session I recom-mended to them the building of a new fort, which they have had under consideration and seems to be approved of, and the committee have reported that to build a respectable fort proper for the purpose will cost £2,500 sterling. Indeed, it's supposed it will require more, but whether this sum or any sum may be granted and raised I cannot yet take upon me to say.

My lord, if we could have a regiment which I suppose to consist of 500 effective men with officers, to be here at Savannah or on the frontiers next the Indians, or elsewhere as occasion may require, and these to be under the immediate and sole direction and command of the Governor as to the duty or services they may be employed upon, I conceive this might answer such purposes as may be most useful; and really, my lord, I should think this necessary for we have not only 3,000 gunmen of the Creek Indians to deal with and keep in order but others. Your lordship has undoubtedly been acquainted with what the back-settlers in North Carolina have done, and we have many in our back-settlements of the same stamp; and as a proof of which I beg leave to refer your lordship to my letters to Mr Secretary Conway of the 31st of January and 1st and 7th of February 1766. And, my lord, troops at St Augustine are of no kind of use to this province or can be, their distance and situation is such; for before we could have any assistance from thence it might be too late as it's well known that the bar of St Augustine is so dangerous and difficult that there is no embarking and transporting troops with any certainty, and a march by land through an unsettled country upwards of two hundred miles is not an easy or expeditious thing. Whereas, my lord, if we had a regiment here and the whole or any part of it should be wanted elsewhere, we have always shipping enough, and they may be embarked in a day's time; and if wanted at Augustine in case that place should be attacked, I'm informed schooners may go within land within 12 or 15 miles of the town of St Augustine, and if wanted in Charleston schooners may go from hence all the way there within land. And if we had such a number of men and a general peremptory order to all the governors to stop the Indian trade and do what else might be necessary, in case the Creeks finally refuse to make satisfaction, I am very certain they would soon do it and I presume not dare to offend again.

And a principal and very material part of our security and defence, my lord, would be in having a ship and sloop of war stationed *at this province* or from Cape Florida *here,* with positive orders when they go into any port to come *here into this river,* and the sloop might come up to the town if necessary. But, my lord, ships stationed as they now are from Carolina to Florida will be of little or no use to this province, for what will it signify sailing along the coast once or perhaps twice a month? Therefore whatever His Majesty may be graciously pleased to think necessary for the protection of this province, I beg leave to repeat again that I request *their orders may confine them to this port only, when they find it necessary to put into any,* for although I understand the orders they now have include this province yet not one of the King's ships now on the station has been here but the *Bonetta,* Captain Wallace, and he not for these two years past. I don't mean this, my lord, by way of complaint against the captains of any of the King's ships, but that we may not have barely the name but real protection in case of war, for be assured, my lord, they will always put in and rendezvous at Charleston, South Carolina, and not here unless their orders are very particular. They cannot go into St Augustine, that bar will not admit of it, and as we have at present no fort that can even beat off or stop a small privateer we may have our town burnt etc. in the night by a little privateer or two, and which cannot be if there is a King's ship in the river. And we have as good a bar and depth of water at this inlet or better than they have at Charleston, and ships may lie as safe at Cockspur and sloops up at this town and be supplied with all necessaries that they can want as well as in Carolina.

And, my lord, if the Assembly should determine to raise money and build a new fort, yet it will probably be eighteen months or more before it's completed, so that we shall be destitute of all safety and protection for that time. Therefore I must earnestly request that if there is a war we may be succoured by sea as soon as possible, and further, my lord, that whatever convoys may be ordered for the Carolina trade may also be ordered to take charge of our merchant ships too, or I am well assured we shall be left to run all risks. I would humbly propose, my lord, that notice may always be given the governor here when the Carolina convoy is to sail, and if we have a ship and a sloop one of them should always convoy the trade from this province to Carolina, and if we should not have two vessels of war here, that one of the King's ships should come from Carolina to this province and convoy the trade back to join the Carolina trade and convoy. This is what occurs at present. *Signed.* [C.O.5/661, fo. 7]

CXXXVIII

Lieut.-Governor William Bull to Earl of Hillsborough (No. 39)

13 December, Charleston

My Lord, this day according to my letter [Vol. II, No. CXXX] No. 38 there was a numerous meeting of planters, merchants and mechanics. After long silence, each party acting in the reserve to receive the first attack, at last one of no note stepped forth and moved that no further regard should be had to the resolutions. Upon which a motion was made to consider whether there should be any alteration or no: the general voice was yea. Upon which Mr Lynch, who came fifty miles to town on purpose, exerted all his eloquence and even the trope of rhetorical tears for the expiring liberties of his dear country which the merchants would sell like other merchandise. He was seconded by his two brethren who were for continuing the Association and proposed importing goods from Holland, but the struggle though strong proved ineffectual. And the only article now talked of as not proper to be imported is tea, and next Monday all the goods that have been stored under the direction of the general committee as contrary to the non-importation agreement are by the committee to be delivered to the proprietors. But I apprehend the Association will now be wholly at an end. Indeed some talk of a new plan of association on principles of sumptuary laws equivalent to non-importation, though I do not suppose it will be of any consequence and probably is intended more to preserve an appearance of reluctance in dissolving their resolutions than with any expectation of succeeding. I thought it my duty to give your lordship this information and I doubt not but when the minds of people are a little cooled most of them will be ashamed of their having been concerned in the Association or in the rash and unreasonable means made use of to enforce the observance of them. I have the honour to be with the greatest respect, my lord, your lordship's most obedient and most humble servant. *Signed*. [C.O.5/394, fo. 34]

CXXXIX

Commissioners for Trade and Plantations to the King

19 December, Whitehall

May it please your Majesty, we have had under our consideration an Act passed in your Majesty's colony of New Jersey in November 1769, entitled "An Act to erect Courts in the several Counties in this Colony for the Trial of Causes of Ten Pounds and under".

Whereupon we humbly beg leave to represent to your Majesty,

That by this Act which is to continue in force for two years, a former Act passed in the preceding year entitled "An Act to Erect and establish Courts in the several Counties in this Colony for the Trial of small Causes" is repealed; and actions of debt and other demands to the amount of ten pounds proclamation money are made cognizable before any one Justice of the Peace, which by the provisions of the former Act were limited to the amount of six pounds only. This Act likewise contains a proviso that in actions where the real debt or demand exceeds the sum of forty shillings either party may demand a jury, the verdict of which jury is to be final; and it further provides that in any judgement given as aforesaid for the sum of twenty shillings or more either party may appeal from such judgement to the next Court of General Quarter Sessions of the Peace to be held for the county, city or town corporate after the judgement given.

We have likewise referred this Act to Richard Jackson, Esquire, one of your Majesty's counsel at law, who in his report to us thereupon submits the following reasons why this Act of Assembly should at this time at least be disallowed, vizt. That summary and domestic justice under the specious pretext of facilitating the recovery of debts necessarily encourages a litigious spirit and frequently the practice of perjury, both highly pernicious in every country, much more so in a commercial one, and the last subversive of every public and private benefit derived from the institution of civil society; that it serves too often to favour the establishment of much petty tyranny in men altogether unfit to be entrusted with such power; and that these reasons have weighed so far with the legislature of Great Britain that this kind of jurisdiction has been always given with caution, sometimes with reluctance, and never hitherto to his knowledge extended beyond the sum of forty shillings sterling; that nothing is of greater importance to every country than that its laws should be certain and depend as little as possible on any man's discretion or affections; that without this certainty law ceases to be what it ought to be, an universal measure of justice, and no longer answers the end of its institution; that the laws of the country cannot be certain unless they are uniform, and they can neither be uniform nor certain where probably more than one hundred judges are to determine, each according to his own notions of justice; that if uniformity is necessary to the public welfare in all countries, it is much more so in a colony where without it it is evident that a conformity to the laws of Great Britain cannot long be preserved, for that the continuance of this conformity can only be hoped for from frequent determinations of the Supreme Court affecting the property in every part of the colony; that if humour and caprice may injure this uniformity and produce injustice, as much at least may be expected from partiality, every plaintiff will naturally resort to a Justice that is his friend: friendship often biases insensibly the honest man but should he be dishonest there seems little remedy in the power of demanding a jury, for the justice may order the jury to be summoned from any town or precinct; that the causes provided for by this Act are not triable in the County Court, the trouble and expense of bringing on a cause there must be much less than the trouble and expense of recovering the same sums in England, even should a writ of error be brought in the Supreme Court, and that one of the mischiefs of the present law is that an appeal is prohibited where there has been a verdict; but that if there is a probability that the mischiefs resulting from the present mode of recovery, as well as the advantages to be expected from the extension of the Act of the preceding year, may be greater than appears to him, it is surely too early after the passing that Act to make so wide a stride; that he made no objection to the former Act because other colonies have extended these laws as far, or nearly so, and this colony has many years had one to five pounds extent, but that this subject is at least one that requires great caution and a slow progress.

These may it please your Majesty are the arguments on which Mr Jackson has grounded his recommendation of the repeal of this Act, which together with the Act itself, we humbly lay before your Majesty, submitting it to your Majesty to determine thereupon as to your Majesty with the advice of your Council shall seem fit. *Entry. Signatories*, Hillsborough, Soame Jenyns, William Fitzherbert, Greville. [C.O.5/999, p. 232]

CXL

Extract from a letter from John Swift, Deputy Collector, and Alexander Barclay, Comptroller, of Philadelphia, to Commissioners of Customs at Boston[1]

20 December,

Honourable Gentlemen, we have received your letter of the 10th inst. and enclosed we now send you copy of the register of the ship *Prince of Wales*, from which you will learn who are the owners, and also copy

1 Enclosed in Robinson's letter to Pownall, 13 July 1771: Vol. I, No. 1393.

of our entry inwards. We had no suspicion when the vessel was entered that any illegal practices had been committed and therefore did not think it material to enquire the names of the seamen, but we will endeavour to learn their names and transmit you a list of them.

Your honours are pleased to say that we ought to have made a proper representation of the riot that happened in this city on 13th of last month to Governor Penn. May it please your honours, we were of opinion that the governor and the magistrates of the city ought of their own accords to have taken the proper steps and have exerted themselves to discover who were the ringleaders and perpetrators of such a notorious insult offered to government; but finding that they did not do it, the Deputy Collector did apply to the mayor and some of the aldermen who with great indifference told him that if he would inform them who were concerned they would do their duty, but they did not think themselves obliged to hunt after business of this kind. He also spoke to the governor about it who told him that he thought the magistrates would have done something in it; he had heard, he said, that they intended it. In short the truth of the matter is the hands of government are not strong enough to oppose the numerous body of people who wish well to the cause of smuggling even if they were ever so well disposed to do it. What can a governor do without the assistance of the governed? What can the magistrates do unless they are supported by their fellow citizens? What can the King's officers do if they make themselves obnoxious to the people amongst whom they reside? Your honours are pleased to authorise us to offer a reward of £50. We don't look upon this as a command and therefore take it for granted that we are at liberty to use our own discretion in the case. We don't think it can possibly answer any good purpose, nobody will dare to inform unless we and they were countenanced by the government. If the governor with the advice of his Council would issue a proclamation and offer a reward, it might perhaps be attended to; but for us to offer a reward in the present situation of affairs will in our opinion answer no purpose but to make ourselves ridiculous. This is not a time for works of supererogation and it will be said that this is a matter that did not immediately concern us and that therefore we had no occasion to make ourselves busy about it. This is our opinion of the matter but if your honours are desirous of having a reward offered we beg you will be pleased to direct the form of the advertisement and send it to us. It will not be too late for we are well assured that the persons principally concerned are inhabitants of the city.

Mr Hatton, the Collector, was here two days ago: he has been sadly harrassed by the magistrates of the county where he resides who have done everything in their power to perplex and plague him. He has now gone to Burlington with a remonstrance to Governor Franklin, setting forth the ill-treatment he has met with from them; and from thence he intends to go to Amboy to take the opinion of the Attorney-General agreeable to your honours' directions. And if we are not much mistaken he would have done just as well if he had stayed at home and whistled to the wind. *Copy*. [C.O.5/72, fo. 266]

CXLI

Governor Lord William Campbell to Earl of Hillsborough (No. 70)

22 December, Halifax

My Lord, proposals have lately been made to me for effecting a permanent settlement in some convenient place near this town of a considerable number of the Indians. This has been an object long held in view and often wished for but the want of influence necessary for the purpose has hitherto discouraged any attempt. At last Mr Bailly, missionary to these people, has not only urged it with the best reasons but has undertaken to use his influence amongst the most considerable of them and to make their place of establishment his residence. When thus collected, my lord, they may be in the power of government, their motions may be watched and prevented if ill-designed, and in time become peacable and useful subjects. Canada and New England afford instances of the advantages which may be derived from such settlements, and if such a settlement shall meet with your lordship's approbation I shall use my best endeavours to forward and carry it into execution.

I should be wanting in justice to Mr Bailly were I not to mention him to your lordship as a man unbigoted, candid, and of a liberal turn of mind. The pains he takes to eradicate the inveterate prejudices, industriously sown amongst the Indians by French priests formerly, and to cultivate in their room the doctrine of obedience to government, though different from them in religion, is a proof of his merit. He has by spending two winters on St John's River impaired his health, which he is now in this town endeavouring to recover and where he officiates to the Indians and teaches them to pray for the King and the happiness of His Majesty's government. I therefore beg leave to recommend him as deserving any token of favour which with propriety may be bestowed on a man in his character. *Signed.* [C.O.217/48, fo. 11]

CXLII

Governor Peter Chester to Earl of Hillsborough (No. 7)

24 December, Pensacola

My Lord, I flattered myself before I left England that upon my arrival at Pensacola I should find His Majesty's 16th Regiment and several companies of the 31st Regiment stationed within the province for our defence and protection; but my hopes were disappointed, as I found here the 16th Regiment not complete and only three companies of the 31st which have lately gone to St Augustine.

The sanguine expectations I had formed of always having at least two regiments within this province have been frustrated by the contents contained in a paragraph of a letter I lately received from Lieutenant-General Gage wherein he says "That they had at home been long wavering respecting the destination of the troops in the Floridas but it is now fixed that one regiment only is to be stationed in West Florida being looked upon as sufficient for the service of the province", so that we are likely to remain in our present state with regard to defence and protection, to wit, with seven companies not complete at Pensacola and two at Mobile. Such a handful of troops in a province situated so near the Spaniards at Orleans and surrounded with numerous tribes of Indians who at present seem to be very discontented will be a great discouragement to its settlement and improvement.

East Florida although by no means so dangerously situated as we are has now two regiments quartered in its capital. This arrangement was probably thought necessary in order that those troops might have been transported much sooner from East Florida than from hence to such of His Majesty's colonies as were in a tumultuous state and in opposition to all government, and where they might have been necessary in order to assist the civil magistrates in maintaining a due execution of the laws; but as those tumults and disorders which have been excited by factious and designing men seem now happily subsided, it may be presumed that as the turbulent are returning to a sense of their duty it will be the means of re-establishing that mutual confidence and affection between Great Britain and her colonies upon which the glory and safety of the British Empire depend. Should this wished for event take place it may then be thought that one regiment from East Florida or from some other of the Northern Colonies will be of greater use to His Majesty's service to be stationed here than in their present quarters, as they can at all times in case of a war or any other emergency be with great facility transported from hence in men-of-war or frigates to such of our West India islands as may be thought necessary which cannot be the case in East Florida, there being so little water on the bar of Augustine as not to admit any of His Majesty's ships into the port.

Should your lordship join with me in opinion and see the propriety of sending another regiment as well for protection as for encouragement to the settlers, who soon find the advantages of such an additional quantity of circulating cash as they will bring into the province, I doubt not but from your representations that we shall soon have the additional regiment required. *Signed.* [C.O.5/588, p. 73]

CXLIII

Charles Stuart to John Stuart[1]

26 December, Pensacola

Sir, I am honoured with yours of 26 August, also that of the 8 November, both which came to hand on the 21 instant. I arrived here a few days ago from Mobile in consequence of some intelligence I had received from His Excellency Governor Chester and Brigadier-General Haldimand, copies of which I now transmit you, and in consequence of which with other informations from the Creek and Chickasaw nations I thought it proper and for the good of His Majesty's service to avoid as much as prudence would admit of the entire confirmation of the peace between the Choctaws and Creeks, notwithstanding that they were within a very few days of meeting at Mobile to a considerable number of each,

1   Enclosed in John Stuart's letter to Hillsborough, 5 March 1771: Vol. I, No. 1032.

in order to take each other by the hand. I had the good luck to defeat their intentions and to send each party away well satisfied with my endeavours to bring them together and not so much displeased with each other but in case of these reports being groundless and that you think proper to confirm the peace, I still have it in my power to unite them in a short time, which consideration induced me and fearing accidents to act as I did as there is no depending on the promises of Indians, and I hope for your approbation: I will take the liberty of assuring you I have that of this province. And the murthers lately committed on the frontiers of Georgia did not a little contribute to the resolution I had taken, joined to the melancholy account Mr Cornall the interpreter gave me of the distracted situation of the Creek nation through a want of some regulation for the trade; without which, and unless some steps are taken and that soon to put a stop to the proceedings of the white people among the Indians and to prevent the vast importation of rum into the nations, I really fear we cannot long avoid breaking with those people. Besides, another great grievance is that of white hunters, a set of people from the northward who go hunting here and are in some measure tolerated through a scarcity of provision, but they do not confine themselves to our grounds at which the Indians are highly displeased, and if this grievance is not removed I shall not wonder that more frequent murders are committed, as the talks given to Indians with regard to those hunters are to seize their property and, if they can, bring their persons without hurting them to the governor who will do them the Indians justice, while on the other side those hunters are resolved to continue their hunts and not to be taken or hindered by Indians; the consequence of which is but too easy to be perceived. I am, however, to lay all these matters in writing before the Governor and Council and the General before I return, at their request, and should any evil consequences ensue through a slackness in the reins of government, it will not be owing to a want of their being put upon their guard by your department, which I think is part of my duty.

You are pleased to mention that you expect a commissary or deputy for the Chickesaws. I can with safety assure you it is much wanted, for I am credibly informed that there are not less than 18 traders and packhorsemen now out a-hunting on the hunting-grounds of that nation the same as Indians, which is contrary to all rule and of which the Indians complain much and are so good a people as not to take satisfaction otherwise than by representation. I am informed those hunters are divided into parties and that they are headed by Messrs. Colbert and Bubbie, and that said Colbert is contrary to His Majesty's instructions establishing plantations in that nation and that he has got cattle, negroes etc. so as even to admit of his having an overseer. Of this also the Indians complain much. I shall acquaint the governor therewith, also of a complaint of Pay Mattaha's against James Bubbie of his having cheated him of eleven horse-load of ammunition sent him in the year 1763 or 1764 by the province of South Carolina. There was 25 horse-load in all sent to be forwarded from Augusta, of which he only delivered eleven, and converted the rest to his own use, and which till of late he never denied but now tells the Leader he cannot and will not pay him who demands satisfaction. You will know the truth of this matter better than I can and make no doubt will see justice done. He is content to take any other goods in lieu.

Mr John McIntosh who is now at Mobile informs me that the Mortar sometime ago sent a talk to the Chickesaws, desiring the Leader to send him the Red Warrior to meet him at a creek called 20 Mile Creek, and which is near the Chickesaw towns. The Leader refused to send him, saying the talks were not good, that he was mad, and that none of his people should take his talks. There had been no more about it when Mr McIntosh left the nation, and it is not yet known to me what is become of the Mortar, but he was in the nation lately and it was supposed he intended going to the Cherokees. I believe he wants support and has not power to carry any scheme he may plan into execution. I shall however be upon my guard and endeavour to defeat anything he may undertake.

Another great obstacle to the proper management of Indians is the difficulty in bringing offenders to justice for want of positive proof, and so very nice are the sentiments of our lawyers that nothing but what is agreeable to the very letter of the law, and as it is practised in England, will take place without any allowance for local circumstances; and if I have influence enough to have a malefactor brought down, there is no such thing as getting those who brought him down paid for their trouble, which makes it difficult to apprehend them and particularly now as they are almost all formed into one company under the firm of the Choctaw and Chickasaw Company. I fear this Company will sometime or other breed disturbance as they do all they can to oppose every other person who may be inclined to trade, and I am sorry to find they are but too well seconded by those people who fit them out, and I could wish such gentlemen were not permitted to visit the Indian nations without some restriction as it is to be suspected that they do no good there but to infuse such notions into the Indians as best suits their purpose and endeavour by magnifying themselves to lessen others in the eyes of the Indians.

I have complaints of Mr Colbert upon this score, and I really think that the most effectual method of riddling the nations of such evil instruments would be by putting them on board a King's ship by pressing them when they come down to renew their licences, and that the information of a commissary who should be a Justice of Peace with the affidavit of one white man should be sufficient proof. I have laid these matters before General Haldimand who is much displeased and desires to have them in writing: he is well acquainted with the truth of them.

I shall by next opportunity transmit to you my last six months accounts, and I wish next year's presents was come, as I am growing short of sundries. However, I shall make shift till they arrive and I flatter myself next year will not be attended with such extravagant issues as this has been, for every Indian who comes to Mobile is sure to come to me and so well they are informed by their white friends with what lies in my department and what not, that they are always provided with their tale and errand, particularly that of the peace and on their way to war, and I conceive it to be my duty and your ideas to keep them in humour and prevent their doing mischief as far as I can. As I have for some time been out of provisions, I have sold at public sale some old and damaged stores to purchase corn, an account of which shall be sent you; and in the estimate I hope you will make provision for the interpreter's two rations per day which he well deserves and of which he has much due as you will see by the returns, and that you will consider the respect I am obliged to show to chiefs and headmen, as also their importunities.

I have for some time past suspected that my residing in a town may possibly draw a greater expense on me than if I was at some distance where I could with equal propriety fulfil the duties of my office. I have therefore mentioned this matter to the General who approves of my scheme. I propose (with your approbation) if I can purchase a small plantation up the Tombeckby River within a few miles of the confluence of the Alibanon with that river to try it for some time. It is more contiguous to all the Indians in my department than where I am and more convenient to the Creeks, besides it will prevent such numbers coming down to Mobile and Pensacola, also any clashing that possibly might arise between the two departments.

Your directions concerning our boundary line shall be particularly attended to, whenever circumstances will admit, and what Emistisiguo meant by white people making fires beyond the line may be owing to two causes: either that lands have been granted beyond what he thinks the line and what possibly may be so, about which I shall enquire, or that he means the white hunters who have camping places undoubtedly beyond it. Mr Cornall informed me that Emistisiguo and the Second Man of the Tallassies had some talks to give me concerning said boundary, but I did not hear them as they did not come to see me. I expect to hear from them soon.

When Emistisiguo, the Second Man, Beaver Tooth King and Little Dick etc. left the nation to come to Mobile to confirm peace, they had not heard of 4 or 5 of their people who had been killed by the Choctaws, of which circumstance I availed myself to keep the wound open as I have already mentioned, and which had immediate effects for Emistisiguo said as did the others that it would be to no purpose to make the peace today and war tomorrow, for they that had lost their friends in that action would surely seek revenge, and that for his part he would return and see how matters stood. Mr Cornall came and acquainted me of their proceedings and as they were to wait his return I sent them the enclosed talk and some ammunition and tobacco, with a new suit to the Second Man who sent me an old coat to mend.

During Cornall's stay the Choctaws arrived who were sorely disappointed and wanted much to have peace. The East and West parties of the Choctaws want much to have peace, but the Six Towns are by no means desirous of it and want a continuance of the war, as do some of the Upper and Lower Creeks. With respect to the Spaniards I have not had any complaints lately, nor are they very desirous seemingly of having any connections with our Indians or rather our Indians with them, and they are not now so rigid as at first to our merchants and others who go to Orleans.

I am sorry to inform you that about 300 lbs. of powder in store is damaged by the wet season, as is all the powder in Mobile. Indeed the magazines are bad and the whole place is falling into rubbish. *Copy*. [C.O.5/72, fo. 179]

NOTE ON INDEX

References are to pages, *not* to document numbers.

The Introduction has not been indexed.

Opinions of correspondents on certain topics have been indexed, e.g. Hutchinson, Thomas, opinion of, on America's capacity to resist. The letters contain so many expressions of opinion that it has been possible to bring within the scope of this index only those on the most striking and important topics.

As in Volume I, Indians have been indexed (a) under national names, e.g. Cherokees, (b) under colonies, e.g. Virginia, Indians, and (c) generally under Indians and Indian Trade.

INDEX

skins, see furs.

slaves (see under E. Fla.; S.C.; Va.; W. Fla.), murderers of, punished by death in some colonies but not in all, 272.

slave trade, damaged by colonial duties, 259, and see under Va.

Smith, Judge, in N.Y., 200.

Smith, Steel, rioter in N.Y., 158, 159, 161.

Smythe, Sir S.S., Trustee for Dartmouth College, 244.

smuggling, on Miss. R., 252, 289; in Philadelphia, 300; in Mass., 133.

Society for Propagating Gospel, 166, 243.

Solicitor-General of England, 76, 231.

Sons of Liberty, see under Charleston; New York; New York City; N.H.; S.C.

South Carolina,

  Acts: Church (1706), 268; Circuit Court, 56–57; Negro (1740), 272; how passed, 56–57; published digest of, 272,

  agent, see Garth, C.; former, see Crockat,

  agriculture, 41, 100–101, 276–278,

  anarchy in, alleged, 152,

  architecture, 276,

  Assembly, 56, 81, 101,

    address of, to King, 80,

    clerk of, appointed by Crown, 269,

    composition of, 269,

    control of money bills and issues by, 172, 179–183, 216, 263–265, 269–270,

    democracy in, 220,

    disputes in, 219,

    dispute of, with Council, 80, 172, 181–182,

    don't begin with prayers, 270,

    not fully representative, 269,

    proceedings of, on Tax Bill, 80, 173,

    resolution of 8 Dec. 1769 passed by, 41–42, 77, 80, 173, 263–264,

    scorn payment, 270,

    Speaker, 78, 270,

    standing of, 269,

    want to know what is said about them, 265,

    won't do business, 180,

  Attorney-General, see Leigh, E.,

  barter widely used in, 279,

  bills of credit, 279,

  boundaries of: with Cherokees, 211, 267, 278; with N.C., 99,

  bounty on hemp paid in, 276,

  canal in, proposed, 101,

  Chancery, Court of, 270,

  Chancery, Master of, 285,

  Church of England in, 267–268,

  Clerks of Crown and Pleas, appointed by Crown, 271,

  climate, 57, 100, 273, 280,

  communications of, internal, 101,

  convoy from, in event of war, 297,

  corn grown in, 100,

Council: as court of appeal, 270; diminished power of, 77, 181–182, 269; dispute of, with Assembly, 80, 172, 181–182; hard to get members, 220; little knowledge of law in, 152; member of, non-importer, 55; recommendations to be of, 152, 220,

  counties of, 267,

  courts, 57, 267, 270–272, 278,

  deerskins, trade in, 101,

  defences of, depend on R.N., 274,

  description of, 266–280,

  Dissenters in, 268,

  ecclesiastical jurisdiction, 270–271,

  education in, 56, 275, 276,

  emigration from, to Miss. R., 192,

  escheats in, 271–272,

  exchange-rate, with England, 279,

  exchequer court, none, 271,

  flax produced in, 276–277,

  flour produced in, 80, 276, 277,

  French resident in, 268, 277,

  gaols and courthouses in, 56, 57,

  Germans resident in, 55, 268, 278,

  Governor and acting Governor (see Bull, W.; Boone; Lyttleton; Montagu, Lord Charles), ecclesiastical jurisdiction of, 270–271; instruction to, of 14 April 1770, respecting issues of money, 77, 172, 179–180, 216, 263–265,

  hemp produced in, 100, 101, 276,

  immigration to, from northern colonies, 273; from Va., 277,

  Indians: hardly any left in province, 279; threat from, outside, 294; trade with, decreasing, 279,

  indigo grown in, 41, 55, 100, 101, 276,

  industry, labour costs too high for, 279,

  inns, 58,

  Irish in, 276–277,

  judges: assistant, or associate, 57–58, 279, 283–285; chief, 57, 287, and see Stokes,

  judicial divisions of, 267,

  juries, how appointed, 271,

  J.P.s, 272,

  land grants: to many, not few, 276; total of, 278,

  lawyers in, 57, 271,

  linen making, 276–277,

  madder grown in, 100, 276, 277,

  manufactures discouraged in, 41,

  martial law not proclaimed in, 273,

  militia: does not serve out of province, 273; negroes serve in, 273; police duties of, 273; reports on, 99–100, 273,

  mills in, 101,

  minerals in, 100,

  Naval Officer, deputy, see Raper, R.,

  negroes: number of, 278; serve in militia, 273,

  non-importation: bad effects of, 286; end of, expected, 56, 297–298; office holders support, 284–286;